THREE JEWISH JOURNEYS
THROUGH AN ANTHROPOLOGIST'S LENS

JUDAISM AND JEWISH LIFE

Editorial board

Geoffrey Alderman (University of Buckingham, Great Britain)
Herbert Basser (Queens University, Canada)
Donatella Ester Di Cesare (Università "La Sapienza," Italy)
Roberta Rosenberg Farber (Yeshiva University, New York),
Series Editor Associate
Simcha Fishbane (Touro College, New York), Series Editor
Meir Bar Ilan (Bar Ilan University, Israel)
Andreas Nachama (Touro College, Berlin)
Ira Robinson (Concordia University, Montreal)
Nissan Rubin (Bar Ilan University, Israel)
Susan Starr Sered (Suffolk University, Boston)
Reeva Spector Simon (Yeshiva University, New York)

THREE JEWISH JOURNEYS
THROUGH
AN ANTHROPOLOGIST'S LENS

FROM MOROCCO TO THE NEGEV, ZION TO THE BIG APPLE, THE CLOSET TO THE BIMAH

MOSHE SHOKEID

Library of Congress Cataloging-in-Publication Data

Shokeid, Moshe.
Three jewish journeys through an anthropologist's lens : from Morocco to the Negev, Zion to the big apple,the closet to the bimah / Moshe Shokeid.
 p. cm. -- (Judaism and jewish life)
Includes bibliographical references and index.
ISBN 978-1-934843-36-9 (hardback)
1. Shokeid, Moshe. 2. Anthropologists--United States--Biography. 3. Anthropologists--Great Britain--Biography. 4. Jews, Moroccan--Israel--Negev--Social life and customs. 5. Israelis--United States--Social conditions. 6. Jewish gays--New York (State)--New York--Religiousl ife. 7. Jewish lesbians--New York (State)--New York--Religious life. 8. Congregation Beth Simchat Torah (New York, N.Y.) I. Title.
GN21.S49A3 2009
305.892'4--dc22
 2009026842

Copyright © 2009 Academic Studies Press
All rights reserved

ISBN 978-1-934843-36-9

Book design by Olga Grabovsky

Published by Academic Studies Press in 2009
28 Montfern Avenue
Brighton, MA 02135, USA
press@academicstudiespress.com
www.academicstudiespress.com

CONTENTS

PREFACE AND ACKNOWLEDGEMENTS 7

PART ONE. INTRODUCTION

CHAPTER 1.
An Anthropologist's Work between Moving Genres 14

PART TWO. MOROCCAN JEWS IN ISRAEL

CHAPTER 2.
Jewish Existence in a Berber Environment 30

CHAPTER 3.
The Emergence of Pseudo-Kin Factions in Immigrant Communities . . . 44

CHAPTER 4.
The Regulation of Aggression in Daily Life:
    Aggressive Relationships among Moroccan Immigrants in Israel . 62

CHAPTER 5.
The Impact of Migration on the Moroccan Jewish Family in Israel 80

CHAPTER 6.
The Decline of Personal Endowment
    of Atlas Mountains Religious Leaders in Israel 96

CHAPTER 7.
    Cultural Ethnicity in Israel:
    The Case of Middle Eastern Jews' Religiosity 115

PART THREE. ISRAELIS IN AMERICA

CHAPTER 8.
One-Night Stand Ethnicity: The Malaise of Israeli Americans 142

CHAPTER 9.
The People of the Song 167

CHAPTER 10.
From the Anthropologist's Point of View:
    Studying One's Own Tribe 191
CHAPTER 11.
In the Company of American Jews:
    An Israeli Observer in a Lower East Side Synagogue.. 201

PART FOUR. GAY JEWS

CHAPTER 12.
The Talmud Circle: Identities in Conflict 236
CHAPTER 13.
    The Women Are Coming:
    The Transformation of Gender Relationships in a Gay Synagogue 251
CHAPTER 14.
When the Curtain Falls on a Fieldwork Project:
The Last Chapter of a Gay Synagogue Study 276
CHAPTER 15.
Closeted Cosmopolitans:
    Israeli Gays Between Center and Periphery 300

PART FIVE. ON METHODOLOGY

CHAPTER 16.
Negotiating Multiple Viewpoints:
    The Cook, the Native, the Publisher, and the Ethnographic Text 320
CHAPTER 17.
What Is There to a Name?
    The Ethnographer and his Moroccan Subjects in Shokeida. . . . 341

BIBLIOGRAPHY. 352

INDEX OF NAMES .388

INDEX OF SUBJECTS 397

PREFACE
AND ACKNOWLEDGEMENTS

As the diversity of essays in this volume suggests, my professional life has departed from the more typical pattern of an anthropologist's career devoted to one or two life-long research projects. Perhaps it's a restless temperament, or a case of intellectual *shpilkes*. But I found it difficult to limit my investigations to a particular institution or society once I had satisfied my interest in the issue that first attracted me to that field.

I began my professional career in the early 1960s as a sociologist with the Jewish Agency Land Settlement Department. There I witnessed firsthand the effects of the dramatic influx of Jewish immigrants of varied nationalities (*edot*) during the first decade of Israel's independence. Drawing on that experience, I chose for a Ph.D. ethnographic project a community transplanted from the Atlas Mountains of Morocco to the Northern Negev. Supported by a research fellowship from the University of Manchester, I remained engaged in that project from 1964 until the mid 1970s. The result was *The Dual Heritage: Immigrants from the Atlas Mountains in an Israeli Village*.

My next research in this field looked at the phenomenon of Jewish immigration from its obverse. It explored a then new and paradoxical reality in Israel's short national history: the exodus of Israeli-born citizens for the Diaspora, and the US, in particular. For two years (1982-4) my family and I lived in Queens, NY, where we were involved with the social and cultural life of Israeli ex-patriots. The result was the ethnography *Children of Circumstances*.

During my stay in New York, I was introduced to an institution that piqued my interest and later became my next research field: a gay and lesbian synagogue in Greenwich Village. Beginning with a full year in 1989, and shorter visits over the next four, I observed Congregation Beth Simchat Torah (CBST)—its lay-led organization, its religious practice, and the meaning it held for its congregants. The result was *A Gay Synagogue in New York*.

This New York research prompted me to look at the circumstances of gay life closer to home. A short study of gays in Tel Aviv yielded an intriguing comparative perspective.

My most recent New York work extended the purview of my study of religious institutions to a modern Orthodox synagogue on the Lower East Side. Beginning in 2004, I participated in the religious and social activities of a congregation devoted to the continuity of a venerable synagogue located in what was once a vibrant center of the city's Jewish life.

In these research fields, my Israeli identity, no doubt, affected how I was perceived, and informed my observations and interpretations. In this regard, the perspective I brought was different from the presumed "neutral" viewpoint of the outsider anthropologist who comes to study a remote "other" society. However, I have no regrets about, or apologies for, what might be viewed as a methodological snare. I sought out lives and cultures that were meaningful to me as an Israeli and a Jew. And I believe any compromise in objectivity was compensated for by an increased access to the field—not just logistically, but also in terms of emotional accord and easier penetration of the codes of the observed behavior.

Drawn as they are from a diverse career, the essays in this volume range from some of my earliest work to my most recent. But even the oldest of them remain relevant. The communities they describe are still ongoing and evolving. Groups and institutions change continuously, some slowly, some more radically. To fully comprehend their developments—indeed, to understand their present—we need a close acquaintance with their past reality.

Chapters 11 and 17 are new and were never published. Most other works in this volume were first printed in European and American journals of anthropology and sociology. Three are taken from my published ethnographies, and two from edited collections. Except for minor corrections and a few short postscripts, they are presented in their original form. As such, one can not avoid some repetitions in a volume of separately published texts.

The seventeen essays—"chapters"—in this volume are grouped into five sections. Chapter 1 comprises Section I. Published in 1992, in the Scandinavian journal *Ethnos*, it inaugurated a series entitled "Key Informants on the History of Anthropology," in which established researchers reflected on their work in a more intimate way. This genre of introspective narrative exemplified the new movement of reflexive anthropology, which encouraged ethnographers to reveal what their experiences and feelings had been during fieldwork.

Except for Chapter 3 (on the feuding *hamula* groups) based on research I conducted during my work as a sociologist of the Negev Region, Chapters 2-6, in Section II, focus on the Atlas Mountain Jews' relocation to Israel. They explore the immigrants' social circumstances in Morocco; the evolution of communal, family and religious life in their new home; and their transformation from craftsmen and traders, to cooperative-village farmers. Chapter 7 takes a broader view, exploring the continuity and change in the religious practice of Moroccan Jews and other "Middle Eastern" Jewish immigrants.

Chapters 8 – 10 in Section III, present my work among Israeli immigrants (*yordim*) in New York. Respectively, they discuss the patterns of social interaction between the immigrants, and their relationships with American Jews; the maintenance of cultural connections while abroad; and discuss my personal response to interacting with Israeli compatriots. In Chapter 11, the field changes. I present my observations as participant in the Lower East Side's Stanton Street Synagogue. This offers a comparison between the patterns of communal life in the US and Israel.

Section IV presents my work among gay and lesbian Jews. The first three chapters refer to CBST in New York. Chapter 12 recounts the evolution in religious observance of a group of veteran male congregants from their early days of radicalism to a later return to orthodoxy. Chapter 13 explores the changes the congregation and its leadership have undergone in recent years, particularly with the increase in lesbian membership. Chapter 14 offers an insight into the transformed relationships between the ethnographer and his subjects. Changing Venues, Chapter 15 presents my small-scale research project of interviews and observations on the existential experiences of gay men in Tel Aviv.

Section V returns to issues implicit in Chapter 1, but now with particular focus on methodological queries and dilemmas. Chapter 16 airs the often fraught relationship between researcher, insiders and editors in the construction of an ethnography—specifically that of the gay synagogue. Chapter 17, the closing scene of my professional journeys, presents the life-long obligation to the first ethnographic journey that also gave me my name—Shokeid.

I am indebted to the many colleagues and friends who made important contributions to this collection by reading and commenting on the original manuscripts of the essays included. I would specifically thank three individuals: my colleague of many years, Shlomo Deshen, who has read most of my writings; Nissan Rubin, who encouraged me to produce this volume; and Sylvia Weinberg, who helped me bring the book to press.

I gratefully acknowledge the following publications in which these essays appeared:

Chapter 1 – "An Anthropologist's Work between Moving Genres," *Ethnos* 57: 233-244, 1992.

Chapter 2 – "Jewish Existence in a Berber Environment," in *Jews among Muslims,* S. Deshen and W.P. Zerner (eds.), Macmillan Press, 1996, pp. 109-120.

Chapter 3 – "The Emergence of Pseudo-Kin Factions in Immigrant Communities," in *Distant Relations: Ethnicity and Politics among Arabs and North African Jews in Israel,* Shokeid and S. Deshen. Praeger and Bergin, 1982, pp. 80-95 (an earlier version was published in *The British Journal of Sociology,* xix: 385-406, 1968).

Chapter 4. – "The Regulation of Aggression in Daily Life: Aggressive Relationships among Moroccan Immigrants in Israel," *Ethnology* 21: 271-281, 1982.

Chapter 5. – "The Impact of Migration on the Moroccan Jewish Family in Israel," in *The Jewish Family: Myths and Reality,* S. Cohen and P. Hyman (eds.), Holmes and Meier, 1986, pp. 82-96.

Chapter 6. – "The Decline of Personal Endowment of Atlas Mountains Religious Leaders in Israel," *Anthropological Quarterly,* 52: 186-197, 1979.

Chapter 7. – "Cultural Ethnicity in Israel: The Case of Middle Eastern Jews' Religiosity," *Association for Jewish Studies Review,* IX: 247-271, 1984.

PREFACE AND ACKNOWLEDGEMENTS

Chapter 8. – "One-Night Stand Ethnicity: The Malaise of Israeli Americans," *Israel Social Science Research*, 8: 23-50, 1993.

Chapter 9. – "The People of the Song," in *Children of Circumstances: Israeli Emigrants in New York*, M. Shokeid, Cornell University Press, 1988. pp. 104-125.

Chapter 10. – "From the Anthropologist's Point of View: Studying One's Own Tribe," *Anthropology and Humanism Quarterly*, 4: 23-28, 1989.

Chapter 12. – "The Talmud Circle: Identities in Conflict," in *A Gay Synagogue in New York*, M. Shokeid, Columbia University Press, 1995, pp. 143-155.

Chapter 13. – "The Women Are Coming: The Transformation of Gender Relationships in a Gay Synagogue," *Ethnos*, 66: 5-26, 2001.

Chapter 14. – "When the Curtain Falls on a Fieldwork Project: The Last Chapter of a Gay Synagogue Study," *Ethnos*, 27: 219-238, 2007.

Chapter 15. – "Closeted Cosmopolitans: Israeli Gays Between Center and Periphery," *Global Networks*, 3: 387-399, 2003.

Chapter 16. – "Negotiating Multiple Viewpoints: The Cook, the Native, the Publisher, and the Ethnographic Text," *Current Anthropology*, 38: 631-645, 1997.

Part One.
INTRODUCTION

CHAPTER 1.
AN ANTHROPOLOGIST'S WORK BETWEEN MOVING GENRES[1]

My romance with anthropology started as a response to a deep disappointment with sociology. I studied sociology at the Hebrew University under S.N. Eisenstadt. He was himself influenced by Talcot Parsons' theories and later directed his students toward the themes of modernization. Actually, my disenchantment was not so much with the abstract theorizing of Eisenstadt. He was quite charismatic as a teacher and I never lost my admiration for his sociological imagination and enormous knowledge. My problems started mainly when I was engaged with research carried out under his guidance. The research project was designed to reveal the patterns of Middle Eastern immigrants' accommodation to the Israeli bureaucratic system. The hypothesis presented by the senior researchers was that, coming from underdeveloped countries, these immigrants maintained an "Institutional Ambiguity" which distorted their perception of how bureaucratic institutions function. We, the junior assistants (third year students) were expected to confirm that hypothesis through our questionnaires and interviews. We were probably so convinced by the wisdom of our supervisors who were our teachers, and so eager to prove our own smartness, that the pilot test we made in the slums of Jerusalem with our self-composed questionnaires proved that the research tools were perfectly adequate. But when we arrived at the cho-

---

1 This chapter was the first article published in a new section in the format of *Ethnos* (vol. 57: 233-244, 1992): Key Informants on the History of Anthropology. I am grateful to Ulf Hannerz, the late Tomas Gerholm and Gudrun Dahl who invited me to introduce my professional experiences in the forum of a departmental staff seminar during my stay at Stockholm University in the Fall of 1992.

sen interview sites in Beer Sheba, Ashkelon and Kiryat-Gat, the new development towns in the Negev, we discovered we were completely wrong. The questionnaires revealed a standard observation: the immigrants have suffered from no ambiguity. However, they wished to talk to us about the many difficulties they confronted in their new country and sometimes with the bureaucrats.

In the state of stress and humiliation arising from the bizarre confrontation with the interviewed, we told our leaders when they visited us in the field, that something was going wrong. I remember the final verdict we presented in the following words: "The questionnaire doesn't work." To our dismay the researcher and our teacher, whom we considered to be the master of methodology, answered: "You do not change horses in the middle of the track." To make a long story short, this was the sentence which literally caused my divorce from sociology. I had learned that sociological wisdom is far more important than the reality of human behavior. (In retrospect, I assume our supervisors were unable, at that stage, to admit the failure of their smart hypothesis).

I was planning to leave the discipline and apply for an apprenticeship with the Foreign Office when, immediately after I completed my BA degree, I was offered a job as a rural sociologist with the Jewish Agency Land Settlement Department. This flattering appointment meant doing applied research in the new *moshav* (cooperative) farming villages. Due to that experience I was also invited to join a team of Israeli experts which went out to Iran after the earthquake in Ghazvin.[2] This is how I first experienced what I would later discover to be ethnographic work.

There was another unsatisfactory facet of the sociological project of modernization in Jerusalem: at that time, theory and research were designed to demonstrate the universal characteristics and variables underlying the processes of modernization in the Third World. Even studies in

---

2   The team included mainly agronomists and water engineers who designed a development project for the Ghazvin region. My report introduced observations on social groupings and a demographic survey in three selected villages. See M. Shokeid (then Minkovitz), Report on the Social Structure of the Ghavzin Area, in The Ghazvin Area Development Project Reconnaissance Report, Tahal, Iran Branch, Tel Aviv, 21 pp. 1963.

Israel therefore showed little interest in the specific social and cultural manifestations which were so obvious and exciting to anyone who was close to the sites occupied by the new immigrants coming from many countries.

When Max Gluckman, chair of the Anthropology Department at the University of Manchester, made a short visit to the Hebrew University in the early 1960s, I attended his lecture at the staff seminar. I was fascinated with his presentation of what I believe were his ideas in *Custom and Conflict in Africa*. I knew this was my solution. Things turned out better than I had expected in my wildest dreams. Max had planned a project of research in Israel supported by Granada Television. As I later discovered, I was on his list of recruits based on the merit of a small article I had published in Hebrew. A "secret agent" who prepared for him[3] a review of the state of the art in Israel, assumed that I was not fully committed to the Jerusalem School and possessed the skills for ethnographic work. Determined to start on a new career I completed my MA studies and managed to get away. In the Fall of 1964 I arrived in dark and rainy Manchester.

My first year in Manchester was marked by a great deal of ambivalence. I knew I was chosen and expected to produce a good ethnography which would be added to the Manchester School's list of books. But although I was too embarrassed to admit it (except to my close friend Shlomo Deshen), the seminars I attended were boring. At the field seminar led by Bill Epstein two students presented their material. They went on week after week introducing observations which, at that stage, lacked the charm of a good narrative and it seemed to me they also lacked any ambition to look for a theoretical raison d'être. The transfer from the Jerusalem grand-theory style to the Manchester style of reporting minute observations was a sort of shock treatment.

---

3   Gluckman had sent out Percy S. Cohen (then a lecturer at Leicester University who had formerly carried out ethnographic research in Israel), to report to him on the studies done and the researchers involved in the Israeli field of immigration. The report was also intended to suggest an outline for the goals of the Manchester project which was later known as the Bernstein Scheme.

I also attended Emrys Peters' seminar where he mainly presented his work among the Bedouin in Cyrenaica. He was a good story teller and he had a convincing theory about the ecological constraints affecting social life and the patterns of marriage in particular. He appeared to fly the Manchester flag that good data equals a good theory about society. This was a lesson he never tired to repeat. At Max Gluckman's seminar the panorama of studies chosen for the process of indoctrination into the ethos of the school was wider. Each student was assigned an ethnography he was expected to introduce in class. Here, probably more than in any other course, I got the message of our apprenticeship. I was assigned Middleton's *Lugbara Religion* (1960) which became one of my favorite books in anthropology.

Although Middleton had been an Oxford graduate, his work could easily be presented as a Manchester show case. At last I was fascinated with the "extended case method".[4] Middleton's beautiful narrative and his imaginative solution to the Lugbara riddle of ghost invocation impressed me far more than the complicated and long ethnographies by the Manchester icons Clyde Mitchell and Victor Turner who had recorded the endless intricate cases of marriage, divorce, conflicts, fission and reintegration in the Yao and Ndembu villages. I just got lost. But probably, had I been assigned to introduce them in class, I might have discovered the power of their presentation and admired their incredible diligence at fieldwork and its transformation into the books which endowed them with their reputation in the school. The staff seminars were another stage of drama and torment where the novices were convinced to believe that behind simple facts another reality and sociological meaning lay waiting to be uncovered by the diligent student.

At last I could regain my belief that in Manchester there was something special which could compete with the results of the education and research of a Jerusalem sociology student. And so the model for a good fieldworker and writer of ethnography was deeply implanted into my

---

4 "The Extended Case Method," a unique contribution of the Manchester School, treated each case as a stage in an ongoing process of social relationships between specific persons or groups engaged in a social system and sharing a culture. See, for example, Van Velson 1967; Burawoy 1991.

cognitive and sentimental education. Moreover, Gluckman treated his students as a sort of close relatives who deserved that treatment because they seemed to be promising anthropologists. We were dined, wined and chauffeured to football matches. This attitude was not only flattering, it actually did affect our self-esteem. How else could I have tried to publish parts of my MA dissertation? I rewrote my Hebrew University modernization-oriented thesis, now influenced by Firth's analysis of factions in Indian overseas communities (see Chapter 3). My first year at Manchester thus turned out to be much more productive than I realized during those days in a gloomy environment.

I was anxious to get into the field which I soon did at the end of my first academic year in the department. I knew there were obstacles, and that even disasters might befall us in the field. A close example was that of my peer from Jerusalem, the late Yitzhak Elam. The most promising student of my Israeli cohort, he insisted on going to the field before he was considered sufficiently trained. He fell ill in the field and never regained his reputation as a promising Manchester anthropologist although he later went back to Africa and produced a very interesting ethnography (Elam 1973).

My return to Israel for fieldwork marked a dramatic change in my methodology and intellectual ambitions. To settle for eighteen months in a remote small village populated by Atlas Mountains Jews was indeed an act of protest if not bizarreness on the Israeli sociological scene. The smallest research design on farming immigrants by Dov Weintraub, an Eisenstadt student, included twelve villages (Weintraub 1971). That sample was supposed to represent the wide variety of immigrant ethnic groups in the various parts of the country. Weintraub launched his research in order to develop Eisenstadt's (1953) theory of the immigrants' predispositions to accommodate with change. I had no sample to represent the majority of the new immigrants from the Middle East or even only from North Africa. Nor had I brought with me a theory or an hypothesis to test and develop. But worse, I was soon worried that I could not observe modes of behavior which might conveniently compare with the world of beliefs and actions observed by my mostly Africanist peers and teachers in Manchester.

However, as it turned out, I observed many conflicts among the villagers and could actually employ the "extended case method". But I confronted one theoretical problem unfamiliar to the Manchester writings and also shared with other works in the British tradition: I could not understand the Romemites' (as I named the villagers I studied) politics without referring to their past history in Morocco. I explained their present competition, quarrels and economic achievements mainly in terms of their constant comparison of their present situation with their status in Morocco. I defined that phenomenon as the "reference situation." Here I felt I was inviting trouble when the day came to present my thesis to a school in which, since the days of Malinowski and Radcliffe-Brown, there had been little respect for "historically" based reasoning applied to societies with no reliable records. I was therefore careful to stress again and again that I did not consider the Romemites' stories about the past as a sort of objective history, but rather treated them in the Malinowskian tradition of myth. I assume my narrative was convincing enough due to the extensive display of events which recorded the villagers' recourse to the past. Some of these events were quite dramatic as, for example, my observation of Yermia Amzlag who was among the poorest residents in Morocco but who did well in Israel. On the Day of Atonement he pleaded with Abraham Sebag, a leader and a wealthy man in Morocco but a poor one in Israel, to forgive him for their fights in the synagogue. By that extravagant show of humility in front of the congregation, Yermia retold the story of the rise and fall of men who came together from the same place. Yermia was publicly claiming his new elevated status versus his lord in Morocco, and Abraham was too old and unfortunate to regain his old position of leadership.

My real ordeal waited for me at the staff seminars. Max was ill and could not attend, so I was left to the mercy of Emrys Peters and the younger enthusiastic lecturers reputed for their skills to tear ethnographies to pieces. They were good at convincing the fieldworker and other listeners that he had completely missed the major aspect which could best penetrate the secrets of the society studied. I must thank Paul Baxter who remained strongly supportive and saved me from the junior wolves ready for a meal. My main concession was to Emrys who insisted that I should look more carefully into the structure of affinal relationships among the Romemites. This demand which seemed so obvious for those brought up in the classical Africanist and Arab literature, meant a lot of work and an additional chapter which actually had little influence on my general arguments. I was merely brought into line. As expected, my thesis was later published by Manchester University Press (Shokeid 1971a).

I took a job at Tel Aviv University, thus also fulfilling Max's project of expanding the Manchester School into new territories. For all practical reasons, Israeli anthropology was founded through Gluckman' enterprising academic vision.[5] This does not mean that all anthropologists in Israel have been Manchester trained and, in any case, only very few remained fully identified with that school of the 1950s and 1960s. As for myself, I retained the legacy of its insistence on dedicated fieldwork. I never lost my taste for immersing myself for a long period in the lives of the people I came to study. I was never content with a short period of observations or with papers based on shallow fieldwork. My disagreement with some manifestations of the new genres was not because of their ideas, but because I sometimes suspected their promoters of not having done their ethnographic work properly and for having compensated for their poor work with grand words. But otherwise, I was never really enchanted with the analytical imagination in much of the Manchester mainstream literature. However, I preferred some of the later publications by its former students, Victor Turner in particular, or Abner Cohen. I found Turner's work inspiring and he published in his Cornell series of *Symbol and Ritual*, a book I co-authored with Shlomo Deshen, where we considered "cultural" manifestations, something beyond the Manchester paradigm of the 1960s and early 1970s (Deshen & Shokeid 1974).

---

5   See Shokeid 2004.

Our interest in the substance of culture was influenced both by social and professional circumstances. First of all, there was our involvement in the Israeli inner discourse following the disillusionment with the melting pot myth and the growing acknowledgement of a continuing cleavage between the dominant veteran Ashkenazi culture and the cultures of the Sephardi newcomers. We published two books in Hebrew which were designed to influence school education (Shokeid and Deshen 1977; 1999; Deshen and Shokeid 1984). We wished to show the processes of cultural continuity, the accommodation and mutual influences of both groups, viewed mainly from the position of our research among North African Jews.

Another source effecting our work has come from our growing contact with American anthropology. Victor Turner was an easy beginning, but the major impact has been my later encounter with Clifford Geertz' work. Geertz embodied the most natural link since I could relate to his work in Morocco (Geertz 1971). For example, his description of the charismatic nature of the Moroccan Marabout as expressed in his *baraka* seemed to me to explain also the power of the Jewish Moroccan religious leader and saint as expressed in his *zekhut avot*—merit of the fathers (see chapter 6). The Geertzian narrative style offered also a license to free myself from the inhibitions of Manchester style and terminology, which did not allow for descriptions and terms not closely tied to the basic "facts" observed. For example, words like "feelings" and "emotions" were not used because we obviously lacked the tools to measure them. These basic words in our daily vocabulary were not considered legitimate in our writings but as a sort of unprofessional intrusion into the psychologist's domain.

The Moroccan field of research had actually revealed a list of other stimulating anthropologists such as Vincent Crapanzano, Dale Eickelman, Paul Rabinow, Lawrence Rosen and others. I was pleasantly surprised to discover that my work among Moroccan Jews in Israel seemed relevant to researchers who went to Morocco from American schools. In his textbook on Middle Eastern anthropology, Eickelman (1981) introduced my ethnography stating that my observations had revealed patterns of behavior which resembled those he observed among Muslims. Another confirmation that my "facts" carried some authority came from another discipline. Actually, I was often worried by what has become a safe ticket to publicity when a newcomer to an already studied community proves that the author of a well received ethnography was completely wrong with his observations. A linguist (Ben-Tolila 1983), who studied changes in the daily modes of speech among the Romemites, discovered differences among the villagers he could not explain before he used my analysis of social competition between the settlers which showed it to be based on their perceived ranked status in Morocco. I felt a sort of satisfaction about the rigorousness of the training I received in Manchester and the confidence I gained there in the reliability of well conducted observations. If one were not intimidated, one might call these "social facts."

My second research project[6] was carried out during the early 1970s among the Arab minority in a major Israeli city. It became my line to choose groups I defined as social minorities. The Arabs who remained in Jaffa after 1948 were by and large disadvantaged compared also with most other Arabs in Israel. They had not retained the kinship networks, the leadership and institutions which remained almost intact in the villages. I employed again the Manchester methodology, but my analysis led mainly toward a cultural-symbolic interpretation. I argued that the Arabs were expressing commitment to the code of honor, a keynote of their culture, as a means of preserving an ethnic identity versus the dominant Jewish society and, at the same time, claiming an affinity with the Arab world within and outside Israel. In *Distant Relations* (1982), also co-authored with Shlomo Deshen, we compared the destiny of two populations of lower ethno-cultural ranking in Israeli society—Arabs and Sephardi immigrants. This sort of reasoning , based mainly on cultural-political-ethnic factors, would not have survived the Manchester staff seminar of the 1960s and 1970s.

---

6   Not represented in this volume dedicated to my study of Jewish communities

My growing alienation from Manchester was part of an erosion of my Anglophile affections. For example, I could not accommodate to the ASA (Association of British Anthropologists) meetings. I probably did all the wrong things, from arriving with out-of-tune papers, wearing the wrong jacket, experiencing my own resentment at the style of discussion, feeling inadequate and lonely. As a sort of consolation I assumed I encountered local ethnocentrism and gave up the idea of ever again attending these meetings.

In sharp contrast, I developed an affection for the AAA (American Anthropological Association) meetings, that huge marketplace of anthropology. It contained the vulgar, the peculiar, the boring and the most exciting. But most of all, at that annual rite of professional integration I never felt I was a stranger. I assume my comfort at the AAA meetings stemmed mainly from the heterogeneity of the American professional scene compared with the British scene. My education as a member of a school and tribe lost its salience upon my departure from England and also as a result of Max's untimely death.

The major research which was more directly influenced by my attraction to the American scene was my work in the early 1980s among Israeli immigrants in New York. I could no longer employ the extended-case method, not because of some new methodological convictions, but simply because it was a different field situation. I wanted to study "a community," but contrary to my expectations, the Israelis in New York were not confined to a territorially bounded community. The ethnography I produced (Shokeid 1988a) focused on people who shared an "ethnicity," a "culture" and memories of experiences from a country they had left. I was not describing a group sharing daily life through close neighborhood and joint institutions. I analyzed the ethnic activities I observed in terms of "cultural performance" which I adopted mainly from Geertz (Geertz 1973); in terms of "one-night-stand ethnicity," a metaphor which I borrowed from the symbolic interactionists' studies of anonymous sex, and in terms of "affective ethnicity." I hope these terms and metaphors added toward a better understanding of ethnicity within the framework of social minorities.

CHAPTER ONE

When I first changed my professional sympathies, I perceived two clearly defined entities, the British versus the American way of "thinking anthropology." But upon getting closer to the American scene, I soon realized that the discipline was undergoing a serious phase of self-searching which showed signs of some chaos. The old major theoretical debates and their protagonists became irrelevant when a new wave of anthropologists, often of a younger generation, were questioning the most fundamental, almost sacrosanct assumptions of the anthropological project. I could empathize with some of their doubts. I was probably among the first who thought anthropologists should inform their readers about their position in the field. Already in 1971 I wrote about my relationships with the Moroccans I had studied. I developed that issue as a sort of protest against the atmosphere of indifference and detachment I felt when I attended the Manchester staff seminars' discussions of reports from the field. Ernest Gellner (then editor of AES) suggested to me the title *Fieldwork as Predicament Rather than Spectacle* (Shokeid 1971b). I did not incorporate that article in my thesis or the book although it was already written. Later too, I kept avoiding the publication of chapters of reflexivity together with the final ethnography although it was now in vogue. I resented another facet of reflexivity which seemed to me to have become far too prominent: the anthropologist in that new genre often emerged as the star of the ethnography.

If, in the beginning, the reflexive anthropologist tried to explain his difficulties with his informants and the misunderstandings of their culture which might have led to serious distortions in the ethnographic text, at a later stage these serious doubts have led to a total debunking of his project. The Ethnographic Text, an attractive terminological change, was of immense importance with regard to the data and meaning of fieldwork and its transformation into a monograph. But often it also deprived fieldwork of much of its previously assumed intrinsic scientific value. The celebration of the past fallacy of positivist anthropology has produced a growing tide of works displaying a new brave anthropologist who has become the center of the ethnography. He might go wrong with the native's point of view and the "facts" he collected, but we are called to celebrate a text based on the anthropologist's true experiences and inner feelings. Although free of a positivist pretension, these ethnographic texts, nevertheless, retain the claim of being able to tell their readers something which does carry the authority of a true story about the natives out there.

For myself, I tried to develop a less heroic and arbitrary approach to the anthropologist's project. In "Anthropologists and Their Informants" (Shokeid 1988b), I analyzed the intricate relationships between myself and those I might have defined as being among my major "informants." In this context I am in agreement with Marcus and Cushman (1982) whose varied writings have often been used in order to legitimize a postmodern approach in anthropology. I argued for a clear presentation of the voices from the field instead of the towering voice of both the old positivist and the young postmodernist anthropologists. In this style I also wrote about my feelings when studying the Israelis in New York (see Chapter 10). But I did not include that piece in my ethnography to serve as an alibi for my reflexive moods.

My debate with some of the studies emerging from the new school free of the pretensions of positivism, was sometimes difficult to separate from my personal identity as an Israeli anthropologist. This has sometimes bordered on the bizarre. I first found out I was accused, together with other colleagues, of expressing our Zionist sentiments when we studied Jews coming from the Middle East and North Africa (Van Teeffelen 1978). No doubt, I was very clear about my personal position already in the ethnography that was first published in 1971, a time when anthropologists rarely revealed their socio-political identity. In the era of reflexivity I should have been congratulated instead for my straightforward revelation of a possible bias. This critique ignored other works which did not correspond with the author's argument. It also suggested a grotesque image of the role of the Manchester School in British anthropology. I came across a similar methodology in a more recent article when the author who carried out research among Palestinians confessed he ignored the ethos of scientific work which demands recording the truth (Swedenburg 1989).

My efforts to express my opinion on these matters met with only partial success. My first attempt to respond was frustrated when the rebuttal I wrote, although accepted for publication, was delayed for three years and finally rejected (Shokeid 1988-89).[7] But more recently, I was given the opportunity to introduce my point of view (Shokeid 1992a). However, this response by a native anthropologist seems to merely anger the apparently liberal and benevolent post-modern Western anthropologist. From his point of view, the local anthropologist must represent the dominant sector of his own society and therefore cannot be relied upon for his observations. It is only the outsider, the neutral, brave and loving anthropologist who can provide the true representation of the society he came to observe. This grotesque pretension which contradicts any claim for authority superior to that of other outside observers or ideologues who do not necessarily wear the scientist's mantle, easily invades our professional forums. I was first amazed, but then somewhat content with the personal attack I received for my review of these works (Swedenburg 1992). I thought the malice and wild use of distorted "data" might convince the sane anthropologists that my claim was not without foundation.

I am grateful for the changes which have occurred in anthropology. They opened the way for me to expand my interests and work in fields I would not otherwise have dared. My recent study of a gay synagogue (Shokeid 1995/2003) has been a most gratifying experience. It allowed me to look into problems of modern life and theoretical issues which for many decades have remained beyond the scope of a "decent" anthropologist. When Goffman visited Manchester in the late 1960s, we were enchanted by his lectures. But I remember telling somebody it was "toilet sociology." No doubt Goffman was peeping through keyholes of doors yet closed to the respectable social scientist. In a previous generation I might have hesitated to take on my gay synagogue project because of the possible suspicions of my inner motives. My attraction to the Atlas

---

7 Written for Dialectical Anthropology it was later published in Israel Social Science Research.

Mountains people was okay because I could not be suspected of a hidden Moroccan agenda.

The new anthropology has opened the doors to the study of society free of old style restrictions and preferences. Not only other societies far away from home, not only the lower classes within our own society, not only the proper issues in terms of our moral education, not only the other. As evidence for the latter, I refer to my experiment in Exceptional Experiences in Everyday Life (Shokeid 1992b). I used events reconstructed from my own life in order to suggest a new dimension to the study of the rites of passage.

I tell myself I am ready to accept the experiments and complaints of a younger generation. But I cannot forgive anyone, however eloquent he might be, if he tries to do that by denying the essence of anthropology as I still believe it to be: the disciplined observation and honest report of human behavior based on a serious attempt to get close to the "victims" of the ethnographer's descriptions and theories.

Part Two.
Moroccan Jews in Israel

CHAPTER 2.
JEWISH EXISTENCE IN A BERBER ENVIRONMENT

During the 1970s historians, sociologists and anthropologists assessed diversely the Jewish situation in Morocco. Polar answers were given to the question whether Jews were a persecuted minority forced to comply rigidly with the more humiliating and severe *dhimmi* regulations, or whether their relationships with the surrounding Muslim society were relatively congenial, particularly when compared with European Jewry. The Moroccan debate cannot be isolated from an assessment of the general scene of Jewish life in Muslim lands, which was permeated with the ambiguity engendered by the *dhimmi* status. That official charter of rights and obligations, applied to Jews and Christians alike, has given rise to contrasting and inconsistent descriptions and interpretations of tolerance versus oppression in Islamic society. Chouraqui was one of the first to emphasize the relatively harmonious elements in Jewish-Muslim relations in Morocco (1958: 54-5), and the controversy gained momentum when Rosen (1972) formulated his hypothesis for the sociological *raison d'être* of these harmonious relationships.

This approach to the Jewish situation in Morocco has been challenged by Stillman (1977) as idealizing the Jewish position and distorting the general Moroccan scene through the application of a hypothesis pertinent mainly to the Sefrou case. Stillman reinforced his argument with historical and folkloric sources which depict the humble and vulnerable legal and social position of Moroccan Jews. Pointing to the pariah status of Moroccan Jews, Stillman contended that they were excluded from many trades and consequently forced into occupations forbidden to Muslims, such as gold- and silversmithing and the particularly despised occupation of money-lending. Stillman also cites records, and brings evidence as to the persecution of Jews. Against the background of these contradictory opinions, Meyers (1977) propounds that there has never been a single paradigm of Muslim-Jewish relations in Morocco. During different periods, as well as in different parts of the country, various patterns predominated, exhibiting different types of co-existence. According to this view, both Rosen and Stillman present only a partial perspective of a situation that is far more complex. An inquiry into the ambiguity of patterns and the general ambivalence in Muslim-Jewish relationships we find in Goldberg's (1978) analysis of the Mimuna ceremony, and this ambivalence of relationships forms the theme of many Jewish Moroccan folktales, in which contacts with non-Jews are tense and contentious.

My own investigation into the particular situation of Atlas Mountains Jews revealed that most of the writers who explored Jewish life under Berber rule in recent generations comment on the Jews' relative safety, emphasizing the cordial relationships with their neighbors. Some of these writers refer to symbiotic relationships between Jews and Berbers. Flamand concentrates on the economic dimension of this symbiosis; Willner, on the other hand, comments in general: "The Jews of Ait Ardar lived in virtual symbiosis with their Berber neighbors, and enjoyed excellent relations with them and a high subsistence level" (1969: 263). These descriptions seem surprising considering the unstable political situation and the more difficult environmental circumstances of Berber tribal areas. The skeptic may query whether the mere fact that Jews continued to survive under Berber rule did not give rise to these idealized descriptions.

Whatever our conclusions on the Jewish situation in the Atlas Mountains and elsewhere, an important factor to be considered, both in past and possibly future debates, is that most of the studies and assessments on Jewish-Muslim relationships have been carried out after the majority of Moroccan Jewry immigrated to Israel or elsewhere. This factor inevitably circumscribed investigation, not only in studies of communities which do not have many written records (particularly communities from southern Morocco) but in other communities as well. Moreover, the collective and individual Jewish experience of the twentieth century, particularly the

CHAPTER TWO

Holocaust, Israeli statehood and, in its wake, mass immigration from Middle Eastern and North African countries, might have colored, in various ways, the views both of Moroccan-born Jews and of those who informed about, or analyzed, the situation of Jews in Morocco.

The arguments of the above scientists and our specific reservations evince a problem rarely treated directly by the various disciplines, namely the interpretative dimension in the presentation and analysis of data. The issue was tackled in anthropology by Geertz (1973: 3-32) who exemplified his argument with observations he recorded in Morocco. The *dramatis personae* in his case were a Jewish trader from the highlands of central Morocco, his patron—a Berber sheikh—robbers from a neighboring Berber tribe who had attacked the trader and his guests, and a French colonial officer. The latter, anxious to enforce French law and order, messed up settlement of the dispute according to Berber custom, which would have granted the Jewish trader considerable indemnification in sheep by the attacker's tribe.

Discussing the quality of interpretation embedded in the presentation and analysis of observed or recorded behavior, Geertz claimed:

> What it means is that descriptions of Berber, Jewish or French culture must be cast in terms of the constructions we imagine Berbers, Jews or Frenchmen to place upon what they live through, the formulae they use to define what happens to them.... They must be cast in terms of the interpretations to which persons of a particular denomination subject their experience, because that is what they profess to be descriptions of (1973: 15).

In analyzing my own data, I was constantly aware of the limitations in the study of the Jewish Moroccan situation. Through the experiences of a community from the Atlas Mountains transplanted to an Israeli village which I called Romema, I tentatively suggest some interpretations for the position of Jews in these parts of Morocco. My observations in Romema were carried out over a period of 18 months—from October 1965 to March 1967, and for three months during the summer of 1976. The people of Romema migrated to Israel in 1956 from Asamer,[1] a village located in the district of Ait Bou Oulli,[2] about 50 kilometers southeast of Demnate. I refrain from discussing the patterns of social and cultural life of Atlas Mountains Jews and possible cultural symbiotic elements with the surrounding Berber society.[3] Rather I concentrate on the basic material circumstances of their lives—residence, occupation, and safety. The present anthropological study will, I hope, further contribute to the descriptive and analytical spectrum of Jewish life in Morocco, through its assessment of the Jewish situation in some parts of the Atlas Mountains.

THE CIRCUMSTANCES OF JEWISH LIFE IN ASAMER

When I began to summarize my data on the relationships of the people of Asamer with their neighbors (Shokeid 1971/1985: 18-23), I realized that these could not be defined in clear-cut terms. The immigrants' spontaneous stories and discussions, as well as their answers to my direct questions, were sometimes reminiscent of the pathetic descriptions of the position of Atlas Mountains Jews by nineteenth and early twentieth-century travelers and geographers (e.g. Thomson 1889; Slouschz 1927; Montagne 1930). In many of these accounts, the Jew is highly dependent on his Berber patron who protects him for his own interest. At times the patron himself might ransack his Jewish protégé's property. Aside from this harsh presentation, there are scores of stories of how the Jews ingeniously contrived to safeguard their wealth and to ensure their personal wellbeing. Often the storyteller, during his narrative, asked God's forgiveness for having duped the Muslims. Others are tales of mutual dependence, based on genuine mutual respect,

---

1   In earlier publications I used a pseudonym, Amran, in order to disguise the identity of the people studied, a standard procedure in anthropological monographs.
2   I used in previous publications a pseudonym, Etgor instead of Ait Bou Oulli. The district of Ait Bou Oulli comprised of several Jewish communities.
3   See my works on kinship, family and religion among Jews in the Atlas Mountains (Shokeid, 1971/1985; Deshen and Shokeid, 1974).

which stress fairplay and personal friendship between the Jewish trader or craftsman and his Muslim client, partner, or patron.

Asamer, an all-Jewish village which prior to immigration, had a population of three hundred and fifty inhabitants, was divided into seven family groups. This familial division greatly overlapped the occupational division in the community.[4] At the top of the economic and social ladder were the traders whose ancestor, according to family tradition, had been a merchant from Demnate, who, upon the invitation of a local sheikh, had settled in Asamer. His sons and grandchildren, like him, were in trade: they contracted farming partnerships with their neighbors for whom they put up capital, and they owned flocks of sheep grazed by Muslims with whom they shared the lambs. However, much of the trade consisted of nuts and the import of sugar, oil, as well as of other items. The senior members of the family of traders had, in recent generations, headed the community and acted on its behalf in dealing with the local sheikhs (in Israel their neighbors have accused them of collaborating with the Muslims).

The other families followed various crafts—cobbling, carpentry, and smithing. The poor and unskilled worked at odd jobs for the wealthier and skilled members of the community. Some of the craftsmen worked at home—particularly those who made embroidered shoes—others plied their craft in nearby or distant Berber settlements. All male members of the community came into direct contact with the Muslim population on an economic basis. There were almost no Jewish communal functions which exclusively provided a livelihood. Also the religious leaders were at times engaged in some kind of economic transaction or occupation. Trade and playing their crafts took the Jews over wide stretches of territories, crossing tribal borders, or, as they put it: "We traveled through different *memshalot* (governments)." A former smith concluded his description of travels in search of work in Morocco with the sweeping statement: "For us craftsmen there were no borders."

---

4   Community life in Romema had been very much influenced by the conflict and competition between the former traders and the rest of the community (see particularly Shokeid, 1971/1985: 23-8, 101-64; Deshen and Shokeid, 1974: 64-94; Shokeid, 1976).

Their houses and the land the Jews usually rented from the Berbers. However, some of the merchants owned property.[5] As far as the people of Romema could remember, they had not paid regular taxes before the advent of the French administration. The wealthy, however, gave costly gifts to their influential neighbors on the occasion of family celebrations or on holidays. They also bribed their sheikh to intercede on their behalf in disputes with their Muslim partners or debtors. Prior to French rule in the region, the local Berber sheikh was elected yearly by a council of the tribal grouping of Ait Mezalt.[6]

Aside from their local sheikh and the landlords, Asamer merchants and craftsmen were not necessarily permanently bound in business or by patronage to particular Berbers. Though they had sometimes developed special relationships with particular Berber families over a few generations, these ties could be cut off and new ones established without formality. However, their strongest ties were with those Berbers from whom they rented houses and land.[7] Their landlords would intervene in disputes with other Muslim families. The Jews, on the other hand, held themselves aloof from any strife in which their patrons' patronymic or tribal groupings were engaged. They would stay at home and wait for the tension to cool off. The trader or craftsman might have moved to another close or distant community upon the invitation of an employer or client to live on his estate. This mobility prompted by the search for livelihood may explain the changing size of Jewish communities in the Atlas Mountains, from less than ten inhabitants to three hundred or more (see Flamand's census, 1959: 329-33).

The landlords and patrons were often intimately acquainted with their Jewish protégés' personal and communal affairs. Thus, for example, the Romemites recall that in settling arguments or disputes between family

---

5   Flamand (1959: 86) also reports that a few families owned land at Ait Bou Oulli.
6   See Gellner, 1972 and Hart, 1972 who describe this system of annual election of tribal chiefs.
7   See also Hart's evidence on the particular relationships between the Berber landlord and his Jewish tenant (1976: 280).

groups in Asamer, particularly between merchants and craftsmen, Berber neighbors were often witnesses or arbitrators. The itinerant craftsman might have remained with his Berber employer for days, or even weeks. His employer saw to his personal needs. Only on the Sabbath might the journeying craftsman have stayed at a nearby Jewish community or visited the synagogue. The Muslims also might come to visit, stay, and partake of food and drink at their Jewish partners' or acquaintances' homes.[8] Friendship was at times expressed in gestures of physical contact, as in the story of the craftsman whose employed kissed his brow, begging him to stay with him overnight.

During the generation preceding immigration to Israel, two Jews from Asamer converted to Islam, both of whom had been itinerant craftsmen. The wife and children of one of them immigrated to Israel. The horrified brethren of the erstwhile Jews explained that the Berber employers of the latter had practiced "witchcraft" on them, while serving them tea. According to the Romemites' stories, however, it would seem that it was poverty and despair, at a particularly hard time, that drove the two to abandon their religion, family and community. Altogether, conversion of individuals to Islam was a problem many communities in Morocco had to contend with.

The wealthier merchants on their major business trips to Demnate, often became the target of robbers: for protection they took with them on these journeys some robust members of the community. Prior to the establishment of French rule, on a number of occasions local sheikhs ransacked the property of the family of traders in Asamer. According to their account, the last time the family was plundered the women were driven out of the house and the men tied up, but none was hurt. However, since the documents of all financial transactions had been well hidden, the family could renew its business, and it continued to thrive. At other times, the merchant could count on his Muslim friends. When the last head of the community was caught by French customs officials with a load of unauthorized fabric,

---

8   See also Flamand who reports on Berbers drinking in the homes of Jews (1959: 99).

a commodity rationed at that time, he stopped on his way to the police station at one of his Muslim acquaintances' home, and managed to leave with him part of his merchandise, loading sacks of straw instead. The eldest son of the head of the community, in his frequent references to Asamer, has vividly drawn the multi-faceted aspects of Jewish life in Morocco, as may be seen in the following succinct comment, phrased in a style often used in Romema in public debates and at ceremonies. This manner of speech interweaves metaphors with a somewhat archaic poetic language.[9] "The Jew even if very rich was stripped of honor in front of the Arab, and had to bow down to his will. But the Jew was always better dressed, better fed, and his house better furnished and stocked!"

On the relative safety of Jewish life in the Atlas Mountains, as perceived by the Romemites, we can learn from the following discussion. One evening, in Romema, while leaving the synagogue after the service, a settler spoke of the Negev Beduin who were crisscrossing the borders of Jordan, Egypt and Israel, smuggling drugs into the country as well as all kinds of heavily taxable commodities. One of the listeners suggested that those who were caught should be "slaughtered." Upon which the son of the last head of the community mentioned above, retorted with astonishment: "But why? The Arabs didn't slaughter us when we were living among them!" Yet on other occasions, people spoke appreciatively of their changed circumstances in Israel: "It is better to live in Israel because it is safe. In Morocco you could be rich, but the Arabs could come any time and rob you of your wealth. Here you are not afraid of anyone; you can shout at, and even throw out, the Jewish Agency people, if you want to!"[10]

The ambiguity in the position of Jews of Morocco, as well as the various modes of relating to their past existence among the Berbers, cropped up also in references by both former merchants and craftsmen to their manner of dress (though their tone and purpose of mentioning that point differed). The Jewish garb was usually white, but the merchants at times wore

---

9   See my reference to that manner of speech in Romema (1971: 134-5).

10 In rural settlements, Jewish Agency representatives were responsible in many matters related to farming, housing, and financial credit.

fancy and colorful clothes similar to the attire of Muslims. The craftsmen in recounting this added, not without a measure of satisfaction, that the proud merchants were the first to be molested not only by the highwaymen, but also by their Muslim patrons and neighbors.

THE INTERMEDIARY ROLE OF ATLAS MOUNTAIN JEWS

Today, when we try to assess what the Jewish situation had been in Muslim countries, we often compare it with the present situation in Israel or in Western countries. This is done also by the immigrants themselves, as evidenced by some of the earlier quotations, or in the following comment by a former shrewd merchant who was wont to speak of his methods of fooling his ignorant Muslim clients, and who, in Israel, had become a prosperous farmer:

> When we came to Israel we thought we would be given a small hut to live in and only bread to eat. I never dreamt we would have electricity and that I would own a refrigerator, a washing machine, and a tractor! There are Jews who return to the country of origin. Not me! I shall not go back to Morocco, even if I get thousands in cash! I shall not return to be cursed again by Arabs!

This former merchant has thus filtered his perspective of life in Morocco, *inter alia,* through his comprehension of personal achievements in Israel. These greatly surpassed his expectations which, at the time of immigration, had been motivated by Messianic beliefs.

This brings us back to our introductory note on the interpretative factor embedded in the informants' apprehension of their past and present situation. But, as demonstrated earlier, the Romemites' recollections were not geared into a definitive formula of positive or negative interpretations of their social position and of their relationships with their neighbors in Morocco. Consistency in interpretation is, it seems, more typical of outsiders, including scholars, or to ideologically motivated "natives." As mentioned, in the Romemites' view of life in Morocco, the Berbers at times played a prominent role in relationships of Jews among themselves.

No doubt the Jews of Asamer did not leave a "paradise" behind them, a notion which may be inferred from those who refer to symbiotic relationships between Jews and Berbers. They were a low-class minority; an inferior status, which, however, did not deprive them in all spheres of life. The Berbers were highly dependent on their many and varied services, which were not confined only to those occupations prohibited to Muslims. The Jews were also not the lowest status group in the Atlas Mountains; lower, for example, were the blacks, the descendants of former slaves, who traditionally were servants or followed such crafts as pottery. Within this framework of economic relationships and interdependence, the prosperous Jew could own land and prove his economic achievements and the special social relationships he had established with influential Berbers through fancy "non-Jewish" dress.

To obtain a broader perspective of Jewish life in the Islamic world we may compare the Atlas Mountains situation with the position of Jews as observed in Iran in the 1960s. Iranian Jews were confined, well into the twentieth century, to the most despised occupations and forced to show humiliating signs of identity, and they were considered of low moral standing. Bodily contact with a Jew was still, in some places, polluting to his Muslim neighbor. A Jew's property, life, and honor was never secure. He learned to hide his material possessions, to look destitute and humble. Loeb (1976) argues that the Iranian Jews' occupations as peddler, moneylender, entertainer, vendor of liquor and prostitution, which lead to interaction with diverse social groups, might have placed him in a position of communicator or disseminator of ideas. As an outcast however—humiliated and polluting—he, in fact, served to insulate the various segments of the population from one another, and thus performed an important service for the Persian elite.

The potential role of the Jew as mediator between various groups in society has been suggested as explaining the position of Jews in two polar extremes of Muslim environments: Rosen (1972) who analyzed the intermediary role of the Jew between Arabs and Berbers, and Loeb (1976) who interpreted the Jew's communicatory potentiality as transformed into an insulating function.[11] Though the approach of the intermediary role of the Jew cannot alone explain the complex Jewish situation, as manifest in Morocco or in Iran, it is a key variable in elucidating the Jewish situation in many places throughout the history of the Diaspora. In our case, the Jew cast in an intermediary role clarifies some aspects of Jewish existence in the Atlas Mountains.

In some parts of Morocco the Jew might have played an intermediary role between the two distinct ethnic categories of non-Jewish society, the Arabs and the Berbers. In the Atlas Mountains, the role of Jews was, *inter alia*, intermediary between different Berber tribal groupings—a hypothesis which calls for further research. The Atlas Mountains Jews were living in what is known as *bled es-siba,* or "land of dissidence" and "disorder". The central administration of the Sultan was not effective in these parts of Morocco and even the advent of French rule had little influence. Only at a late stage of French occupation—since the second quarter of the last century—were changes imposed. The surrounding Berber society was segmentary, organized agnatically, and in continuous inter- or intra-tribal conflict (see Gellner, 1972; Hart, 1972, 1976; Burke, 1976). Basic to the political tribal system were the *ingurramen* (marabouts), members of holy lineages, who did not belong to the tribal groupings, mediated in disputes, and applied tribal customs (such as the election of chiefs by rotation). They were endowed with *baraka* (divine grace), pacific, and their person was safe (Gellner, 1969, 1972).

The Mosaic of Berber society, aside from these holy outsiders, comprised another network of communities of pacific and secure outsiders—the Jews—who rendered vital economic services, yet were powerless due to their lower status, which was manifest in their humble behavior.

---

11 This comparison is obviously limited by the particular influence of Iranian Shi'ism on the position of Jews (Loeb, 1976).

Therefore services rendered by Jews or trading with them was not socially committing, which would not have been the case had the interaction been with a Berber from another patronymic group, and that might have been degrading for one party. Lack of commitment was especially significant in partnerships with Jews, who put up the capital in farming and herding enterprises; but also in day-to-day trading with the Jewish merchant who extended credit to his clients. This vital interaction with the Berbers placed the Jewish merchants and traders in Ait Bou Oulli, in an advantageous position evidenced, by their superior station in the Jewish community.

Hart's study of Jews shortly before immigration to Israel, and his recording of comments made by Berbers after the mass departure of Jews, succinctly encapsulates some features of Jewish existence observed from the other side:

> The keynote of Jewish behavior was that of safety in humility; conversely, for a powerful man to have 'his own' Jew was considered a sign of prestige. Because the Jews stood entirely outside the political system, and because their occupational services were much in demand, many informants said that to kill or even to molest a Jew was an infinitely worse offense than to kill a fellow tribesman (Hart, 1976: 280).

Although these two sets of records, my own from Israel and Hart's from Morocco, do not originate with the same group of Jews and their Berber neighbors, they reflect complementary interpretations of some elements of Jewish existence in Morocco. As it appears from the Romemites' experience, the Jewish craftsman, peddler and merchant could live in his community or travel with little risk involved, and he was welcomed, though he did not enjoy an honored position, in nearby or remote Berber settlements.[12]

---

12 The Jews, as other members of pacific groups (of lower or higher status), were exempt from payment of *dhazttat,* the protection fee a traveler paid to go from his own tribe into the territory of another (see Hart, 1976: 303-4).

The course of peaceful coexistence might have been intermittently interrupted, but the Jew could normally rely on the protection of his patron, employer, or client, and draw some sense of security from the local cultural code which specified rules to safeguard the weak and helpless, such as women and Jews. This position of the Jew, comprising both the inferior status and circumstantial advantages, opened the doors of Berber homes and tribal and sub-tribal territorial borders to the itinerant Jew. "For us, the craftsmen, there were no borders," remarked to me one of Asamer's former smiths, and thus elucidated the situation he experienced in Morocco.

CONCLUDING NOTE

We started our discussion by presenting a polarity of opinions about the position of Moroccan Jewry. Our case does not fully support either of these viewpoints. It seems as if both Rosen and Stillman described a "true" but partial reality of the Jewish situation. That perception of reality is not modified by the contradictions of daily existence which some scholars might view as "non-data," as, for example, the intervals of economic and social interaction and cooperation between a subordinate ethnic minority and a dominant majority. Accordingly, Rosen and Stillman have drawn clear-cut conclusions; the harmonious perspective versus the conflict perspective in Jewish-Muslim relationships. I have suggested some additional situational and structural factors which affected the position of Jews and their relationships with their neighbors. I emphasized the interpretative element embedded in the Romemites' perception of their experience in Morocco. Their perceptions and interpretations yield a complex image of Jewish-Muslim interaction evidenced by their paradoxical accounts of harmony and conflict. These presentations are genuine expressions of the existential experience of Atlas Mountains Jews, which cannot be dismissed because of apparent inconsistency. Thus, while most scholars have tried to formulate consistent paradigms, representative of at least some geographical areas or certain historical periods, such consistent paradigms may be nonexistent.

Also certain rabbinical texts, or other forms of extant records, sometimes arouse disagreement when used as sole bases for interpretation. The verbal communications which I collected about life in Morocco offer a kind of data which is rarely recorded. That type of material, if it survives at all, is with the passage of time, absorbed into such forms of discourse as folklore and folk tales.

CHAPTER 3.
THE EMERGENCE OF PSEUDO-KIN FACTIONS IN IMMIGRANT COMMUNITIES

Familism became a familiar feature of the Israeli political and social panorama soon after the establishment of the State of Israel. Kinship groups, known as *hamulas*, came to the fore among two very distinct, and apparently different, populations living under very diverse conditions: Arabs in traditional villages, and Middle Eastern Jewish immigrants in newly established rural settlements.

A Cohen (1965) identified the revival of corporate action of *hamula* groups in Arab villages in Israel (these groups having apparently been muted during the British Mandatory period), which he interpreted as a reaction to the new political and economic environmental constraints. My own observations in a number of villages of Middle Eastern immigrants revealed the quasi-kinship structure, and the transient nature of some of these *hamula* groups which, as later explicated, I define as a particular type of faction. The revival of *hamula* action might, to some extent, have been anticipated in Arab rural society and culture, but the occasional agitation of *hamula* groups in many of the Israeli Middle Eastern Jewish immigrant villages, which was widely publicized, took the Israeli public by surprise. The settlement authorities tried to suppress—in most cases unsuccessfully—the vociferous banding of *hamula* groups which deeply contrasted with the social ideals of the *moshav*, a smallholders' cooperative, to which the immigrants were expected to conform and adjust.

Factions have become a fertile field of research for the social scientist.[1] Studies of factions in rural societies seem to proffer the view that a fac-

---

1   For a developmental perspective of the study of rural factionalism see Lewis (1954), Firth (1957), Siegel and Beals (1960a, 1960b), Boissevain (1964), Nicholas (1965), Mayer (1966), Shokeid (1968), Buyra (1973), Schryer (1975), Silverman and Salisbury (1977).

tion is an ephemeral group which emerges in order to advance a specific aim (this is its cohesive element) or to rally around a specific interest in a dispute. People join one faction or another mainly for personal interests which often instigate the dispute or are the cause of the rivalry, or because the aims of the faction are a suitable vehicle for their personal aspirations, and not because of any prior connection between its members, such as kinship ties, religious affiliations, or belonging to the same caste. According to this view, it follows that when a faction develops into a more stable group bound by permanent criteria of membership, such as kinship ties or ideological commitments, it ceases to be a faction.

The research on which this discussion is based was carried out in two new rural immigrant communities in Israel. I tried to reconstruct the history, and identify the conditions under which factions first emerged and then disintegrated over a period of ten years. At their emergence these factions appeared to be aggregates of relatives referred to by outsiders, and by their own members, as *hamula* groups. The discussion will explicate the role played by family ties in initiating corporate action in situations of environmental pressures and of ambiguity in social relationships, thus relating the phenomena observed in Arab and in Jewish rural societies.

The reconstruction of the emergence and disappearance of family factions calls for a description of a considerable number of participants and of the many activities which took place over a long period. I shall present only the main lines of the process and this in greater detail only in one of two villages I studied, named here "Merhav,"—the other I have called "Misgav."[2] The inhabitants of the two villages were from different provenances. The Merhav settlers came from Morocco while those of Misgav were from Iranian Kurdistan. Despite the social and cultural differences between these two communities, the development of factionalism and its structural features were similar.

The two villages were planned by the settlement authorities according to the *moshav* pattern. This type of settlement was introduced into Israel

---

2   For more details about Misgav, see Shokeid (1968); for more details about Merhav see also Weingrod (1966).

in the 1920s by young European Jewish pioneers who wanted to establish a new society. The *moshav* is an agricultural settlement organized on the basis of moderate economic and social cooperation. The land belongs to the nation, but each family cultivates its farm and privately owns the household and farm equipment. The national institutions, administratively in charge, allocate to each farmer the same facilities and amount of land. While the *moshav* ideology intends its members to remain economic equals, in practice economic differentiation may occur as a result of individual efforts, enterprise, and skills, or of familial demographic factors. Economic cooperation takes place in many important activities, such as the marketing of agricultural produce, the supply of farm and household needs, and in sharing such services as dairies and granaries. The most important administrative organs are the village committee and the general assembly. There are also a number of other committees with specific and limited functions. Members of the committees and the incumbents of all offices are elected democratically each year.[3]

CASE STUDY — MERHAV

Merhav began to be settled in December 1954 by two groups that had immigrated from Morocco earlier the same year. One group, composed of fifteen families, had already experienced some of the trials and tribulations of the melting pot policy[4] when they lived for a few months in the neighboring village of Shefa, which was populated mainly by East European immigrants. The meeting of different cultures in Shefa was infelicitous and the Moroccan immigrants asked to

---

3   For more details about immigrant *moshavim*, see Weingrod (1966), Willner (1969), Shokeid (1971), Weintraub et al. (1971).

4   The melting pot policy aimed at a speedy integration of the various Jewish ethnic groups arriving in masses in Israel during the 1950s. Instrumental in welding a common Israeli cultural identity was the establishment of ethnically mixed settlements where the daily contact was expected to dissolve separate cultural identities. That policy however caused many difficulties during the 1950s. Since then, the Settlement Department has preferred to establish ethnically homogeneous villages.

be transferred to a village inhabited by fellow countrymen. The members of the Shefa group, as they were later called, had first met on board ship on their way to Israel.

The second group of settlers in Merhav, also fifteen families, was sent to the village immediately upon arrival in Israel. Of this group, apart from five families which came from Askaria, Morocco, some of whom were relatives, the rest had met in the transit camp in Marseilles. Banded as a group by their arduous experience of migrating together to Israel, they were called the Askaria group because the main cluster of families came from there.

In May 1955 five families, named Dahan, who were consanguineously related (two brothers, their two grown sons, and a daughter wedded to a sister's son) joined the village. In the Atlas Mountains they had lived as an extended family; they continued this household in Casablanca where they had moved the last few years before immigrating to Israel. On arrival in Israel, in 1954, they were immediately sent to a remote *moshav* in the Negev. Looking for a better place to live, they decided to move to Merhav. A few months thereafter they were joined by the three sons of another sister, named Danino, who on arrival had been sent to a different Negev village. By 1957 this group called the Dahans has recruited three more families, a married daughter, a brother-in-law, and a friend from Casablanca. In 1957 a Dahan boy married a local girl from the Shefa group, and her family also came to be identified with the Dahans. One of the two elder brothers, a skilled *shoheit* (ritual slaughterer), became the leader of the group.

With the arrival, in November 1955, of four interrelated families named Nahum, a fourth group began to settle in Merhav. The Nahum families came from Nurim, a *moshav* in the Galilee where, since 1954, a number of their relatives, all of whom hailed from the same town in Morocco, had settled. Similar to the Dahans, before immigration to Israel, some of them had lived a few years in Casablanca. Upon arrival they had been sent to Nurim whose population, consistent with the melting pot policy, originated from various countries. Social strains, which exacerbated the severe economic conditions, soon came to the fore, and the four Nahum families asked to be transferred to Merhav where one of them had

CHAPTER THREE

distant relatives among the Askaria group. The latter, in time, became the leader of what came to be known as the Nahum group. Within a few months four more families left Nurim for Merhav and by the beginning of 1957 this new group equaled the Dahan group in size. Apart from the eight families from Nurim, four families from the Askaria group were identified with the Nahums.

In comparing the kinship structure of the Dahans with the Nahums, we observe a major difference. Most of the Dahans were paternally or maternally related. Eight heads of families were descendant from the same parentage, while only four were related affinally or otherwise. In contrast, most of the Nahums were affinally related (including recent marriages) and only a minority consanguineously (see Charts 1 and 2).

Meanwhile about a third of the first two groups in Merhav, the Shefa and Askaria groups, gradually left the village, others joined the Dahan and Nahum groups, while the rest lost their group cohesion. These changes in the village composition prompted a new framework of relationships in which the Dahan and Nahum groups became dominant. Those settlers who identified with neither group were called "neutrals."

During the first year of settlement, Merhav was administered by instructors from the Settlement Department. The settlers were represented

Note: Charts 1, 2, 3, 4 include in the present generation all males above the age of 18 and only married females who live in the village.

Chart 1: The Genealogical Structure of the Dahan Group of Relatives

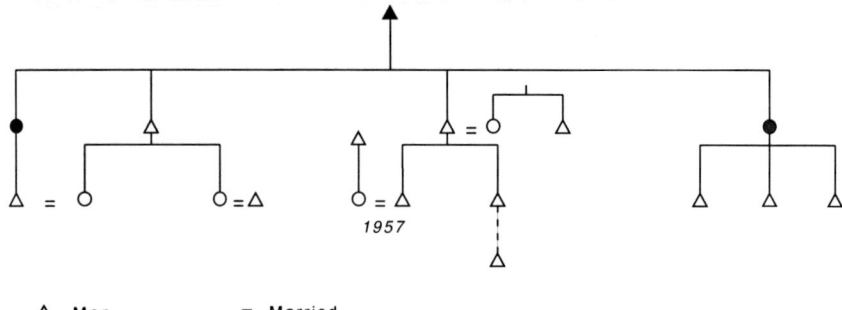

△ Men   = Married
○ Women   ▲ ● Deceased
--- Related by ties of friendship

THE EMERGENCE OF PSEUDO-KIN FACTIONS

Chart 2: The Genealogical Structure of the Nahum Group of Relatives

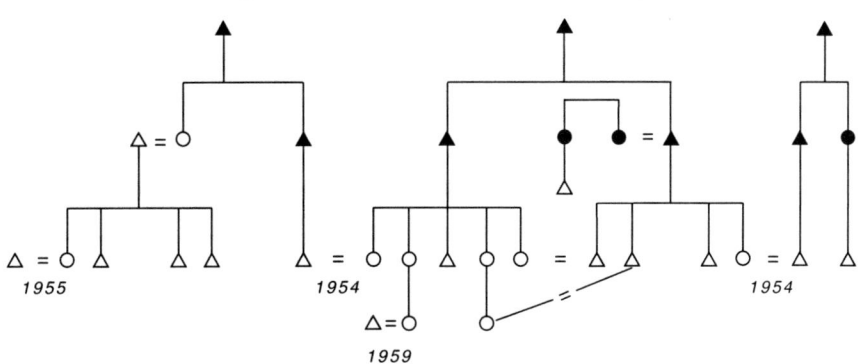

by the respected elders of the first two groups. Since the settlers knew little about farming, only ten dunams (two acres) were allocated at the beginning to each family, while most of the land was temporarily cultivated by a regional company. Severe economic conditions obliged most of the settlers to work as daily laborers at poorly paid, menial jobs (which were subsidized by the government), on the regional farm, in the village, or in its vicinity. This employment was assigned by the instructors, and later by the secretary of the village. Feelings of discrimination in the allocation of work formed a permanent source of complaint and bitterness.

The arrival of the Dahans drastically changed the framework of local leadership. Within a few months one of them was appointed *moshav* secretary, another agricultural store manager, while the leader of the group was installed in the office of rabbi. Only the defense organizer was not a Dahan. The Dahans proved to be diligent farmers who cultivated their land cooperatively. They also carried out the functions of their public offices efficiently and the instructors, impressed by their initiative and entrepreneurship, willingly offered them support. Although there were no other settlers in the village equally qualified and energetic, the takeover of the positions of influence by the Dahans, and the displacement of the Shefa and Askaria elders from leadership fermented rancor. During this period of scarcity in economic resources, the public offices, apart from their prestige and regular income, were also a means for providing important privileges, such as control over employment assignments, and the easy attainment of agricultural supplies and tools. The quickly growing influence of the Dahan group increased suspicions and feelings of discrimination and deprivation among the rest of the settlers.

The arrival of the Nahums at this time of increased tension had important consequences. Among them were men with initiative and skills who could compete with the Dahans. Family ties with a number of the first settlers assured them the support of many neutrals. Therefore, the numerical, as well as influential, growth of this group did not arouse opposition, rather the contrary—they were welcomed. The power of this new grouping and its support by many veteran settlers found expression in the demand to replace the Dahan secretary with a Nahum candidate. A complaint sent at that time to the Settlement Department by a settler not associated with either of the groups highlights this demand:

> The Dahan party, which counts nine families, sticks closely together, its members help only one another, making fun of the rest of the villagers. One of them is secretary; he saw to it that his brother be appointed store manager of agricultural produce. Each of them earns IL150. a month. These two see to it that their families are assigned the better jobs and get more work days.

The firm opposition of the majority of the villagers, who backed the new cohesive core group of the Nahums, forced the Dahan secretary to resign, and the leader of the Nahums was immediately appointed to the post. This replacement led to open rivalry between the Dahan and Nahum groups, which the instructors and the settlers called "*hamula war*," (*milhemet hamulot*).

In 1957 a few members of the Dahan group jointly bought the first tractor at Merhav. Although it was small, it symbolized that group's achievements, and gave the Dahans an important advantage in cultivating their farms. At the same time it provided them with a new source of employment and income since the services of their tractor were in demand by the other farmers. This augmented the animosity toward the Dahans which was further exacerbated when they brought in a new settler, in spite of the village committee's refusal to approve his candidacy. At the end of 1957, the committee demanded the demission of the Dahan agricultural store manager. They claimed that he abused his position to benefit himself. He was forced to resign and his duties were added to those of the grocery storekeeper, who was an outsider. The tendency to spurn them and force them out of public offices aroused the Dahans' ire, and they refused to continue to cooperate with the village institutions. They stopped marketing their produce cooperatively with the rest of the villagers and ceased to pay municipal taxes. As a result, they were also at odds with the settlement authorities who supported and supervised the activities of the *moshav* and were interested in smooth functioning of the village institutions, particularly the cooperative marketing. The representatives of the sponsoring agencies, who had previously supported the Dahans, now considered them troublemakers. In January 1958 they were even willing to help the village committee sue the Dahans for selling their produce privately and for not paying taxes. The mounting tension climaxed when the two groups came to blows in the synagogue, sparked by a quarrel between the Dahan rabbi and a Nahum congregant. A few in the brawl were injured, the police intervened and took members of both sides into custody. The case came to court and the participants were fined. In the wake of this clash, the rest of the villagers refrained from contact with the Dahans, refusing even to pray with them, and to use the rabbi's services.

Socially isolated and deprived of the *moshav* services and of the support of the settlement authorities, the Dahans began to look for the possibility of moving to another settlement. But they were unwelcome in other villages due to their reputation for aggressiveness. The settlement authorities, who valued the Dahans' industry and enterprise, were anxious to reconcile them with their neighbors. Toward the end of 1958, after a few months of peacemaking efforts, a compromise was reached between the two parties. The Danans, for their part, agreed to market their produce through the village institutions and to pay their taxes. The Nahums, on the other hand, conceded to the Danans the privilege of the village to buy a big tractor tax-free and on easy credit terms. This turn of affairs was facilitated by the growing influence of one of the younger and more genial Dahans.

By the end of 1958, the competition and animosity over public offices had greatly eased, but discontent and tension now mounted because the Dahans had monopolized the tractor services of the village. The settlement authorities had gradually completed their allocation of land to the Merhav settlers. At the end of 1957, the central farm was discontinued and each farmer received an additional eleven-dunam plot. The size of a farm was now twenty-one dunams (two-thirds of the planned farm) with the last eleven dunams to be allocated in the autumn of 1959. The Dahans' tractors became an extremely lucrative enterprise since the other farmers came to be increasingly dependent on their services.

Only at the beginning of 1960 did three Nahum farmers jointly buy a tractor. They had to pay the full price since the village was not entitled to another tax-free tractor on convenient credit terms. A few years later the Nahums' leader proudly described to me that purchase:

> Our purchase was the body blow that broke the barrier. The Dahans thought that none but they could buy farm machinery. We showed them it was possible. We decided to oppose power with power and we bought a lot of tools. We busted the fence.

The purchase of this tractor was soon followed by another, which severely damaged the Dahans' interests. One of them told me: "They bought a tractor only to vex us, so that our tractors would not be hired." Thus the old rivalry over public offices was transmuted into a struggle between the owners of tractors. This competition was particularly exploited by the neutrals who gained cheaper tractor services; but the competition as such caused much damage to the owners of tractors on both sides.

A dramatic change in the relationships between the groups occurred in 1961 when a partnership, under the name The Cooperative, was formed between the owners of tractors and other vehicles of both sides, three Dahans and three Nahums. This unexpected development was facilitated through the intervention of a new Nahum settler, a skilled mechanic, who had had no part in the *hamula* rivalries. Soon after his arrival, he participated in the Nahums' purchase of farm equipment and strongly urged that they form a partnership with the Dahans to open a tractor station that would provide for all the needs of Merhav and the neighboring villages and would prevent unprofitable purchases and competition.[5] The new Nahum settler was the most likely candidate to head the enterprise. In 1962 the secretary of the *moshav*, a Nahum who was also a partner, voluntarily resigned and a young settler whose family was not connected with the *hamula* feuding became secretary. Thus the most conspicuous and painful symbol of dispute between the Dahans and Nahums disappeared.

The Cooperative survived two years and was peacefully dissolved when the manager left Merhav. The enterprise had not been as profitable as envisaged, particularly since many more settlers gradually bought farming equipment which stymied a monopoly and reduced the dependence on, and the competition over the competition, machinery services.

These developments also influenced relationships within the groups. Thus, for example, the three Danino brothers, nephews of the Dahan elders, who had not been partners in the new machinery enterprise, realized that the long *hamula* struggle had not been equally profitable to all. Their uncles and cousins, who had become well-to-do farmers, had profited much more than they. Since the establishment of the tractor station, the Dahan group had lost much of its esprit de corps. But the sudden reconciliation between the groups had an even more telling effect on the solidarity of the Nahum group, the group having initially been motivated by external constraints exerted by the Dahans, rather than by spontaneous solidarity.

Since the mid-1960s, the *hamula* phenomenon has hardly had any major effect on village life. The public offices which previously had been such issues of contention interested the core of the *hamula* groups much less, as well as other *moshav* members, because they were now economi-

---

5   The Dahans entered their bigger tractor into the partnership, the Nahums two medium-sized tractors. The latter were sold and in their stead the partners acquired a caterpillar tractor and a truck.

cally secure and could not spare the time. Those who did look for jobs preferred to take a position outside the village, possibly with the regional economic and administrative institutions,[6] which was more prestigious and more lucrative. The village committee, consisting of a Dahan, two Nahums, and two former neutrals, functioned smoothly. They were no longer elected as representatives of groups according to a fixed quota, but by virtue of personal merits and ties.

CASE STUDY—MISGAV

Settlement in Misgav, a village about twenty kilometers distant from Merhav, began in 1953 with two groups of immigrants from Iranian Kurdistan. For three years after their arrival they had lived in Israel under the depressing conditions of transit camps (*ma'abarot*),[7] located on the outskirts of Jerusalem and Rehovot. Their expectations for a quick improvement in their standard of living were painfully shattered when they came to Misgav. The houses and farms were not ready, and for a long time they worked in menial jobs, subsidized by the government.

Eliezer, the leader of the Jerusalem group, began to recruit relatives from various places to the *moshav*. Within a year they formed a cohesive group called Hamulat Eliezer, which showed itself to be forceful and ingenious. The group contrived, *inter alia*, to purchase tax-free and on easy credit terms the tractor and truck allocated to the *moshav*. Its members disrupted the orderly functioning of the village institutions. Gradually a second group emerged from among the other settlers, called Hamu-

---

6 Thus, for example, the Nahums' first leader and secretary of the *moshav* has, since the mid-1960s, managed a regional industry, while one of the younger Dahans took a position with an important administrative organization where he represented the Negev villages.

7 The *ma'abarot* were transit camps initially established to cope with the shortage of housing during the mass immigration of the early 1950s. This temporary arrangement extended in most cases over a long period. In a sense, the *ma'abarot* degenerated into organized shanty towns. During that period there was also a shortage of work, and the residents of the *ma'abarot* were mostly employed in menial jobs as daily laborers.

THE EMERGENCE OF PSEUDO-KIN FACTIONS

lat Mahbati. The formation of this group was made possible particularly through the marriage between members of two small family groups.

Similar to our findings in Merhav, the kinship ties within each of the *hamula* groups were not consistent and included relatives from various descent lines and genealogical distances (see charts 3 and 4). The deep animosity between the two groups reached its climax in a series of violent outbursts. Gradually, the Mahbati group gained the approval of the rest of the villagers, the neutrals, who opposed the Eliezer group which they considered aggressive and which monopolized positions and economic assets. This general support was reinforced by the marriage of a Mahbati boy to a girl from among the neutrals.

In 1960, some Mahbati members and a few neutrals bought their first tractor. This purchase was of particular importance since in 1960 the settlement authorities also completed the full allocation of land per farm. It also made a breach in the Eliezer monopoly and marked the beginning of the gradual breakup of the Eliezer group, a few of whom even left the village. Now a majority, the Mahbati group and their supporters succeeded in appointing one of their members to the office of secretary, which facilitated the orderly functioning of the village institutions. In the mid-1960s villagers thus described the decline of *hamula* groups: "Today, the *hamulas* are like the smell of tobacco."

Chart 3: The Genealogical Structure of the Eliezer's Group of Relatives

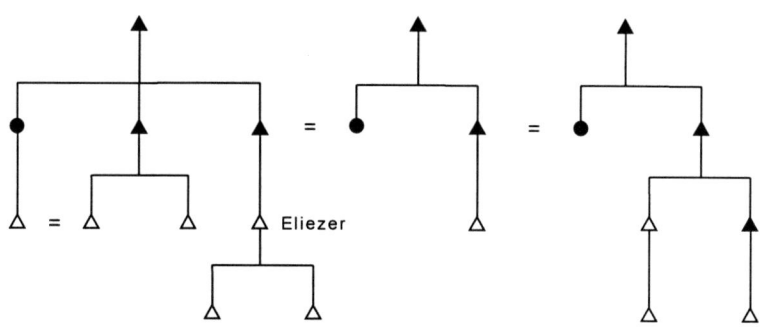

CHAPTER THREE

Chart 4: The Genealogical Structure of the Mahbati Group of Relatives

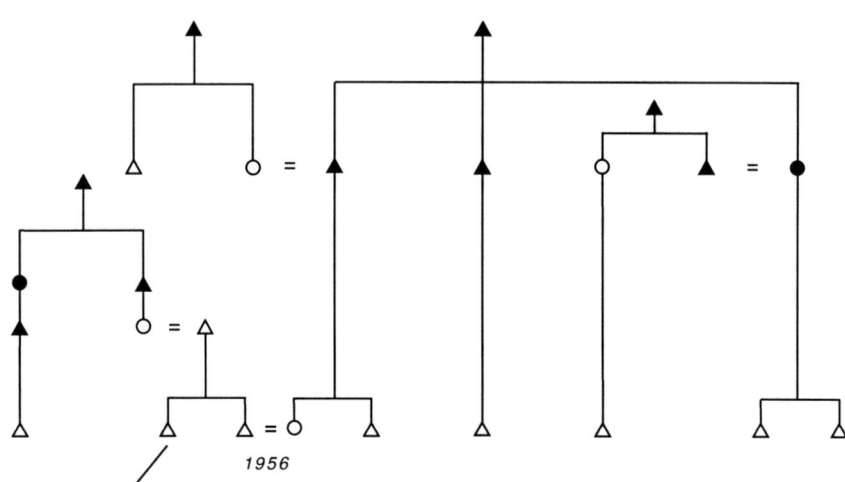

* Married a girl from among the neutrals in 1958.

HAMULA GROUPS—FACTIONS IN TRANSITION

The processes of development and dissolution of *hamula* groups in Merhav and Misgav represent factionalism as earlier defined. A focused summary of events in both villages emphasizes the familiarities of that particular faction phenomenon, in spite of the apparently different cultural background of the settlers.

The majority of the settlers arrived in the villages with the expectation of improving their economic situation and social standing. They came either from other villages where they had been sent by the authorities and where they had met with economic difficulties and social deprivation, or from the depressing *ma'abarot*. The first settlers clung together during immigration and the first stages of their absorption in Israel; the common experiences—on the boat, in the villages structured on the melting pot theory, and in the *ma'abarot*—provided the basis for concord among them. But the road to success in farming proved to be long and difficult.

Once settled, they had to share the limited resources allocated to them within the framework of a cooperative organization.

A few newcomers to the social ideology of cooperation, and who had no inclination to comply with it, tried to grab for themselves the limited resources allocated to the village as a whole. The formation of a novel type of social grouping, based on kinship (the Dahan group in Merhav and the Eliezer group in Misgav), rendered this feasible. This new grouping, called *hamula*, provided its members with considerable advantages.

The immigrants had known this type of organization among their Moslem neighbors in their countries of origin, but most of them had not practiced it before immigration. Paradoxically, its revival was initiated by those better adjusted to the new economic constraints and who, before coming to Israel, had experienced important changes. They had left their communities of origin in the Atlas Mountains, in Southern Morocco, or in mountainous Kurdistan and had settled in the larger cities of Morocco and Iran.

New groupings of relatives, apparently taking their cue from the first, soon organized (the Nahums in Merhav and the Mahbaties in Misgav), imitating their modes of action. This profound change in social action altered the principle of social organization in these villages that, at settlement, had been based on the common traumatic experiences of people thrown together by the circumstances of immigration. Instead, these quasi-family *hamulas,* confronted each other belligerently, competing over the administrative positions and other material resources allocated to the village. The principle of kinship, employed to recruit new members to the groups, was flexible and manipulative. All sorts of relatives joined either from afar or from within the village through marital alliance.[8]

---

8   A manipulative element in kinship affiliation has been observed in the immigrants' Muslim host societies as demonstrated by Eickelman (1967: 99-102, 105-207) and Spooner (1965). The development recorded in our study parallels, however, the situation in many growing urban centers in Africa where people are united by cognatic and affinal links which replace more specific types of kinship ties, see Epstein (1961).

Due to competition between groups of relatives, which encouraged economic initiative and the agricultural burgeoning as the result of a full allocation of farm land, there gradually evolved a new situation which greatly affected relationships in the *moshav*. Individual economic achievements created new interests which, on the one hand, sometimes divided members of the same *hamula* group but, on the other, were common to members of the opponent *hamula* group. These developments inevitably led to a change in the framework of social association and challenged the modes of behavior based on the principle of kinship which, until then, seemed to have been a stable guide for behavior. Particularly noticeable is the partnership formed to establish a tractor station in Merhav, a new interest group which cut across the previous family groups. Thus, on the whole, these *hamulas* were temporary groupings, organized to promote certain interests of their members.

Sociologists and anthropologists who have studied factions in small communities offer various, sometimes contradictory, explanations. Already at the inception of faction research, in the late 1950s, there were two divergent and contradictory approaches. Siegel and Beals (1960) who studied factions which emerged in long-established communities argued, for example, that these are symptomatic of social maladjustment. They explained their emergence as an outcome of physical and cultural external pressures converging with internal strains inherent in the social system. Firth (1957), on the other hand, basing himself on data collected in newly established communities, interpreted factionalism as a social mechanism which enables individuals to reach their goals in a situation in which they are separated from their traditional groups.[9] Both these approaches have been elaborated on in more recent studies which have examined the relevance and structure of factionalism under different types of strain and conflict, and have been applied to the growing data of social mobilization and community change.[10] Elements of both approaches are useful to

---

9 This line of analysis Firth (1957) shared with researchers of overseas Indian communities, such as Benedict (1957), Mayer (1957, 1961), Morris (1957).

10 See, for example, Yadava (1968), Schwartz (1969), Gross (1973), Schryer (1975).

our cases. We find that *hamula* factions emerged when individuals had to react to severe external pressures in a situation where institutionalized role expectations and mutual relations between the members of the community had not yet been established. They had to survive on meager resources which dashed their hopes for a quick improvement of their economic conditions, and were compelled to adjust to principles of cooperative settlement alien to them. In confronting these constraints, they were in the company of people most of whom they had not known before or had met only recently, during immigration, after they were separated from their traditional groups and associations. In sum, they did not feel a deep commitment toward their new compatriots on whom they could not rely for support and were engaged in a situation of ambiguity as to the rules and norms of social interaction. The revival and recruitment of kinship ties, as crystallized in a *hamula* pattern, provided a familiar, and relatively stable, framework for social interaction and corporate action.

As Siegel and Beals have observed, and in our cases, at least during the first stage of settlement, factions were indicative of maladjustment since they accelerated tensions, initiated strife, and hampered the functioning of village services and institutions. However, similar to Firth's findings, we too observed that the first faction in every *moshav* which tried to monopolize the limited resources available was also a pacemaking group of "economizing attitude"[11] displaying enterprising characteristics among people who, on the whole, were ignorant of, and apathetic to, the new economic conditions. The motivations, aspirations, and stratagems of the pacemaking groups were imitated by the other settlers.

However, these *hamula* groups lacked many of the characteristics such groups had had in their traditional setting. The incentives that led to the formation of the studied *hamula* groups, which were apparently built on traditional elements, were mainly rooted in the interests and needs generated by the particular conditions related to the settlement of the immigrants. Therefore, when the constraints which had spurred the formation

---

11   A concept developed by Shils (1958).

of these groups changed, the groups underwent a deep transformation. External as well as internal developments contributed to the changes. External developments were particularly those related to material means as, for example, the completion of the allocation of irrigated farm land and the many more opportunities for diverse work in the vicinity of the villages. Among the internal changes of particular importance are individual material achievements and the unequal accumulation of wealth which gave rise to conflicting interests among the members of each faction.

Our study identified *hamula* factions as transient frameworks for corporate action which emerged at a crisis of anomie, in the wake of the breakdown of the traditional social order on immigration, and evolved between unrelated people coping with difficult, new economic and social conditions. The factions operated as a selective mechanism which combined values and modes of behavior chosen from the past social structure with those demanded by the new environment. Though the factions were inconsistent in their selection and open to internal conflicts, strains, and changes, they nevertheless played a vital role in the initial adjustment to the new environment, as well as in the transition to a more coherent and meaningful system of values and norms of behavior.

We cannot present here the detailed data needed to demonstrate the revival of *hamulas* in Israeli Arab villages. I shall briefly describe the background situation that gave rise to them. During the Mandatory period, as explicated by A. Cohen (1965), a few families owned most of the land in Arab villages, while the bulk of the population worked for them. The growing disparity of wealth in the village led to association between groups of equal social status that crossed *hamula* boundaries. Intermarriage between these groups forged bonds between economic and political equals. However the inclusion of these villages within the frontiers of the State of Israel led to drastic changes in the processes and patterns of the distribution of wealth and power in Arab rural society. The amount of land at the disposal of Arab landowners diminished considerably; the poor landless peasants, on the other hand, now had ample opportunities to improve their standard of living through wage labor in Jewish villages and towns. Besides this tendency toward a leveling of income, candidates for political positions in the village were now elected by secret ballot. These positions, such as village councilor, the chairman of the village council, or the administrator of the labor exchange office, carried much prestige and power. The former alignment between the prosperous notables of various *hamulas* broke down, giving way to the recruitment of the rank and file of each *hamula* to support its candidates in the competition over public offices and political appointments. *Hamula* division was not emphasized and the *hamula* entity was jealously guarded through the insistence, at time compulsion, of marriage solely within the *hamula*. Members were mobilized to take sides in interests and events till then considered the private affairs of the parties concerned.

In spite of the many differences between the *hamula* factions we observed in Jewish Middle Eastern immigrant villages and *hamula* groups in stable Arab rural society, one is struck by some similarities in the process of their emergence and performance. Although *hamula* groups in Arab village society do not conform to the usual definition of factions, the circumstantial revival of these *hamula* groups calls to mind some of the new approaches and the criticism leveled at the usual anthropological perception and analysis of kinship groups in Arab societies. Schneider (1971), Rosen (1972a), and Eickelman (1976), for example, emphasize the contractual basis of kinship relationships in Arab society. Our observations help to sharpen that perception of the stratagems and situational elements imbedded in what often appears to be a primordial compelling force of behavior in Arab and other societies.

CHAPTER 4.
THE REGULATION OF AGGRESSION IN DAILY LIFE: AGGRESSIVE RELATIONSHIPS AMONG MOROCCAN IMMIGRANTS IN ISRAEL

Moroccan Jews, the largest group of immigrants to have arrived in Israel since the establishment of the State in 1948, have long been stereotyped as hot-tempered and uncontrollable. During the 1950s and early 1960s, this was symbolically represented by the appellation *morocco sakin* (literally, Morocco knife).

Their violence was interpreted as a sign of the breakdown of family and communal ties; the continuation of a process of disintegration that started in Morocco with the migration from rural areas to the coastal cities. Thus, Bar-Yosef (1959), commenting on an outburst of riots and violence by Moroccan immigrants in an urban slum, notes that the migration to cities has led to the breakdown of the traditional Jewish economy in Morocco, a growing identification with unattainable middle-class ideals and standard of living, and a desire to achieve political equality. Those who came to Israel transferred these aspirations to their new society, but their hopes of quick improvement in economic, social, and political status were soon shattered. Moreover, the notion of relative deprivation grew immensely with the change of reference group. Marx (1976), who studied Moroccan immigrants housed in a new town with limited employment opportunities, interpreted minor personal violence as a strategy employed by the individual for extracting material benefits from bureaucrats responsible for the allocation of various resources; or as a way of attracting the attention of other members of the family and community to his predicament and to his inability to provide for his family. Existing studies have thus mainly emphasized the situational aspect of Moroccan violence, based on a somewhat vaguely defined hypothesis of social disintegration and aggression.[1]

Another common view has considered Moroccan violence a product of the conditions of personal danger that, for many generations, typified great parts of Morocco, due to the weakness of the central government (see, for example, Marx 1967: 33). However, studies carried out in Morocco (Rosen 1972; Geertz 1973) and my own data (Chapter 2) substantiate a common anthropological observation: the weakness of central governments does not necessarily imply chaos and lawlessness in the lower levels of social organization, and particularly in the life of local communities. Studies on the relationships between Jews, Berbers, and Arabs in Morocco demonstrate that, except during particular instances of political turmoil, violence was carefully checked at the local level, even in the most remote tribal areas. Moreover, in this social environment there were no strangers, in the sense that travelers were easily identified as members of certain social units (Jewish or Muslim), whose relatives and patrons would demand revenge or compensation for any damage or injury.

Approaches to the study of aggression are varied. Social anthropologists have usually queried the social context of the more extreme manifestations of violence, such as homicide and suicide.[2] Others have considered those cases of aggression which triggered competition, feud, vendetta, or war between groups of relatives, neighboring tribes, or other societal groupings.[3] Cultural anthropologists have been particularly interested in the manifestations of national character.[4]

Sociologists have mainly considered aggression in terms of group violence which expresses social protest and which may develop into a social movement, or in terms of delinquency and crime. In considering the latter context, which is the more relevant to the present discussion, they have concentrated on the distribution and characteristics of reported crime,

---

1   See also Weingrod 1960; Palgi 1966; Elam 1978.
2   See Bohannan 1960; Firth 1961.
3   See Gluckman 1963; Peters 1967; Nettleship, Givens, and Nettleship 1975.
4   See, for example, Mead 1935; Montagu 1967; Levy 1973; O'Nell 1979.

which obviously cannot cover all manifestations of aggression. Moreover, they have often concentrated on crime associated with specific populations, such as juvenile delinquency, or white-collar crime.[5]

Psychologists have queried in particular the sources, triggers, and types of human aggression. Is aggression an instinctive biological drive, as Freud (1975) assumed? To what extent are aggressive acts conditioned by frustration? How can one disentangle the expressive, hostile, and instrumental properties of aggression?[6] Most of these studies, however, were carried out through experimental laboratory manipulations, which even psychologists admit have certain limitations (Stonner 1976: 254-256).

In sum, neither anthropologists, sociologists, nor psychologists have provided a thorough examination of the varied expressions and distribution of personal aggression and violence in daily life, which only selectively appear in official crime records. Minor outbursts of aggression and violence, while not completely neglected, were largely considered in terms of particular institutional spheres, as in Bakan's (1971) and in Steinmetz and Straus' (1974) descriptions of marital and parental relationships.

In contrast, my approach deals with the totality of aggressive acts rather than with specific types of aggression, as this permits a better understanding of aggression as part of the mechanisms regulating affect in society. The composition of the study population further facilitates this objective as it is composed of two separate communities both of which were less subject to acute processes of social disintegration and economic deprivation than were the Moroccan groups analyzed in other studies. The Moroccan immigrants that I observed seem to have been highly selective in their targets for both verbal and physical aggression. Under similar circumstances of dispute and provocation, they more frequently and more violently attacked those individuals with whom they were involved in a web of social ties. Our findings, which indicate the social and cultural constraints that regulate the direction of aggression among

---

5   See, for example, A.K. Cohen 1955.
6   See Scott 1958; Feshbach 1964; Wolfgang and Ferracuti 1967; Quanty 1976.

Moroccan Jews in Israel, may offer a methodological and conceptual tool for the study of those elements which regulate the various patterns of aggressive behavior in other human groups.

BACKGROUND OF RESEARCH

My study is based on participant observation among Moroccan settlers in two villages, which I call Romema and Yashuv. Most of the Moroccan settlers in these villages migrated in 1956 from Asamer, a single community in the Atlas Mountains.[7] In Morocco, the Jews of Asamer had worked as craftsmen, peddlers, or merchants serving the Berber population. In Israel they all became farmers in moshav communities, a settlement form developed in the 1920s by young European pioneers, and based on moderate economic and social cooperation between smallholders. The moshav is administered by elected officials and committees, and major decisions are ratified by the general assembly of the village.[8]

On arrival in Israel, all newcomers from Asamer were settled in Yashuv, but a large group soon split off and settled in Romema. The houses and farms they vacated have since been settled by immigrants from Eastern Europe. In 1979, Moroccans comprised about 50 per cent of Yashuv's population. Public life in Romema was dominated by three family groups who competed over the allocation of resources and positions of power in the moshav organization. A similar phenomenon occurred in Yashuv, which was dominated by two family groups. In earlier analysis of strife in Romema I focused on intragroup cohesion and intergroup aggression.[9]

---

7   Fieldwork extended over 21 months (October 1965 to March 1967, June 1976 to September 1976) in Romema. Research in Yashuv was conducted during sporadic visits over one year (1979),

8   For more details about the moshav pattern of settlement and about the adjustment of Middle Eastern and North African immigrants to that model of organization see Weingrod (1966), Willner (1969), and Shokeid (1971a; 1980a).

9   See Shokeid 1971a, 1976; Deshen and Shokeid 1974.

In contrast, I now compile all cases of personal verbal aggression and physical assaults that I observed or that became public knowledge during my fieldwork, whether the cause was domestic, economic, territorial, administrative, or political.

INCIDENTS OF AGGRESSION

Aggression as discussed here, refers to raising the voice followed by the manifestation of anger in facial and bodily expressions, whether in expressing personal accusations of misconduct or of disappointing behavior or in reaction to illegitimate claims. The outbursts discussed generally attracted the attention of bystanders or passers-by, who tried to separate the protagonists and calm them down. Sometimes, however, these verbal outbursts escalated to involve the use of force.

Table 1 presents all cases of verbal and physical aggression according to the sphere of activity in which they occurred and the social relationship between the protagonists. The latter variable includes three categories: disputes involving members of the same family group; disputes involving members of different family groups (three in Romema and two in Yashuv); and disputes involving an outsider (working in the service of the moshav, representing an outside agency, or, in Yashuv, Eastern European settlers).

With the stress on personal aggression, these cases are distinct from the frequent disputes during meetings of the village committee or the general assembly. In these settings the target of aggression was usually more diffuse (for example, the bitter complaints against a particular family group for its apparent desire to monopolize positions of office, rather than the direct personal attack at a particular contender for a specific office).[10] Nevertheless, a few of the cases described did take place at such public meetings.

---

10 See Romanucci-Ross (1973) who differentiated between bound conflict, when individuals act as members of a larger unit, and unbound individual conflict, when the individuals act on their own behalf.

TABLE 1. VERBAL AND PHYSICAL AGGRESSION, BY FIELD OF
CONFLICT AND SOCIAL RELATIONSHIP BETWEEN PROTAGONISTS

	Intrafamily		Interfamily		Strangers and Outsiders		Total	
	Verbal	Physical	Verbal	Physical	Verbal	Physical	Verbal	Physical
Domestic and family	6	2					6	2
Neighborly	5	2	1				6	2
Partnership	1	1		1			1	2
Service		1			7	2	7	3
Communal Organization	2		3	2	2		7	2
Economic Resources	1		3				4	
Other			2				2	
Total	15	6	9	3	9	2	33	11

PHYSICAL ASSAULTS

In Morocco, members of the Asamer community had once killed a Muslim robber, and one community dispute almost ended in a fatality, but since their arrival in Israel no one had ever been charged with severe physical assault. No weapons were ever used and any injuries were slight; such incidents were always the result of the spontaneous escalation of verbal disputes. In most cases of strife between kin, non-kin, strangers (such as Eastern European settlers in Yashuv) and outsiders, aggression was mainly verbal. While the contenders would often get very close and scream at each other, their faced reddened by anger and their bodies tense, they usually refrained from the final move towards violence.

Table 1 shows that nearly 50 percent of all aggressive encounters (31 out of 44) involved close relatives. Physical assaults, particularly the more violent, were also more frequent among kin; three of the four physical assaults which left clear marks involved close relatives. The fourth, like most other physical assaults in which both protagonists were locals, involved women who intervened in their husbands' disputes. The only other minor physical assault, in a dispute between two men from Romema, involved distant relatives. Unrelated Moroccan members of the community or strangers, usually from other ethnic groups, were only rarely (and then only slightly) injured.

Thus, Daniel Sebag, Romema's marketing manager, faced bitter opposition from the rival Biton family. Yet, the only violent incident during his period of office was instigated by his two first cousins, who objected to his criticism of their vegetable sorting. In the ensuing fight, Daniel was slightly injured, and the case was brought to court. But sometime later, the two cousins made a sumptuous conciliatory feast and the relationship returned to normal. Another violent incident in which close kin were involved concerned the breaking-up of a sheep-farming partnership between two first cousins despite the local conviction that only partnerships between kin could succeed. In contrast, the only long-standing partnership was between two settlers related only through distant affinal ties. The eventual peaceful dissolution of this partnership belied the predictions of violence that had been rife in Romema for years.

The only case of severe violence involving unrelated Romema settlers occurred when two members of the village committee came to inspect a settler's alleged encroachment on communal land. The settler, Aziz Sebag, was the eldest son of the last head of the community in Asamer. The change in the family status in Romema made him especially touchy about perceived disrespect. While the men were arguing, Sebag's wife suddenly leaped forward and bit the owner of the cart on which the investigating delegation had arrived, leaving him with clear marks on his arm and face. No formal reconciliation ever took place, and the stigma contributed to the decline of Aziz Sebag's status in the community.

Only two incidents of violence toward strangers were recorded in Romema, and both were rather minor. In one case, a farmer hit the manager of the moshav shop (a Tunisian from a neighboring moshav) who refused to supply goods until an outstanding debt had been settled. The shopkeeper, who was offended rather than injured, reported the attack to the police, and the farmer was fined. In another case, aggression was directed towards the rabbi, an outsider appointed by the Ministry of Religious Affairs, who took off for a few days, leaving the congregants without a ritual slaughterer just before a festival. On his return one of the settlers, protesting this action, gave the rabbi a light shove; again, causing offence rather than injury.

These incidents illustrate that while the Moroccans studied might physically assault close kin, they generally refrained from assaulting members of their own community with whom they had no family ties. However, there were some incidents of violence involving outsiders. It seems that the defensive stance adopted by outsiders in response to their Moroccan protagonists' deafening screeches and bodily expressions, which they perceived as expressions of imminent violence, in fact exacerbated the dispute, and triggered off a counter-reaction which might otherwise not have taken place. Even so, the outcome was generally oral rather than physical injury. This observation is supported by Marx's (1976) findings with regard to Moroccan immigrants' action towards officials.

VERBAL AGGRESSION

While physical assault was never considered excusable, and was an embarrassment to all concerned, verbal aggression was unanimously considered natural, a sign of purity of motives and sentiments. This attitude was expressed in statements such as: "Dirty mouth—clean heart," "he who has evil in his mouth does not have evil in his heart," "I scream but I don't keep a grudge," "our people don't know how to talk, they don't conceal their thoughts." Other common sayings stressed the connection between verbal aggression and reconciliation: "if we scream at each other we can later meet and talk again, that's how we are," "as much as we Moroccans quarrel, when we eventually meet at a celebration we eat together and make up." This was given impressive expression in the frequent parties in Romema, many of which were arranged by those involved in disputes as a gesture of conciliation for wild mouths.[11]

This mode of behavior was clearly demonstrated by a wealthy farmer in his late forties, a shrewd politician who was frequently carried away by violent outbursts of anger and was involved in more disputes than anyone else (eleven incidents, including two physical assaults). He was, however, a generous party giver; after a quarrel with the rabbi he insisted on holding the annual party of the Zohar (text of Jewish Gnosticism) Study Circle in his house and at his expense, even though he rarely attended their meetings. In contrast, the very few settlers who refused to reconcile with their disputants were condemned and regarded with suspicion by the rest of the community.

Frequently, verbal aggression appeared to express a fleeting emotion, and its impact was no less fleeting. Having screamed out their protest, settlers would frequently calm down and head for home, or engage, often good-humoredly, in discussion on another issue. The people of Asamer were inclined to interpret more permanent disaffection in terms of a wider political confrontation rather than personal enmity. Thus, Daniel Sebag, experiencing Levy Biton's persistent opposition to his taking office in the moshav organization (opposition which had severe personal consequences for Daniel Sebag, as it meant the loss of badly needed money as well as prestige), interpreted it not as personal animosity but rather as part of the Bitons' resentment of the Sebag family's aspirations for leadership. In arguments with Biton, Sebag was very careful to suppress the release of the

---

11   Shokeid 1976.

frustration and anger apparent in his facial and bodily expressions. Sometimes, at the peak of a heated argument in the village meeting, he would leave abruptly so as to avoid the escalation of a personal dispute. Later, he would rejoin the meeting and resume discussions with the participants, Biton included. Sebag's great control in encounters with Levy Biton and other members of the Biton family was in sharp contrast to his lack of restraint in arguments with his own relatives. Thus, at a public discussion of a decision made by the village committee, he rudely attacked his elder first cousin and brother-in-law, Shlomo, as stupid and incompetent; but within a few weeks the two were reconciled at a family celebration. By that time, Daniel had told his close associates that his attack on Shlomo was in fact a strategy he employed in order to gain Levy Biton's support in another matter, beneficial to the Sebags, which he would have otherwise opposed. Shlomo seemed inclined to accept this face-saving interpretation. Had Daniel expressed his anger with Levy Biton in the same uncontrolled fashion, reconciliation would have been much more difficult. This restraint in verbal disputes with unrelated individuals, despite longstanding rivalry contrasts keenly with the uncontrolled aggression with close relatives. As such, it is akin to the pattern observed in physical aggression.

AGGRESSIVE NEIGHBORS—FORGIVING RELATIVES

Eight aggressive encounters (18 percent) between members of nuclear families, in-laws, and other relatives followed disputes over the neglect of family responsibilities and family commitments. Thus, for example, Levy Biton beat his wife and threw her out of the house for nagging him to switch off the radio as an act of respect for her father who had been taken to the hospital. The furious woman and her children found shelter at an uncle's house. Despite talk of calling the police, the woman was back home within a few hours of the incident. Someone suggested that her husband must have been drunk. This was an unlikely explanation, since he rarely drank, but it was a welcome face-saver for all concerned. Reuben Mahluf carried on a bitter quarrel with his relative and neighbor, Yehuda Mahluf, because the latter offered to supply water to a Sebag to farm land ceded to him by Reuben as the result of a village decision. Reuben claimed emphatically that Yehuda, as a kinsman, should not have helped the Sebag who had taken his land.

While the farmers preferred close relatives as neighbors, residential proximity between kin was a constant cause for dispute. Disputes between neighbors from different families were frequently far milder than those between neighbors from the same family group. Thus, Daniel Sebag had two Mahluf families (Yehuda and Itzhak) as next-door neighbors, while his first cousin Nahum Sebag lived opposite. Daniel's contacts with his Mahluf neighbors were usually cordial but his relationship with his cousin gradually deteriorated, largely because of Nahum's habit of borrowing farm tools without asking permission. When Itzhak Mahluf died, a young, still unmarried, first cousin of Daniel Sebag moved into the house. To Daniel's astonishment, the newcomer soon claimed that Daniel's hot-house (built a few years earlier) encroached on his land. Unable to resolve the dispute, which escalated under its own momentum, the two finally sought legal advice. Daniel's bitterness was exacerbated by the fact that his cousin only received the house because he, Daniel, and his brother had persuaded the other members of the village committee to make an exception and allocate a house and farm land to an unmarried candidate.

Family disputes were not limited to the Sebags. Thus, while Yehuda Mahluf got along fine with his Sebag neighbor, Daniel, he was continuously involved in disputes with his neighbor and relative, Reuben Mahluf. Yehuda complained, for example, that Reuben's poultry battery was too close to his courtyard, and the refuse too close to his windows. Thus, while Daniel Sebag and his Mahluf neighbors seemed to avoid aggressive encounters, both were engaged in disputes with neighbors from their own family group. But, as a teenaged Sebag commented, "Sebags do quarrel, but within a fortnight it is all forgotten," or as Aziz Sebag commented disparagingly, "the Mahlufs conceal their envy and contempt of each other, unlike the Sebags whose mouth is a true agent of their heart." Thus Aziz tried to justify his own frequent involvement in disputes as an expression of affective relations with his kin.

While most Romema settlers were involved in one or two disputes during my fieldwork, six men (five of them Sebags) were involved in five or more incidents of aggression. The high frequency of intrafamily incidents of personal aggression among the Sebags seems paradoxical in the light of the high frequency of intrafamily marriages and the geographical concentration of Sebag farms and dwellings. However, even flagrant aggression was rarely reported to the police, and another Sebag or the rabbi would act as mediator. More often the protagonists cooled off and belittled the whole issue, in deference to family solidarity.

As much as the Asamer people were quick to support their relatives when in dispute or competition with strangers, they sometimes competed with their own kin. Thus, for example, a young settler in Yashuv was concluding negotiations for the acquisition of a farm from a retiring European settler. To his dismay, he discovered that his older cousin had tried to interfere with the deal in order to get the farm for his unmarried son. Nevertheless, he did not consider severing his relationship with his relatives. This incident was one of several between them, of which the most serious had occurred about a year earlier, when the same cousin had beaten the informant's sister and mother. The aggressor's ten-year-old son had called the other's sixteen-year-old sister a whore. She lashed out and spanked him, and the child ran home to his father. The father ran straight to the girl's home and hit both her and her mother (his aunt). When interrogated by the police, he claimed that the violence of his action was provoked by his aunt's grabbing his genitals. However, in spite of the injury and abuse, the aunt finally decided to drop the case.

This unseemly behavior never caused the long-term deterioration of family relations; and those Moroccans who had no close relatives in the community complained in desolation, "I have here no one of my blood, no one of the main source. I have here only friends who may not recognize me tomorrow."

CHAPTER FOUR

Analysis of the descriptions of family relationships in the folktales of the different ethnic groups in Israel adds supportive data.[12] The proportion of tales whose theme indicates intrafamily confrontations (mainly between husband and wife, parents and children, siblings and in-laws) is significantly higher among North African and Middle Eastern Jews than among European Jews. According to Shenhar (1972: 406), this is due to the prevalence of the extended family in North African and Middle Eastern society; a situation prone to dispute because of the conflict which stems from the contradiction between individual goals and the structure of social and economic cooperation. The results obtained from the analysis of Moroccan folktales seem compatible with the observed high frequency of conflict and disputes among relatives who, in their new environment, seem to continue practices associated with the traditional extended family.[13]

In the search for an explanation for the observed frequency and intensity of aggressive acts as related to the social distance between the protagonists, we should consider two major variables; structural expectations, and bystanders' reactions. Thus, opposition, lack of support, or inconsiderate behavior from close relatives, shattered patterns of social relationships and norms of role expectations. The perception of breakdown in the social and moral order intensified the reaction of the individual who felt himself wronged, and affected his control of aggressive expressions.[14] Second, in cases which involved members of different family groups or strangers,

---

12 According to Shenhar (1972), of the 455 folktales recorded among Moroccan immigrants, 24 per cent (108) deal with intrafamily confrontation, as compared with 27 per cent among the folktales of Tunisian immigrants, 55 percent among Iraqi immigrants, and 25 per cent among Yemenite immigrants. Among European Jews the proportion is much lower; for example, 11 per cent Among Rumanian Jews, 10 per cent among Russian Jews, and 8 per cent among Jews from Poland.

13 In fact, aggression and violence involving strangers and outsiders are rather rare in the general corpus of Moroccan folktales.

14 Bilu (1979), in his study of demonic explanations of disease among Moroccans in Israeli villages, observed that fights and quarrels constituted a frequent context for the emergence of demonic disease. But most interesting, the impact of these discords and their development into a demonic disease have been influenced by the fact that they have

any relatives who happened to be present acted almost automatically to restrain the escalation of conflict and the release of aggression. But in those disputes in which the protagonists shared a common and close-knit social network, confused loyalties on the part of bystanding relatives and an unwillingness to get involved on the part of outsiders delayed the restraining mechanism. However, in disputes involving strangers, even if the bystanders were members of the community not closely related to the local protagonist, they would sometimes intervene to restrain him, thus assuming the shared status of Moroccan community members.

CONCLUSIONS

The Moroccan Jews studied here did not undergo the acute process of family and community disintegration characteristic of a large segment of Moroccan Jewry, nor were their experiences in Israel as traumatic as those described in most other reports. The absence of these situational factors in this study may therefore permit better insight into the culture of aggressive behavior among Moroccan Jews.

The data reveal two main observations. First, in spite of a cultural code which apparently allows for and professes the free release of verbal aggression, in practice the release or restraint of either verbal or physical aggression seems to be conditioned not so much by the extent and type of provocation, but rather by the social relationships connecting the protagonists. Second, as with the cases of more severe violence, homicide in particular (Bohannan 1960; Wolfgang and Ferracuti 1967), the outburst of uncontrolled verbal aggression and minor violence has an intragroup characteristic. The individual encounters numerous aggressive stimulations in the cycle of daily life involving close or distant relatives, co-villagers from the same or different ethnic groups, or outsiders who render him various services. Although these encounters may be considered equally frustrating, he nevertheless tends to select as targets

---

"usually evolved within the patient's inner social circle and rapidly escalated to physical violence" (Bilu 1979: 369).

for the release of aggression those with whom he is integrated in a web of social relationships.[15] While the Asamer people were easily triggered toward aggressive responses, their control in the selection of target and the extent of the aggression released is indicative of great restraint in that sphere of expressive behavior.

A third observation is the high frequency of Sebag men involved in aggressive incidents, which supports the conclusion that membership in a more dense social network is associated with higher incidence of intragroup aggressive encounters. Aggression thus appears to incorporate an element of affectiveness in reverse, which could be metaphorically defined as the right to offend and hurt one's relatives. Aggression and violence, usually a compelling sign for the termination of social relationships, is tolerated by its frequent victims—close relatives—in the communities studied. This type of privileged aggressive relationship resembles the affective phenomenon of joking relationships which anthropologists have identified in many societies as both a privilege and a mechanism of tension release between certain categories of relatives—particularly in-laws—whose relationship involves both attachment and separation (Radcliffe-Brown 1952: 90-104).

Another observation has been the role played by women in aggressive encounters. While the men refrained from the escalation of dispute with unrelated disputants, women were less inhibited by social distance. Moreover, women sometimes intervened in disputes involving their menfolk where the men themselves had refrained from the release of aggression. Their actual or reputed aggression involved embarrassing acts such as biting or grabbing the men's genitals, but probably their low status in the community may explain the widespread toleration of such spontaneous outbursts.

Marx (1976) considered aggression among Moroccans in an immigrant town mainly in terms of strategies to obtain material and social

---

15   This is reminiscent of witchcraft accusations, which also tend to involve people who are closely related, particularly by consanguineous, affinal, or territorial ties (e.g. Gluckman 1963).

support. Debating some leading psychological theories, and particularly the frustration-aggression hypothesis, he searched for the social context of aggression and came to emphasize the goal-directedness and rationality of aggressive behavior. Thus he states (p. 109): "Most of the aggression I studied served a more or less clearly defined purpose...the aggressors sought to produce some effect on their social environment." No doubt, some forms of aggression, like other affective mechanisms, may be instrumental in reorganizing the social and emotional order (see chapter 3). Moreover, the circumstances in the town Marx studied may have left the immigrants with few alternative effective personal resources. However, it is most noticeable that under the relative prosperity of the moshav, most outbursts of aggression could not be interpreted in terms of rationality and of instrumental goal-directedness; rather, it was the control and inhibition of aggression that carried an element of rationality.

Elam (1978), in comparing the patterns of violence among Georgian Jews with the cases of violence in the town described by Marx, argued that the Moroccan aggressors, in using force, were actually trying to establish a particular social relationship with the universalistically-oriented bureaucrats, which is consistent with our view. While research among Moroccans settled in villages demonstrates that family ties provide the individual settlers with a powerful asset (see also chapter 3) it appears that in towns, family ties lost much effect and came to be replaced by growing dependence on the services and support provided by government and municipal officials. During the period with which I had contact with the villages presented here, there were no attacks on bureaucrats representing outside agencies, such as the Ministry of Agriculture, the Jewish Agency Land Settlement Department, and the regional municipal and economic organizations, among others. This is in stark contrast to the frequency of aggression directed against relatives, even though they provided major sources of support to the individual settler in his claims on outside agencies and in his struggle for economic and political resources in the moshav organization. In contrast with the relatively advantageous economic and organizational conditions in the moshav, the bureaucrats in Israel's new and often depressed towns have assumed the roles of benevolent, yet often incomprehensible sponsors responsible for the individual allocation of most material resources (such as employment, housing, and welfare). Considering the evidence available from other studies of Moroccan Jews, it appears that when aggression was employed by Moroccan immigrants it may have implied the cognitive confusion of social categories. In that liminal stage of social passage, when the instrumental and affective perception of the role of relatives is considerably reduced, clients grant bureaucrats an affective property which often forces them to react also in terms of personal relationships.

A clear indication of this is found in Cooper's (1978) study of Moroccans in a development town. He states that "kin roles are sometimes projected beyond the range of real kin and applied as formulas for generating behavior" (p.156). He brings the case of a desperate man, married to a blind woman and father of eight children, who jumped on a table and shouted at the town council chairman "Micha, you are my father, you must find me a job" (p. 47).

Storr (1968) has suggested that aggression is probably as indispensable to human nature as sexual expression. While I cannot assess Storr's suggestion, his comparison of the release of aggression with sexual expression seems acceptable if viewed in terms of the regulation of affective mechanisms in society. Although aroused by numerous sexual targets, the release and manifestation of sexual stimulation are culturally and socially defined and directed; so here the release of aggression is channeled into prescribed modes of expression and defined sets of social interaction. If aggression were the inevitable manifestation of the aggressive instinct or of frustration, as is often suggested by psychologists, it could not explain the selective dimension so apparent in this study.

Human aggression has been, for many years, a continuing source of scientific and ideological discourse: is it a biological drive, or rather a product of society and culture? I have considered the affective dimension of aggressive behavior which is socially and culturally defined and chan-

THE REGULATION OF AGGRESSION IN DAILY LIFE

neled. I also suggest that drastic changes in economic and social circumstances influencing the patterns of interaction and commitment between individuals and groups soon influence the modes of action and the social application of that type of affective behavior.[16]

---

16 The Ik (Turnbull 1972) offer an extraordinary example of immense fluctuations in affective relationships effected by extreme environmental changes.

CHAPTER 5.
THE IMPACT OF MIGRATION ON THE MOROCCAN JEWISH FAMILY IN ISRAEL

The analysis of various socioeconomic and cultural phenomena in Israel has usually been based on a comparison between Jews of European extraction (*Ashkenazim*) and those of Asian and African extraction (*Sephardim* or *Mizrahim*—Orientals). While most scientists posit the overall stability of the Israeli family, they all use for their research the comparison of the European versus the Asian and African Jewish populations. Their main findings point, however, to the growing similarity of the rates of marriage and family size between these "two major ethnicities."[1]

I intend to examine a few patterns of family life in one particular ethnic group from among those aggregated in the category of Asian-African Jews. The Moroccan case discussed here suggests that similar examination of other specific groups may produce some more revealing conclusions concerning continuity and change in family life than do the all-embracing statistical averages which point, for example, to the apparently growing similarity of birthrates between Ashkenazi and Sephardi families.

MIGRATION AND SETTLEMENT

More than 200,000 Moroccan Jews have arrived in Israel since the mid-1950s. At present numbering more than 500,000, they represent the largest group of Middle Easterners in the

---

1   See, e.g. Friendlander and Goldscheider (1978), Peres and Katz (1981), and Goldscheider (1981).

country. The Moroccans are particularly noticeable in farming villages (*moshavim,* shall-holders' cooperatives) and development towns (*ayaron pituah*) which were set up during the period of their arrival. In the larger population centers they have been less noticeable as a group, having settled in the more ethnically mixed suburbs of immigrant residence.[2] However, a few urban slums, centers of social disturbance and political agitation, have carried the image of Moroccan neighborhoods.[3]

During the late 1950s and throughout the 1960s, Moroccan Jews in Israel maintained a stigmatized public image. Often described as inadjustable and violent, they were also attributed with the signs of communal and family breakdown. Scientific research has apparently confirmed some elements of this stereotype. For instance, in studies of the distribution of delinquency and prostitution according to country of origin, Moroccans were highly represented.[4] Some studies have related these phenomena to the rapid social and cultural changes that they have undergone since the recent trend of urbanization in Morocco and with immigration to Israel.[5]

This chapter will examine the situational position of Moroccan Jews' family life, drawing upon a series of community studies I and others have conducted during the 1960s-1970s. These explored patterns of family life as they emerged under different economic, social, and ecological circumstances. A few of the anthropological studies of Moroccan Jews, mainly in the villages and development towns, have already discussed the position of

---

2 On arrival, about a third (some 85,000) of all North African immigrants have been settled in development towns. About 50,000 have settled in villages and the rest, more than 80,000, have settled in the older and larger urban areas.

3 The best-known are Vadi Salib in Haifa, where violent demonstrations broke out during the late 1950s (see Bar Yosef 1959, 1970) and Musrara in Jerusalem, where the Black Panthers movement was established during the late 1960s (see Cohen 1972).

4 See, for example, Shoham and Rahav (1967) and Shtal (1978) concerning the high frequency of prostitution among North African Jews. For information about the high frequency of juvenile delinquency among North African Jews, see for example, Amir and Shihor (1975) and publications of the Youth Probation Service (1977, 1978). For information about the high frequency of North African adults involved in criminal acts, see Statistical Abstract of Israel (1980: 565).

5 See, for example, Bar-Yosef (1959, 1970); Weingrod (1960); Palgi (1966).

the family in these communities.⁶ My two decades of research on a community transplanted from the Atlas Mountains, and settled in the villages that I call Romema and Yashuv, conducted since the mid-1960s, introduces a dynamic element and a perspective of process to the study of Moroccan immigrants. In considering Moroccan family life in Israel I shall query the patterns of transformation of a number of major structural features, in particular the position of the extended and nuclear family, the division of labor between the sexes, and parental authority.

FAMILY LIFE IN TOWNS AND VILLAGES

The stigmatizing stereotype of Moroccans has emerged from reports on their poor economic accommodation and aggressive behavior in towns, witnessed mainly during the first years of settlement in Israel. Studies of those Moroccans living in urban slums and new development towns (most of which have remained underdeveloped to this day) described isolated nuclear families, often with many small children. Their adult men—the breadwinners—were usually unskilled in terms of Western technology and science, poorly paid at their manual or semiskilled jobs, and often dependent on welfare.⁷ These disadvantaged men expressed their frustration at bureaucrats who controlled such resources as employment, housing, and welfare, at themselves (in suicide attempts), and at other members of their nuclear family (their spouses in particular).

The studies that were carried out during the same period in villages present a radically different situation.⁸ The immigrants' transformation from peddlers and craftsmen to farmers—however difficult and, at times, degrading—was not an impossible task. Intensive instruction and industry

---

6   See Shokeid 1971a, b; Deshen and Shokeid 1974: 122-50, 210-36; Marx 1976; and Cooper 1978..

7   For the situation of Moroccans in development towns in particular, see Berler (1970), Deshen (1974), Marx (1976), Spilerman and Habib (1976), and Cooper (1978).

8   For the situation of Moroccans in villages, see Weingrod (1966); Willner (1969); and Shokeid (1971a)

turned most settlers into competent farmers within a few years. Moreover, *moshav* farming offered economic independence and even affluence.

But settlement in villages also carried an important social characteristic absent in towns: according to the policy of settlement applied since the mid-1950s, which intended to establish homogeneous village communities, settlers were sent to their villages of destination immediately upon disembarkation at Haifa port. Consequently, the settlers sent to a certain moshav often originated from the same village or town in Morocco, and therefore included many family members. Moreover, these settlers often reorganized family groups by recruiting their relatives who had been settled elsewhere, or established new groupings by contracting marriage ties with their new Moroccan neighbors (see chapter 3). These groups supported the individual in competition with members of other groups for the limited resources available in the economic and other spheres of the moshav organization. Thus, revival of familism helped to reinforce traditional patterns of relationships between close family members and among groups of relatives.

My later observations, however, made in the same villages during the 1970s, reveal a growing ambivalence toward family corporate action. Family groups no longer functioned, as they did during the late 1950s and the 1960s. Many of the hesitant novices in agriculture have become competent and affluent farmers; they no longer needed their relatives' support. Furthermore, with the passage of time, another intrafamily development emerged: married brothers who in Morocco shared a joint household, organized according to seniority or age, now headed independent households; their economic interests, achievements and social standing in the community were rapidly growing apart.

Nevertheless, the tension often observed in the relationships between relatives never caused the long-term deterioration of family relations, and those Moroccans who had no close relatives in the community felt themselves at a disadvantage: "I have here no one of my blood, no one from the main source; here I have only friends, and they might not recognize me tomorrow." The villagers looked forward to visiting or hosting relatives settled elsewhere in the country. These visits carried the features of pilgrimages; the guests traveled long distances and once they arrived were continuously entertained and richly fed for days by their relatives, who pressed them to prolong their stay.[9] They were thus sustaining a noted characteristic of Moroccan culture (Geertz 1979).

In the meantime, however, the social composition of the development towns has been crystallized. With the withdrawal of many of the settlers from other ethnic groups, a considerable number of towns have become noticeably North African in their composition. In fact these towns have turned into "extended villages," exemplifying particular social characteristics that have been identified in Moroccan Israeli villages.

DEMOGRAPHIC STABILITY OF THE NUCLEAR FAMILY

Considerable demographic stability, if not expansion, of the Moroccan nuclear family has been observed both in villages and in development towns. The continuing tendency of a high fertility rate in the older generation of immigrants who were already married on arrival may be explained by their basically traditional orientation. The growing size of these families was also due to the improved medical and related social services which drastically reduced the high rate of infant mortality. However, there is clear evidence that this trend continues among those who married in Israel within the first decade after their arrival. Moreover, there are some indications that the pattern persists among many of those who married more recently as well. Those who married in Israel, many of whom served in the army and were educated in Israel, often criticized the older generation for their uncontrolled family size; nevertheless they have gradually increased their own families.

One woman who married in Israel, already mother of five children, who considered herself a modern woman and aspired to a better standard of living, claimed that she "never said that a new baby was the last

---

9   See Deshen and Shokeid 1974, 210-36.

one—whoever comes may he be blessed!" In fact, she had had her fifth child against strong medical advice to avoid another pregnancy. On the other hand, she criticized her neighbor, a woman in her early forties and mother of eight, including a few grownup children, who was looking for a remedy since she could not conceive more children. It appears that within a vague norm of "reasonable" family size, influenced in particular by the age of the eldest children, the continuing birth of children was as acceptable to men and women of the younger generation as it had been to their parents. Only when her eldest son was conscripted into the army (at age eighteen) or once her eldest daughter reached marriageable age (at about twenty), was it considered shameful for a woman to give birth.

We find substantial support for our observations in demographic research based on national surveys. The scientists who produced those data, however, did not consider country of origin separately and in fact neglected it altogether. Thus, according to data presented by Friedlander and Goldscheider (1978: 316) it appears that among immigrants from African countries (the majority of whom are Moroccans), the younger marriage cohorts have retained high fertility levels more than other ethnic groups (particularly in comparison with immigrants from Asian countries). For example, we find different patterns among Asian and African immigrants when the 1945-49 (immediate pre-immigration) and 1960-64 marriage cohorts among immigrants from Asian countries are compared. Among Asian immigrants, 55 percent of the earlier cohort had large families (5+ children), while in the younger cohort only 20 percent had large families. Among immigrants from African countries, 61 percent in the earlier cohort and 49 percent among the younger cohort had large families.[10]

A similar finding appears in Goldscheider's more recent evidence as he proved that North African urban women in Israel exhibit the highest rates of desired and achieved family size.[11] Another indication of the relatively high fertility rates among Moroccans in Israel is offered by Inbar

---

10 Friedlander and Goldscheider (1978: 316, Appendix Table 3).
11 Goldscheider (1986).

and Adler (1977), who compared the status of Moroccan Jews who immigrated to France with that of their siblings in Israel and reported, inter alia, on family size. Thus, the average family size in France was 3.88, while in Israel it was 4.79. It is also interesting to note that the association for rights of large families—Zahavi—is led by Moroccans, and is city based.

While the frequency of large families is not considered a "social problem" in the relatively affluent situation of the moshav, it has often been perceived as one of the severe problems of development towns. However, Cooper's (1978) study among Moroccans in a poor development town demonstrated the economic viability if not the economic rationality of a large family in that environment. The accumulation of income from a large (though often low-salaried) labor force, as well as the possibility of home manufacture of various products, tax reductions, and other privileges granted by governmental authorities (including welfare support) contributed to the smooth, though not affluent, running of the large family enterprise.

In the village, the management of large families seems to be easier, even when economic circumstances are particularly difficult. An example is the case of the poorest family in Romema. In 1976, Mr. Elgazi was fifty-four years old and his wife, who married him in Morocco in her early teens, was forty. They had ten children, the three oldest married with children, living elsewhere in Israel, and the youngest a two-year-old girl. When they arrived in 1962, Mr. Elgazi, who was a silversmith in Morocco, refused to take on the responsibilities of an independent farmer. Expecting a transfer to an urban environment, he was employed as a daily laborer on his neighbors' farms. In 1972 he underwent a minor operation, after which he has never returned to normal functioning, going to work only occasionally. Mrs. Elgazi worked regularly, either on their neighbors' farms or at various manual jobs in the nearby school. The older children at home were also employed on their neighbors' farms. The family received some welfare assistance.

Eventually, Mr. Elgazi requested, and received, a farm and full membership in the moshav organization. Although he did not take on active farming, his nominal farming and the privileges accompanying the new status afforded him another modest contribution to his family's budget. Their table was regularly as abundant with meat, soft drinks, and alcohol as that observed in the wealthiest homes in the villages. The Ministry of Housing expanded and refurbished their house as part of a special project carried out in most villages. There is currently no equivalent kind of support in towns. In fact, Mrs. Elgazi refused to let the work be finished in their house until she convinced the officials at the ministry that they were entitled to a larger house, although she was only in the first months of her last pregnancy. Sarcastic about the ministry's rules, she was also critical about the architects it employed, who designed large living rooms with no separating corridors and doors from the entrance to the house and other rooms. She exclaimed jokingly: "This is nice for the Ashkenazim who have two kids at most, but we Moroccans have at least ten children who roam around all the time." While Mr. Elgazi appeared somewhat pathetic, his wife was usually convivial, looking forward to the available possibilities to benefit her family.

WOMEN'S INVOLVEMENT IN ECONOMIC ACTIVITIES

The Jews in Morocco, in line with the Muslim code of honor, segregated the women from the company of unrelated men; therefore, women did not participate in economic activities outside of the home. There is not sufficient information about the patterns of women's employment among North African immigrants in towns; in villages Moroccans easily accommodated with the economic constraints which necessitated women's participation in outdoor farming activities. They were recruited to help on their family farms as well as on their relatives' farms. But women were also regularly employed as farming laborers regardless of family ties. Even the most traditional men eventually succumbed to economic pressures and came to accept the employment of their wives, mothers, sisters, and daughters.

In the 1960s, I was struck by the vast participation of women in most farming activities; ten years later, their withdrawal from farming was equally striking. Since 1967, with the growing affluence of farmers and the availability of cheap Arab labor from Gaza and the West Bank, the farmers could gradually manage without their women's labor. In some cases, however, women continued to participate in the farm's activities as overseers of its Arab employees.

Particularly illuminating was the reaction of a successful Romema farmer whose wife was regularly employed on their farm during the 1960s. An outspoken woman, I recorded her in 1966 commenting at a family gathering that "nowadays women are more important then men since they work both at home and on the farm." However, during my stay in Romema in 1976, the farmer, while acknowledging the immense improvement in his economic and social position since he came from Morocco, categorically denied that his wife had ever worked on their farm. Thus, with the change in economic circumstances, some ideological elements of the traditional family patterns were cognitively reinstated.

The broader field of relationships between spouses is not considered here; I have dealt with it more extensively elsewhere.[12] My data do, however, point to the growing accommodation with the impact of Western norms of behavior concerning equality between the sexes.

CHANGING PATTERNS OF MATE SELECTION

Most marriages in Morocco, as well as most of those contracted during the first decade in Israel, engaged close relatives or other members from the same community. However, no marriages since then have involved close relatives or members from the same community. Since the mid-1960s, Romema and Yashuv have been completely exogamous.[13] Moreover, a few girls have married men from other ethnic groups (Iranians in particular). It seems that this phenomenon is

---

12   See Shokeid 1971: 165–215; Deshen and Shokeid 1974: 122–50.
13   This tendency of marrying out of the community negates Matras's (1973) findings in other ethnic groups and his conclusion that endogamy may continue in transplanted communities.

THE IMPACT OF MIGRATION

related to another change: engagements are no longer arranged by parents. Those girls who do not attract suitors by their own devices cannot rely on their parents' intervention. The implications of this new situation were clearly demonstrated in the case of an affluent and influential Romema farmer whose three daughters were approaching their mid-twenties with no husbands in sight. His wife suffered mental depression, attributed by relatives and neighbors to that family predicament.[14]

Most girls in the villages I studied met their future husbands in school, at work, and through friends. This rapid change of a basic aspect of family life was adopted relatively easily. The villager mentioned earlier, who denied that his wife ever worked on their farm, told me about the engagement of his daughter: she was employed as a nurse in a nearby development town where she met a local Moroccan boy. The boy's elder brother came with one of Romema's leading settlers to tell her parents about his brother's serious intentions. Since the girl consented to the marriage, the father accepted her wishes, but stipulated one condition: they should not meet outside the village until they got married. However, when the boy later asked permission to take his fiancée to visit relatives and spend a few days in another village, her parents discussed the matter and agreed that "things are no longer as they used to be in Morocco where the bride and groom did not meet until the wedding ceremony." As a matter of fact, they thought it might be an opportunity for their daughter to become better acquainted with her future husband. The girl was advised about proper conduct when she was away—particularly that she shouldn't let the boy touch her. Soon after the trip the young couple were married.

This phenomenon of parental tolerance toward the changing modes of relationships between boys and girls and the rapid accommodation

---

14 The eldest daughter, who was not considered particularly bright, refused any kind of matchmaking. The second daughter was not good-looking but was considered clever; her occasional suitors made great financial demands on her father, who therefore suspected their motives. The third girl refused to marry a cousin from another village who had asked for her, apparently because of medical apprehension about offspring of closely related Parents. Eventually, the two younger girls married just before they were considered too old for a normal first marriage.

with Israeli youth culture, which we observed in a prosperous and relatively cohesive Moroccan community, has been even more strongly demonstrated among Moroccans settled in the more heterogeneous urban environment.[15]

CHANGING PATTERNS OF INTERGENERATIONAL RELATIONS

In Morocco, married sons usually shared the household with their parents and siblings; this pattern was given up immediately on arrival in Israel. The change was greatly encouraged by the policy employed by the Jewish Agency in villages and towns alike, which entitled all immigrant couples, young and old, to separate lodgings. Although most old couples in villages did not take up independent farming, they did receive their own homes and land. Those who had only one mature son (not uncommon, considering the high rate of infant mortality in Morocco) transferred their farms to them. Consequently, these sons became owners of two farms. Moreover, in these families old couples generally worked on their children's farms. This generation of old parents adjusted easily to the reversal of roles and authority; it actually increased their involvement with their sons' families.

However, the parents of the younger generation in Israel (as observed since the late 1960s) refused to share their farms with their maturing sons, in spite of the absence of vacant farms in the village, which often forced the departure of a son. In response to the suggestion that he share his farm with his only son, an aging father replied: "Am I already dead?" This attitude prevailed in spite of the pressure exerted by the settlement authorities to involve young farmers in the farms of aging parents. The settlement authorities even offered generous financial support for construction of

---

15 In a study of Arabs and Jews in an Israeli mixed city, I observed, inter alia, the freedom gained by Middle Eastern Jewish girls among whom Moroccans were particularly noticeable. The situation probably represents the more extreme circumstances of loss of parental authority (Shokeid 1980b , and Deshen 1982: 35, 40)..

separate homes on the farm for a son's family, a pattern that has been institutionalized in more veteran—mostly Ashkenazi—moshavim.

In towns, the rapid breakdown of joint households is not surprising. Adult children could not usually stay in their parents' small, crowded apartments after marriage. Neither were they expected by governmental and municipal authorities to stay on with their parents. In the villages, on the other hand, one could expect at least a partial reconstruction of the traditional pattern of joint households. It seems, however, that Moroccan parents who have given up authority over their children's major decisions, as for example with mate selection, have refused to forfeit their economic independence and authority over their farm enterprise (Shokeid 1990).

I should emphasize, however, the apparently paradoxical phenomenon of the overall muting of intergenerational conflicts as observed in villages. Parents seem to be remarkably permissive and tolerant toward their children's behavior, including minor forms of delinquency. They did not enforce their ideological convictions (such as religious conformity), nor did they often demonstrate parental authority in other spheres of daily life. Thus, for example, when the son of a leading farmer insisted on driving his van although he did not yet have a driving license, the farmer commented ambivalently: "Here you can't say anything to children, but Shimon is a good boy—he does not surpass limits.[16]

Levy Biton, among the most successful men in Romema and uncompromising towards his opponents, did not contest his nineteen-year-old son who often hinted at the father's religious naiveté when Levy was performing or expressing traditional Moroccan practices and beliefs. But another Romema settler became the laughingstock of the community when he

---

16   He went on in a pleased mood to tell about his reaction when he was informed that Shimon was playing soccer on the Shabbath. He immediately went to the playground and shouted at him: "Shimon, why don't you throw away your skullcap and leave school?" With that he turned away. Shimon ran after him, stopped him, and swore that he was only playing basketball. (Soccer players, though unintentionally, apparently perform acts that resemble work religiously forbidden on the Sabbath, such as digging and weeding). The father was obviously extremely satisfied with his son's reaction, which apparently proved his obliging character

stubbornly nagged his rebellious teenage son to adhere to religion. It was amusingly related that he complained to the police about the boy's refusing to wear a skullcap.

The eldest son of my closest neighbor in Romema refused to help his father (a hard-working farmer with seven children at home) on the farm when he finished his army service. Likewise, he was unwilling to take a job as a mechanic, a skill he had acquired at school. Instead, he asked his father for a considerable loan, which he invested, together with a friend, in a secondhand van that they bought for their own business. Their venture failed and the boy returned home penniless. Still, the son would not consider helping out on the farm. The father related that recent calamity, which had cost him the bulk of his savings, with no recriminations against his son but with the notion of bad luck which struck his family.

The few cases of juvenile delinquency reported in Romema and Yashuv were usually attributed by the settlers to the parents' indulgence, thought to encourage the youths' demanding and unrestrained behavior. However, the attitudes of parents and siblings toward delinquent youth were akin to the attitude expressed toward the few cases of mentally disturbed adults. Searching for the particular circumstances that made the victims gravitate to misfortune, they viewed them with pity rather than contempt or disdain. It was apparently bad luck rather than bad nature that caused misconduct and delinquency.

The loss of parental authority among immigrants has often been described as a grave phenomenon effected by their economic and social failures. In this study, however, the apparent loss of parental authority emerged as an accommodation achieved with no real battle between generations, in the framework of overall economic success and the particular conditions that were relatively congenial for social and cultural continuity.

The description of family life among the Moroccans presented here points to a few major—though sometimes apparently contradicting—findings. These include rapid accommodation with changing environmental conditions, as represented by emergent familism in villages during the first stage of settlement and the gradual decline of that type of intensive family cooperation. Similarly, the relatively easy introduction of women into regular farming activities contrasted with their withdrawal from farming at a later stage. Rapid accommodation has also been observed in the confrontation with social and cultural pressures affecting intergenerational relationships. Old and young rapidly adapted to the Israeli norms of nuclear family independence as well as to the new modes of relationships between the sexes and the overall independence of youth from parental authority.

The tendency of rapid accommodation with environmental constraints and cultural pressures of the dominant group in society is not a new phenomenon among Moroccan Jews. Moroccan Jewry present a remarkable example of a large Jewish group that survived in spite of its accommodation and actual acculturation for many generations with social and cultural characteristics of the Muslim host society (Sharot 1976).

At the same time, there are indications of the persistent continuity of a family orientation. First, a relatively high birthrate has been maintained, even among the younger generation. Second, in spite of the decline of intensive family cooperation, family ties within large networks of relatives still carry much importance in the life of individuals. Third, severe tensions and conflicts do not characterize the relationships between parents and children. The widespread persistence of family orientation among Moroccans is also indicated by observations of religious behavior in these communities—a subject discussed in the following chapters.[17] In stark contrast to the stereotype of family breakdown among Moroccan immigrants, my observations suggest that the Moroccan family has greatly preserved its position as the center for affective relationships in society.

---

17 As presented in chapters 6 and 7, my observations among Moroccans in villages and in a Tel Aviv suburb, as well as information available in the mass media, identify a certain pattern of religious behavior, anchored in the family life and family traditions. I suggest that the religiosity of Moroccans in Israel demonstrates the viability of Moroccan family characteristics and sentiments.

CHAPTER FIVE

My research was carried out mainly in the relatively affluent Moroccan farming communities; this may apparently explain both the viability of family organization and its apparently smooth transformation. Yet there are indications that this trend applies to other Moroccan groups in Israel as well. For example, the high birthrate among Moroccans has been confirmed in nationwide surveys. To the extent that the various Jewish ethnic groups carry particular primordial social paradigms, some elements of which survive under changing circumstances, Moroccan Jewry seems to transmit to its members a deep sense of family ascription and allegiance as well as a diffused commitment toward relatives. The Moroccan case demonstrates overall continuity of a family orientation which seems to have been relatively unaffected by the exigencies of immigration and the cultural pressures of the "melting pot" ideology (which actually presents as model the lifestyle of the veteran and secular Ashkenazi segment of the Israeli population).

This conclusion may appear to contradict the data concerning the high rates of delinquency and prostitution among Moroccan Jewry in Israel. However, as shown by Shtal (1978) a similar phenomenon, demonstrated by far more impressive figures on the rate of prostitution and illegal traffic of women by Jewish gangs and pimps, was observed among Eastern European Jews in Europe and America at the turn of the century. These figures were analyzed as the result of the social and economic difficulties which confronted Eastern European Jewry at that period. Do these figures, reliable as they seem to be, convince us about a tendency of prostitution and the breakdown of family life among Eastern European Jews, either then or now? No doubt, the particular situation of the exodus of North African Jewry to Israel, which often entailed severe economic and social difficulties, for the older generation in particular, and which also often influenced the loss of parental authority, has produced the circumstances for various types of deviance. But the rates of deviance do not necessarily reflect the position of the family in society, or negate the viability of a strong family orientation.

Beyond that somewhat evaluative concern, it seems necessary to carry out more sensitive demographic surveys and to interest more sociologists and anthropologists in the study of Moroccan Jews under various conditions as much as of other groups which compose the undifferentiated category of Jews of Asian and African extraction. This may identify those groups which, similar to the Moroccans as here presented, do carry a strong family orientation as compared to those groups which have experienced drastic changes in their traditional family life style. This approach will test the validity of the present use of the "Ashkenazi-Sephardi" ethnic dichotomy as major categories for demographic and sociological research. More important, it will help reveal the processes and the conditions that mold the patterns of family life in various groups.

CHAPTER 6.
THE DECLINE OF PERSONAL ENDOWMENT OF ATLAS MOUNTAINS RELIGIOUS LEADERS IN ISRAEL

Social and cultural changes undergone by Middle Eastern immigrant communities in Israel have been a fertile field of study. Most of the anthropologists and sociologists who worked in Israel have, however, geared their studies to questions and propositions on acculturation and modernization. Consequently, much has yet to be learned about the way this major wave of newcomers and their descendants have reacted in religious terms to the reality they confronted in Israel: they became Israeli citizens, but at the same time were Jews, bred in the historical tradition of the Promised Land, a tradition kept alive from generation to generation by religious beliefs and practices. Could religious observance and its perpetuators withstand the tests of the host society whose European leaders were mostly secular? How did the immigrants who sensed the incompatibility of their religious convictions with their new experiences fill the void created when they discarded old traditions?

An important contribution to this neglected aspect of anthropological research was made by Deshen (1970) who observed the manipulation of religious symbols during an election campaign. This paper, however, concentrates on the conflicting forces at work in the organization of religious life in a transplanted community of immigrants from the Atlas Mountains.[1] Immigration to Israel for this traditional community was a maze of perplexing physical, social and spiritual experiences. I try to analyze symptoms and reactions indicative of the deep changes in the position of

---

1 For the detailed ethnography see Shokeid 1971.

the old communal religious leadership. These religious leaders—imbued with charismatic attributes often inherent in some patronymic groups—in Israel left their community of old, apparently voluntarily; in fact, however, they were eased out and they had to seek their livelihood and residence elsewhere. At a geographic distance, the religious leaders of old could continue to wield some of their past spiritual and moral authority; while their adherents from Morocco, who were in the throes of change, expressed through chaos in ritual, were probably struggling to arrive at a new modus vivendi in their religious order.

TRANSPLANTATION OF A COMMUNITY

The data presented here were collected during eighteen months of fieldwork (from October 1965 to March 1967) and during periodical visits thereafter, in Romema,[2] an agricultural settlement in the semi-arid zone of the northern Negev, in southern Israel. The Romema settlers had come from Asamer,[3] a small, remote, all-Jewish village in the Atlas Mountains of Morocco, situated near the larger center of Demnate. In Asamer many of them had worked for surrounding Berber population as shoe-makers, carpenters, blacksmiths, tailors or as peddlers of sugar, candles and oil. Others had been merchants, some of whom had partly financed the farms and herds of Berbers. The unskilled and poor had usually been employed by the more prosperous businesses or as domestics. It had been natural for a son to take up his father's occupation, especially since he had had little choice.

Jewish culture and religion in Asamer kept alive mainly though oral tradition, had hardly been influenced by Talmudic developments in other parts of the Diaspora in recent centuries. Faith was couched in mysticism[4] and folklore. Belief in spirits, demons, sorcery and the evil eye was widespread.

---

2   Romema and all names of persons are fictitious.
3   In earlier publications I used the pseudonym Amran.
4   An important religious activity in Asamer was the expounding of the Zohar, a thirteenth century text of Jewish Gnosticism, in small reading circles. Though written in an esoteric language, the Zohar stimulated strong feelings of sacredness and piety, and people of

In 1956, the entire population of Asamer migrated to Israel; in 1957 thirty-three families settled in the *moshav* of Romema.[5] The *moshav*, a smallholders' cooperative, introduced in Israel in the 1920's by young European pioneers who wished to forge a new way of life, is established on national land and organized on the basis of moderate economic-social cooperation. Each family cultivates its own farm and privately owns the household and farm equipment. The national institutions, which founded and supervised *moshav* communities, allocated to each farmer the same facilities and same amount of land, and although the moshav ideology intends its members to remain economically equal, differentiation might occur as a result of individual efforts, enterprise, skills and household composition. There is economic cooperation in many important activities, such as the marketing of agricultural products, the supply of farm and household needs and the sharing of such services as dairies and granaries. Administration is by committees and offices and appointments by a majority vote of the village general assembly.[6]

Upon the settlement, the people of Romema defined themselves—and were identified by others—as members of three groups of relatives, here called Sebag, Biton and Mahluf. (A few members of other patronymic groups, such as the Amzlags, attached themselves to one of these). In Asamer, the Sebags had been wealthy merchants who had been better off economically and socially than the Bitons who had been the poorer itinerant craftsmen and the unskilled residents. The Mahlufs, who had held an intermediate position, had been skilled in the more specialized crafts and had been among the better educated in the community. In Romema, the Mahlufs gradually declined in number and in status; the Sebags tried

---

Asamer believed that by reading the text, mystic powers could be invoked to cure the sick or for the general welfare of the community..

5   Upon arrival the people of Asamer were settled in Yashuv (a fictitious name), a village in northern Israel. Due to internal conflicts, the majority left for Romema and only thirteen families remained (for full details see Shokeid 1971: 35-47)

6   For a more complete description of the social and economic bases of the moshav, see Ben-David 1964, Weingrod 1966, Weintraub *et al.* 1969, Shokeid 1971.

to maintain their former superior position; and the Bitons attempted to reverse the lowly status they had held in Asamer. The groups were soon involved in fierce competition in the economic sphere, over leadership positions in the moshav, and in the area of ritual.[7]

ELEVATION IN PERSONAL STANDING VERSUS DECLINE IN RELIGIOUS BEHAVIOR

All Romemites strictly followed religious practice. However, soon after my arrival, I realized that their observance was fraught with paradoxes: they often would fervently express their conviction that their individual religious standing had risen immensely in Israel, yet they might also complain that religious and moral behavior had greatly deteriorated.

Their religious experience was most dramatically affected by the revival of the Hebrew language, which they learned to speak in their new home. The holy books and prayers, written in Hebrew, now were intelligible to them. Barukh Mahluf, who had been a poor cobbler in Morocco told me, for example,: "In Morocco we said Grace after Meals as if we were performing a duty demanded by a landlord, without understanding the reason. Here, thank God, when I intone *Barukh Eloheynu sheakh-balnu mishelo ubetuvo hayiniu* (Blessed be our God of whose bounty we have partaken, and through whose goodness we live), I grasp what I am thanking God for". Barukh's face shone as he pointed out what was a revelation to him.

On another occasion, Aziz Sebag, the eldest son of the last head of the community of Asamer wanted to fetch a book from home to substantiate his argument with the local rabbi. Before leaving, he commented: "In Morocco, we were a nation of the head (*am ha-rosh*); in Israel, we have become a nation of the book (*am ha-sefer*)". In Morocco, he said, they had recounted stories only from memory; in Israel, they could verify them in books. This new literary revelation, a source of deep religious satisfaction

---

7   See Shokeid 1971: 99-162; 1974: 64-94; 1976.

to many Romemites, gained further scope because an increasing number of farmers, particularly those who had been poor and of low standing in Morocco could afford to buy religious texts—as, for example, a *Zohar* set or *Torah* scrolls; the latter, an expensive investment, at that time cost about IL.2,000 or $650. There were nine Torah scrolls for less than forty families in Romema in 1966, a quantity far in excess of that required for regular ritual activities and communal prayer, and of the average number in neighboring villages and towns.[8]

The Romemites' religiosity and sense of achievement in Israel found an outlet also in substantial donations and gifts to the synagogue, and generous contributions at the selling of *mitzvoth*.[9] While the Romemites would complain about taxes and sometimes refuse to pay them or to contribute to the institutions and services of the village, they showed largesse to charities, to little-known religious institutions whose emissaries visited them regularly, and to itinerant scholars of Moroccan origin who invoked the right of *zehkut avot* (merit of the fathers),[10] who came to Romema and stayed with local families for a Sabbath or during the festivals. Their hospitality and generosity were however exploited more than once by unscrupulous imposters.

All the males of Romema attended prayers at the synagogue on the Sabbath and on the festivals and were absent only when ill.[11] On weekdays however, only a small number, mainly the older congregants who did not own farms, regularly came to the morning, afternoon and evening services. Most adult Romemites who did not attend the communal services

---

8   At most, three Torah scrolls are needed for a communal synagogue service which includes reading from the Torah.

9   On the Sabbath and the festivals, as well as on Mondays and Thursdays, the synagogue service requires a reading from the Torah. The privilege of being called up to the Torah was preceded by a contribution to the synagogue funds. The practice, common in many synagogues is called "the selling of *mitzvoth*", but is performed only on the Sabbath and the festivals.

10 The idea of merit of the fathers is mentioned in the Bible and in rabbinic literature.

11 Women did not participate in synagogue activities, and there was no seating arrangement for them in the synagogue. For more details about women see Shokeid 1971: 165-215.

THE DECLINE OF PERSONAL ENDOWMENT

at the synagogue apparently prayed at home—I observed many of them doing so during trips. It would seem that synagogal attendance in Israel did not fall much from what it had been in Morocco, where the men had often worked or traded in neighboring villages on weekdays, returning home only for the Sabbath and the festivals.

In 1965 a large body of congregants seceded from the communal synagogue to form what came to be known as the Bitons' synagogue. It was thought that now the bitter and lengthy quarrels which had disturbed the services would cease, but the wrangles over leading the prayers and reading from the Torah continued. Either the rabbi was rudely accused of being incapable of keeping order during prayers, or a few older congregants were blamed for their obstinate desire to always lead the prayers and not allow other congregants to take their turn. Neither congregation had an appointed *hazan* (cantor) to conduct the services: old and young alike led various parts.

A frequent source of discord was old Abraham Sebag, the formerly wealthy and powerful head of the Asamer community in Morocco. Though now a poor and ailing shepherd, he was still bitterly resented by his erstwhile employees and subordinates. During ritual, oblivious of the fact that in coming to the Promised land he had lost his fortune, power and privileges, he took his seat on the almemar bench together with the rabbi, the beadle and visiting dignitaries.[12] Whenever he wished to lead the prayers or to read from the Torah, he did so, deaf to protests. Even his sons and relatives, who usually defended the caprices of an old and unfortunate man, tried to persuade him to consider other congregants' complaints, but in vain. Matters came to a head on those occasions when Abraham Sebag irritated Yirmiya Amzlag, his one-time employee in Asamer and now a successful farmer, who had also seated himself on the almemar. Abraham

---

12   As in most Middle Eastern and North African synagogues, the congregation was seated along the walls of the prayer hall. The Holy Ark was placed against the northeastern wall (facing Jerusalem), while the *bima* (almemar), a platform on which there was a reading table and a bench, was in the center. For an illustration of this type of synagogue see Shokeid 1971: 150.

101

CHAPTER SIX

did not heed the angered Yirmiya, who, just as stubbornly, refused to surrender his right as an equal congregant to lead the prayers.

The discord among the worshipers caused a dissonance in chanting, which, amounted almost to a cacophony at times, until finally there rose a general outcry of complaints and loud insults. The rabbi was a favorite target for abuse—not only because of the disorder during services, but because he was thought to misappropriate synagogue funds to buy books for his personal use. At other times, he joined in quarrels: On one of the festivals he told Aziz, Abraham Sebag's eldest son, that he was vying over mitzvoth not for the "sake of God", but for the "sake of pride". In the ensuing argument, one of Aziz's cousins went so far as to whip off the rabbi's hat and to push him off the almemar.

The synagogue often became the scene of quarrels about village and farming problems—as, for example, when in the middle of the Sabbath service Shlomo Sebag, a member of the village committee, warned the owners of herds not to damage the village orchard. He pointed at particular congregants, who vociferously denied his accusations.

While the overt purpose for the establishment of the Bitons' synagogue was to eliminate quarreling during ritual, the secession was greatly prompted by the competition between the Sebags and the Bitons. Peace and quiet did not reign at either house of worship.

The services at the Bitons' synagogue were mainly disrupted by the occasional shouting of David Biton, the leader of the congregation and an ordained *shoheit* (ritual slaughterer of food animals). However, in contrast with the communal synagogue, services at the Bitons' synagogue generally proceeded smoothly because David held the congregation strictly in check. For that reason the congregants tolerated David's coarse behavior. His rudeness to his own aged father however, they could not forgive. On one of the festivals, which happened also to be the anniversary of the death of his grandmother, David tried to prevent his father from reciting the *haftarah*,[13]

---

13 The haftarah is a portion from a book of *The Prophets* which is read after a reading from the Torah.

saying that the old man was incompetent. The shocked congregants in vehement protest forced David to let his father recite that part of the service. Subsequently, the entire congregation did not attend the Bitons' synagogue for a few weeks. This was a blow for David; he was found crying in the synagogue one night, and he even fainted in the communal synagogue. When his father was called to his bedside, David pleaded, "Father, why have you forsaken me?" Touched by this act of contrition, most of the congregants returned to his synagogue.

The Romemites—including those who were the cause of the disturbances—were unhappy about the religious and moral behavior of clergy and laymen alike, and they tried to make amends. The rabbi, for example, was often invited to dinner by those who were insolent to him: He was also given generous portions of meat when he acted as *shoheit*. He in turn tried to appease and reconcile his opponents, and to forgive those who had offended him. Aziz Sebag preached unity and comradeship. One Sabbath, when referring to the approaching festival of *Shavuot*, which commemorates the giving of the Torah on Mount Sinai, he told the congregation that when God gave the Torah, he told Moses that the Children of Israel *yihyu safa ahat* (would be one language), meaning that they should be united. Shlomo Sebag confided to me that those who yelled the loudest, meaning himself, might have a "clean" heart —might be kind-hearted and good. Although he himself did not attend the Zohar circle,[14] he offered to throw a party for the group (which included the rabbi), since it had completed a reading cycle, and it is customary to celebrate the occasion.[15] On *Yom Kippur* Yirmiya Amzlags publicly asked Abraham Sebag's forgiveness.[16]

In lamenting the deterioration of religious life in Romema, the Romemites constantly harked back to the strict ritual orderliness which had prevailed in Morocco under the guidance of venerated leaders. None

---

14 See note 4.
15 For a description and analysis of parties and peacemaking occasions in Romema, including that specific event, see Shokeid 1976.
16 See detailed case in Shokeid 1971: 151-154.

was now living among them. They had either not come to Romema or had left after some time.

DISPERSAL AND DECLINE OF RELIGIOUS LEADERS

Before settlement, the Romemites had planned to give the three public offices—secretary, defense organizer and rabbi—to a representative of each of the three main family groups (Sebag, Biton and Mahluf). The post of rabbi was the first office in the moshav organization immediately open to a local. However, neither of the two local, competent candidates—a Biton and a Mahluf—were approved for the position. The Bitons and the Mahlufs could not agree as to whose candidate should be appointed, and the third group, the Sebags, refused to allow a representative of only one group to hold a position of leadership. At one stage of the dispute, the Bitons and the Mahlufs came to an understanding: the younger of the two candidates was to sit for the requisite external examination and thus be formally appointed, but for all practical purposes, the two candidates were to share in the role and the salary of the rabbi's office. The plan failed, mainly because the Sebags opposed it, and the two candidates left Romema after a few years, to take up rabbinical office elsewhere. At that time there was no Romemite qualified for the office of rabbi and the present rabbi, a man in his early thirties who came from an urban milieu in Morocco, was appointed by the Ministry of Religious Affairs, which also paid his salary.[17] Since the departure of the two candidates, the Romemites have been without the type of influential and guiding religious leadership they had known in the old days. A rabbi, formally appointed by external agencies, introduced to the Romemites the

---

17 The position of district rabbi in Israel is that of a religious functionary who supervises the practice of ritual law (*halakhah*). He also has pastoral duties. A rabbi is appointed by an electoral body of local dignitaries; among the requirement are rabbinic ordination and approval by the two Chief Rabbis. The salary is paid in part by the Ministry of Religious Affairs, and in part by the local community. At the time of the establishment of Romema, due to the incessant quarreling among the different family groups, the appointment of the local rabbi was made solely by the Ministry of Religious Affairs.

bureaucratization of religious leadership and helped to undermine their traditional religious order.

The structure of religious leadership among Jews of the Atlas Mountains differed greatly from that of the *kehillah*—a complex organization which had paid officials, especially the rabbi—which became fully institutionalized among European Jewry in the sixteenth century.[18] Israel adopted the European pattern of communal organization since European immigrants to Palestine during the decades preceding 1948 greatly outnumbered those from the Middle East. Thus both the religious and the secular authorities assumed that every immigrant moshav should have a rabbi.

In the Atlas Mountains the practice of tradition and the behavior of individuals was guided and controlled by informal religious leaders. Their authority, based on their reputation as men of learning (*hakhamim*) and piety (*tzadikim*), also drew to a great extent, on their ancestors renown for piety, scholarship and miraculous deeds. The aggregate of their personal and their forefathers' virtues and encapsulated in *zekhut avot*,[19] an attribute which, though hereditary, was at one and the same time an inherent trait of moral superiority possessed by those descendants who chose the religious calling. The more distinguished among them were endowed with charismatic characteristics: it was said *hem hayu medaberim ba-shamayim* (they conversed with heaven). Some engaged in regular economic activities; others were supported by their families or by contributions and payments for such services as ritual slaughtering and circumcising. The stories that the Romemites told reflect the great moral force and wisdom of their illustrious rabbis[20] and stress their occult powers, such as their

---

18 For a description of the European *kehillah*, see Katz 1961. For a description of the situation in the Atlas Mountains, see Shokeid 1971: 15-33; Shokeid and Deshen 1977: Chapter II.

19 *Zekhut avot* and the tendency of hereditary transmission of religious leadership, as manifest in Asamer were also observed in other communities of the Atlas Mountains (see Willner 1969).

20 I use the term "rabbi" for the convenience of presentation although Atlas Mountains religious leaders commanded religious authority informally and were not officially appointed. The term "rebee" is used wherever it forms part of the religious leader's appellation.

ability to punish malicious Gentiles, to communicate with heaven and the world of spirits, and to perform miracles. These are popular themes in Moroccan Jewish folk tales.[21]

The organization of religious life of Jews in the Atlas Mountains was distinct from that of the surrounding Moslem-Berber society.[22] However, the charismatic characteristics of their religious leaders and their recurrence in particular families has a parallel in the religious leadership of the host society, among whom charisma[23] was the quality of an individual as well as of a family patrimony. *Zekhut avot*, ascribed to Asamer's venerated rabbis might be compared to *baraka* (blessing), the virtue of sacredness attributed to the Moroccan Marabout and his living descendants. According to Geertz, the baraka is not evenly distributed among his descendants; only a few—to judge by their wonder-working capacities—have been imbued with it; and they are the true living Marabouts. In describing baraka, Geertz states: "the best analogue for baraka is personal presence, force of character, moral vividness—baraka is a gift which Marabouts have in superlative degree" (1968: 48-50).

In Asamer, the more important religious leaders belonged mainly to two families or, rather, to two "rabbinical dynasties". During the years immediately preceding immigration, each of these families had two active, highly revered rabbis. Two minor religious figures were engaged mainly in ritual slaughtering (these were the two candidates who vied for the position of rabbi in Romema). All four eminent religious leaders came to Israel; the two older, a Mahluf and an Amzlag, were referred to in charismatic terms. The Mahluf rabbi, who became the spiritual leader of Yashuv,[24] died a few years after his arrival and was succeeded

---

21 See particularly stories nos. 5, 29, 37, 38 and 50 in Noy 1964.
22 See Gellner's (1969) and Eickelman's (1976) description of a contemporary High Atlas Mountains Berber community, and Geertz's (1968) overview of religion in Morocco.
23 Weber (1947: 329) describes charisma as "a certain quality of an individual personality by virtue of which he is set apart from ordinary men and treated as endowed with supernatural, superhuman or at least specifically exceptional qualities."
24 See notes 5 and 35.

by his younger brother. The second venerated leader, the Amzlag rabbi, settled in Kiryat Gat, a new town in the Negev. He was usually adoringly called Rebee al'Aziz (Arabic meaning "beloved" or "precious"). Two older Romemites, when relating Rebee al'Aziz's *zekhut avot*, recounted one of the miraculous deeds of his grandfather, Rebee David. One day, while passing through the district, a sheikh noticing Rebee David teaching Torah to young students, enquired, "Why is this Jew making all that noise?" The enraged rabbi wished that the Moslem's star fall to earth and break. The curse took its toll for on the following day the sheikh lost his whole fortune.

Another old Romemite recalled that Rebee al'Aziz visited Asamer's neighboring Jewish communities on weekdays, but would always return to Asamer for the Sabbath, even if he were eight traveling days away; he thus achieved *kefizat haderekh*, a miraculous contraction of the road.[25] Old and young in Romema respected Rebee al'Aziz. A young farmer told me, for example, that whenever he went to see his sister in Kiryat-Gat, he first visited Rebee al'Aziz.

Once when Barukh Mahluf was ill, his brother-in-law took him to a hospital in a nearby town, but the doctors, not finding anything wrong with him, sent him home. The brother-in-law then went to Kiryat Gat to consult Rebee al'Aziz, who told him that Barukh had been harmed the previous Friday when he had unintentionally crossed the path of a spirit that loved him. He sent Barukh an amulet to wear. Upon being told this, Barukh recalled that at midnight, the previous Friday, he had heard a strange noise coming from the sheep pen, and struck the animals to quiet them. The following day he had fallen ill. Barukh added that the spirit whose path he had crossed while angrily hitting the sheep had not intended to harm him, for it was his age counterpart; every living man, he explained, has a mate of the same age in the world of spirits. When he returned to the house, the spirit, whom he had unwittingly hurt, followed and watched him, its every glance, like a flash of pain, piercing him. Thus

---

25 See also Willner's records 1969: 295.

CHAPTER SIX

Rebee al'Aziz proved to be not only clairvoyant, but capable of communicating with spirits.

While the younger rabbis from Asamer became village rabbis, or *shohatim*, Rebee al'Aziz was not gainfully employed, but could count on gifts from his adherents to supplement his social welfare allowance and the support he received from local religious funds. The Romemites also took up collections for him in his absence, and on one occasion donations for him were made in Romema's communal synagogue on Yom Kippur. In all other cases, contributions to scholars were made in their presence.

Rebee Joseph Amzlag, Rebee al'Aziz's kinsman, who also lived in Kiryat Gat, was likewise venerated, but not as his relative. Both had arrived in Israel about a year before most of the other Romemites. Rebee Joseph had been sent to a village of immigrants who hailed from communities near Asamer. However, finding no suitable post, he moved to Kiryat Gat, where he was *shoheit* at the local abattoir. The Romemites visited him in Kiryat Gat and sometimes invited him for the Sabbath or the festivals. While they collected cash donations for Rebee al'Aziz, they showed their reverence for Rebee Joseph more subtly: some of those who owned herds gave him a lamb each year, which they raised for him and which he either slaughtered for his own use or exchanged for goods or cash. It is remarkable that although Rebee al'Aziz and Rebee Joseph were deeply revered, neither seemed ever to have been offered the post of rabbi in Romema.

In contrast to the qualities of religious leadership of Rebee al'Aziz and other rabbis from Asamer, Romema's appointed rabbi could lay claim neither to religious statute, nor to moral authority. A government functionary, skilled in Jewish law and ritual, he had neither *zekhut avot* nor personal charisma. The two local farmers, David Biton and Eliya Sebag, who had qualified as *shohatim*, after the departure of the two Asamar candidates, had pretensions to religious leadership, but neither had *zekhut avot*. David, not a very successful farmer, was a man in his mid-thirties, whose father, a poor blacksmith in Asamer was far from being considered a man of learning. His two older brothers had little education, but in Israel their economic position had improved, and one of them had become very influential in the Biton group. David's aspiration to religion leadership suited his family's social ambitions, and he built his synagogue mainly with the financial help of his brothers. But David, though well versed in religious affairs, did not have the personal virtues necessary to promote his ambition. He was thought high-strung (*atzbani*—nervous), even by his close relatives, and was rude to his followers. Apparently on a mere whim, he one day refused to continue slaughtering. That decision, together with the offense to his father, was proof to his friends and foes alike that he was unsuited for religious leadership. He also dressed shabbily and he rarely entertained congregants at home. In sum, compared to Asamer's religious leaders, some of whom were still alive, he cut a pathetic figure.

Eliya Sebag, the other newly qualified *shoheit*, a middle-aged successful farmer, had belonged to the wealthiest family group in Asamer. However, his ancestors had not been distinguished by any special attributes, and he therefore did not have *zekhut avot*. His modest and courteous behavior and his detachment from political strife, in which all his relatives engaged, endeared him to the Romemites. They favored Rebee Eliya—as he was often called —as *shoheit* over Romema's rabbi.

Although esteemed, Rebee Eliya was not placed on a level with Asamer's religious leaders. A respected old Romemite, referring sarcastically to both David and Eliya, told me: "In Morocco these two were not considered *hakhamim* (religious scholars); only in Israel have they become *hakhamim*. In Morocco, their scholarship would have been questioned mercilessly, but here they get away with anything *aviera be'alma*, thin air)". Nor did the old man revere the rabbi, but held him in some esteem for he was said to be well versed in the Talmud (Talmud scholarship had been rare in Atlas Mountains Jewish communities). Thus, the rabbi, although a man of learning, could not command religious authority while the local pretenders lacked inherited and personal authority.

Since the Romemites apparently still revered traditional religious leadership, we must examine the reasons why the leaders of Asamer did not settle in Romema. We also have to examine whether their absence alone can explain the disturbances during the synagogue services.

CHAPTER SIX

THE WEALTHY AND POWERFUL DETACHED FROM RELIGIOUS PRIVILEGE AND LEADERSHIP

Besides the absence of venerated religious leaders, other changes in the community's traditional social order—such as the dissolution of the social ranks that had existed in Asamer society—also led to religious disruption. Although a clear distinction had existed between the politico-economic and the religious elites in Morocco, the wealthy Sebags, who had been among the better educated in the community, had close social relationships, welded by marriage ties, with the Mahluf and Amzlag rabbis. Not only the revered rabbis, but Abraham Sebag and a few of his relatives, who also owned Torah scrolls, had wielded authority in their community in Morocco.

Aziz Sebag, Abraham's eldest son, who had been brought up to inherit his father's position, tried to uphold his former status. He spent large sums on mitzvoth (thereby embarrassing his contestants), was ostensibly observant, and was most hospitable to itinerant scholars. It was Aziz who was particularly blamed for undermining the plan to have the post of rabbi shared between the Biton and the Mahluf candidates. I assume that the Sebags resented the plan partly because the candidates were not closely related to them by marriage or by other social bonds. These candidates did not fit into the traditional order which had existed in Asamer through the interconnecting ties between the religious and the politico-economic elites. That pattern of relationships and independence was confirmed by Rebee al'Aziz when I asked him about life in Morocco and who had had the main say in the affairs of the synagogue in Asamer; he answered firmly, "the Sebags, who were very rich". The wealthy and powerful in Asamer society helped to maintain the venerated religious leaders who, through that close association, legitimized the favored position of the wealthy.[26]

---

26 Eisenstadt advances the hypothesis that "the sources of prestige, of the deference which people render to others, are rooted not only in their organizational (power, economic, etc.) positions, but also in their differential proximity to those areas which constitute the institutional foci of charisma, that is, the various types of centers (political, cultural,

Thus, when Aziz Sebag initiated contributions for Rebee al'Aziz on Yom Kippur, he was prompted by the norms of the old order.

In Israel, the politico-economic elite of Asamer had lost its power, while those who prospered strove for equality in every sphere, including the religious. Yirmiya Amzlag, for example, among the poorest and least important in Asamer, now asked to be treated as the equal of his former wealthy employer, Abraham Sebag. He constantly wanted to show that he was as proficient in ritual as the man who had been the lay leader of the Asamer congregation. Similarly, the synagogue of the Biton brothers symbolized their new status and independence.

Unlike religious leaders in other parts of North Africa, the Atlas Mountains rabbis had not received extensive formal training, as, for example, their Tunisian counterparts[27] and their position had not been formally institutionalized. This factor had been significant in the accommodation of the other North African religious leaders to the Israeli religious bureaucratic system.[28] On arrival, the Atlas Mountains immigrants were met and assisted by Jews who were only too anxious to "demystify" their perception of the world and to promote secular ideologies and Western science.[29] The revival of the Hebrew language, which they were so proud to understand, was instrumental in "demystifying" religious ritual, and in laying bare the intellectual limitation of the Moroccan leadership. Asamer's religious leaders were unsuited for holding offices within the Israeli organization of religious functions. They also could not look to their close partners of old, who, with immigration, had lost their source of power and were struggling

---

etc.) and in the degree of their participation in those areas" (1968: XXXIII). Through this frame of analysis, we can see the wealthy and powerful being offered easy access to those endowed with charisma.

27 See Shokeid and Deshen, 1977: Chapter II.
28 In contrast with the evidence from Atlas Mountains communities, Goldberg's account (1972) of a transplanted traditional community from Libya showed a remarkable degree of social and cultural continuity.
29 For an example of the confrontation between beliefs of Atlas Mountain Jews and Western science, see Shokeid, "The Emergence of Supernatural Explanations for Male Barrenness amount Moroccan Immigrants", in Deshen and Shokeid 1974: 122: 150.

not only with the new economic constraints, but competing with their former inferiors as well. Had the venerated rabbis of Asamer settled in Romema, they most likely would have been driven into fierce competition over formal religious leadership. That competition might have been most detrimental to their reputation and as bitter as that observed between the other Romemites, who were constantly fighting over economic resources and managerial positions in the moshav organization.[30]

The religious leaders were therefore out of tune with the new external (religious bureaucracy) and internal (turmoil within the community) circumstances, and were unable to react meaningfully and authoritatively to the overwhelming experiences engulfing the rank and file. They drifted toward a more heterogeneous environment where there were more varied occupational opportunities.[31] Some of them, in time, found a place within the new religious establishment. Away from their autochthonic community, they also regained some of their old confidence and former stature. Distance of place and time allowed them to handle better the changing destinies of their former flock, and to react more forcefully to their needs. They no longer underwrote the legitimacy of the rich and powerful, whether old or new, but concentrated on current existential problems confronting their still admiring adherents. For the Romemites, the social restructuring, the equalization of ranks and the equal access to various positions and resources in their community were made possible, *inter alia*, by the fact that the religious leaders of old lived away from the community but were equally accessible to all their followers.

---

30 In *The Dual Heritage* (1971: 101-162), I discuss the process of introducing into Romema a system of democratically elected officials and members of committees to function in the farming and municipal organization of the moshav. The introduction of this system was followed by constant competition and disputes during which offices were often stripped of value and local officials were disgraced. Some important positions were held by outsiders, such as that of secretary of the moshav.

31 Deshen in this study on a Negev town and its synagogues (1969) observed many religious dignitaries who have moved away from their autochthonic communities. Some of them became pathetic figures. Among these "leaders without a congregation", Moroccans were most prominent.

This combination of centrifugal forces may explain why Asamer's rabbis were not called upon to fill an office in Romema, and why the more venerated did not even stand for office, though they were not appointed elsewhere to high-ranking positions. The gap left by their absence prompted the lesser religious figures and the new pretenders[32] to aspire to the position of rabbi—now a job among the offices of the moshav organization. The chaos during ritual in Romema I thus interpreted to be indicative of the process of transformation from a communal order based on the interdependence of charismatic leadership and the oligarchy of wealth into an egalitarian order of elected or appointed trained officials in all spheres of life, including the religious.

As for the individual congregants in Romema, their previous close contact with their religious mentors—who not only had guided them in their daily living, but had mediated between them and the spiritual realm—had been severely disrupted. The rabbi appointed from the outside, or the new "self-ordained" local aspirants to religious leadership, did not have the spiritual capacity of the venerated old leaders.[33] The Romemites had to travel long distances, or be visited by genuine dignitaries or impostors to sense again the spiritual aura of past leaders. The growing popularity of pilgrimages to holy sites, such as Meron,[34] may be related to the Romemites' sense of communal loss.

The transition from personal religious authority to bureaucratic appointment is a noticeable sign of the religious change undergone by Atlas Mountains communities in Israel[35] The constraints of change seem

---

32 Formal professional training and sitting for the examination did not damage the reputation of the aspirants, but invested them with some measure of authority.

33 During my visit to Romema in later years, no change seemed to have taken place with regard to the position of rabbi.

34 For a description of the pilgrimages made by the Romemites, see Shokeid 1974: 64-94.

35 The impact of the new environment on the traditional religious leadership was not as severe in some cases, such as where Atlas Mountains immigrants were a minority in the new moshav settlements. In these villages, Atlas Mountains immigrants were competing bitterly with other groups of immigrants (either from other parts of Morocco or from other countries) over various resources, positions and prestige. In fact, they tried to have

CHAPTER SIX

to have irreversibly shattered the previous communal order. However, the present mode of accommodation with the organization of religious life is characterized by a sense of malaise. Atlas Mountains immigrants probably share with many other communities in Israel,[36] and elsewhere, some of the existential problems which followed the breakdown of their traditional order. The anthropologist who studies this type of field situation has a better opportunity to comprehend the processual element in social accommodations, being aware at the same time that he is recording but a fraction of the moving picture of social life.

---

their religious leaders appointed as rabbis in these villages. See Weingrod 1966; as well as the case of the rabbis from Asamer who stayed with their closes of kin in Yashuv, which, since the departure of the majority of the people from Asamer (those who settled in Romema) had become a multiethnic community. Remaining a minority in Yashuv, they tried to have their relatives appointed to the post of rabbi (Shokeid 1974: 210-225).

36 Interesting research has been carried out by Zenner (1965) in Jerusalem with veteran residents who originated from the Middle East, particularly Aleppo.

CHAPTER 7.
CULTURAL ETHNICITY IN ISRAEL: THE CASE OF MIDDLE EASTERN JEWS' RELIGIOSITY[1]

INTRODUCTION

National myths and public policies in Israel long assumed that the country's diverse Jewish immigrant groups would all eventually, and indeed within a short span of time, be absorbed and fused into a unified social, economic, political and cultural entity, but this expectation is now giving way to widespread doubts as to its feasibility. Some of these doubts were expressed already during the 1970s in a series of studies which demonstrated not only that there were still gaps between Israelis of Middle Eastern and North African extraction (often called Sephardim or Oriental/Mizrahim Jews) and those of European extraction (Ashkenazim), as regards occupational and residential mobility, income and educational achievements, political representation, and social prestige, but that the gaps were widening.[2] The growing disillusionment on the part of Middle Eastern Jews (North Africans included) was dramatically revealed in the 1981 general elections by the emergence of a new ethnic party, Tami, which seemed to have better prospects of success and survival than any previous

---

1   I am grateful to Shlomo Deshen, the late Jacob Katz, Robert Chazan and Menachem Friedman for their helpful comments.
2   See, for example, Hartman and Ayalon 1975; Spilerman and Habib 1976; Smooha 1978; Svirski and Bernstein 1980. These observations have been confirmed also in later publications.

ethnic party. Moreover, the results at the polls obtained by most of the other parties seemed to reflect an intensifying ethnic polarity.[3]

A growing number of sociologists have been concerned with the social, economic and political factors that have led to the emerging ethnicity in Israel, but they have usually refrained from discussing more specifically the cultural elements that characterize Israeli ethnic divisions. The sociological perspective derived from the theories of modernization of the 1950s and early 1960s, which regarded Middle Eastern Jews as representing traditional societies and cultures, and expected them inevitably to move out toward the modern axis (which was apparently represented by the veteran European and mostly secularized Israelis),[4] had been seriously challenged,[5] but no alternative theoretical framework for understanding the dynamics of cultural continuity and change had been suggested. The absence of a clear treatment of these processes has possibly been influenced by the prevailing general sociological approach, which seems to perceive emergent ethnicity as an ephemeral phenomenon of little consequence. This has been interpreted, *inter alia*, in terms of the exigencies of survival and the structure of opportunity (such as the result of residential and occupational enclaves) rather than as the manifestation of a common heritage.[6] Alternatively, Gans (1979) interpreted contemporary American ethnicity in terms of "symbolic ethnicity", which influences leisure-time activity, does not need a practiced culture and is "largely a working-class style".

Leaving aside intuitive assumptions and stereotypes, we know relatively little about the cultural components that characterize the ethnic structure of contemporary Israeli society.[7] Anthropological studies of Middle

---

3   The major contest in the 1981 general elections involved the Labor Party and the Likud. It has been confirmed, however, that a higher proportion of voters of European extraction voted Labor while a higher proportion of voters of Middle Eastern extraction voted Likud. See, for example, Arian 1981; Diskin 1981.

4   See, Eisenstadt 1954; Weintraub and Lissak 1964; Bar-Josef 1968.

5   See, for example, Smooha 1978; Bernstein 1978; Ram 1993.

6   See, for example, A. Cohen 1974; Yancey, Ericksen and Julian, 1976.

7   See Goldberg, 1972.

Eastern immigrants have provided detailed information about specific institutional characteristics, such as the patterns of family and kinship or the patterns of communal and religious leadership in particular communities of immigrants from Tripolitania, Djerba or the Atlas Mountains.[8] However, because of the inhibitions and limitations inherent in the methodology of intensive participant observations in small communities, the authors of these studies have usually refrained from deducing relevant trends to wider ethnic populations.

Deshen, (1974), who gave more specific attention to the status of the ethnic cultures, observed during the late 1960s and early 1970s the revival of some ethnic customs and traditions among Tunisian Jews. He interpreted this phenomenon as indicating a process by which cultural ethnicity has been replacing political ethnicity among Middle Eastern immigrants. These observations and interpretations suited the euphoric, optimistic national mood following the 1967 war, which for some time camouflaged the persistence of social gaps. A few years later, Weingrod (1979) suggested the emergence of a working-class culture which involves Middle Eastern Jews in particular. He related this culture mainly to certain typical leisure activities, such as the growing popularity of national ethnic festivals, the enthusiastic attendance at football games, the popularity of particular forms of music, etc. This observation requires, however, a closer investigation of various dimensions of behavior that may constitute a more complex definition of culture.

I do not intend to propose a specific definition of culture here. There is no doubt, however, that we cannot conceive of Jewish society at any stage of its history without considering the Jewish religion as a major component of its cultural presentation. The aim of this article is to indicate some trends in the cultural processes that characterize contemporary ethnic developments in Israel, as demonstrated by the role of religion in the life of Middle Eastern Jews. The religious component of Jewish culture has

---

8 See, for example, Deshen 1970; Shokeid 1971; Goldberg 1972; Deshen and Shokeid 1974; Shokeid and Deshen 1982.

become increasingly problematic and a source of acute tension in recent generations as a result of the decline of social and cultural homogeneity in Jewish society at its various centers. This trend has been noticeable in Europe since the emergence of the Jewish Enlightenment (*Haskalah*) in the eighteenth century.[9] Among Middle Eastern or North African Jewry, however, the process started much later, in some places at the end of the nineteenth century, in other places not until the beginning of the twentieth century, or even later.[10] In Israel, the question of the role to be played by religion in the nation's life has become a major source of conflict. A large segment of the population (and particularly those associated with the socialist elite which dominated the country for many decades) sees religious orthodoxy as an archaic survival of little relevance. Ashkenazi orthodoxy in its various shades, however, has demonstrated extraordinary viability. Apart from the ultra-Orthodox, who are concentrated in exclusive communities (such as Jerusalem, Benei-Berak, etc.), the more moderate "neo-Orthodox" group seems to have strengthened its hold on the younger generation,[11] as witnessed by the recent expansion of its modern rabbinical high schools (*yeshivot tichoniyot*) and the growing involvement of its youth with the Gush Emunim nationalistic movement.[12]

We are not concerned here with an analysis of religious change, as expressed, for example, in terms of secularization versus traditionalism. For the purposes of the present discussion we consider religious behavior to be an integral part of a broader cultural and social repertoire, although it is often arbitrarily separated from its more comprehensive context and analyzed independently in exclusively religious terms. Just as the changing position of religion in any particular group reflects on processes mainly related to the religious domain, it reflects no less on fluctuations in the status and the existential circumstances of the people involved. Thus,

---

9   See J. Katz 1961.

10 See, for example, Weingrod 1960.

11 See Deshen 1978.

12 A movement mainly dedicated to the establishment of Jewish settlements on the West Bank.

for example, A. Cohen (1969) demonstrated the Islamic religious revival which supported the ethnic-economic interests of the entrepreneurial Hausa traders in Yoruba towns. In a study of a transplanted Atlas Mountains Jewish community, I found that the field of religious activity is a very sensitive vehicle for expressing the changing circumstances, aspirations and achievements of individuals and groups.[13] This was demonstrated by changes in the style of worship. A different situation is described by Deshen, who revealed that the abandonment of religious symbols by Tunisian immigrants in an Israeli town was as a result of their considering themselves religiously unworthy to perform the observances related to these symbols.[14] Their feeling of religious unworthiness reflected, however, a wider notion of failure and self-depreciation derived from the circumstances of their new environment. The role played by religion in expressing social developments and political conflicts has again been recently demonstrated in various parts of the Middle East, Israel included. Thus, on the one hand, certain revivalist religious trends have been identified among young Muslims in Israeli villages and towns, and on the other hand, religious activism among young, mostly Ashkenazi Jews has been the energizing force behind the establishment of new settlements on the West Bank. It is therefore interesting to find out whether and how Middle Eastern Jews express in religious terms their status in Israeli society.

HYPOTHESIS AND METHOD

The first encounter between Middle Eastern immigrants and the country's secularized dominant sector, as represented in particular by the major national bureaucracies, must have been a traumatic experience for the newcomers. Moreover, their concurrent meeting with the Ashkenazi religious establishment was by no means genial. Although the latter provided them with religious services and tried to

---

13 See Shokeid 1974.
14 See Deshen 1974.

recruit their youth to its educational institutions, the contacts between the Ashkenazi religious establishment and the Middle Easterners were disappointing, often painful, and ultimately of little consequence. On the whole, Ashkenazi orthodoxy in its various shades have little regard for the standards or religiosity and the ethnic traditions of the newly arrived co-religionists who had become its clients. Therefore, it could not reinforce their traditional religious patterns and did not succeed in recruiting many of the younger immigrants.

Social scientists assumed that Middle Eastern Jews would tend to assimilate with the dominant Ashkenazi segment of Israeli society. The observations providing the basis for the prediction that the Middle Eastern Jews would eventually be secularized were, however, greatly influenced by a perspective of religiosity which was anchored in the Ashkenazi tradition of orthodoxy as experienced or stereotyped by the researchers. This perspective inevitably has led to the conclusion that Middle Eastern Jews will eventually abandon their religious commitment completely, a conclusion that was supported for many years by the absence of noticeable trends of religious revival and the lack of institutions of religious education among Middle Eastern Jews, in contrast to the remarkable vitality observed among the various sectors of Ashkenazi orthodoxy.[15] As a result of these assumptions, the newcomers became to an extent "religiously invisible". Against this evaluation of the religious situation among Middle Eastern Jews, we argue that they have nevertheless developed a strategy of cultural accommodation with the surrounding dominant society, a strategy also employed by Middle Eastern Jews in earlier centuries. According to our observations, this has produced a religious path which appears to be midway between Ashkenazi orthodoxy, on the one hand and Ashkenazi secularism, on the other. The symbolic presentation of this style is distinctive and appealing to the extent that it carries the potential of influencing political life in Israel, but it is not provocative

---

15 See, for example, the discussion of religious education among Ashkenazi and Middle Eastern Jewry by Deshen 1980.

and exclusivist to the extent of contradicting the national ideal of social integration. These observations, we hope, may also expand our understanding of the role and strategy of emergent ethnicity in contemporary civilization in general.

The data I draw upon are varied and it may not always satisfy a strict doctrinal approach. I report on participant observations which I carried out during the late 1960s and late 1970s in villages inhabited by Moroccan immigrants. During 1979 I carried out observations in several synagogues located in two neighborhoods of Tel Aviv, and in 1981 I interviewed supporters of the new ethnic party, Tami. I also draw upon ethnographic data produced by other anthropologists, the available sociological surveys and interviews with leading Middle Eastern Jews recorded by the mass media. My discussion is supported by the reconstruction of Jewish life in the Middle East provided by historians and social scientists. These observations seem to have predicted later developments in Israeli society.

PRECEPTS VERSUS TRADITION

The expansion of anthropological research in Israel since the mid-1960s had been accompanied by an increasing interest in the religious life of Middle Eastern Jews. In a study of an immigrant town, Deshen (1969) reported on the viability of ethnic synagogues: the regular participants, however, were mainly youngsters under fifteen years of age and adults above thirty-five. Thus the generation of young adults was absent. Another observation, mentioned earlier, indicated that the immigrants' notion of religious depreciation reflected their deteriorating position in other spheres of life. We may assume that this low self-esteem also influenced parental authority over children's religious behavior, which may explain their absence from synagogue activities as well as the growing intergenerational disparity in religious conformity, as reported by Herman (1970). It is not surprising that ten years later Deshen (1980) reported that the ethnic synagogue had lost most of its thriving viability. Its regulars appeared to be mostly aged, while the younger generations participated only occasionally and mainly at festivals and family celebrations.[16]

Interpreting these observations, Deshen employed Sharot's (1976) comparison of the level of acculturation with the host culture among Jewish communities in Europe, the Middle Eastern and the Far East. Middle Eastern Jewry occupies a midway position on a scale of acculturation whose extremes represent, at one end, the high acculturation of Far Eastern Jewry (such as the now defunct Chinese Jewry) and at the other end, the Jewish communities of Europe, which until the nineteenth century remained remarkably segregated from their host societies. Sharot argues that the general disposition of the host religious doctrine toward minority religions determined the degree of the Jewish acculturation: the greater the tolerance demonstrated by the host society, the stronger the tendency on the part of the Jewish community toward accommodation with the host doctrine. This analysis is supported by the observation that the traditions, rituals and beliefs of most Middle Eastern Jewish communities often displayed elements in common with those of their Muslim neighbors. To this assessment of the characteristics of the religiosity of Middle Eastern Jews, Deshen (1980) adds that oral tradition, as opposed to written tradition, played a greater role in the transmission of Middle Eastern Jewish culture. That is to say, as compared to East European Jews,

---

16 In the 1960s, however, a few sociologists began to include in their surveys questions about the religious attitudes of Middle Eastern Jews. Thus the data produced from a national sample of eleventh-grade school students reported by Herman show that while Middle Eastern children were less religiously inclined than their parents, the proportion of Middle Eastern youth who considered themselves religious was higher than among Ashkenazi youth (34 percent vs. 22 percent). In addition, considerably more Middle Eastern youth defined themselves as *mesoratiim* (lit. "traditional")—a common term for believers who observe religious precepts selectively—44 percent versus 22 percent among Ashkenazi youth. The survey also revealed noticeable differences among the various groups of Middle Eastern Jews: Yemenite youth were highest in considering themselves religious (63 percent), North African youth second on the scale (44 percent) and other Middle Eastern youth came lowest on this scale (21 percent). However, the majority of Middle Eastern youth who did not consider themselves religious defined themselves as *mesoratiim*. See also Matras 1965.

Middle Eastern Jews were less likely to regard learned texts as depositories of culture. He therefore concluded that the religion of Middle Eastern Jewry was less differentiated externally vis-à-vis Gentile culture, as well as internally, from other facets of Jewish culture. The conclusions derived from these studies may provide an explanation for the patterns of religious behavior observed among Middle Eastern Jews in Israel. Since they are apparently predisposed to a relatively easy accommodation with the cultural pressures of their host society, whether Muslim or Israeli-Ashkenazi, they soon seemed to acculturate to the secular culture of the dominant veteran segment of Israeli society and accommodated with no protest to the attitude of superiority demonstrated by the orthodox establishment.

An anthropological study which I carried out during the late 1960s and again during the late 1970s among Moroccan immigrants in villages revealed a phenomenon different from what was observed in the town environment. The economic affluence afforded by farming, which eradicated the old communal stratification, enabled the families that had once been poor to utilize the religious sphere as a means of displaying their achievements in Israel, as, for example, through the acquisition of expensive Torah scrolls. Moreover, all generations participated regularly in synagogue activities.

In many parts of Morocco religious leadership was exercised by scholars whose authority was vested as much in their personal charismatic traits as in their family patrimony (i.e. *zekhut avot*—"merit of the fathers"). The attribute of *zekhut avot* was hereditary but at the same time was an inherent trait of moral superiority possessed by those who chose the religious calling. Such leaders were not formally appointed and did not receive a regular salary, but they were reputed for their extraordinary deeds and the power of their blessings. The characteristics of this leadership had a parallel in the religious leadership of the Muslim host society: *zekhut avot* might be compared to *baraka* ("blessing"), the virtue of sacredness attributed to the Moroccan *marabout* and his living descendants. It was not easy for leaders of this type to accommodate to Israel's bureaucratic religious system (Chapter 6). Moreover, while in Morocco the local communities had each supported several religious leaders who catered individually to their clients, in Israel the Ministry of Religious Affairs appoints only one salaried rabbi to each community. The unsuitability of the traditional leaders for this highly formalized system, as well as the tensions and conflicts resulting from the inevitable competition between the candidates who were available for such appointments, often led to the departure of the authentic communal leadership, whose members settled in the more heterogeneously composed new towns. Meanwhile, the ministry appointed its own candidates, who often did not gain the respect and affection of their congregants (Chapter 6).

During the late 1970s I carried out observations in two suburbs of Tel Aviv. One was a decaying public housing project dating from the 1950s. Its residents, of low socioeconomic status, were mainly of Middle Eastern extraction. The second suburb, situated nearby, was mainly composed of privately owned apartments, and its residents, a younger population of both European and Middle Eastern extraction, had moved in since the early 1970s. Eight ethnic synagogues were regularly operating in the old neighborhood: one Iranian, one Afghani, one Iraqi, two Egyptian, two East European and a joint congregation of Tripolitanians and Moroccans.[17] Although spacious and richly decorated, the synagogues were usually poorly attended by the younger generations, who had moved out to better neighborhoods or did not feel obligated to attend services. The scene seemed to confirm Deshen's observations about the decline of ethnic synagogues. Nevertheless, these observations did not appear to represent an irreversible process.

In the nearby new neighborhood, I observed two ethnic congregations—one Moroccan and the other Yemenite. The congregants assembled in the local school, where they were allowed to use two classrooms for the daily early morning and evening prayers as well as for the Sabbath

---

17 The suburb was mainly settled in the early 1950s, before the major immigrant from Morocco in the mid-1950s. Therefore, the small number of residents of Moroccan extraction, who could not establish a separate Morocco congregation, joined the Tripolitanian synagogue.

and festival services. The congregants were exerting pressures on the Ministry of Religious Affairs and the Tel Aviv Municipal Religious Council to provide the sites and financial means necessary in order to build proper separate synagogues. The Moroccan congregation, which I observed more closely, had been started by a forty-year-old congregant from Casablanca. He was the son of a religious leader in Tafilalt and had brought along a Torah scroll when he came to Israel in the early 1960s. On arrival he had settled in a development town, where he was employed in various teaching and clerical jobs. He moved to Tel Aviv in 1976 and soon after started to organize a *minyan* (ten adult males) for regular services. At first the *minyan* met at his home, but with the growth of the congregation it was allowed to operate in the school. In 1979 the congregation already owned four Torah scrolls, which had been provided by the ministry and by individual residents. When I attended Sabbath morning services during July (the peak of the summer season), twenty young and older men were present. The leader told me that usually thirty men attended services regularly, "but now there are some members who prefer to go to the beach". He added that he was careful not to burden the younger congregants with heavy religious demands. He knew that some of them did not wear a skullcap on weekdays and probably drove cars on the Sabbath, "but what is really important is that they come to the synagogue". He also told me that on the High Holidays many more residents of Moroccan extraction asked to participate in the services. On these occasions the services were held in the school's gymnasium. The holiday services provided the congregation with new recruits who sometimes became regulars. He did not hesitate to recruit new congregants whom he knew "were not particularly religious". Thus, for example, a regular congregant of about thirty years old told me that he did not wear a skullcap on weekdays but in the last few years had stopped driving his car on the Sabbath. "I keep the tradition which I got at Father's home", he ended as a sort of explanation.

At the end of Sabbath prayers the congregants went together to perform a short ceremony at the home of a non-member family which was mourning the loss of an elderly relative. On the way the leader mentioned that the congregants and other residents often invited him to perform family rituals and also consulted with him on various personal matters. He ended the conversation with the statement: "They treat me like a rabbi". Although the appearance and bearing of this congregational leader were "modern", his performance was very similar to that of traditional Moroccan religious leaders. His authority was personal, rather than based on formal criteria of learning and ordination, and also seemed to contain some features of *zekhut avot*.

During the High Holidays, the synagogues in the old neighborhood came to life. This phenomenon of religious revival was particularly noticeable amongst the Iraqi residents. The Iraqi synagogue, which was poorly attended most of the year, was fully packed, including many young adults and youth. Moreover, a new congregation was organized for the holiday season in the gymnasium of the local school. In addition, crowds of men, women and children gathered around the synagogues during the services, so that each one appeared to be the center of a lively communal festival. Within the synagogues, large sums of money were contributed for the right to perform various honored parts during the service. The emergent congregations manifested noticeable features of communal bonds.[18] On Succoth (Tabernacles), when the attendance dropped considerably, I carried on a conversation with a group of regular congregants about religious life in Iraq and Israel. The beadle, an impressive man in his early sixties, argued somewhat impatiently: "There is no difference; it is all a matter of family comportment. If the father attends the synagogue, the children go along. But if the mother spends her time playing cards and the father whiles his time away in similar pursuits, the children will do just the same. And there are also the uncles whose behavior carries some influence as well. So you see, it all depends on the blood that runs in the family". He added that the attendance at the synagogue in Iraq was also not regular, "but Rosh Hashanah and Yom Kippur are different days!" He was thus

---

18 This type of High Holidays communal congregation differs from that observed in many Ashkenazi synagogues, where the swollen congregations during the festivals are usually composed of unrelated participants.

implying that in Iraq also, the attendance of congregants on the festivals was much more impressive.

Another congregant, in his early fifties, reacted as follows: "In Israel there are many parties [*miflagot*]: Iraqis, Iranians, Egyptians, etc. Everyone establishes his own synagogue; there is even another Iraqi synagogue here [on the High Holidays]. But on weekdays you can't assemble a *minyan!*" Although the latter expressed some bitterness about the organization of religious life in Israel, neither man complained about changes in the extent of religiosity among their compatriots, nor did they look back nostalgically.

The personal experiences of the historian Yehuda Nini are revealing in this context, reflecting similar characteristics among Yemenite Jews. He was born in a veteran village of Yemenite residents, which he left at a later stage for a nearby town. He was often questioned by observant older relatives about his absence from the synagogue services on the Sabbath. He answered in astonishment that he could not attend on the Sabbath because of the distance of the synagogue from his home. With no hesitation they suggested that he should come by car and park near the entrance to the village. He was also invited by relatives to participate in the Sabbath and festival services in another village whose residents had arrived from Yemen in 1948. They also suggested that he lead the prayers on the festivals. They knew he could not accept their invitation unless he came by car on these occasions. Eventually he came by car, parking at the center of the village. He was warmly received and was treated during the service as a guest of honor.[19]

Pertinent support for our observations is provided by Tessler (1978) who carried out a study in Morocco during the early 1970s. He reports that most of the Jews who remained in Morocco's towns (many of whom had migrated from villages), "are observant, but often by tradition rather than conviction" (p. 371). Ninety-two percent of his respondents kept

---

19   I am grateful to Prof. Yehuda Nini of Tel Aviv University, who gave me permission to publish this information.

kashrut at home, sixty percent attended synagogue every Sabbath, but only twenty-five percent observed the Sabbath strictly. When they were asked to report on aspects of daily life which most frequently reminded them that they were Jewish, the majority pointed out factors relating to family, friends and the social milieu as often as those relating to worship and observance. This information recalls the many interviews with Jews of Moroccan extraction (the largest group of Middle Eastern immigrants) on Israeli radio and television or appearing in the daily newspapers. The interviewees recurrently confess their attachment to *masoret* (lit. "tradition"). Such statements are often made by leading young figures who are not considered religious by most listeners and readers. For example, Mr. Shaul Ben-Shimhon, president of the Association of Moroccan Jews stated in a newspaper interview:[20] "Although I smoke on the Sabbath, I adhere to tradition [*ani masorti*]. I am secularized, nevertheless, I fast on Yom Kippur. I attend synagogue during the festivals and I perform *kiddush* [the blessing over wine] every Sabbath. I consider the Sabbath feast as holy of holy [*kodesh hakodeshim*], and I dedicate the Sabbath completely to the family [*Shabbat kodesh lamishpachah*]". A similar attitude was reported by Mr. Raphael Edri, who at the time of the interview (1979) was the manager of a large national building concern and had later served as a Labor member of the Knesset. He also defined himself as "traditional" [*mesorti*]. He told his interviewer[21] that, although he drives a car on the Sabbath, he often dons phylacteries.[22] "It has been planted in our blood", he explained and continued: "My children attend a secular school, but during the Sabbath feast I make the blessing over the wine and the children wear skullcaps". Most revealing is Aharon Abu Hatzeira, son of the most venerated religious leader of Moroccan Jewry, who at the time of

---

20 Levy Itzhak Hayerushalmi, *Ma'ariv* weekend supplement, Nov. 9, 1979, p. 30.

21 Hayerushalmi, *Ma'ariv* weekend supplement, Nov. 9, 1979, p. 30.

22 It seems that the interviewees attributed an equal value to most religious actions, as well as to their transgressions. Thus, for example, the *Kiddush*, smoking on the Sabbath, fasting on Yom Kippur, the wearing of a skullcap, driving on the Sabbath, and donning phylacteries are presented as equal alternatives.

the following observation was serving as minister of religious affairs. At a political rally which he held on the campus of Bar-Ilan University[23] before the 1981 general elections, soon after he broke away from Mafdal (the National Religious party), he explained the meaning of the name of the new party he headed, Tami, whose initials stand for *Tenu'at Masoret Yisrael* (The Movement of Israel's Tradition): "Mafdal opened its ranks to those who observe *taryag mitzvoth* [the 613 commandments prescribed in the Pentateuch; the word *taryag* is made up of the Hebrew letters *taf* = 400, *resh*—200, *yod*—10, *gimmel* = 3]. But there are many people who do not observe all the *mitzvoth* (precepts), yet they do consider themselves Jews as the followers of Israel's tradition. Why should we close our ranks and exclude them? *Taf mitzvoth* [400 precepts] or *resh yod mitzvoth* [210 precepts] are also sufficient!!" A similar interpretation of Tami's ideology was offered to me by a young school principal whose family arrived in 1956 from the Atlas Mountains: "Tami is a party which cherishes tradition [*Tami miflagah mesoratit*]. Oriental Jews [*edot hamizrah*] are not extremists: they did not reside in the ghetto. If the Arab grew long hair, the Jew cut his hair and left a beard only. If the Arab wore a white gown, the Jew wore a black gown instead. But the Jew lived *with* [*hai'im*] the Arab!" Referring to the complex reality of Jewish life in many Muslim countries, he was describing both a philosophy and a strategy of existence which had sustained Jewish cultural survival through an unabashed accommodation with social and cultural constraints (as forcefully phrased in his statement: "But the Jew lived with the Arab"). He was at the same time implying that the Ashkenazim tend toward extremism, as demonstrated both by their orthodoxy and by their secularism.[24]

---

23   June 3, 1981.

24   He went on to explain the pattern of voting in his village (composed of Moroccan settlers), which was divided between Tami and Likud (Premier Begin's party coalition). He though that those who voted for Likud had acted against their own economic interests, since as farmers they were more likely to prosper under a Labor government, "but the propaganda presented the Labor party as the old Mapai [the Labor party, mainly under Ben-Gurion's leadership]. Mapai represents secularization! This is the party which, many years ago when the settlers arrived in the country, was suspected of prohibiting the learning of the

Quite in line with this type of religiosity is the continuing popularity, particularly among North African Jews of pilgrimages to the tombs of venerated scholars and saints, whether of ancient or more recent vintage. This phenomenon has been noticeable since the first years of immigration, the period which seemed to reflect most profoundly the weakening of religion in the life of Middle Eastern Jewry. Thus, for example, by the early 1960s the pilgrimage to the tomb of Rabbi Shim'on bar Yohai in Meron on Lag B'Omer was already the largest spontaneous gathering in the country. More than 100,000 pilgrims, the majority of Moroccan extraction, came to the annual celebration.[25] Tunisian Jews also hold lavish celebrations in honor of their late scholars.[26] The pilgrimages and celebrations attracted a noticeably large number of younger people. Drawn, among other things, by the entertainment and social activities which the gatherings offered, the younger people were participating in these activities at the very time when they were neglecting synagogue life (as indicated by Deshen). The popularity of the pilgrimages continued in spite of the objections of the religious establishment, which also in North Africa had unsuccessfully objected to this phenomenon of folk religion. Manifestations of folk religion have not decreased since the 1960s. On the contrary, new pilgrimage sites have become popular. Particularly noteworthy are the North African scholars and saints whose spirits have apparently moved to Israel in recent years, as revealed in the dreams of their disciples. Ben-Ami (1977) for example, observed that the worship of saints intensifies in times of crisis. Immediately after the 1973 war he recorded instances of young soldiers and their parents expressing gratitude to family saints for the miracles they had performed on the battlefield.[27]

Torah and which was enthusiastic in conscripting girls to the army". In accordance with this interpretation, the Labor Party was now rejected because of its image as representing extreme secularization.

25 See Shokeid, 1974.
26 See Deshen, 1974.
27 See Bilu (2003) for more recent developments in the field of saints worship.

Besides the spontaneous revival of traditional patterns of folk religion, a new type of ethnic-religious celebration has been evolving since the late 1960s: the Moroccan Memuna, the Kurdish Saharanei and the Iranian Ruze-Baque. Although based on traditional elements, these celebrations have been greatly encouraged by the Israeli political establishment.[28] The largest celebration, the Memuna, on the day after Passover, has been held in Jerusalem.[29] The Saharanei celebration, which began during the 1970s, is held during Succoth at a more secluded country site.[30] The Ruze-Baque, the most recent of the celebrations, is also held on the day after Passover, in Ramat Gan's National Park. These gatherings, which originally were family and communal events, have been transformed into nationwide ethnic-political festivals. They are regularly attended by national leaders and politicians, including the president, prime minister and the leader of the opposition. Although the activities at these celebrations bear little resemblance to the traditional family and communal festivities in Morocco, Kurdistan and Iran, both the organizers and the participants perceive them as part of their diaspora heritage. This heritage is so intertwined with religious aspects of the celebrations, that in 1980, accepting the inevitable, the Sephardi chief rabbi publicly gave his blessing to the Memuna.[31]

FAMILIAL AND COMMUNAL ANCHORAGE OF RELIGIOUS ACTION

The data suggest that religious vitality differs according to the extent of homogeneity or heterogeneity in the ethnic composition of settlements. Thus, a larger percentage of youth seem to participate in synagogue life among ethnic groups whose members are more

---

28 See Weingrod 1979.
29 For the origins and pattern of the Memuna, see, for example, Goldberg 1978.
30 See Halper and Abramovitch 1984.
31 There are two chief rabbis in the country, an Ashkenazi and a Sephardi. This system of rabbinical leadership was established during the British Mandate in Palestine.

concentrated in villages or urban suburbs.[32] But religion is not dying out with the passing of the older generation in the more heterogeneous settlements. Despite the shattering cultural crisis that Middle Eastern Jewry experienced in Israel, which involved, among other things, a depreciation in the status of their religious leaders and a diminution in the authority of religious observances in daily life, the religious domain still forms an important element in the cognitive, perceptive and affective layers of social existence for a considerable portion of Middle Eastern Jewry.

In order to clarify these propositions we will first elaborate the sociological definition which indicates the features of religious activity among Middle Eastern Jews. The definition, largely developed by Deshen (1980) relates to the minimal differentiation of religion from other cultural domains among Middle Eastern Jews. This definition, which has greatly contributed to our understanding of Middle Eastern Jewish religiosity, fails, however, to consider the extent and the consequences of Middle Eastern Judaism's anchorage in the family and the community web of commitments. We argue that this type of lesser differentiation between religion and other social domains, which has deeply anchored Middle Eastern Judaism in familial and communal action, offers the religious domain indispensable support under changing circumstances that deprive religion of many of its own resources. This perspective on the structure and content of religious action leads us toward a different interpretation of contemporary observations of Middle Eastern Jewish religiosity and toward a different evaluation of the prospects for religious life among Middle Eastern Jewry.

In Muslim countries, several factors related to the social environment and to material existence lent much binding force to the individual's familial and communal commitments. Genealogical bonds and territorial ascription were among the most important indicators of the social position of the individual in Muslim society (Rosen 1979). Although the Jews did

---

32 This may explain, for example, the higher frequency of self-designations as religious among Yemenite youth as opposed to North Africans and members of other groups.

not adopt the ideological elements that sustained this system, the organizational components of the host society were, nevertheless, incorporated to some extent into Jewish society. The importance of genealogical and territorial bonds was particularly noticeable in small, remote and isolated Jewish communities. Moreover, in many parts of the Muslim world, the weakness of the central political organization was reflected in the inability of the Jews to develop national or regional organizations. These constraints naturally buttressed the familial and communal dimensions in the composition of the individual's Jewish identity. The essential position of the family and the community is also indicated in the style of Middle Eastern synagogue services; for example, the seating arrangements, and the social activities that take place in the synagogue. Thus, all congregants, including children, participate as soloists in leading sections of the service, regardless of their musical skills or religious competence. The congregants are mainly seated along the walls of the synagogue hall facing each other, in contrast to the seating arrangements in Ashkenazi synagogues, where the congregants sit in rows facing the holy ark, and consequently can only observe the backs of most of the other congregants. Similarly, in the Middle Eastern synagogue service, those who have been called to take part in the reading of the scrolls of the Law make a round of the hall and greet each congregant before returning to their seats. The various modes of greeting (e.g., shaking hands, kissing cheeks, kissing on the brow) reflect the particular relationship with each congregant: kinship, friendship and deference.[33] Traditionally, the old men in the community, regardless of their religious competence and economic and social position, were treated with respect and were attributed with the power of blessing reminiscent of the reverence reserved for the religious scholars and sacred objects. The deference expressed toward the old men buttressed their position as heads of their families and enforced family loyalties.

Economic life, however, more directly affected the patterns of religious life, social comportment and identity. Itinerant peddlers and craftsmen

---

33   See Goitein, Vol. 2: 145; Shokeid 1971: 149-152.

who stayed for days, weeks and even months with their Muslim clients could not regularly participate in synagogue life (Chapter 2). These difficulties were acknowledged by local religious leaders as shown, for example, by the exception made by a Sefrou scholar for employees who could not attend public prayers.[34] Moreover, we do not find among Middle Eastern Jews pressures similar to those prevalent in European Jewish society regarding the severe avoidance of social relations with Gentiles, which aimed in Europe at maintaining religious and social barriers even when Jews were obligated to associate with Gentiles.[35] The data which I collected among Jews from southern Morocco demonstrate the frequent and relaxed contacts with Muslim patrons, neighbors and clients. Since the religious leaders in the tribal and rural areas were not given full financial support by their communities, they too were usually obliged to interact regularly with Muslims with whom they had an economic relationship. Therefore, the religious leadership was not as remote as the European Jewish leadership from the reality of mutual relationships between Jews and Gentiles. Also, in their physical appearance and clothing the Jews in the Middle East were not ostentatiously different from their neighbors, unlike orthodox Jewry in Europe for many generations.[36] These observations indicate that Middle Eastern Jewry did not develop a life-style of observances and prohibitions which consistently limited and stigmatized social interactions with Gentiles. The religious culture of Middle Eastern Jews, particularly in North Africa, was probably influenced by the Sephardi tradition developed by the Jews in the Iberian Peninsula until their expulsion in 1492. It was this tradition that also contributed to a more accommodating approach to the surrounding society and culture.[37]

---

34 Deshen 1983: 69; Ovadia 1975: 90
35 See Katz 1961: 33-34.
36 See Goitein 1955; Shokeid, Chapter 2.
37 H.J. Zimmels in *Ashkenazim and Sephardim*, 1958. He claims, inter alia, that "as a general rule the Ashkenazim were stricter than the Sephardim" (p. 158) and, "while as far as general culture was concerned the Sephardim were certainly superior to their Ashkenazim brethren, the latter surpassed them in religious and moral conduct". (p. 261).

Sharot (1976) and Deshen (1980) analyzed the close affinity of Middle Eastern Jewry to the culture of their host society in terms of its impact on the patterns and content of their religious activities. My approach, however, emphasizes the relevance of this affinity in generating a mode of religiosity that is highly interwoven with the individual's bonds of family and community affiliation. Moreover, in spite of the economic, social and political changes they underwent prior to their immigration to Israel (such as those following the process of urbanization in Morocco), Middle Eastern Jews still represented to a great extent a homogeneous society, in terms of a shared world view, maintained by all classes, in which a prominent position was occupied by the familial, communal and religious realms. Although the same processes of social differentiation and communal disintegration that had occurred much earlier in European Jewry had already begun in some parts of Middle Eastern Jewish society, their impact and consequences were not, as yet, comparable. Similarly, while the close-knit kin and community networks of Middle Eastern Jewry disintegrated somewhat as a result of immigration, the extent of dispersion and actual decline of the family and community was by no means so pronounced as among European Jews in Israel. The immigration from Europe starting at the end of the nineteenth century was usually composed of individuals and small families, and this became irreversible as a consequence of the Holocaust. In stark contrast, Middle Eastern Jewry's immigration was usually composed of communities in their entirety. Although these communities often became dispersed in Israel, and in spite of the various constraints that affected the daily life of the immigrants and their offspring in their new environment, the individual Israeli of Middle Eastern extraction has not become dissociated from the actual bonds and obligations as well as from a general orientation toward a wider network of kin and community members (Chapter 5).

We relate the symbiosis of the religious, familial and communal domains in Middle Eastern Jewry society in the diaspora, which survived until recent times, to the presence of a deep attachment to a diffused concept of *masoret beit abba* ("the tradition of the father's home") that is usually connected with synagogue life and, more specifically, to religious details connected with family ceremonial life on the Sabbath and the festivals. No doubt, the impact of religious obligations and the authority of religious leaders have greatly diminished, but the intensity and scope of family and communal ties, which have been traditionally interwoven with religious activities and meanings, have provided an important source for a diffused identification with religious symbols and an incentive for partial participation in religious activities at this stage of societal reorganization. The interpretations suggested by Sharot and Deshen for the apparently easy accommodation of Middle Eastern Jews with the secular culture of Ashkenazi Jews ignore the impact exerted by the factors of familial and communal commitments in the process of religious change and adjustment among Middle Eastern Jews versus Ashkenazi Jews. The lack of powerful family and communal orientations may offer an explanation for the dominant patterns of religiosity among Ashkenazi Jews in Israel, which do not encourage the modes of "partial religiosity". It should be emphasized, however, that the Ashkenazi scene in Israel is considerably different from that in the United States and Western Europe, where partial religiosity is acceptable to the Reform and Conservative denominations and is not consistently denounced by the orthodox sector.[38]

Particularly revealing have been our observations of the expressions of tolerance by Middle Eastern Jews toward partial participation in synagogue life. The attitudes of the leader of the Moroccan congregation that I observed in the new Tel Aviv suburb are reminiscent of the attitudes expressed by Moroccan leaders in earlier generations, as, for example, the Sefrou scholar mentioned above who made allowances for congregants who could not easily attend prayer services. The mere identification of individuals with the synagogue congregation through partial participation, without acceptance of the full range of *mitzvot* in public and at home, was accorded by the leader a religious value in a scale of religiosity which

---

[38] For an analysis of the phenomenon of ethnicity in American cities in terms of structural factors, see Yancey, Ericksen and Juliani, 1976.

ranks and rewards every believer according to his particular existential circumstances. The congregants perceive this scale as the natural order of religious life which endows contemporary leaders, as well as the scholars and saints of the past, with the spiritual power to supplement their religious deficiencies. These figures provide seasonal opportunities for religious evaluation, as, for example, during the pilgrimages to the saint's tombs and other celebrations.

This mode of religiosity is characterized by spiritual and emotional involvement and the notion of belonging, rather than by the strict practice of religious observances. The general reaction of Middle Eastern Jewish religious leaders seem to provide some support for this approach. Even those of them who succeeded in preserving their leadership status in Israel did not encourage the kind of isolationist tendencies or more aggressive manifestations among their followers that are observed among certain segments of Ashkenazi orthodoxy. This accommodating reaction does not by any means imply that the Middle Eastern leadership is weak or has lost control under the new circumstances. Nonetheless, it is difficult for those whose expectations and evaluations of religious comportment are anchored in the Israeli Ashkenazi tradition to comprehend this seeming religious tolerance and the modest religious demands presented to the congregants in daily life. From the Ashkenazi perspective, there is not much religious substance in the selective preservation of religious observances that are mainly of folkloric value. The low evaluation in religious terms accorded to the modes of behavior reported here leads naturally to the conclusion that we are actually witnessing a process of secularization.

MASORET RELIGIOSITY AND ETHNIC ACTION

Beyond the possible debate about the religious value to be accorded them, Middle Eastern patterns of religiosity may indeed express distinct symbols of an ethnic culture. Congenial circumstances for the development of that symbolic estate are provided by certain structural factors, and particularly by the tendency of Middle Eastern

Jews to concentrate geographically in villages, development towns and urban suburbs. Moreover, this concentration in ethnic neighborhoods is associated with a shared socio-economic status among residents.[39] *Masoret* religiosity as here described may both express and satisfy the growing dissatisfaction among Middle Eastern Jews and their increasingly more outspoken demand that their culture be recognized as a legitimate alternative to dominant Ashkenazi culture which is supposed to represent Israeli society. The melting pot ideology in Israel, as in other countries, has apparently aimed at social unification through a single, homogeneous culture. This ideology aimed no less at quick acculturation of the recently arrived groups, whose members were often considered backward and traditional, into the social order and the cultural repertoire of the dominant veteran sectors. Secularization has been one of the most noticeable characteristics of the veteran Israelis of Ashkenazi extraction. It was they who staffed the governmental, municipal, Jewish Agency and party bureaucracies that monopolized and allocated to the immigrants the major resources of livelihood and prestige. Among these bureaucracies the Labor party, which ruled the country for many years, was particularly influential. Actually, Middle Eastern Jews could usually choose between two alternatives offered, if not forced on them, by the Ashkenazi political establishment: firstly, the secular parties (preferably Labor), and secondly, the religious parties (preferably Mafdal). Therefore, it is not surprising that Tami, an ethnic party that went to the polls for the first time in 1981 and showed better prospects than any other ethnic party that has emerged since 1948, has chosen to identify itself by the term *masoret*.[40]

---

39 The election advertisements of Tami utilized the slogan "*masoret* is the thread which links all *edot* [ethnic groups]"; see, for example, *Ma'ariv*, June 11, 1981. The *edot* were identified in another advertisement as follows:: "... those who came from North Africa, Egypt, Libya, Iraq, India, Cochin, Kurdistan, Yemen and other Diaspora lands"; see, for example, *Yediot Ahronot,* June 12, 1981.

40 For an analysis of Israeli ethnic parties, see Herzog, 1984.

The emergence and disappearance of ethnic parties in Israel has usually been analyzed in terms of situational factors.[41] The new party's choice of its name appears to be consistent with our observations of the wide use of the term *masoret* by Middle Eastern Jews in explaining their religious situation. The concept of *masoret* conveys the symbols of a religio-familial-communal culture which is supposed to include also those who observe only *taf mitzvot* or *resh yod mitzvot*, as was openly declared by the party's leader. Thus, addressing itself to the vast constituency of Middle Eastern Jews, Tami made itself the representative of a distinct culture different from both the Ashkenazi secular culture which has conspicuously and aggressively dissociated itself from traditional Judaism, and the Ashkenazi exclusivist orthodoxy, which compulsively observes *taryag mitzvot*. The symbols and messages utilized by Tami offered indications about the characteristics of the cultural aspect of the developing ethnic-political framework of contemporary Israeli society.

Emergent ethnicity in Israel and elsewhere often seems to be a temporary phenomenon, as usually suggested by contemporary research. Thus, for example, it provides the first generation of immigrants with an instrumental means for claiming a larger share of public resources, and the third generation with a nostalgic return to their ancestral culture.[42] I do not claim that the emergent ethnicity is a revival of an authentic ethnic heritage. It certainly is not, though it reflects traditional elements and influences. Nor is it the mere ephemeral outcome of structural opportunities, or a primarily leisure-time activity of a working-class culture, though it has certainly been influenced by structural opportunities and does sustain a type of leisure-time activity that often characterizes "working classes". The fact that "ethnic" and "working-class" cultural manifestations often filter upward (e.g., American black folk culture) indicates their role in creating new symbols which also attract the mainstream and may even-

---

41 As suggested, for example, by Yancey, Ericksen and Juliani on "Emergent Ethnicity" (1976).

42 M.L. Hansen (1938), and "The Third Generation in America", *Commentary* 14 (1952): 492-500.

tually be transformed into major national cultural symbols. The *masoret* religiosity adopted and proclaimed by Middle Eastern Jews, which has been influenced by their diaspora heritage as much as by their family, community, residential and other structural opportunities in Israel, may under certain circumstances develop into a symbolic linkage with the more dominant cultural stream. With the growing disparity between the expanding Ashkenazi orthodoxy and the dominant secular sector on the one hand and the growing notion of cultural need concerning the symbolic realm of Jewish identity in the secular sector, on the other, *masoret* religiosity may be more than an ethnic peculiarity. Regardless of its possibly temporary nature, emergent ethnicity could have an important impact on mainstream culture, much beyond what has usually been assumed.

POSTSCRIPT

My observations and conclusions about the patterns of religiosity among Israelis of Middle Eastern extraction (the Mizrahim) and their position in mainstream society have not been rebuffed about a quarter of a century later. Tami was succeeded by *Shas*, a successful party in national politics, led by the widely venerated charismatic leader, Rabbi Ovadia Jossef (a former Sephardi Chief Rabbi). The party that made a claim to revive old Jewish traditions of religious education and social morality could thrive on the existential experiences and cultural sentiments nourished by many of the immigrants and their children. No doubt, Middle Eastern Jews have made a lasting impression in the social, political and cultural fabric of present day Israeli society.[43]

---

43 For further developments in the religiosity of Middle Eastern Jews in Israel see, for example, Leon 2008.

PART THREE.
ISRAELIS IN AMERICA

CHAPTER 8.
ONE NIGHT STAND ETHNICITY:
THE MALAISE OF ISRAELI-AMERICANS

On the basis of common interests and cultural heritage the sojourner tends to associate with people of his own ethnic group. He and his countrymen, if there are enough of them, very likely live together in a racial colony or cultural area. "Little Tokyo", "Little Sicily", "Greek Town" and "Chinatown" in this country, for example, are their ghettos.

(Siu, 1952: 36)

INTRODUCTION

The survival of ethnic presentation in the United States has been possible, as suggested by Park and Miller (1925), Siu (1952) and others, through the immigrants' geographical concentrations and their establishment of voluntary ethnic communal institutions and national organizations. The *landsmannschaften* of East European Jews are only one example of this tendency. Park and Miller (1925) have emphasized, however, that Jews have been particularly creative in institution building, commenting that, "From the standpoint of organization the Jews are the most interesting of the immigrant groups" (p. 237). Sociologists and anthropologists have often discussed the function of ethnic traditions and organizations in the process of immigrant absorption; for example, Eisenstadt (1954: 18) suggested, "Thus all such associations serve not only as foci of tradition, but also as channels of communication with the absorbing country".

From a different vantage point, Van den Berghe (1981) commented a few decades later that:

> The importance of ethnic ties can become especially crucial in the impersonal, anomic environment of a large city, where an ethnic group can be the main and only mediating institution (outside the nuclear family) between the isolated individual and a cold, hostile urban jungle.... Assimilation is not a simple function of 'urbanization', 'modernization", Westernization', or any of these glib concepts that were so popular in the social sciences of the 1950s and 1960s (p. 257).

In any case, ethnic organizations could not have come into being had the individuals concerned not been willing to meet regularly, to communicate and to negotiate with their compatriots, not only within the intimate circles of relatives and close friends, but also within the wider contexts which bring together casual acquaintances and strangers.

This chapter examines the absence of communal organizations and ethnic corporate action among Israeli emigrants in New York. Although their numbers in Queens and Brooklyn have increased considerably within a short period, and although some shops even have Israeli names, they have not created a "Little Tel Aviv" or an Israel Town. The image of a lively ethnic community as a common characteristic of both early and more recent waves of immigration to New York certainly cannot be applied to the Israelis. They differ greatly from their coreligionists who, a few generations earlier, were singled out for their organizational skills, and who are still noted for their ethnic solidarity.[1] They differ no less from other new ethnics who reside close to them and who make their ethnic presence prominent, as for example the Koreans in Flushing.[2] Ethnic presence also persists in Queens neighborhoods among European groups of immigrants; for example, the Greeks in Astoria.

---

1   See, for example, Yancey, Ericksen and Leon (1985: 113), who commented on the survival of Jewish ethnic solidarity even under high levels of residential mobility.
2   See, for example, Kessner and Caroli, 1981: 123-143.

The recent wave of Indian immigrants to the United States offers an illuminating comparison. As early as 1975, there existed twelve associations for fewer than 50,000 Indian immigrants residing in the New York metropolitan area. The proliferation of Indian associations has brought together members of varied educational and occupational backgrounds who come from afar to participate in political, religious, professional and recreational activities.[3] For a similar, or possibly larger, population of Israelis concentrated in smaller areas, not even one active voluntary association existed in New York during the years 1982-1984.

Furthermore, unlike the massive Jewish immigration waves during the later decades of the 19th century and the new ethnics who arrived since the late 1960s, the Israelis have not developed easily identifiable economic enclaves. The Koreans, for example, rapidly appropriated a considerable share of fresh produce marketing in New York.[4] The Israelis do not seem to have evolved an economic footing that would both manifest and strengthen their ethnic solidarity.[5]

This phenomenon of "submerged ethnicity" must relate to deeper layers of the existential experience of the American Israelis. As suggested by Isaacs (1975:34), "the function of basic group identity has to do most crucially with two key ingredients in every individual's personality and life experience: his sense of belongingness and the quality of his self-esteem". The Israelis who, as described in this article, do not attach themselves to the vast and prestigious network of American Jewish national

---

[3] See Saran and Eames, 1980; Fisher, 1980; Saran and Leonhard-Spark, 1980.

[4] See also Light's (1985) description of the ethnically based economic expansion into specific businesses, as demonstrated by the Koreans and other new ethnics in Los Angeles.

[5] Popular assumptions have often emerged about Israelis concentrating in particular businesses in New York: for example, taxicabs in the late 1970s. More recently, Israeli movers have become visible. But these occupational preferences have proved to be emphemeral and, in any case, have not become an ethnic monopoly. See Ben-Ami's (1992) description of Israeli workers in the moving companies in New York. They are mostly young men (recently discharged from the army service) on a trip around the world, who leave the United States after a relatively short time.

and communal institutions, and at the same time refrain from expressing a separate ethnic presence, seem to be out of tune with the mainstream of ethnic behavior in America. That phenomenon seems closely related to the Israelis' problem concerning the legitimacy of their emigration, their self-definition and self-esteem.

Ethnicity has usually been considered in terms of visible and continuing group activity carrying economic, political or cultural consequences.[6] Sociologists and anthropologists in particular have naturally been attracted to studying those immigrants and ethnics who get together in order to build communal institutions, who stake political or economic claims, or participate regularly in festivals and ceremonies.[7] When I first planned to study the Israelis, I assumed that they too would be immersed in the hectic routine and close networks of a lively community.[8] As it turned out, my major problem was accommodating my research method to the absence of a viable Israeli community.

Why do Israeli-Americans differ from most other groups of immigrants? Are they unique in this pattern of ethnic behavior? Immigrants who refrain from consistent organized and visible ethnic activity are considered to be absorbed, assimilated, acculturated, etc; that taken for granted, breaking away from ethnicity should be reconsidered. The case of Israeli-Americans enabled me to explore a field of observation and a type of social determinants which are only rarely considered in the repertoire of ethnic field studies and the variety of factors that affect ethnic behavior. Moreover, it made me aware of the methodological and theoretical affinity between the research of ethnic groups and the sociological

---

6 For the representation and review of these studies and its theoretical approaches, see for example, Barth, 1969; A.Cohen, 1974; Yancey, Ericksen and Juliani, 1976; Van den Berghe, 1981; Shokeid and Deshen, 1982.

7 See, for example, Avner Cohen, 1980, regarding the West Indians' London Carnival and other publicly displayed ethnic activities.

8 There are, of course, some studies which refute this generalization. Thus Eidheim (1969) introduces the interesting case of the Lapps, who, as a minority in Norwegian settlements, try to abandon or cover up those social characteristics which Norwegians take as signs of Lappishness..

research of other social minorities whose members share the problem of identity management.

METHOD AND SETTING

According to estimates of the Harvard Encyclopedia of American Ethnic Groups (Thernstrom, 1980:597), 300,000 Israelis had immigrated to America in the three decades following the founding of the Israeli State in 1948. Half of these settled in New York and another large contingent in the Los Angeles area. The rapid increase of Israeli emigration to the United States is comparable to that of other recently arrived groups. Thus, for example, during the late 1970s the newly emerging Asian-Indian group constituted about 250,000 people (Varma, 1980); the Dominican, 350,000 (Ugalde, Bean and Cardenas, 1979); and the Korean, 300,000 (Kessner and Caroli, 1981: 23). They, too, represent various social strata, including a large population of professionals and members of the middle class (Glazer and Moynihan, 1975: 23). It is interesting that most writers on contemporary immigration trends in the United States have failed to pay attention to the Israeli immigration,[9] in contrast to the attention paid in Israel itself, where the growing wave of emigration to the U.S. and elsewhere has become an issue that elicited great public concern. Emigration has been pejoratively labeled in Israel *yerida* ["going down"], and its participants are called *yordim* ["those who have gone down"].

Recent studies suggest that the vast majority of Israelis in New York City reside in Queens and Brooklyn. It is assumed that the socio-economic

---

9   Thus, for example, they are not mentioned in Bryce-Laporte's *Sourcebook on the New Immigration* (1980), in Caroli's review "Recent Immigration to the United States" (1982), not included among the portraits of new immigrants presented by Kessner and Caroli (1981), nor among the groups introduced in Foner's volume (1987). They are also not mentioned in later volumes which deal with immigrant populations, such as in Liberson and Waters (1988), Waters (1990), or Rumbaut and Portes (1990). The special issue of *Time Magazine* dedicated to the "Newest Americans" (July 8, 1985) indicates the presence of Israeli immigrants in Queens and Brooklyn (map, pp. 36-37), but the reference in the text is restricted to the presence of 8,000 Israeli engineers in the United States (p. 35).

status of Israeli residents of Brooklyn is somewhat lower in comparison to that of the Queens' residents.[10] Taking into account the various estimates of the Israeli immigrant population in the United States in general, and in New York in particular, the Queens population may range from 30,000 to 40,000.[11] Israelis in Queens tend to concentrate in the neighborhoods of Rego Park, Forest Hills, Flushing and Kew Gardens, a close chain of residential areas in the center of the borough that contains bigger and smaller apartment buildings, as well as blocks of semi-detached and ranch houses. For many years these neighborhoods attracted Jewish residents, but they are now increasingly occupied by Asian immigrants and middle-class members of minority groups.[12]

The fieldwork on which the following portrayal is based was carried out while I held a two-year fellowship at the Center for Jewish Studies at Queens College of the City University of New York. Between September 1982 and August 1984, I and my family rented an apartment in Kew Gardens. I first tried to identify settings frequented by Israelis, where I could observe their social interaction. There did not appear to be an Israeli "street corner society" (Whyte, 1955) or a "Tally's corner" (Liebow, 1967), the renowned observation units employed by urban anthropologists; the amorphous field situation in Queens lacked any resemblance to an anthropologist's expectations for an ethnic study.[13] My Israeli field was gradually constructed and defined through my growing involvement in Israeli activities and the slow expansion of a network of Israeli acquaintances.

---

10 See, for example, Korazim, 1983

11 See, for example, Ritterband's (1986) review of these estimations. As we discussed that topic in August 1993, Ritterband suggested there were no more than 30,000 Israelis in Queens.

12 See Sanjek's (1988) exploration of the history of Queens and the changes in its ethnic composition.

13 My previous urban study engaged an Arab population residing in a suburb of an Israeli city (Shokeid and Deshen, 1982). See also Epstein's (1981) reflections on the difficulties encountered by an anthropologist carrying out research in an urban environment, and Sanjek's (1978) comments on the methodological issues involved: "In evaluating urban ethnography one must always ask: On what basis, whether explicit or not, has this selection been made? Where is the ethnographer, and how does she or he trace their behavior?" (p. 257).

An Israeli family occupied another apartment in the same building and we gradually struck up a friendship with them and several other Israeli families residing within walking distance whose children were enrolled in the same school as my children. In time, I recognized most of the Israelis on our block, as we must have been recognized by them. Some were easily identifiable, but others, particularly the singles and young couples without children, were more difficult to distinguish; on the whole, the Israelis—dressed in sneakers, jeans, sweatshirt or suits—were indistinguishable from other New Yorkers. This knowledge of our neighbors' origins did not involve much sociability, since a shared neighborhood did not appear to be a sufficient stimulant for friendship. The neighborhood did, however, encourage social ties when relationships were sustained by other common elements, such as professional interests, children at the same school, or acquaintanceships carried over from Israel. Our stay in what seemed to be an "Israeli neighborhood" was important to the study, since it enabled us to strike up many acquaintanceships and offered insights into the Israelis' style of life.

Reaching out for the Israeli constituency, I approached Israeli-owned businesses and services in various parts of Queens, such as the garage where I bought my car and where I remained a client throughout my stay in New York. I often visited a nearby Israeli pizza shop, an Israeli pediatrician, and an Israeli travel agent. A major source of both casual and close acquaintances was the Israeli club at the Central Queens Young Men's and Young Women's Hebrew Association [YM & YWHA] in Forest Hills, which at the time was the only institution of its kind. A "social club" maintained its major activity, which took place once a week and was usually a lecture. It also organized parties for the major festivals, and once a month, an Israeli film show. Another place where I met Israelis was among the faculty, administration and students of Queens College. I also initiated contacts with several Israelis about whom I had heard from mutual acquaintances.[14]

New York City offered many occasions for brief meetings with *yordim* at the various "Israeli" gatherings sponsored by American Jewish

---

14   See description of Israeli informants in Shokeid, 1988b.

organizations or official Israeli agencies, such as the Israeli Film Festival and the annual Salute to Israel Parade on Fifth Avenue. Performances by Israeli artists and entertainers and visits to Israeli restaurants and nightclubs offered similar opportunities. These events were, however, frequented more by American Jews than by Israelis. In addition, I often encountered Israelis in public places such as the subway, department stores, the Lower East Side shops and in Central Park.

The population of the present study was largely the outcome of the natural evolution of a social network and occasional contacts of an Israeli resident in New York. My occupational life as an Israeli academic associated with a local university was not unusual in the Queens environment. Neither was my family life in any way different from that of many other Israelis in Queens. My contacts were mostly with Queens residents, and these encompassed a wide spectrum of its Israeli residents' occupational and social characteristics. From this viewpoint, my research population is probably more representative than that of most previous studies concentrating on specific populations.[15]

SOCIAL RELATIONSHIPS OF YORDIM

For many years Israelis have attached the epithet *yordim* [those who go down] to their compatriots who leave Israel, a rather degrading national designation which is also associated with presumed base motives of greed and cowardice. This was most strongly demonstrated

---

15　Some researchers have concentrated on students and professionals (Ritterband, 1969, Fein, 1978; Elizur, 1980). Kass and Lipset (1982) do not clarify the method of their sampling; while Korazim (1983) selected Israeli families according to the criteria relevant to the problem of services utilization. Y.Cohen (1988) relied mainly on the INS official data. Sobel (1986) interviewed applicants for immigrant visas in Israel. Tzabar (1996) interviewed a group of former kibbutz members in the Silicon Valley, and most later studies (e.g. Gold, 1997; Lev Ari, 2008) have relied on surveys or samples of Israeli immigrants studied by formal methods of research (questionnaires and interviews). In contrast, I did not screen my research population through any formal criterion and endeavored to disregard any preconceived view of the "typical" Israeli immigrant. For more details about the population studied, see Shokeid, 1988a, pp. 22-33.

in 1976 by the then prime minister, Mr. Rabin, who, during a television interview on the Day of Independence called *yordim* "the left-overs of weaklings" [*nefolet shel nemushot*]. His statement shocked Israelis residing abroad, and the term remained implanted in the memory of a generation. Since the mid-1970s, Israeli newspapers and periodicals have continuously dealt with the issue of *yerida*. I quote only a few citations from this enormous corpus of writing:

> Yerida is not much different from the cowardly flight from the battle field. If yordim are not completely deprived of human and national feelings, they will suffer for the rest of their life from a sense of guilt and from an inferiority complex. They shall be cast out by their children and friends [Gothalf, 1976:19]

> The *yored* is a miserable figure, a one-dimensional man or even less, oriented toward one goal—material gain. He is a caricature of a person, uprooted from everything which binds a human being to his geographical, social and cultural environment (Bar-Yosef, 1976:84).

> … you have given up a dream, a most beautiful dream, not only of the Jewish people but of the entire human race… You are, in fact, a deserter. Of course you have a right to desert, to try to replace one destiny by another. By your choice you have surrendered your superiority over all other animals. Just like them you have chosen life. You are a handsome, skilled and well-behaved animal and I have no doubt as to your future success. But I don't envy you… (Keinan, 1976:5).

However, since the war in Lebanon in the early 1980s the Israeli media has gradually become less hostile toward *yordim*.[16] The Lebanon war seems to have indicated the end of an ethos of a national consensus regarding

---

16 See, Har-Even (1989), who studied changing attitudes in the Israeli media toward *yerida*.

major societal issues and goals, such as relationships with the Arab world, the future of the Occupied Territories, etc. The growing political conflicts and the persistence of unresolved social gaps and divisions in Israeli society also contributed to a less critical attitude toward those who left the country. That emergent tolerance, however, had not yet had an impact during my work. Those who have written about *yordim* or spoken on their behalf emphasize the stigma which they carry and the feelings of guilt which they themselves nourish. This notion of guilt experienced by *yordim* was indeed expressed in my presence, though usually as relating to other Israelis and sometimes in a scornful manner. This labeling of Israeli emigrants is also reflected in their relationships, as observed in the following three fields or domains of communication and interaction.

YORDIM AND AMERICAN JEWS

American Jews and Israeli *yordim* regard each other with little sympathy.[17] *Yordim* aspiring to the economic and social position gained by American Jews are, nevertheless, inhibited by their inherent Israeli disdain of Diaspora Jews (see, e.g. Yehoshua, 1981) and their deep contempt of being identified with them. Reaching out to American Jews by joining their synagogues and other organizations demands the transformation of a crucial part of the *yordim*'s identity and self-perception vis-à-vis Diaspora Jews. Their sense of real or assumed rejection by American Jews seems to support the self-image and identity of *yordim* as being closer to the Israeli axis of identity, their present status as Diaspora Jews notwithstanding.

American Jews on the other hand, are bewildered by the presence of Israelis in their midst. Apparently, Israeli citizens who want to settle in America introduce an anomaly with which it is difficult to come to terms. For many generations Jewish communities everywhere have always

---

17 I cannot introduce here the observations relevant to this assessment, but only suggest a general overview. For more details see Shokeid's ethnography (1988a).

extended help to their fellow Jews who were held in bondage or lived under conditions of physical risk. American Jews have traditionally been particularly generous in this regard, as shown by their recent assistance to Russian Jews, even though these are the least "Jewish" in terms of educational and religious outlook. The *yordim*, however, although mostly secular, introduce a totally new dimension to the definition and categories of Jewish identity. On the one hand, they openly repudiate Jewish tradition, assuming instead a superior Hebrew culture, while on the other they forsake the Jewish homeland and the cradle of the culture which they claim to represent. In addition, the arrival of well-fed, skilled and often affluent Israeli immigrants who have left their Jewish homeland raises doubts as to the *raison d-être* of Zionism, while at the same time appearing to threaten the viability and security of Israel.

Yordim represent a social aberration, which can be perceived in terms of Douglas' (1966) discussion of the phenomena of anomaly and ambiguity that threaten the cultural categories of a social structure and moral order. American Jews who want to restore the categories and definitions which constitute the order and values of the respective Israeli, Jewish and Zionist identities, employ a subtle strategy: they ignore the *yordim*, they avoid associating with them, and express their disdain and resentment as much as their code of civility allows.[18] My own more intimate relationships with American Jews were mainly confined to colleagues on the various New York campuses. They informed me that their acquaintances felt little love towards *yordim*. I heard, for example, that Israelis were sometimes called "Fish", the abbreviation of "fucking Israeli shithead".

There is no doubt that the confrontation of American citizens with a new wave of immigrants of the same ethnic origin often generates ambivalent emotions. The arrival of the masses of poor, religiously-traditional

---

18 American Jews permit *yordim* to join their institutions, particularly if this affiliation seems profitable. Thus, for example, Israelis have joined the YM and YWHA in Forest Hills, where they make use mainly of the sports facilities (the swimming pool in particular). But the Y's management was not prepared to support programs for the Israeli constituency unless funded by the Federation of Jewish Philanthropies.

Eastern European Jews at the turn of the century also raised considerable anxiety among German Jews in America. The latter were worried about the possible adverse impact of the ghetto-image of the newcomers on Gentile Americans. Even so, they did extend help to their needy coreligionists. The newcomers, for their part, were well aware of the wide gap separating them from the affluent and assimilated German Jews (Wirth, 1928).[19] In the same way, Israeli emigrants are at a disadvantage in comparison with the social and economic achievements of American Jews, although on the whole they do not constitute a needy group of newcomers. It would appear, therefore, that both sides can afford the present situation of mutual resentment and separation.

YORDIM'S CONCEPTION OF YORDIM

The alienation from American Jews represents, however, only one facet, albeit major, of the *yordim*'s interaction in their new social environment. At this point, I want to introduce some observations describing their interaction with their American compatriots which show their own continuing dilemma of perceiving and defining the borderline between the *yerida* (emigration from Israel) as a type of collective behavior of which the immigrants, themselves, disapprove and *yerida* as a private action taken by individuals confronting particular existential problems. The disapproval of *yerida* as a type of collective behavior makes it difficult for the *yordim* to put up with the company of other Israelis in national or local ethnic associations.

This attitude was expressed, for example, by a recent arrival, an entertainer (who, when not performing, drove a taxi cab). While waiting

---

19   Ambivalence and conflict between the newcomers and old-timers of the same national origin have also been observed among other groups; for example, Kessner and Caroli (1981: 223) reported that "New Italian immigrants rarely foresaw the possibility of conflict with Italian Americans. Yet it is a division that marks relationships at all ages". See also Smith's (1978) description of tense relationships between old and new Portuguese in a New England town.

for his act during a party he commented: "Here you have the Bronx Zoo. You have here hawkers from the Carmel market [Tel Aviv's biggest open-air food and clothing market]. They are well disguised, but behind their masks you can smell them". The party took place in a Queens hotel, and the participants looked quite prosperous. On the same occasion I met Hanan, an engineer married to an American woman, who had come to the party together with two other couples. He also seemed unhappy with the surrounding company, which he considered noisy and vulgar. I myself was unable to differentiate between his own prosperous appearance in a three-piece suit, and that of most of the other participants.

A similar attitude was expressed by Eli (a retired artist), although his social life was completely confined to the company of Israelis. He told me that he had stopped attending performances by Israeli entertainers, because,

> I got depressed on these occasions. I love the sensation of Israel as experienced in Israel, but I hate the presentation of Israel as experienced in New York. I enjoy watching an Israeli crowd in Tel Aviv, with groups of people from all walks of life, whereas here you see a vulgar crowd of Israelis who talk Hebrew in high-pitched voices and get excited at meeting acquaintances they haven't seen for a long time.

Nevertheless, during my stay Eli did go once more to an Israeli evening, at which several popular entertainers performed. In the event, the occasion turned into a scandal, with the audience noisily demonstrating its dissatisfaction with the performance. Eli regretted having been tempted to attend this event against his better judgment (his wife was visiting her ailing parents in Israel at the time, and possibly he felt lonely and nostalgic for Israeli culture).

> When I looked at the crowd I subconsciously saw myself in the mirror. When you see other Israelis screaming in Hebrew, you

realize that you may possibly look the same. Unfortunately, I rediscovered the ugly Israeli.

During a Saturday evening gathering attended by five couples, those present referred to the "Israeli cancer". All agreed with the assessment of one participant that "every Israeli who arrives at Kennedy Airport believes that he already knows everything better than anyone else". A similar mood dominated another Saturday evening meeting. Excluding their close friends, our hosts, Joseph and Rina (employees of a Jewish organization) described the Israelis in New York in unflattering terms: although not very knowledgeable, the *yordim* were self-assured about their capabilities, which they assumed surpassed those of everybody else. Moreover, the Israelis were described as exploiting the American environment, infecting it with their own poor standards of discipline and work ethic. They also accused their compatriots of taking advantage of the sheer size of American society in order to evade the law.

Those looking for new acquaintances who to them represented "nice Israelis" were often disappointed. While attending a party at the Israeli club we met an Israeli in his late twenties who Hanan thought looked like a kibbutz member or a combat officer. Our new acquaintance actually turned out to be a graduate of the Israel's Wingate College of Sports and Athletics. According to his story, he had soon tired of his teaching job, and set out to look for new opportunities in America. Starting as an assistant in an electronics shop, he had eventually established his own business importing records and video films from Israel. Hanan was very disappointed to discover this transformation of an athlete into a "trader like anyone else". He lamented the Israeli reality in New York, commenting: "Whatever we do, even if we are born as peasants (*falachim*), we'll end up again in the old Diaspora Jewish tradition of trade and commerce".

One snowy evening, Arik (an engineer) was too bored to stay at home and watch television. This sort of weather made him, miss Israel more than ever and he suggested that we go to the Israeli club at the Central Queens YM &YWHA. Finding the club was closed, we decided to visit Dani (a craftsman), who lived a few blocks away. While

CHAPTER EIGHT

discussing the family and business affairs of some close acquaintances, Dani exclaimed,

> Looking around me, I suddenly see strange faces. If I would paint a picture of all this [implying his Israeli acquaintances in New York], it would turn out to be a frightening Kafka painting. And if someone hung this painting in his living room, anybody who came in would run away as fast as his feet would carry him.

On our way home, Arik asked me if I intended to write a book about the Israelis and their life in America. Noticing my hesitant reaction, he told me that I should write one in order to tell the "truth" about the Israeli reality in New York (which he considered to be rather depressing).

Although those quoted all sought out Israeli company, they failed to be satisfied. The Israelis with whom they came into contact appeared to be representative of the undesirable *yordim*. For that matter, they themselves were often similarly perceived by their acquaintances. Most of them were deeply attached to Israel and to Israeli company, so that their vehement criticism of their compatriots in New York, demonstrated neither a strategy of distancing themselves from Israel, or of legitimizing their own departure. They were, however, distancing themselves from other *yordim*, who were seen to represent the worst of Israeli society. Through their verbal descriptions and active avoidance of Israeli associations (as described below), they seemed both to adopt and confirm some of the common attitudes and stigmatized perceptions of *yordim* as expressed by the Israeli media and by Israelis in Israel.

PARTICIPATION OF YORDIM IN ISRAELI ACTIVITIES

The growing Israeli population in the city and its suburbs has resulted in the establishment of restaurants and coffee bars advertising Israeli food (mainly Middle-Eastern favorites such as *falafel*, *humus* and *techina*). Here, apart from enjoying the "ethnic cuisine", Israelis can also obtain information or advertise apartments, furniture, cars, babysitters, jobs, etc. Naomi's Pizza on Flushing's Main Street in Queens is a good example of this kind of establishment. The place carries the name of a woman of Yemenite extraction who runs the restaurant together with her husband, other family members and hired workers, all of whom speak Hebrew. Although the place is frequented by many Israelis, it lacks the familiar characteristics of an ethnic club. A fast-food restaurant, it caters to both Israeli and American clientele. More impressive is the growing number of popular Israeli troupes, performers and entertainers who, since the early 1980s, have discovered the commercial potential of New York's Israeli community. These performers often come to the United States for just one or a few shows. This new wave of Israeli artists appears at hotels and other halls able to accommodate large audiences.

The Israeli club at the Central Queens YM & YWHA in Forest Hills represents a completely different type of institution. It was designed to offer a more intimate environment for continuing social and cultural activities. Its geographical location makes it easily accessible to the residents of some of the densely populated Israeli neighborhoods in Queens, particularly Forest Hills, Rego Park, Flushing and Kew Gardens. The club was launched in June 1982 with the financial support of the Federation of Jewish Philanthropies of New York, and it is open to both members and non-members of the "Y". Its activities included a weekly Wednesday program (the Social Club), festival celebrations and an Israeli film on one Saturday night a month. I observed the club's social activities for nearly two years, from shortly after its inception during the 1982 fall season, through the 1984 spring season (the club did not operate during the summer recess of August-September).

The social club met in a large room on the Y's top floor. Most Wednesday evenings no other activities took place on this floor, and the sense of seclusion lent support to the illusion of a non-man's land. However, despite the many attempts made by the Israeli manager to offer attractive cultural and recreational programs and create an Israeli ambiance, the club failed to recruit a stable membership or initiate close social relationships between the participants.

CHAPTER EIGHT

When the club's new program for singles was launched, seventy men and women, including large numbers from Brooklyn, showed up for its inauguration party, which was held on a Saturday night. The few volunteers from among the club's regular participants, who had helped prepare for the party, were greatly disappointed with what seemed to them a small attendance, particularly from the Queens area. These disappointing numbers were discussed at the following Wednesday meeting. A twelve-year resident of Queens (a taxicab owner), whose own participation was very infrequent, exclaimed, "How is it possible that, with a few hundreds of thousands of Israelis living in our neighborhood, we don't manage to attract 150 participants for every meeting of our club?" Several more observations by the participants emphasized the reluctance of their compatriots to commit themselves to communal activities. Arik, seven years in New York, commented,

> You always see a small group of regulars, while all the rest are newcomers. They usually say they enjoyed the evening and promise to come back, but they never show up again. The Israelis are just looking for entertainment.

Hanan, an infrequent participant, told me.

> A visit to the club is a pain-relief tablet for the Israelis. I come because of the interesting lectures advertised in the programs. The Israeli institutions [implying the club, Naomi's Pizza, etc.] are an important support to the Israelis who live in America.

Even so, his emphatic statement did not indicate a wish to establish a stable relationship with the Israelis who frequented these institutions.

Sarah, a good-looking, well-dressed, pleasant and outgoing middle-aged academic, once told me about her growing predicament after more than twenty years in America.

> I feel as if I'm going crazy! In America you work with the same people at the same place for years, you talk to them, you laugh together, but they never invite you home. The club is no differ-

ent; at the end of the evening's program everyone goes his own way. I have tried to establish ties, but it is useless. I can't stand it any longer, I must go back to Israel.

When during a sing-along evening Sarah complained bitterly that both the singing and the social meetings at the club were no more than a "substitute for the real thing", a bystander reacted sarcastically: "But it's cheaper than the $600 airfare to Israel".

I myself was at times baffled and frustrated after a seemingly promising conversation with a friendly new visitor or couple. They would seem to be impressed with the club, and expressed an interest in pursuing our acquaintance. We would say good-bye with the clear intention of meeting again the next week or the week after, but no other meeting took place—at least not at the club.

Yaffa, who very rarely accompanied her husband during his frequent visits to the club, argued,

> Only the desperate go to the club. Israelis are scared to let others see that their integration into American society has failed. They prefer to hide in their holes, instead of coming out and identifying themselves.

On another occasion she explained her own reluctance to visit the club as follows: "The fact that people speak Hebrew isn't sufficient to make them friends. I am entitled to select my own friends". Her husband, Eli, who was among the club manager's few confidants, argued however that,

> The Israelis will flock in great numbers to hear Naomi Shemer [a popular Israeli lyricist, composer and singer], and they would gladly accept an invitation for a meeting with a high-ranking Israeli army officer. An Israeli prefers discussing the latest news from the Israeli stock-exchange with his close friends over talking about the American economy, but he won't attend the club. He prefers to keep a low profile because he feels guilty about being here.

CHAPTER EIGHT

Attendance at the club manifested a paradoxical mode of behavior. On the one hand, the participants were noticeably open and friendly toward their new acquaintances, and often expressed a desire for an Israeli social atmosphere contrasting with the more reserved American style of interaction. On the other hand, they often failed to grasp the opportunities that they appeared to be looking for, and they were very careful in striking up close friendships. Their irregular attendance prevented a growing commitment to the place and its visitors, and obviated the development of intimate relationships. Most of the participants were unable to sustain extensive close-knit networks of relatives and friends like the ones many of them had experienced in Israel. To the extent that they looked for Israeli company beyond the small circle available, they were reluctant to become involved in social ties that might entail certain obligations and commitments. At the club, the majority preferred the "one-night-stand" type of participation. Even those who attended Israeli activities more regularly did not develop close ties with other regulars. Regulars who stopped coming and were never seen again were rarely mentioned by other regulars.

In sum, although *yordim* refrained from acting out and advertising their Israeli-ness in formally established ethnic institutions, they did participate, on the basis of a "one-night-stand" relationship, in expressive activities featuring Israeli culture and sentiments. They flocked to concerts or performances by Israeli artists, attended the annual Israel Parade on Fifth Avenue, infrequently visited an Israeli club or restaurant, expressed deep emotions during community singing of Israeli folk songs, and they might have read the New York weekly Hebrew language newspaper *Israel Shelanu* [Our Israel], or listened to the evening broadcasts on 98 FM, WEVD of *Kan Israel* [Here is Israel]. The club's visitors proved to be attracted to those meetings which enabled them to display or observe Israeli expressive modalities. They arrived as individuals or couples who, upon entering, appeared to leave behind their American experience and status, but who at the end of the evening's Israeli activity, marched back into their American reality.

My observations have been supported in a later survey by Mittelberg and Waters (1992), who studied kibbutz-born Israelis in the United States. Nearly 90% of those surveyed reported little or no contact with Jewish or Israeli voluntary organizations (pp. 423-424).[20] Mittelberg and Waters emphasized in particular the Israelis' difficulties in identifying with their proximal hosts' (American Jews) major components of ethnic definition. Not having developed a surrogate Israeli ethnicity, the authors maintain that, "The Israelis spend much energy trying to be 'invisible immigrants'" (p. 429).

CONCLUSIONS

Discussing the process of assimilation, Van den Berghe (1981) started his thesis with the assumption that maximization of individual fitness is best guaranteed by behaving nepotistically and therefore ethnocentrically. Thus, he claimed, only a powerful force can motivate people to behave otherwise (p. 216). He suggested the following profile of the group most likely to assimilate: "an immigrant group similar in physical appearance and culture to the group to which it assimilates, small in proportion to the total population, of low status and territorially dispersed" (p. 219). Israelis in New York, however, are the least ethnocentric of immigrant groups in the United States, although there are apparently no powerful external constraints or benefits to motivate their rejection of ethnic alliances. In addition, they only partly accommodate Van den Bergh's profile of a group most likely to assimilate. The sources of their avoidance of ethnocentricity lie elsewhere.

Israeli emigrants appear to be severe critics of their compatriots who share their own immigrant status. They disapprove, or even detest, *yordim* as individuals who do not conform to their image of decent Israelis. The attitudes they express and their behavior, as observed at Israeli activities, appear to demonstrate the characteristics of stigma management suggested by Goffman (1968):

---

20 The data were collected in 1987-1988 from a representative sample in a survey administered through mailed questionnaires.

> Whether closely allied with his own kind or not, the stigmatized individual may exhibit identity ambivalence when he obtains a close sight of his own kind behaving in a stereotyped way, flamboyantly or pitifully acting out the negative attributes imputed to them (p. 131).

But Goffman goes on to suggest a counter-reaction:

> The sight may repel him [the stigmatized individual], since after all he supports the norms of the wider society, but his social and psychological identification with these offenders holds him to what repels him, transforming ashamedness itself into something of which he is ashamed. In brief, he can neither embrace his group nor let it go (pp. 131-2).

The phenomenon under observation seems comparable with observations made of members of another stigmatized minority who also share a problematic identity, although not constituting an ethnic group. Despite obvious differences between the two groups, the impersonal sociability observed among American Israelis nevertheless appears to me to resemble the phenomenon of impersonal sex as reported in studies of gay society. Members of both minorities appear to have a choice between three modes of dealing with a complex situation of identity and its display. They can: 1) divulge their identity and associate mainly with their own kind; 2) refrain altogether from any public exposure of this identity; or, 3) confront their concealed identity in secluded settings carefully separated from their usual fields of activity, so that they may display their hidden selves without seriously threatening their otherwise well-managed public identity.

Both the impersonal sex during occasional visits to bars, saunas, parks and restrooms and the impersonal sociability at the Israeli club, Israeli restaurants and shows, offer a similar outlet: instant gratification of a deprived identity, without the burden and risk involved in obligations and commitments to the partners in the activity. You will recall the remark of Hanan, a "regular-irregular" club participant, quoted earlier, that a visit to the club or to Naomi's Pizza was like a pain-relief tablet. The sarcastic visitor's reaction to a complaint about the club—"But it's cheaper than the $600 airfare to Israel"—comes close to Humphreys' assertion about tea-room sex: "This encounter functions, for the sex market, as does the automat for the culinary, providing a low-cost, impersonal, democratic means of commodity distribution" (1975: 154). Impersonal sociability also has a democratizing effect, in that younger and older Israelis, men and women, Ashkenazim and Sephardim, professionals and businessmen, craftsmen, taxi drivers, secretaries and shop assistants, can communicate comfortably about their work experiences and other personal details, while enjoying a joint display of "Israeli-ness".

Admittedly, during my stay in New York, not all the participants came to the club for impersonal sociability only; there were those who expected to make more lasting contacts within an Israeli social network, or to strike up friendships with individuals of both sexes. This attitude was also revealed by Styles (1979) in his study of a setting characterized by impersonal sex. A third of those he interviewed at a bath claimed that they went there for sexual contact, but also to look for a long-term relationship that would extend beyond the setting of the specific encounter. A few of his informants reported that they regularly met with the same person whom they saw only at the bath. In both settings under comparison, the expectations of a long-term relationship were often frustrated, the expectant visitor ending up with another "one-night-stand" experience. Our discussion does not exclude the sporadic informal socializing of Israelis in small circles of friends. But that form of sociability also lacked a supporting system for its continuation over the long run as experienced in the Israeli context.

The comparison between these two situations of impersonal encounters and identity management extends to the ethos displayed on occasions of expressive manifestations, but a discussion of this issue falls outside the scope of this presentation. The point I wish to emphasize, however, is that, despite the increasing flexibility and subtlety in considering factors which effect ethnicity, most researchers still perceive ethnic phenomena in terms of a unique biological, political, cultural, economic or situational manifestation. This approach, which relates mainly to organized ethnic action, also separates ethnicity from the sociological analysis of other social minorities whose members share the problem of identity management.

"One-night-stand" ethnicity, which offers little support for corporate communal action, also lacks the compulsion and the resources for the survival of ethnic culture at home, and might actually turn into "one-generation ethnicity". The demise of Hebrew among the children of *yordim* offers an important indication in this direction. This observation has also been made in other parts of the Israeli diaspora.[21] Of course, the resistance of children to speak their mother tongue and their rejection of their parents' Old World ways have been reported long ago among other groups of immigrants (see Hansen, 1952; Van den Berghe, 1981: 258). But the striking inability of American Israeli parents to preserve some proficiency in their native language in the home environment is influenced considerably by their reluctance to support ethnic organizations (Hebrew schools included) or to join American Jewish religious institutions or their educational systems. It seems pertinent to repeat here the statement made by Yancey, Ericksen and Leon (1985: 94-95): "An ethnic group is composed of individuals with some common characteristic *who associate with one another*" [our emphasis]. Unless future research finds them victims of "ethno-less symptoms", the second generation of American Israelis may prove to be one of the fastest groups of immigrants to have assimilated into American culture. This conclusion seems particularly plausible in view of the fact that Hansen's thesis (1952) about the resurgence of ethnic solidarity among the third generation has not received empirical support in resent research (Roche, 1984; Yancey, Ericksen and Leon, 1985). Israeli youth lack the background which might foster even the less noticeable features of "symbolic ethnicity", as observed by Gans (1979) among third-generation Americans.

---

21 See McNamara's (1987a.b) reports on the massive shift to English among the children of Israeli immigrants in Australia. McNamara commented, "Israelis in my study had a low perceived ethnolinguistic vitality, so low as to amount almost to a death wish" (1987b: 13).

Former Israelis would not be the first group to disappear from the American ethnic scene. The Germans represent a similar and relevant case. Glazer and Moynihan (1970: 311-312) have suggested a number of factors which handicapped the development of a German ethnicity; among these were, in particular, the heterogeneity of this immigrant group vis-à-vis the relative homogeneity of other groups (in terms of religion, education and professional skills). The German immigrants "... reflected, as it were, an entire modern society, not simply an element of one". Israelis also reflect an "entire modern society", but this alone cannot explain the process which may lead to the fast disappearance of Israeli ethnicity. Indeed, the case of the Asian Indians raises some doubt about the validity of the conclusion drawn by Glazer and Moynihan. Although a highly heterogeneous group, the Asian Indians in the United States have nevertheless evolved a strong ethnic presence within a short time. Van den Berghe (1981: 220), on the other hand, in commenting on the rapid assimilation of German immigrants in the United States, noted their low social status on arrival, but this suggestion does not seem a sufficient explanation for either the Germans or the Israelis. This model of explanation, based on structural, socio-economic and other measurable factors (though not always actually assessable), seems therefore insufficient to explain some more complex cases of ethnic behavior.

Recent studies employ a more sensitive approach, as for example, Roche (1984), or Yancey, Ericksen and Leon (1985), who measure the degree of ethnic awareness among those classified in the ethnic category, rather than concentrating on the assumed ethnic categories or the apparent signs of "emergent ethnicity". Yet these studies of attitudinal ethnicity scores are limited to the scope of issues and questions traditionally related to ethnic studies. "One-night-stand ethnicity", a metaphor I introduced in order to describe and comprehend the Israeli-American case of submerged ethnicity, will not, I hope, be taken as a mere "sexy" contribution to the terminological inventory of ethnic research. This pattern, and its metaphorical image and social analogy for impersonal sociability will, I believe, expand the observational scope of ethnic phenomena, and proffer an insight into the missing factors affecting certain forms of ethnic behavior.

POSTSCRIPT

Since my observations during the 1980s, the position of Israeli immigrants has greatly changed in the Israeli public perception. The term "*yordim*" has lost much of its stigmatizing connotation. Many Israelis have close relatives and friends who live permanently or only temporarily outside of Israel, and the bitter notion of betrayal and of shame for deserting Israel has gradually evaporated. Those who left in recent years, are not perceived any longer as endangering the security of Israel. The trend of globalization, the growth of international business, science and technology, help accommodate with the torrent of citizens who commute forward and back, though many stay on permanently away from their homeland.

However, my observations of the absence of Israeli institutional life in New York remain true to this day. I assume the reasons for this present day avoidance of communal life are not directly related to the "*yerida*" stigma of the "old days". No doubt, most Israelis of Ashkenazi extraction in particular, are secular and are unable to join American Jews', synagogues and other cultural institutions. It calls for further research in order to reveal the social, cultural and other constraints that handicap these days the development of Israeli institutional ("ethnic") life in the New York diaspora.

CHAPTER 9.
THE PEOPLE OF THE SONG

The Gatherings of Israeli emigrants (nicknamed *yordim*) centered around the singing of Israeli folk songs were among the events that most puzzled and impressed me during my stay in New York (see Chapter 8).

Folk songs are a standard part of Israeli youth movement education and I myself sang at the *kumzitz* gatherings during army service and afterwards. These songs are regularly broadcast on radio programs, particularly during the annual celebrations of the Day of Independence. On this festive day, the main streets and squares of most villages and towns entertain thousands of people walking and dancing under the spell of blaring loudspeakers playing their repertoire of old and new songs. During the late 1970s and early 1980s Israeli television aired a few *shira betzibur* programs (sing-alongs). These were recorded on the grounds of a kibbutz, thus evoking nostalgia for a different Israel than that of my own urban upbringing. It was Israel as depicted on posters, untainted by the harsh realities of mounting economic, political and social problems.

After my arrival in New York, I sang more in one year than ever before. At long last I had occasion to experience the passion associated with the kibbutz, albeit in a situation that appeared to be diametrically opposed to kibbutz ideals—in Forest Hills, Flushing and Rego Park. I first became involved in communal signing at the Israeli Club in Forest Hills. The club's weekly Wednesday meetings, with their lectures on Israeli-related subjects, usually attracted a crowd of less than thirty participants. The crowd attending the monthly gatherings of *erev shira betzibur* (an evening of communal singing), however, rarely included less than fifty participants. Moreover, on particular occasions, such as the parties scheduled for the national holidays (Chanukkah, Independence Day and so on), at which

CHAPTER NINE

communal singing was a major activity, attendance reached a few hundred. The participants were neither kibbutz nor *moshav*[1] veterans, but mostly former residents of the major urban areas in Israel. In Israel, these same people had rarely, if ever, participated in regular communal singing. Sometimes they spoke of being puzzled that in New York they sang ten times more than they had in Israel. This enthusiasm could not be attributed to David, the club's manager; he was not at ease with singing, dancing and other kinds of expressive activities, and after introducing the musician who would lead the singing, he left to attend to administrative tasks.

Communal signing was an important aspect of most other gatherings of Israelis I attended in Queens. It took place whenever a crowd of Israelis met for entertainment or celebration either informally at home or at more public occasions. Other resident Israelis in New York reported the same observation to me.

Although the audiences at the sing-alongs usually included both young and old participants, the majority were in their late twenties to late thirties. Most of them had left Israel within ten years after their army service and had been living in the United States for at least five years. Many had been there for more than ten years.

Members of the Israeli community of official delegates (*shlichim*) and their families—who represent a wide variety of Israeli cultural, political and economic institutions—participated in the weekly meetings of the Israeli folk dance program held at the Central Queens YM-YWHA, which was also attended by many American Jews. *Shlichim* also sometimes attended specific lectures held at the Israeli Club. But apart from the occasional participation of one delegate's wife, no other Israeli belonging to this community ever attended the sing-alongs. One American man attended regularly. He hoped to settle in Israel and came to the sing-alongs and other programs "in order to be exposed to the Hebrew language and to the Israeli people".

---

1   A small-holders cooperative.

The majority of Israelis, either in Israel or abroad, rarely remember the lyrics of folk songs, the corpus of which is enormous.[2] Most are familiar with the chorus of some songs and only a few words or lines from others. Since they do know most of the tunes, they usually mumble words and lines as close as possible to the original text. When the sing-along is well prepared, the participants, led by a musician usually playing the accordion, are aided by songbooks or photocopies of texts of selected songs. Alternatively, they may read the lines of the songs projected onto the wall by a slide projector. The slides are sometimes illustrated with pictures relevant to the specific songs, such as views of Jerusalem's monuments, farmers at work, the figure of a smiling young soldier carrying a rifle.

The texts of songs distributed at sing-alongs were usually taken from songbooks containing two hundred songs. The slides added another fifty to a hundred songs to that corpus. The sing-alongs I observed in other places included a similar repertoire of songs. During a regular sing-along about forty songs might be sung altogether.

CLASSIFICATION OF ISRAELI FOLK SONGS

I do not classify the Israeli folk songs most often sung by Israelis in Queens according to their literary and musical structure, but rather according to the following categories: (1) songs associated with pre-state *Yishuv*[3] society (sometimes referred to jokingly as "the songs of the first *aliya*");[4] (2) songs associated with the War of Independence (sometimes referred to as "the songs of 1948"); (3) songs associated with the post-1948 army troupes; (4) songs associated with popular professional troupes, musicals and festivals, as well as with individual singers; and (5) the corpus of songs written and composed by Naomi Shemer.

---

2   See, e.g. the collection of 600 songs (in three volumes) by Pesachzon and Eligon (1981, 1983, 1984), 250 songs by Ephi Netzer (1983) and 130 songs (in three volumes) by Naomi Shemer (1967, 1975, 1982).
3   Prestate, twentieth-century Jewish society in Palestine.
4   The first wave of modern Jewish immigration to Palestine.

CHAPTER NINE

SONGS OF THE YISHUV

This category includes a considerable number of foreign folk songs, particularly of Russian origin, the music of which was often borrowed and dressed up with new Hebrew lyrics. Most participants in the sing-alongs regarded these songs as authentic Israeli songs. Some of the most popular songs to this day, which often open an evening of communal singing, are of Russian origin. The main themes of the early Russian songs include love, war and the beauty of nature. The first songs usually performed in this series are "Katyushka" and "Zivonim" (Tulips). "Katyushka" is a melodious song about love and nature:

> The pear and apple have blossomed.
> The mist has covered the river
> And Katyushka took a walk
> To a beautiful beach.
> The girl was longingly singing
> A song, her sweetest song
> About her most beloved one....[5]

"Zivonim" is probably the only joyful song about war in the Israeli song corpus:

> Mother said to Vania:
> My dear son Vania
> Stop strolling in the streets
> Looking for red girls to love
> Vania, my dear Vania,
> Take me to the war.
> You will be a red commisar
> And I will be a devoted nurse.[6]

---

5   Hebrew lyrics by Noah Pniel, copyright © by Noah Pniel.
6   Hebrew lyrics by Levin Kipnis, copyright © by Levin Kipnis.

The group of popular songs also includes "Zoya", "Lushinka" and those less noticeably Russian, such as "Rina" and "Ruach Mevaderet" (The wind blows her skirt). The same themes appear in many, if not most, of the songs in all categories, excluding, to some extent, the professional performers category, in which the themes are more varied. Many refer to Israeli battles, the love of young soldiers, the attraction of and commitment to special sites and scenic views in Israel. Representative of these among the prestate songs is "Veulay" (and perhaps), written by the young poetess Rachel, who was struck down with tuberculosis and forced to leave the Kibbutz on the Kinneret (Lake of Galilee). From her deathbed she expressed her tragic longing to return to work in the fields and to the scenes of her beloved lake. The poem ends:

My Kinneret, oh, my Kinneret,
Were you really there, or was it a dream?

Another song in this category is "Shir Ha'emek" (Song of the valley):

Rest has come to the weary
And calm to the worker.
A pale night spreads
Over the valley of Yizrael.
Dew below and moon above,
From Beit Alfa to Nahalal.
Oh, what a night of all nights,
Nothing stirs in the valley of Yizrael.
Sleep, oh, valley, glorious land,
We shall be your guards.[7]

Similar songs are "Yesh li Kinneret" (My Kinneret), "Anachnu Sharim Lach" (We sing to you, homeland and mother), "Shir Ha'avodah" (Song of work). This last popular song includes the lines

---

7   Hebrew lyrics by Nathan Alterman, copyright © by Nathan Alterman.

CHAPTER NINE

> Blue is the sea of water
> Lovely is Jerusalem.
> The sky sheds its light
> Over the Negev and Galilee.
> The song - stand up
> Play with hammers
> Play with plows.
> There is no end to the song
> It starts right now.[8]

SONGS OF THE WAR OF 1948

The war of 1948 produced many songs that have not yet lost their popularity either in Israel or in New York. These include, for example "Shir Hafeenjan" (Song of the coffeepot), a Russian melody based on a Hebrew poem, a song closely associated with *kumzitz* gatherings, and "Shir Hapalmach", a song of an underground organization (Palmach) during the British Mandate whose recruits were mainly kibbutz members. Palmach recruits combined the ingredients of both pioneerism and heroism best represented in their dedication to the land:

> Around us the storm rages
> But our heads are unbowed
> We are always prepared
> We are the Palmach
> From Metulla to the Negev
> From the sea to the desert
> Every man is combat-ready
> Every man on guard.[9]

---

8   Hebrew lyrics by Nathan Alterman, copyright © by Mifalei Tarbuth Vekhinuch.
9   Hebrew lyrics by Zerubavel Gila'd, copyright © by Mif'alei Tarbuth Vekhinuch.

Another popular song of 1948, "Lech Lamidbar" (Go to the desert), tells of the young men who conquered the Negev Desert:

> Go to the desert
> The roads will lead you,
> Before nightfall
> Go, my friend, to the desert.
> Barren, windy and hostile land
> The warriors have returned like a storm,
> To the desert, land without water,
> Oh, my land, we have returned to you.[10]

Another song, "Haamini Yom Yavo" (Believe me, the day will come), tells the story of love and war:

> Today is our war, sister,
> Therefore I am far away.
> Celebrate our meeting
> In our little kitchen.
> Believe me, the day will come
> I promise you I will be back
> I will come and embrace you
> And make you forget all thoughts of war.
> And if you can't fall asleep
> Sing this little song
> Then you will hear the song of our land.[11]

---

10 Hebrew lyrics by Hayim Hefer, copyright © by Hayim Hefer.
11 Hebrew lyrics by Rafael Klatchkin, copyright © by Negev Publishing Company.

CHAPTER NINE

ARMY TROUPE SONGS

Since 1948 the army troupes have become a very important institution in Israeli entertainment. Some of the most celebrated Israeli artists are graduates of these troupes, which have given rise to new songs dedicated to love, the consequences of war and the commitment to the land, including the sites gained in the Six-Day War in 1967. Particularly popular are the songs performed by troupes of the Nachal regiment, whose volunteers combine regular army service with kibbutz life. One of their famous songs is "Mool Har Sinai" (Opposite Mount Sinai):

> It is not a legend my friends
> And not a passing dream,
> Here, opposite Mount Sinai
> The bush is burning.
> It is glowing in song
> On lips of regiments of men.
> This day should be recounted, my brothers, as
> The day the nation returned to stand at Sinai.[12]

Another of the Nachal songs is "Shir Lashalom" (A song for peace). Its poetry is difficult to translate, but its message is clear and powerful:

> Let the sun rise
> Let the morning shed its light.
> Sing a song of peace for those
> Who have fallen.
> Bitter tears, pure prayers and songs of praise
> Will not return them to life.
> Only peace will vindicate their death.[13]

---

12 Hebrew lyrics by Yechiel Mohar, copyright © by Yechiel Mohar.
13 Hebrew lyrics by Jacob Rotblit, copyright © by Jacob Rotblit.

Among the army troupes' popular songs are a number of love songs that also portray scenes of nature and army life, such as "Ma Avarech" (What shall I bless) and "Beeretz Haavati" (In the country of my love). "Ma Avarech":

> What shall I bless the boy with?
> The angel asked
> And he blessed him with eyes
> To see all flowers and birds
> And a heart to understand
> All views and images.
> And he blessed that his hands
> Would tend the flowers and
> Would learn to handle the power of steel.[14]

The songs on this list gain particular force from a lyrical style that emphasizes polar existential conditions and personal qualities, such as peace versus violent death, softness versus toughness. Love of the land is also obvious: "tend the flowers… handle the power of steel".

PROFESSIONAL PERFORMERS' SONGS

Professional troupes, musicals, films and festivals, as well as the growing number of individual performers, have all introduced a wider variety of themes and more humor into Israeli folk singing. Their songs often contain observations of Israeli daily life which have led to the infusion of social parody into folk songs. The festivals, which originated in the annual song competition held for many years on the Day of Independence, have produced songs that display personal, individualistic characteristics, as well as traditional national themes.

The Ayalon troupe, for example, introduced a popular folk song and parody about what has become the Israeli national food, falafel:

---

14 Hebrew lyrics by Rachel Shapira, copyright © by Rachel Shapira.

CHAPTER NINE

> Every country in the world
> Has a national dish
> We have falafel, falafel, falafel
> Once when a Jew came to Israel
> He kissed the earth and prayed.
> Today when he gets out of the plane
> He immediately buys falafel.
> The preparation of falafel is an art
> Well known to every Yemenite.
> But falafel prepared by Ashkenazim
> Carries the strange taste of gefilte fish.[15]

The various festivals and the Chassidic song competition have also produced many popular songs, such as one based on a line from the prayer book:

> He [God] will bring peace upon us
> And upon all the people of Israel.

Popular songs first introduced by celebrated singers include, for example, "Simona from Dimona", about a girl with a pseudo-North African name and who resides in a new town in the Negev. The song gives a romantic aura to the Israeli melting pot and the settlement of new immigrants in remote towns. It was first introduced by Yaffa Yarkoni, who has entertained army units since 1948 and who holds the unofficial title "Singer of Wars".

> Every day on the heights of Dimona
> There she stands sorrowful.
> She is suntanned and her name is Simona
> And she is waiting for her mate.

---

15   Hebrew lyrics by Dan Almagor, copyright © by Dan Almagor.

> I shall wear a hat
> I'll drag my feet in the heat
> I'll climb eight hundred meters
> To my Simona, from Sodom.[16]

The song "Bashana Habaah" (Next year) was first introduced by Ilanit, one of the younger generation of Israeli performers:

> Next year we'll sit on the balcony
> And count migrating birds.
> Children on vacation will play hide-and-seek
> Between the house and the fields.
> You will see, you will see
> How good it is going to be
> In the coming year.[17]

A more individualistic mood is represented, for example, in "Erev Shel Shoshanim" (Evening of roses), a love song first introduced by a pair of popular singers known as Hadudayim:

> It is an evening of roses
> Let us go out to the grove.
> Myrrh, spices and frankincense
> Are the threshold at your feet.
> The night falls upon us slowly
> And a breeze of roses is blowing.
> Let me whisper a song to you
> A song of love.[18]

---

16 Hebrew lyrics by Hayim Shalmoni, copyright © by Hayim Shalmoni.
17 Hebrew lyrics by Ehud Manor, copyright © by Ehud Manor.
18 Hebrew lyrics by Moshe Dor, copyright © by Moshe Dor.

CHAPTER NINE

These last two songs, although apparently neutral in their themes, nevertheless suggest an Israeli environment: the balance where Israeli city dwellers spend their leisure time at home during the long summer, and the fragrance of the groves on a summer evening.

SONGS BY NAOMI SHEMER

Naomi Shemer holds a unique position in Israeli folk culture. Although audiences rarely identify the lyricists and composers of folk songs, songs with lyrics and music by Naomi Shemer are usually recognizable as such. For more than forty years, Naomi Shemer (1930-2004) has been the most prolific and popular songwriter in the country. Distinctly nationalistic in her political views, she has written two songs whose popularity has almost no precedent in Israeli folk singing: "Yerushalayim Shel Zahav" (Jerusalem of Gold), which coincided with the 1967 war, and the more recent "Al Hadevash Veal Ha'oketz (On the honey and the sting). The latter's first performance coincided with the bitter debate on the peace treaty with Egypt, which committed Israel to evacuating all Jewish settlements in the Sinai.

> On the honey and the sting
> On the bitter and the sweet
> On our baby girl
> Do guard my good God.
> Don't uproot the planted
> Don't forget the hope
> Bring me back and I will come
> To the good country .
> Preserve, my God, this house
> The garden and the wall
> From sadness, from sudden fear
> And from war.[19]

---

19 Hebrew lyrics by Naomi Shemer, copyright © by Naomi Shemer.

Another engaging love song by Naomi Shemer is set in the fields of Bethlehem on the West Bank:

> The moonlight shines on the mountain,
> A white night spreads over the fields of Bethlehem,
> A stone lies upon my heart
> Like the stones in the fields of Bethlehem.
> Somewhere at the end of the road
> You will be waiting until dusk.[20]

The songs sung at most sing-alongs included a selection from all five of the above categories. Together, these five categories of lyrics, melodies and performers capture the recent history of a nation. Although some participants complained that the collection represented "old songs", closer observation revealed that while the proportion of old and new songs might vary with particular musical leaders or special events, the repertoire usually represented all categories.

SPECIAL INTERVENTIONS AT SING-ALONGS

A sing-along evening was not entirely controlled by its musical leader, nor was it strictly a singing event. First, the participants might request to sing particular songs not included in the list prepared by the leader. Second, particular songs often stimulated verbal commentary, jokes or mimicry. Last, the participants might sometimes call for a "solo", the performance of one or more songs by a participant. These songs, usually of a comical-theatrical type, were often unknown to the other participants (the musical leader included).

Comments on the content of particular songs alluded either to the discrepancy between the message of the song and the reality of life in New York, or to that between the message and reality of life in Israel. Thus, for example, the singing of a popular prestate song revealed a paradox:

---

20 Hebrew lyrics by Naomi Shemer, copyright © by Naomi Shemer.

> Here in the cherished ancestors' land
> All hopes will be materialized.
> Here we'll live and here we'll create
> Life of freedom and liberty.
> Here the Divinity will reside,
> Here will flower the language of the Torah.[21]

While the crowd proceeded enthusiastically with the song, Dani pointed his finger downward, his face shining with mischief, and exclaimed loudly: "Here, here" [in America]. All those next to him burst out laughing. A perceptive participant told me about a similar experience he had witnessed at a sing-along elsewhere in the United States at which the musical leader was singing ecstatically "From the Summit of Mount Scopus". As he sang the last lines of the song his face and body expressed the anguish and determination of his feelings: "Jerusalem, Jerusalem, I will not move from here!" At this point his listeners collapsed into hysterical laughter, since the reference seemed to be to the spot where he was standing, which they all shared as home for the foreseeable future.

The words of the song "Shekhav Bni" (Sleep, son) are a mother's narrative; they include the stanza "You will grow up in the Land of Israel; like your father, you will be a worker". When this was being sung at the club an amused participant remarked: "The person who wrote this song was an optimist". He thus implied the growing involvement in the Israeli economy of Arab workers from the West Bank and the supposed preference of Israeli Jews for white-collar jobs. The remark evolved smiles and laughter.

Jokes that interrupted the singing often revived the repertoire of Israeli army jokes with sexual connotations. These interruptions also included jokes about the political situation in Israel, taken from Israeli newspapers or from popular Israeli comedians. No complaints were ever made about these jokes, even by those who may have favored those be-

---

21 Hebrew lyrics by Yisrael Dushman, copyright © by Yisrael Dushman.

ing ridiculed. Thus, for example, much laughter followed a stingingly anti-Likud joke told by Arik: "Why do Mr. Begin's supporters keep their fists tightly clenched when they shout in the streets, 'Begin! Begin!?' Because if they opened their fists they would fall off the trees!" The joke contained an ethnic reference to Begin's constituency, which was assumed to include most of the less-educated, Middle Eastern Jews.

The most effective interruption by participants occurred, through not very often, when an individual volunteered or was encouraged to entertain the audience with his own private repertoire of songs. These "natural performers" had often played a prominent role at sing-alongs in Israeli youth movements and army units. One such "natural" made a particularly successful appearance during a party held at the Israeli Club on Independence Day. The party, organized as an indoor, candlelit *kumzitz,* turned out to be an ecstatic sing-along evening. The volunteer performer was a newcomer of unusual appearance—he had a clean-shaven head and dressed in a worn T-shirt and tight jeans. He started with a well-known song about a Yemenite girl who is worried about her father's reaction to the news of her love affair. He was cheered enthusiastically and encouraged to perform another "solo". He proceeded with a song unknown to most participants, which turned out to be a parody of an Israeli tour guide who manipulates a naïve American female tourist into a trip to various sites and finally to a secluded Mediterranean beach, where a sexual encounter leads to a happy ending. Greatly amused by his narrative and performing skills, the audience demanded more. The newly discovered star complied and informed his fans that his next song would be a tribute to his buddies, the paratroopers of his former army unit in Israel. He said that the song was the private anthem of his unit. The song, which borrowed the music of a popular 1948 song, "Feenjan", tells the story of a parachutist who, during action, was daydreaming about his girlfriend's intimate parts. Excited by these sweet thoughts, he forgot to land properly and, alas, ended up with broken legs.

Both the participants and the musical leaders were usually reluctant to end the sing-along on time (10.45 p.m.), as requested by the club's director, who was anxious to let the janitors clean and lock up the building. Finally, everyone had to be almost thrown out in the cold Forest Hills night.

PARTICIPANTS' REFLECTIONS

Not surprisingly, various participants and other observers commented on the love of folk singing shown by people who did not seem otherwise inclined to singing and who had not been particularly enthusiastic about it in Israel. The following remarks, made during or immediately after singing together, seem representative of such comments. A successful businessman in his late forties: "What makes Israel special is the army. People there share experiences". A taxi driver in his early thirties: "The songs remind us of the army and the *kumzitz* gatherings". A housewife in her late thirties: "The songs are the connecting thread". A nurse in her late thirties: "The songs are reminiscent of our youth". A professional in his mid-thirties: "Singing together should come from the soul. It expresses something which people cannot otherwise say". More complex was Nira's reaction: "We need this bond. Although communal singing touches on our nerve centers, it is only a small part of my life now. I need it from time to time, but no more than that. We've been brainwashed with Trumpeldor's[22] testament that 'It's good to die for our country', but that's going too far".

Eli commented analytically: "These people, who used to be part of a majority, have become a minority here. Singing together they have a two-hour opportunity to experience being a majority again". But although he was well aware of the temporary duration and artificial nature of this activity, Eli himself was much moved by the communal singing at the Independence Day *kumzitz* mentioned above. He said that had we closed our eyes and listened to the singing, we would have thought we

---

22 A national hero who was killed in 1920 while defending one of the first settlements in Galilee. It is commonly believed that Trumpeldor's last words were: It is good to die for our country", which has become a popular motto of Israeli national education.

were at a *kumzitz* at Tanturah Beach (an attractive spot on the Mediterranean between Tel Aviv and Haifa). Alex commented less excitedly: "It was one more evening of singing together", to which Eli reacted: "No, it was a state of spiritual elevation [*hitromemut ruach*]!" The only participant I met from the community of Israeli official delegates, a woman in her mid-thirties, told me: "The songs give us strength. They were written during days of war. The songs make us forget our pain".

When I presented the material in this chapter at a conference in New York, an Israeli social scientist employed at a local university who had been living in the United States for more than twenty years confessed to me that my presentation had made her shed tears. The songs could thus arouse a flow of emotion even when translated into English and presented in a detached manner inter-woven with irony and humor.

American Jews who sometimes observed the Israelis singing together were usually impressed by this flow of emotion. Partly amused, partly sympathetic, the husband of an Israeli woman once exclaimed: "Poor things, they miss home so much!" But a newcomer to the United States who represented an Israeli cultural institution, upon visiting the club, angrily exclaimed for everyone to hear: "I don't need to sing in order to feel that I'm an Israeli, I am an Israeli!" Like most other Israelis on an official appointment, she never showed up again.

Benny, who had left Israel ten years before and was now in his early thirties, had an amused and derisive reaction: "I would rather attend an American club than listen to a Hebrew singer or sing about the Negev Desert with other Israelis". He avoided the company of Israelis, who he called *yordim*, and in fact, two years earlier, he had purchased an apartment in Israel for which he was still repaying the debts. A year after making the above statement, he returned to Israel with his Israeli wife and two children.

My own reactions are relevant here. I usually enjoyed communal singing and often openly expressed my pleasure and displeasures with particualr songs and the way they were performed. Sometimes I was amused, as, for example, when the singers enthusiastically repeated the lines of a song that begins with the command "Go, go to the desert, the roads will lead you there", while the night lights of the American metropolis could be seen through the glass windows of an overheated room. But sometimes I shuddered at the singing of songs that alluded to the death of soldiers at war. At these moments my thoughts carried me back to Israel, reminding me of people I knew whose sons had died the summer before in Lebanon. I also thought about my own two young sons, who one day would join the Israeli army. On other occasions I remembered nostalgically my home in Israel and even recalled some neighbors I had never liked. At these moments I suddenly felt alienated from the other participants some if not most of whom might go on for years coming to the clubs, hotels and apartments in Queens, singing about the sacredness of Jerusalem, the beauty of the Golan Heights and the Negev Desert, and about the heroic deaths of handsome young men.

I realized, however, that I was not the only one sensitive to this incongruity. Once I attended with a few close friends a concert of Israeli songs during which the audience often joined in with the singers. I suddenly noticed that the woman seated next to me, who had lived in New York for more than ten years, remained silent while the rest of the hall, bursting with emotion, sang a famous war song. She was usually a devoted singer of Israeli songs and an enthusiastic participant on these occasions. I commented on her silence and she answered: "There are some things which are inappropriate". Had she been inhibited by my own reserved reaction or was she also disassociating herself from the audience of *yordim*?

COMMUNAL SINGING AS CULTURAL PERFORMANCE

Susanne Langer (1953) has described music as a "significant form" with the characteristics of a symbol: "A highly sensuous object .... feeling, life, motion and emotion constitute its import" (p. 32). "Music is a tonal analogue of emotional life" (p. 27). Langer also claims that when words and music come together in a song, music swallows words: "Song is not a compromise between poetry and music .... song is music" (p. 152). There can be no doubt that even the best Israeli lyrics would not have survived without evocative melodies, but the emotional effect of most Israeli popular folk songs is produced through a striking combination of words and music. The audience is usually well aware of a song's content which arouses various emotional moods and sometime provokes comments, mimicry and jokes.[23]

Participants in the sing-alongs seemed to be involved in a collective experience of nostalgia in the purest sense of "a painful yearning to return home" (Davis 1979:1).[24] This could be seen, for example, by the American observer who exclaimed: "Poor things, they miss home so much!" They appeared to be using the occasion to revisit their lost youth, immutably linked, in particular, to memories of their army service. But this simplistic view of their nostalgia does not represent the full repertoire of the behavioral expressions and the symbolic contents displayed at the sing-alongs, nor does it accommodate the sociological perspective of nostalgia.

Few of the memories evoked by the songs had, in fact, been experienced by the participants. In addition, the "nostalgic content" revealed in the songs related to recent phenomena in Israeli life, including, for example, the dedication to territories regained or settlements established after many of the participants had left Israel. Moreover, the revived past was never compared to deprived and lamentable present conditions. Such a comparison is the main feature of nostalgia as defined by Davis (1979: 18): "A positively toned evocation of a lived past in the context of some negative feelings toward present or impending circumstances". For most of the participants the yearning or homesickness was clearly demarcated from the pressing needs and hopeful plans of their present lives.

---

23 In the following discussion I do not analyze the participants' responses to the musical stimulus per se. See Meyer (1956) and Feld (1982) for discussions of the emotional response to music in general and to folk music in particular.

24 See also Paz 1981: 208.

From that vantage point, they were not so different from New York Orthodox Jews, who in their prayers express their yearning and dedication to the Temple in Jerusalem and to a code of observances prescribed for those who live there. Neither Israelis at a sing-along nor orthodox Jews at prayer evaluate their present life in New York as particularly disadvantaged, nor do they actually try to retrieve the subject of their yearning, although it is accessible. In most other cases of personal and collective nostalgia, the subject of yearning is beyond reach.

There was, however, more to the sing-along evenings than the expression of nostalgia. Participants were making a cultural claim and expressing an existential predicament. They were deeply absorbed in a type of activity that Singer (1955), Geertz (1973), Heilman (1983), and other have defined as a "cultural performance". As suggested by Geertz, the participants in a cultural performance express, approve, experience and communicate moods, motivations and metaphysical concepts that form a perspective for a world of beliefs. Expanding on this approach, Heilman, who observed Talmud *lernen* circles,[25] argued that "listening to himself and his fellows brings to life the voice of the Talmud, the participant publicly reflects, communicates, perpetuates and develops the patterns of meanings and inherited conceptions that define traditional Jewish culture" (p. 61). Although the term "cultural performance" has usually been applied to the context of religion and rituals, Geertz himself suggests that it may also apply to non-religious contexts.[26] The symbolic activity carried out by Israelis at sing-alongs may seem relatively simple when compared with complex Indian rituals, Balinese dramas and games, or the *lernen* of Talmudic texts. But the significance of a cultural performance cannot be properly evaluated through comparative analysis, which tends to attribute greater value to what appears to be less comprehensible in terms of the observer's own culture.

---

25 *Lernen* is a Yiddish word for the Ashkenazi Jews' pattern of study of the Talmud.
26 Geertz 1973: 113.

The Israelis observed singing together, either at scheduled programs of singing or on less formal occasions, formed in Goffman's terms (1961: 9-10) a "focused gathering" that, in common with other observations of cultural performances, was clearly demarcated from the usual routine of daily life. Such gatherings, though often consisting of a crowd of strangers, stimulated communication through a particular language of signs. This form of communication informed close situational familiarity. For a few hours participants became united through the flow of sentiment, bursts of laughter, the winks and mimicry that communicated shared understanding of the imagery and moods expressed by the songs' Hebrew texts and their melodies, as well as those evoked by the comments and jokes. During the singing encounter, not only did the participants free up suppressed emotions and their longing or "nostalgia", which is probably the most obvious interpretation, but, as suggested by Geertz (1973: 444), they "displayed" these emotions and the plethora of imageries and sensations lying at their roots.

The absence of members of the official Israeli community at these gatherings is important in assessing the symbolic significance of the sentiments evoked. The songs introduced a world of Israeli history as taught, told, mythicized and experienced, as well as a core of intimate bonds with sites, landscapes and a way of life (its ironies included).[27] Israelis on a "legitimate visit" to the United States, or those *yordim* whose return to Israel was imminent, found it emotionally difficult to recreate and display this world in the company of those who, in their eyes, had voluntarily given up the commitment to share the realities, the responsibilities and the dangers of daily life in Israel. An Orthodox Jew who

---

27 Feld (1982) analyzes the songs of the Kaluli people (of Papua, New Guinea), which echo bird sounds and bird words as expressions of social sentiments and personal emotions that evoke a desired state of identification with a particular place and geographical history. The conspicuous differences in their ecological, societal and cultural contexts, in the patterns of song composition and performance and in the intentional messages of the Israeli and Kaluli songs make an analogy between the sing-alongs and the "bird songs" seemingly spurious. Nevertheless, the Kaluli evidence supports my contention that an expressive modality can display and communicate a cultural ethos and a social identity.

prays devotedly for "next year in Jerusalem" has a different city in mind than that experienced by the secular Israeli. But an Israeli who has acquired an alternative citizenship (or other arrangements of permanent residence in the United States) and who is ecstatically absorbed in singing "From the Summit of Mount Scopus" or "Jerusalem of Gold" is conceived by his Israeli compatriots as expressing his longing and affinity for a Jerusalem of flesh and blood. As suggested by Deshen's typology of religious symbolic changes,[28] a single symbolic action may convey different meanings to the persons involved in it, depending on the different social situations of the actors. Here too, though in a nonreligious context, the devotional singing of Israeli residents in New York was an act of profanation for those Israelis who were on an official visit (albeit of long duration) to the United States.

Though subjectively experienced, I assume I was not unique among the Israelis in associating some of these songs with, for example, the death of particular young men, as well as with the sense of danger that the return to Israel may bring to one's own children or other loved ones. This was a clear manifestation of the sentimental education embedded in a collectively sustained symbolic structure as suggested by Geertz, whereby, using a vocabulary of sentiment, singing together relates to Israeli destiny, a destiny that offers the gift of extreme happiness inseparably interwoven with deep sorrow. By attending sing-alongs, the participant "learn[s] what his culture's ethos and his private sensibility look like when spelled out externally in a collective text" (Geertz 1973: 449). Singing together, the participants not only evoked their national ethos through familiar symbolic repertoire, but also updated their stock of songs and incorporated new symbolic references to present-day Israel.

The participant who commented that if we closed our eyes and listened to the singing we would have thought that we were at Tanturah Beach was indicating the potential power of communal singing to transform reality, a process pertinent to most rituals and cultural performanc-

---

28   In Deshen and Shokeid 1974: 151-72.

es.²⁹ As already suggested, visiting Israelis were reluctant to share this transformation of reality with the permanent residents of Flushing and Forest Hills. The participants themselves were sometimes aware of this process, the spell of which they broke through the airing of comments and jokes during singing. They thus reminded themselves and their fellow participants of their paradoxical reality as Israelis in America. Through this participation and the ambivalence revealed, they supported each other by expressing the shared dual reality: an identity rooted in a country and a way of life left behind and, at the same time, a growing commitment to a new identity associated with a country and a way of life adopted through their own free choice. At these events, uninhibited by the presence of "official Israelis", they could act out an existential predicament rooted in a state of social and cultural liminality in both American and Israeli societies.

The Israeli who leaves Israel for New York whether as a result of planned immigration or mere circumstance, no longer takes along the holy books his forefathers carried in early migrations. But he does take along the songs. However, are these songs sufficiently to sustain the "vessel" of Israeli ethnic identity?³⁰

---

29   See, e.g., Geertz 1973: 112; Heilman 1983: 65.
30   In Barth's terms (1969: 14). See also Shokeid and Deshen, 1982: 76.

CHAPTER 10.
FROM THE ANTHROPOLOGIST'S POINT OF VIEW: STUDYING ONE'S OWN TRIBE

Malinowski, the deposed prince of modern British anthropology, made his second coming and perplexed the world of anthropology with his field diaries published by his widow (1967). Once again he strode the stage of anthropology and provided a new subject for methodological discourse. Shaking up the assumption that anthropologists are deeply attached to the people they study and can see things "from the native's point of view", Malinowski posthumously broke a major professional taboo and shattered an arsenal of deeply-rooted beliefs associated with his life-long work.

The ethnographic tradition did not require anthropologists to relate their fieldwork experiences. After all, the taste of the fish on our plate is not affected by the fisherman's personal trials. Anthropologists who did not harbor happy memories from the field usually kept this apparent professional failure and moral deficiency a secret. Following the revelation of Malinowski's contempt, a growing number of anthropologists "came out of the closet" and confessed. The ethnographer as anti-hero became a popular figure. The anthropologist's predicament, however, was now diagnosed in terms of an inevitable confrontation between the ethnographer and his informants, a clash of selves as well as of cultures. Anthropologists were called upon to adopt reflexivity since "It is through the understanding of self-to-other that the investigator comes to examine culture" (Myerhoff and Ruby, 1982, 18). Thus, in this way too, Malinowski radically altered the position of anthropologists. The observers had now themselves become subjects of observation.

Geertz (1973), Rabinow (1977) and Dumont (1978) dealt with the anthropologist's limited ability to penetrate the "native's point of view". Crapanzano (1977) and Marcus (1982), however, revealed the missing part in the construction of ethnographic reality, namely, the anthropologist's point of view.

Crapanzano, who suggested that the writer of ethnography writes "to talk to himself, though wanting to be heard" (p. 72), argued that the ethnographer is affirming an identity by addressing and reifying thereby the other. He claimed that the writer of an ethnography addresses two audiences: the audience of other professionals, "his own people" and the silent audience, "those illiterate others on his fieldwork", by which he affirms his identity as an ethnographer and obtains his sense of self (p. 72). Understanding an ethnography is therefore a venture into the story of another (informant or people), as much as into the story of the writer himself.

I intend to explore the "self-to-other black box" in a case where the other is not a silent audience of illiterate or literate others, but rather a significant part of the ethnographer's own social world. This situation involves a few interrelated problems: particularly, is the ethnographer, as an insider, confined to "experience-near concepts" and therefore, as suggested by Geertz (1973, 227), left "awash in immediacies as well as entangled in vernacular"?

The following text introduces moral dilemmas that are indispensably interwoven with professional issues as experienced by an Israeli anthropologist who had chosen to study his emigrant compatriots in America. I was both the native and the stranger among people I studied; I was the detached anthropologist studying others, but also an involved individual who carried along his commitments, biases and doubts that were closely related to the subjects and the issues of his research.

I was brought up on the ethos that one should take part in the march of history. This educational imprint appeared to me to be a logical reaction to the apparently disastrous passivity of Jews for nearly 2000 years. I was maturing when the echoes of momentous events in Jewish history were still being heard. The 1920s and 1930s witnessed the expansion of Jewish settlements in Palestine. The Holocaust took place during the first ten years of my life. I was far too young to participate in the 1948 long war, but mature enough to understand its historical meaning. The mass immigration to Israel from Europe, the Middle East and North Africa followed hard upon the heels of that war and the establishment of the State in 1948. When I was drafted into the Israeli army in the mid-1950s, Israel's destiny was in the process of being shaped for years to come. I was thus a close witness to the major dramas of modern Jewish experience. My parents' generation regarded my generation of Sabras (Palestinian-born youth), as the promising fruit of Jewish rejuvenation. For my part, I felt I had been allocated the less heroic role of an observer. I could not actively participate in and share the experiences of those who had made history.

I chose to become a professional observer which is the expertise and privilege of anthropologists. When I came to choose my own territory of anthropological fieldwork, however, I was no longer excited by the idea of sailing to distant lands to discover an exotic society completely dissociated from my own life experiences. Instead, I employed my anthropological education to search for exotic tribes hiding in my own backyard.

My first fieldwork project during the late 1960s dealt with the consequences of the last event which had taken place before my eyes: the mass immigration of North African Jewry. I selected what seemed to be an exotic Jewish society, the immigrants from the Atlas Mountains in Morocco, who had been settled in a Negev village in Israel.

However, towards the late 1970s, a new phenomenon that seemed the most paradoxical in the contemporary Jewish and Israeli experience was the growing wave of emigration from Israel to the United States. This phenomenon had been labeled *yerida* ("descending") and its participants were nicknamed *yordim* ("those who descend").

Within the span of one generation I thus witnessed both the massive flow of Jews from many corners of the earth who wished to participate in the renewal of Jewish independent nationhood and the turning-point, in which many children of that revolution, as well as newcomers, took again to the boats and planes, but ones which carried them back to the Diaspora. At this point I was no less intrigued than at my first meeting with the Atlas Mountains Jews who had exchanged their homes of many generations among the Moroccan Berber tribes for new homes in the as yet barren and semi-arid Negev. I did not yet know when and how, but I targeted New York for my next fieldwork, the metropolis which seemed to have become a major attraction for the new exodus.

When I tried to interest the Ministry of Absorption, the embarrassed reaction I encountered surprised me. The Ministry had absolutely no desire to draw attention to this delicate subject. *Yerida* was posing profound ideological dilemmas, and official circles preferred to evade an issue which might shatter certain basic tenets of Zionism at home and abroad. I therefore made my own arrangements for spending a sabbatical leave in New York. Queens College of the City University of New York offered me a fellowship, which subsequently was extended for two years (September 1982 - August 1984).

Yerida was regarded with disdain both by the Israeli media and by the majority of Israelis. Moreover, this disdain was mixed with a profound anxiety. The Israelis who had left for America were considered greedy failures, who looked for an easy way to better themselves; tax evaders, who had slipped out; exploiters, who had decided to smuggle out their fortunes made at Israel's expense; Jews, who had once again forgotten the lessons of history; and cowards, if not traitors, who refused to share the risk of living in a country surrounded by enemies. The last accusation was the most emotionally charged. The departure of Israelis, whatever their skills, talents or morality, threatened the survival of Israel besieged by foes whose material and human resources greatly outnumbered its own.

What was my stand regarding these accusations and the deep contempt? When I left Israel in the 1960s for graduate studies in the United Kingdom, some of my friends assumed that I would not be back. During those years in the U.K., I experienced, however, the hostility towards Israel that could not be dissociated from the dubious role that my host country had played as a mandatory power in Palestine. Although I admired the British way of life, I was overwhelmed by the national euphoria in Israel which followed the threat and the victory of 1967. The anxiety and alarm which engulfed me during the weeks that preceded the war made me aware of the depth of feelings and the binding loyalty which I nurtured for Israel and its people. I returned to Tel Aviv, my birthplace where I joined the ranks of the newly-established university.

I was soon disenchanted by many of the social and political developments in Israel. I was astonished that I had returned to Tel Aviv of all places. I now realized that I have fully accepted my sojourn in Israel as a journey's end. Apparently I have more in common with my forbears who came to Israel than I ever believed. How strange it now appears to me that I passed up an option to get away from a country and a place from whose politics and economic conditions I had become so thoroughly alienated and against whose patterns of interaction in various spheres of life I nourished such a deep aversion. Leaving would also have allowed me to escape the pressures of a small and familistic society. Even so, I could not bring myself to take the rational step and move out. I knew then, as I know now, that the effort to release myself from the bonds of a city and a state that frequently makes me feel a persecuted stranger will forever be an effort that is a losing battle.

This background of a reluctant Zionist prepared me, so I believe, for taking on the role of a sufficiently impartial observer among other Israelis who, for various reasons, had broken the spell that had held its power over me. I was therefore very different from an Israeli colleague, a social psychologist from another faculty, who phoned me one day in New York and told me he had come to study *yordim*. He had convinced himself that most *yordim* pretend to be successful and thereby pressured others to prove a similar achievement. Consequently, they are too ashamed to return. He decided to implement his research through what he considered impartial research agencies, ones that refused to employ as interviewers Israelis or Jews, who would be suspected of emotional involvement. He added that he would make his findings available to writers who would describe the "true situation" of the *yordim* - and thereby discourage the continuing flood of *yerida*. He himself appeared to have no doubts whatsoever about the emotional and instrumental components that constitute the bonds between a person and his environment. The naïve conception of this social scientist demonstrated a predominant folk belief, the profound anxiety and the threat which *yerida* evokes in Israel.

One day I took a telephone call in my office at Queens College and identified the caller as an Israeli woman who was looking for the secretary of my department. As not unusual among Israelis, we started a conversation, I told her about my stay in New York and about my interest in the Israelis in America. I mentioned my belief that people live in Israel, as in New York or New Zealand, because this is the place that suits them. I told her that I had studied the Jews who had come to Israel from the Atlas Mountains, adding a common Hebrew reference to the mystical location of the lost tribes, "who arrived from beyond the mountains of darkness". I continued, "I am curious about those Israelis who have again crossed the mountains of darkness", thus referring to the difficulties involved with the new exodus. She corrected my ironic figure of speech, saying, "Oh no, crossed the ocean", adding in a casual tone, "You have passed the test". This impromptu conversation was the starting point of a close relationship with a family that would not otherwise have welcomed a researcher of *yerida*. The presentation of myself during our first conversation could not have been convincing if it had lacked honesty.

To be sure, I have experienced moments of bitterness and contempt towards *yordim*. There were certain Israeli songs, particularly those relating to fallen soldiers, which I could not bring myself to sing in their company. During such moments I could not escape the thought that my own sons would one day serve in the Israeli army. The mortal risk romanticized in these bitter-sweet lyrics was enthusiastically echoed in my presence by men and women who had placed themselves outside the reality of living in Israel and most of whom would not be exposed to the experience of which they were so movingly singing. I realized, however, that I was not the only one to sense this incongruity. I attended a concert of Israeli songs with a few close friends, during which the audience often joined in the singing. I noticed that the woman seated next to me, who had been in New York for more than ten years, remained silent while the hall was bursting with emotion as the audience loudly joined a famous war song. She was a lover of Israeli songs and an enthusiastic participant at these occasions. When I commented on her silence, she answered: "There are some things which are inappropriate". Was she inhibited by my reserved reaction, or was she also dissociating herself from the audience of *yordim*?

I was bitter and resentful during discussions in which *yordim* supported nationalistic policies, such as the expansion of Jewish settlements in the West Bank or the Lebanon War. Here they were safely sitting in New York, while expecting me and my children to pay for the political, economic and physical damage resulting from the ideology that had produced these policies. For a long time I refrained from publicly stating my opinions on various issues, particularly at meetings where many Israelis were present. Some of my acquaintances were surprised at my silence. I once attended a lecture by the Israeli writer, Rachel Eitan. Describing literary approaches, she portrayed the author as a traitor of his close relatives, whom he observes during his childhood and subsequently introduces in his books. As we left, one of the participants asked me why didn't I speak out during the long discussion dealing with the American Jews' attitude towards Israeli literature. Borrowing the lecturer's metaphor, I answered: "I am the traitorous anthropologist".

Only at a later stage of my fieldwork did I become less restrained in expressing my opinions during hectic discussions. I knew that similar conflicting ideas existed in Israel, and that *yordim* were expressing beliefs shared with many Israelis in Israel. I also became aware that the support of nationalistic policies was a way of expressing loyalty to Israel. Therefore, whenever I openly expressed my disagreement and resentment about politics, for example, it was within the framework of the style of argumentation and debate that Israelis use among themselves in their own country. In fact, I discovered that disagreement did not prevent the development of social bonds.

The sole rupture of communication following the discovery of my personal political opinions occurred when I deliberately challenged an official Israeli delegate who advocated the construction of housing projects in the West Bank. Assuming that I was a *yored*, he closed the conversation saying contemptuously: "You have no right to speak (*ein lecha zechut ledaber*); those who stay here have no right to speak!! (about Israeli political issues)". He thus revealed the deep resentment the official Israeli delegates have to the *yordim*. Unintentionally, I gained the sympathy of the bystanders who observed my encounter with the prominent official.

When I studied Moroccan Jews in an Israeli village, I thought my research situation differed greatly from that of other anthropologists who travelled far to study "other" societies (Shokeid 1971b). I now discovered how much closer one can get to the subjects of one's research. Regardless of the educational, professional and other characteristics in which I differed from many Israelis I met in New York, the impact of shared elements on our mutual relationships predominated. In addition, the fact that I had occupied a temporary university position and taken up residence in a densely populated neighborhood of Queens (unlike my colleagues most of whom lived in Long Island's more homogeneous suburbs), offered me a better chance to get involved in a more heterogeneous company of fellow countrymen than ever before in Israel. There I made friendships of the kind I believed I was no longer capable of. These were affective relationships with my peers and with younger and older people from various other walks of life. I was not going native; I was a native careful to preserve the perspective of the observer betwixt and between the invisible borders separating the anthropologist from his subjects.

My growing involvement with Israeli activities did not allow me to maintain the "don't touch me" stance of the unaffiliated alien anthropologist. Thus, for example, I felt I could not avoid performing in a play which, at first glance, I totally disliked. It was staged by a few of my close friends in the Israeli Club at the Central Queens YM-YWHA in Forest Hills. They had almost finished rehearsals when they became convinced that I was the only suitable replacement for a key part. I disliked the play, which presented a far-fetched Israeli environment, and even more the particular role in which I had to appear on stage. I no less resented the idea because of the unexpected forced departure from the role of observer to

CHAPTER TEN

that of a full participant. For a while I resisted the pressure but then succumbed to the feeling of loyalty towards my friends. The resentment expressed in my acting must have made me better suited for the role, since my performance was considered a success.

Did I betray my friends through the same kind of deception that Rachel Eitan suggested writers use? Some of my close friends were well aware that I was going to record my New York's Israeli experiences. My role and intentions became fully clear, when I presented a paper at a conference on Israelis in New York, convened by the City University. The conference took place in the fall of 1983, halfway through my stay in New York, and was heavily attended by my acquaintances from the Israeli club. As far as I can judge, it did not affect my relationships with the Israelis who attended the lecture and could identify the setting and the type of activities I described.

I indeed wrote my ethnography having two audiences in mind. Right until the final stage of proofreading I made changes, omitting details which I thought might offend "my natives". Even so I assume that a few among the Israelis in New York will find certain parts of my description and interpretations unacceptable. There are indeed two audiences, but only one ethnographic text. Once the "silent audience" reads it, the ethnographer can no longer rely on the double layers of meaning he wished to express, one of which is only implicitly expressed.

Our family's stay among Israelis, the majority of whom seemed to have made a successful adjustment outside the borders of Israel, had been a permanent test of our own loyalties. New York, the contemporary Rome of western civilization, a colossal stage for both the exalted and the vulgar, and only the gateway to a vast continent is indeed the antithesis of its faraway and much smaller counterpart in the Mediterranean. Israel has for many years been the focal point of an international conflict, the stage of continuing wars, a country increasingly dependent upon American economic and political support, and a nation divided by diametrically opposed ideologies and cultures (religious versus secular, national maximalists, the "hawks", versus minimalist "doves", Ashkenazim versus

Sephardim, etc.). Particularly painful to me had been to observe the continuing erosion of Israel's moral standing.

The life stories of the Israelis whom I had studied had taught me at least one thing: that the longer I stayed, the more the prospects of a return to Israel would fade away. I have no clear explanation for my decision to go back. I shall only quote my then five-year old son, who after more than one year in America on our return from a pleasant visit to Boston, which included the adventures of staying at a motel, the happy stops at McDonald's and the rest of America's inventions suddenly asked: "Why don't we already go back to Israel"? I was stunned. We were just approaching the Whitestone Bridge that he so loved to see. We had not been talking about Israel, so why on earth did he mention it at that particular moment? I asked him why he wanted to return to Israel. He answered: "I want to see my grandmother and aunts".

Whatever the reasons for my yearning for particular people, views, a climate and a way of life, and whatever my notion of duty, the sentimental imprint of education, and the self-punishment which caused me to return, I do not carry a grudge against those Israelis who have chosen to stay away and whose experiences I have described in the chapters of "Children and Circumstances" (1988). As much as I observed them, I was observing myself. This may have been the real motive for my choice of conducting fieldwork in New York. At the end of my journey to "*yordim* land" I had reaffirmed my commitments, or at any rate become reconciled with the circumstances of my Israeli existence, apparently as a result of free choice.

Observing the desperate efforts of *yordim* to preserve the vestiges of their "Israeliness" may also have raised my own sensitivity and longing for the uniqueness and enchantments of my own culture. Therefore, my search for the context and content of the *yordim*'s Israeliness actually involved a search for the meaning of Israeli identity on both sides of the ocean. An "experience-near" situation had not necessarily crippled my work, leaving me "awash in immediacies as well as entangled in vernacular". As much as I admire Geertz's ethnographic work and his eloquent writing, through which he introduces one into the secrets of other cultures, I sometimes wish he had tested his skills in a field closer to home.

Anthropologists are usually the only witnesses to the data reported in their ethnographies, as well as to the reflexive knowledge they divulge. They actually grant their accounts on reflexivity the same sort of authority according to their accounts of the lives of "others". I was fortunate to be able to show this paper to Shlomo Deshen, a close colleague of many years whom I first met during undergraduate studies. He raised a number of reservations about the accuracy of my account in relation to my perception of the "free choices" I had made at some critical stages of my career. His questions enlighten us about the nature of texts on reflexivity as much as about the limits of our knowledge of "others" (our friends included). No doubt, his queries made me more keenly aware that my choices might have been affected by additional motives, or constraints. However, I neither concealed nor faked details in order to enhance my professional life history. It does seem, however, that I produced a less complicated, more coherent and meaningful script directed firstly at satisfying my own search for inner harmony. We are continuously looking for the meanings and order in the lives of the "others" we study; it is only natural we do the same with our selves. This tendency is almost inevitable, since the data we use about ourselves is only partly recorded in fieldnotes, neither do we write these accounts under the guidance of an analyst.

For that matter, my biography is not important enough to as yet add the missing details in the above account. This would not change in any case the interpretation of reality, and the essence of the message from the "ethnographer's point of view". We have already reconciled ourselves with the limits of the ethnographer's knowledge of the "native's point of view". After all, ethnographers are not photographers.

CHAPTER 11.
IN THE COMPANY OF AMERICAN JEWS: AN ISRAELI OBSERVER IN A LOWER EAST SIDE SYNAGOGUE

Only the rich and the poor can have authentic buildings. The rich can afford to build well and keep it up, and the poor don't have the money to patchke around.

(Elissa Sampson, September 17, 2004)

DISCOVERING THE STANTON STREET SYNAGOGUE

It was an accident. I was invited to a Friday night Sabbath dinner by friends on the Lower East Side. My hosts, Jonathan Boyarin and his spouse Elissa Sampson, suggested we meet beforehand at their local synagogue on Stanton Street (Congregation Bnai Jacob Anschei Brzezan).

I agreed, thinking it might be an interesting experience. Though I gave up religion shortly after leaving my Tel-Aviv religious elementary school (*Tachkemoni*), in later years I was often engaged in the study of Jewish religious life. Early in my career, I studied the religiosity of Moroccan Jews in Israel (chapters 6, 7), and more recently I reported on the gay synagogue in New York (chapters 12, 13, 14). However, as it turned out, between that encounter at a March 2004 service and one in December 2005, for about six months during my sabbatical stays in New York, I attended services regularly—Friday nights, Saturday mornings and afternoons (*mincha and maʼariv*), holiday services, several congregation dinners and other social activities. Like most other congregants, I did not attend all services, and in particular, I abstained from the early morning (6:30 am), *shachrit* services on weekdays. However, I was often invited for Sabbath meals and other events at the homes of congregants. In spite of my sporadic attendance, I was considered a member and was invited to vote, also by proxy, on a few major decisions. If all went well, it took me thirty minutes to get to the synagogue by subway or bus, but sometimes it took much longer. Though not at first, I did not hide from my close acquaintances the fact that I used transport, violating Orthodox restrictions, in order to attend on the Sabbath. They seemed to tolerate my religious misconduct.

Why did I continue to attend services in a dilapidated old synagogue located at a distance from my apartment in New York? In the following pages I try to explain my attraction to this site that seemed to represent some intriguing issues in the life of American Jews and their brethren in Israel.

I started recording my observations with Elissa Sampson's words (quoted above)[1] in a feature in *The Jewish Week* that reported on a congregational fund raising party. That sentence encapsulated the story of a nearly 100 year-old synagogue that was revived shortly before it was lost under the ravages of time that had left it to decay after the demise of most of the people who had built and sustained it for many years. The children and grandchildren of these original congregants had left for more prosperous places in the suburbs and elsewhere. The building was almost a ruin when it was saved by the few veteran members still around together with a group of younger people, newcomers to the neighborhood, who decided to bring it back to its better old days. What Elissa insinuated in the Yiddish term *patchke* (around) was an assessment of the character and the project of the founders and of the new Jewish arrivals who had come now to restore the place. Neither then nor now, could the congregation afford to invest in an artistic taste, adding elegance and comfort to a site that was originally built as a communal

---

1   Unlike most of my ethnographic reports, I kept the names of all congregants mentioned in the text. I consider it a tribute to their dedication and continuing contribution to the survival of the synagogue. I am grateful to their warm welcome and candid openness.

shul (a Yiddish term for a small, intimate, synagogue). I have been familiar with the word '*Patchke*' from my early youth, when Yiddish was still often in use by my parents and their associates. It meant, derogatively, messing around, wasting energy in painting, mending, and doing other jobs of little value.

The *shul* on Stanton Street was not a monumental structure (as some other Jewish sites in New York that were built originally as synagogues or as churches), but, founded in 1913, it was authentic as synagogues of the period go. In a count taken in 1905, there were 350 congregations functioning in the Lower East Side, and sixty buildings that had been expressly built or converted to be synagogues (Kaufman 2000:116). Among the few that survived, the Stanton sanctuary also maintained the special aura of naive art. Elissa, who became a volunteer tour-guide in the Lower East Side, enjoyed to emphasize to the visitors the elements of folk art beautifully expressed in the sanctuary's decorations. These were fashioned in a style popular in Eastern European synagogues, but borrowed from non-Jewish sources. This was evident in the decaying wall paintings that presented the twelve-month, symbolic images *(mazalot)*. There was no time and money to *patchke* around now except for a basic re-enforcement of the deteriorating structure (the leaking roof in particular). This was true for the founders, Anschei Brzezan, the people (*anschei* in Hebrew) who came from Brzezan, a shtetel in Galicia (in the eastern part of the Austro-Hungarian Empire), and started a new life in America. It was no less true for the younger congregants who came in recent years to live in the Lower East Side, the cradle of Jewish life in New York during the early decades of the 20th Century. The love of Jewish traditions, the search for a community, and frugal in their life style were the hallmarks of those generations of past and present who made the Stanton Street Synagogue a focus of their social and cultural cravings.

I will now proceed to describe the congregants, their social and cultural agenda as custodians of the Stanton Street Synagogue, a place and a tradition. As I witnessed, it was not an easy task. I admired their investment of time, money and emotion. Though, still with one eye of the addicted anthropologist, I was sucked into their project as observer participant, rather than the usual "participant observer."

I am not the first secularized Jew to have been drawn to the Jewish heritage of the Lower East Side. Many books and films have been dedicated to this modest-looking neighborhood that became a myth of a lost Jewish Town in America (e.g. Boyarin 1996; Diner 2000; Diner, Shandler, and Wenger 2000). The Jews did not imitate their close neighbors, the Chinese, who preserved their ethnic enclave in New York and in most other major cities in the United States. Paul Cowan in his *Lost in History* (1982), for example, described his return journey to Judaism, which was particularly influenced during his search for the history and remnants of Jewish life in that neighborhood. Moreover, he visited the Stanton Street Synagogue and developed a close relationship with Rabbi Singer, who continued to lead the *shul* until its near demise a quarter of a century later. Cowan, however, remained the hero of his story. Although the following pages also tell about myself, as the author, nevertheless, I hope "my story" will be mostly dedicated to the people I met at this site.

THE VETERAN CONGREGANTS

The core of the congregation, as much as the wider network of more casual participants, contained a mix of veteran residents—men and women of advanced aged, in their seventies, eighties, and nineties—together with a larger constituency of younger men and women who were mostly in their twenties, thirties and forties. There were also a few in their fifties and sixties. Members of the core group were engaged in the long fight to save the synagogue from being sold as a building site, a plan orchestrated by the last rabbi's family. Under the pressure made on an old dedicated rabbi by his greedy offspring, the rabbi asserted that there was no congregation left at Stanton to claim ownership rights. Therefore, the rabbi's family argued, the synagogue had reached the end of the road.

I was immediately captivated by Benny, the eighty nine-year-old President of the congregation, who was instrumental in his efforts to rescue the synagogue. Benny arrived in America in 1933 from Poland, at the age of eighteen. At 85 he had retired from a tough job as butcher only because he had to take care of his incapacitated wife. He had worshiped at Stanton for forty-five years. It was his immaculate and formidable appearance in court that convinced the public agencies involved and the judge who presided over the case that the sale of a synagogue based on the claim that it was "without a congregation" was a charade. As I soon learned, this apparently a simple and unassuming man was endowed with immense personal powers.

Benny spoke good English though in a somewhat Yiddish intonation that was often laced with words in Yiddish. He thus set a tone suitable to a synagogue with a history that went back to the founders, who, in the beginning, must have communicated mostly, or only, in Yiddish. Actually, Elissa used to show in her tours the two versions of the synagogue's book of constitution. The first, formulated in 1905, was only in Yiddish. The second, in 1954, was both in Yiddish and English. In spite of his advanced age, Benny maintained a firm body and preserved the looks of a handsome man. He projected an image of the quintessential father-figure. He carried an aura of authority, though always gentle in his approach and manners. He also revealed a subtle sense of humor. In poetic terms, he was a man of today as much as of yesterday. When I left New York for an unspecified period, Benny invited me for an *aliya* (one of seven blessings, and an honor, during the Sabbath reading of the Torah) and commented that he would have given me another one had I stayed in town. I was as gratified by his gesture, as if I had gained a prize for a good publication.

Abe (or Abie as he was fondly called) was another old man who fascinated me. Ninety-four years old, he was small and thin, the size of a young boy, but he was remarkably agile, always in a good mood, and loved by all. He opened the synagogue's gate and the inner doors every morning, before 6.30 a.m. He arrived early enough to prepare coffee and some pastries for the *shachrit* early morning service participants. He opened the synagogue also for all other services and was thus always the first congregant on the premises. Abie also made it his responsibility to take care of the Torah Scroll's cloth cover when it was taken off during the reading at the Sabbath services. Abie had none of Benny's regal appearance and authority. But the young children loved him, and he was always happy to amuse them and let them play with the cane he sometimes used in winter.

Abie arrived in America as a ten-year-old, in 1921, with his widowed mother. Abie's mother's older sister helped them come over. I was told by another old congregant that Abie, who had some hearing difficulties, was considered retarded by his teachers, who kept him in a remote corner, missing the smartness of that little boy. He had worked in various blue collar occupations, and since retirement had served as a volunteer assistant in various charity organizations. He was very proud of his only daughter, who had occupied an important role in the city's education administration. Younger congregants arriving earlier to services enjoyed listening to Abie's stories of his past employment, and other memorable events. He seemed to be a miracle of mental sharpness and happy spirit in spite of the difficulties he must have endured throughout his life.

Abie never missed a service. Actually he was the only one among the older men who attended the evening services. All the others, including Benny, rarely attended the Friday and Saturday evening services. Benny could not leave his invalid wife, who had no nursing help at night. The other older men preferred to attend synagogues closer to their homes and avoid the hazards of the weather in the winter and the city streets dangers at dark hours. But nothing could stop the widowed Abie, who lived alone, from coming to the synagogue at any hour of service, early morning or late evening. He told me once that he must walk, anyhow, in order to avoid the loss of his limbs' agility. Abie was present in the sanctuary at all times that it was open to the congregation, as much as the Holy Ark and the Torah Scrolls inside.

Very different in his demeanor was Gedaliah, a man in his late seventies, a robust Holocaust survivor. We gradually developed a particular chemistry as he looked for my company during prayers. As he told me, he came out of the war a very young man (probably sixteen or seventeen years old). He survived together with his father and older brother because they managed to keep escaping both the Germans and their Polish collaborators. His father had served in a fighting regiment in World War I, which left him a few Gentile friends. They had warned him about the danger posed also by close neighbors who might betray them. Gedaliah had many stories of his escapes and also of the revenge he took sometimes when threatened by Germans and Poles. No doubt, he learned to take care of himself. Moreover, when they came back home after the war, he discovered that their Polish neighbors had no compassion for the few surviving Jews who wished to retrieve their property. As they prepared to leave, he wanted to put their village on fire. But, Gedaliah's brother stopped him from committing that violent act of farewell that he thought did not comply with Jewish morality.

For many years Gedaliah had a hardware store, and, as he told me, President Nixon made a mistake not calling on his services to break into locked doors more skillfully. He had a better opinion than many people of that demoted leader because Nixon had stood by Israel at its dark hour in 1973. Gedaliah was prominent and self-assured enough to chat with me (and others) during prayers and the sequences of Torah reading. He reminded me of Benny with his impressive stature, physically and mentally, and with a candid sense of humor. Gedaliah resented Jewish intellectuals, who, defending social causes, have also often expressed in his view anti-Israeli feelings. He had not much faith left for other nations' love for Jews, either. We remained on friendly terms in spite of my own critical view on the present Israeli government's policies in the occupied territories.

I felt free to confront Gedaliah with a question that often came to my mind during services at Stanton, and particularly when listening to Gedaliah's stories from the Holocaust. What makes Jews continue pray to a God that deserted them in the dark hours of Auschwitz? Gedaliah answered me in his direct style: "It is ingrained in the Jewish psyche." He knew it was not a rational way of thought or conduct. On another occasion Gedaliah quoted an idea apparently voiced by Churchill that "the Jews have a stiff neck" meaning that they stick with their beliefs and traditions in spite of all impediments (actually, "stiff necked" is a direct translation of the biblical term *am kshe oref*). His response, however, was not much different from other answers I got, though presented in different styles, from the younger congregants in particular. Basically, they all expressed the notion of continuity, the respect, honor and affection that also the present cohort of practicing Jews owes to the many generations who brought them along.

The veteran congregants managed to develop amicable relationships with their non-Jewish neighbors on the block, primarily poor Latinos. It seemed normal for congregants to call on an employee from a nearby store, or even approach innocent by-passers, and ask them to switch off lights, or start the air-conditioner, etc., in the synagogue—forbidden tasks for Orthodox Jews on the Sabbath.

THE NEWCOMERS TO STANTON

Among the younger generations, I have already mentioned my friends who introduced me to the synagogue, the middle-aged Jonathan, an anthropologist of reputation engaged in Jewish Studies, who writes evocatively also about his experiences at the Stanton and other synagogues (e.g. Boyarin 1996). His spouse Elissa (quoted above), is a computer expert and a rare type of a conservationist of the local environment and of Jewish historical sites in particular. Jonathan was eager to taste different styles of worship and to also help other struggling congregations in the neighborhood. He often attended services in other synagogues and arrived late to join with Elissa and other friends. But he often led services, read from the Torah, or gave a talk between services on the Sabbath afternoon.

Elissa, who attended the *shul* more regularly, was instrumental in particular in taking care of the *kiddush*, a light meal (*nash* in Yiddish) that concluded the Sabbath morning service. But she was also much behind the scenes of most activities and decisions taking place at the synagogue. Elissa never tired of making the Stanton place a beacon of a Lower East Side Jewish treasure. When she discovered that another synagogue was going on sale, she retrieved some of its old furniture for Stanton. Jonathan and Elissa had moved to the Lower East Side as a young couple when it was still a low rent area. Now, they could be defined as "veteran newcomers."

Jonathan had often expressed his amazement and pride at the "miracle" of the continuity of Jewish culture in spite of all the suffering and the temptations to defect. I remember one Friday evening service, as a few congregants including himself, his eighteen year old son, Abie and others were dancing in a small circle during a joyful prayer, Jonathan called out jubilantly: "Look, they have been doing it for the last 2000 years!!"

Among the surprises awaiting me on my first visit was meeting Jeff, an old acquaintance from earlier engagements in New York whom I had not encountered for many years. An officer of high rank in the city education administration, he had moved to the neighborhood a few years earlier after separating from his spouse. Jeff, in his early 50s, was reared in a family with little Jewish education, but had gradually become Orthodox. He told me that he was surprised himself of having discovered a belief in God. He felt an inner drive to dedicate himself to Jewish survival. As he moved to his new location he also departed from his former mid-town Orthodox synagogue. During my nearly two years association with the Stanton Street congregation I witnessed Jeff's growing involvement with the synagogue's affairs. He actually became a major force in the community next to Benny. I could sense also the deep affection that developed between the two men.

As it gradually became evident, to me and to other congregants, Benny seemed to depend more and more on Jeff to execute the synagogue's routine affairs in ritual and administrative life. In turn, Jeff depended on Benny's moral authority among the congregants to support him with the growing tasks at his domain as the elected Vice-President. Jeff learned to deal with Benny's sometimes overbearing expectations. The affection and trust between the two also made Benny accept Jeff's decisions even when these did not fully suit his wishes. Jeff, who had lived a few years in Israel, had acquired a good knowledge of Jewish liturgy and ritual. He thus maintained a position of leadership based upon both his managerial skills and his expertise in Judaism.

CHAPTER ELEVEN

Jeff made no compromises and abides by the rules and practice of Orthodox Judaism. One Friday evening, as we walked out of the synagogue, he discovered he had money left in his jacket's inner pocket. He immediately called on a bartender in a restaurant next door and left with him the notes of about $20.

Already at an early stage, Jeff told me that the Stanton *shul* differed from other synagogues, which were far more homogeneous in the character of their congregants. "Here," he explained, "no one comments about others' behavior." He tolerated my own transgressions on the Sabbath and encouraged me to attend services, inviting me for meals at his meticulously kosher home. Jeff believed his investment of time, energy, and other resources at Stanton were "an answer" to the other Orthodox synagogues around: "Here I feel at home. I always looked for *Yiddishkeit* (Jewish ambiance) and hope we will build a movement here." Jeff also often employed the image used by others to explain the attraction for newcomers: "It is *heimish* (cosy)." A visitor—a friend from Jeff's former synagogue—commented: "It is a synagogue that one doesn't need another one to go to". He was thus referring to Jewish jokes about the synagogues needed to satisfy one's sympathy and antipathy.

Jeff, however, was not the only younger congregant who turned to orthodoxy without prior exposure to a rigorous Jewish life-style. Among the younger congregants I developed a friendship with Jonny. A gregarious podiatrist, in his early thirties, and his spouse Annie also a medical professional. Jonny's parental family had been only minimally dedicated to Jewish life, but his mother had decided to enroll him in a Jewish day school. As his father told me on his visit to the synagogue, Jonny became engaged in Judaism far more than his parents. Actually, it was Jonny's wife, Annie, who had spent a year in Israel and who insisted on observing a traditional Jewish home when they had discussed their prospective life together. The couple got a modest apartment owned by their parents who had kept it after they moved out to the suburbs. A few other congregants had similarly gained access to an apartment in the neighborhood.

At a High Holiday meal to which Jonny invited also my visiting son, Annie talked about the importance of joining and supporting the synagogue. It offered a community within a metropolitan city, she explained, and pointed out that they might have otherwise been isolated as was typical of the majority of New Yorkers.

Jonny became a leading member in the synagogue. He was ready to invest time, labor, and money in operating various functions, such as supervising the food catering for the *kiddush* and other communal celebrations. In his hectic schedule and family obligations (having two young children), he still found the time for various odd jobs, such as replacing the old refrigerator at Stanton. Jonny was always in a good mood ready to joke, welcoming and offer hospitality to newcomers. He usually arrived with one or two of his young children who roamed around the synagogue and became a regular attraction among the congregants. When a reporter of *The Jewish Press* newspaper published an article about an art exhibit at the synagogue, Jonny sent out an e-mail message expressing his pleasure in "...the small *shul* that has a big place in my heart..." Jonny's stout figure made that image seem real. As much as with Gedaliah, Jeff, and a few others, my relationship with Jonny was not affected by my "Leftist" positions concerning Israeli politics. Elissa overheard an intense discussion I was having with Jonny on the eve of the disengagement from Gaza. She commented to me in a tone tolerating both interlocutors: "Jonny is liberal with every social issue, except for anything related to Israel."

Another remarkable young congregant was Baruch. When I first saw him, I assumed he was a bum, almost a teenager in his eccentric appearance and demeanor. In his mid-thirties, he was often dressed in the provocative style of ethnic neighborhoods, with new caps and colorful parts of clothing at each service. He approached me when he first saw me, asked about my background and started joking about himself. I was surprised to discover that he was then in the role of Vice-President of the synagogue. However, I soon learned it was his *shtick* (amusement) to impersonate the role of a clown. Baruch came from a *"frum"* (fully observant) family, and two of his younger brothers have been to rabbinical schools. He had had a good Jewish education and had spent some time in a yeshiva in Israel. He was successfully engaged in business and was a generous contributor to the synagogue. When he married, he moved to the Lower East Side, and, together with Neal, a friend who had moved at about the same time, they checked out the synagogues operating in the vicinity (about fifteen altogether). It was at Stanton, where they felt their needs for Judaism and community were best suited.

In spite of his seemingly vulgar behavior, Baruch was instrumental in recruiting several more participants. He approached everybody who got close to the site or entered the premises and easily broke barriers of age, gender, and status. His humor, warmth, and unassuming presentation of self gained him the affection of many congregants, who tolerated his somewhat uncouth demeanor. He was too energetic to sit still during services, and instead, he often moved around and chatted with old and new acquaintances. Benny put up with his hyperactive conduct—he knew he could also rely on his more serious performance when needed. Baruch was particularly pleased to arrive on time to the Friday night service with a bottle of good alcohol to lift up the spirits of the younger congregants assembled for *Kabalt Shabat* (welcoming the Sabbath). He was thus promoting the atmosphere of a party and feelings of *communitas*, which must have separated the Stanton *Shul* from most other Orthodox synagogues in the neighborhood. Baruch had often raised old Abie out of his seat and took him for a dance in front of the Holy Ark. With others joining them, adults and young children, it became a symbolic ritual of the bond of generations at Stanton.

When I asked Baruch for his opinion on why Jews continue to worship a God who deserted them so many times, he answered me in his maverick style and in a voice intended to be heard by those in the near seats: "God wanted always to keep for himself a limited number of Jews only. This is also why he wants also the homosexuals among them." No doubt, as much as intended to amuse, Baruch made a statement about his position on issues recently debated in the United States (gay marriage in particular). I assume he also expressed his tolerant attitude about the acceptance of gay and lesbian congregants. Baruch, who often traveled to foreign countries, seemed remarkably free of racial, gender and sexual prejudices.

Peretz, a lawyer, in his early forties, became a regular and took on various responsibilities at the synagogue. During my stay, he was elected to the board of trustees. Coming from a Modern Orthodox family background, he was for many years a member of an affluent mid-town Orthodox congregation. He was introduced to the Stanton synagogue when he met Jeff at a mutual friend's birthday party. He liked the place as he told me, because he had had enough of "a congregation of strangers." He made it a habit to shake hands with everybody, familiar or newcomer. It was his conviction that newcomers in particular should be warmly approached to make them feel welcome. This was also a strategy he believed that might help to expand the membership so needed for the congregation.

Peretz could testify for the embodiment of a community of friends at Stanton as a social reality, not just an image. More than once, he had experienced the benefits of warm relationships at Stanton. When he fell ill, he called on Elissa and Jonny, who immediately provided him with medical advice and urgent medication. Peretz admitted it was not a religious drive that had mainly drawn him to the synagogue, but rather the search for a community. To reach that goal, he was ready to invest time and money. Nevertheless, he sometimes felt a need to take a short break and return for a service at the mid-town synagogue. "Here I always feel a pressure—they need me—but there, I can sit, relax, and meditate."

David was single when we first met. An artist and art teacher, he had spent some time in Israel. On his return and while seeking an apartment in the neighborhood, he was also looking for a synagogue. He was recruited by Baruch whom he met at a Sabbath dinner. "Here they don't check you out" he said succinctly in explaining his attraction to the Stanton *shul*. He often performed as cantor and I liked his pleasant voice and gentle style of prayer. As he told me, he would not have dared perform as cantor in any other synagogue. It was the feeling of security and friendship he experienced at Stanton that allowed him to try and improve his skills.

I met also David's father, who came for a visit from Chicago. The father, an impressive professional, seemed to represent a cohort of successfully integrated American Jews who were also proud of their cultural heritage. His father expressed disappointment about prevalent attitudes among Israelis who emigrated to the US, but they felt no connection to American Jews or to Jewish culture. I agreed with him, since I had made similar observations in my earlier study of Israelis in Queens (chapter 8).

The last couple I introduce: Dov, a lawyer, and Sharon, a pediatric neurologist. Both had a good Jewish education. Dov enjoyed sharing with me his appreciation of the beauty of the Hebrew language as displayed in the Torah and prayer texts. I was surprised to discover his wide knowledge of Jewish scripture and his sensitivity to the subtlety of Hebrew, which often surpassed my own. The poetic style of prayers, sometimes raised his excitement and a sense of longing, such as the phrase and the traditional tune of *hashivenu venashuva*—"take us back (God) and we will return (to you)." Sharon had attended medical school in Tel-Aviv, and she made me proud with her happy memories of life in my home town. Like other congregants, Dov and Sharon often used to invite families and singles to join their table for a Friday night or Saturday meal.

Dov had been born in the neighborhood, but joined the synagogue by coincidence. He came to attend a lecture, was warmly received, and gradually came to feel obligated to attend services. He told me he was not scrupulously religious, but attending services at Stanton gave him the assurance of continuity of time and space. Abiding by the traditions of his ancestors, who for millennia had developed and preserved these texts and rules, he had defined his personal position in the universe.

There were many more singles and couples who attracted my interest and who treated me warmly. These included, in particular, the dedicated young treasurer, Neal, and his wife Harriet. Neal was brought up in a Conservative family, but, when he went to college, "I gave up religion." However, when he left college and was getting married, he decided to return to tradition. He and Harriet were also thinking about the cultural environment of raising children (during my stay they had a one-year-old baby boy). They had chosen Stanton because it was a synagogue "where no one tells you how to dress." I once overheard a conversation between Baruch and Neal when Baruch said, "It is not the ritual that I feel for, it is the social," to which Neal responded: "It is both the ritual and the social."

Another regular congregant was Moishe—single, in his early 30s—who had also been recruited by Jeff. He came from an Orthodox family and felt at home at Stanton. He told me that sometimes he felt he was "in wonder-land"—that it was a synagogue for people who could not go anywhere else. Actually, he was among the few newcomers who could claim roots at Stanton. His grandparents (his father's parents) had prayed there a few decades earlier.

Neal's comment about the lack of a mandatory code of dress at Stanton was an image often used to describe the inclusiveness and tolerance typical of their synagogue. Actually, one could observe that image also in practice as male congregants attended services in a large variety of clothing styles, from suits to jeans, wearing conservative hats, yarmulkes, or baseball caps. Nevertheless, I sometimes thought they shared "a Jewish look." Some congregants reminded me of the first painting I bought many years ago that, surprisingly, was by Moshe Berenstein, a painter , whose subjects were taken from the lost shtetel. I still have it in our living room, the profiles of three young men with caps who could be Yeshiva students, or rather blue collar Jewish workers. Was it my subconscious mourning for the Holocaust? Have I retrieved the shadows of that lost society at Stanton? However, among the women at Stanton, a few were dressed up in a period fashion reminiscent of an earlier Lower East Side elegance.

THE WOMEN AT STANTON

Built as an Orthodox synagogue, the original structure used the second floor for the women's gallery. Later, however, no one considered maintaining the tradition of letting the women climb up the uncomfortable staircase. That seemed out of tune with modern times. Instead, the entry section of the main sanctuary containing about 8-10 rows came to be reserved for women. The women's section (*ezrat nashim*) was separated from the larger men's section (with the *bimah* and holy ark) by a *mechitza*, a divider made of a light lace-like curtain, that left the men and women separated but in full view of each other. Moreover, the *mechitza* left open the way between the two rows of benches along the sanctuary. Consequently, the space was open for the young children to run along the open path between their mothers and fathers in the front and back seats.

I invited a female friend, a feminist, active at a gay synagogue, to attend a Friday service. She was the only woman attending that evening. On his way to his seat, Dov almost automatically, with a friendly smile, moved the *mechitza* curtain "separating" the women's section. My guest who was acquainted with Dov and Sharon (we were also both invited to have a Sabbath dinner with them), accepted that gesture in good humor. She told me later: "they are unique in separating between religious orthodoxy and political liberalism."

Women are not obligated to participate in public prayers in Orthodox Judaism and only very few showed up at the Friday (*kabalat Shabat*) services. Their number fluctuated on the Sabbath morning service, but they attended in a great number at the *kiddush*—the social hour at noon following the Sabbath morning service—when they joined the men or came on their own. The *kiddush* included light food, drinks, a *dvar* Torah (a homily), and the recent local tradition of singing the national anthems of Israel and the USA. Also very few women attended the Sabbath afternoon and evening (*mincha* and *ma'ariv*) services. But many women attended services on the major holidays. The only opportunity for women to take an active part in a religious activity was during the *kiddush*, when a few women often presented the *dvar* Torah. Among these women was a graduate of a rabbinical school who usually based her talk on the Torah *parsha*—the chapter read at the morning service. Some women related to other Jewish sources, to literature, or issues of Jewish ethics.

Although the women's attendance was limited compared with the men, and they had little part in public ritual, nevertheless, they had taken a major role in the maintenance and running of the synagogue. They fully participated in the board and communal meetings. In the annual meeting I attended, women presented the more sensitive issues, such as the need to raise the annual fees. In their arguments they particularly emphasized the importance of the synagogue in the lives of its members. They were always raising awareness of the responsibility of keeping "our *kehillah*" (community) strong. The term *kehillah* evokes feelings of shared sentiment and affection. As we were leaving the synagogue after a Friday evening prayer, I asked a woman who seemed to be in her early forties how she felt about the peripheral position of women in the ritual of an Orthodox synagogue. "It doesn't bother me. There are many other ways for women to engage themselves in the synagogue," she responded with no hesitation.

CHABAD'S EMISSARIES

Almost every Sabbath later in the afternoon, two young men clad in black suits and black hats made their way to Stanton. I assume that was part of Chabad's policy to help and influence Jewish constituencies in the near and far away communities. The weekly visitors to Stanton were usually very young, unmarried Yeshiva students. Pale, thin, and in black adult attire, they seemed as guests from a long lost East European *shtetel*. They came sometimes early enough to help start the *mincha* service, however, they usually arrived during the break between the *mincha* and *ma'ariv* services. This was the time for the traditional *seu'da shlishit* (the "third meal" of snacks, nuts, and cold drinks) during which some kind of cultural activity took place. Jonathan, for example, used to read aloud from literary sources in Yiddish. The Chabad visitors were always expecting to offer a *devar* Torah, that usually ended with the promise of the near coming of the Messiah.

I suspected that most listeners had little appreciation for the intellectual depth of these presentations. Some of the congregants busied themselves in various odd jobs that kept them away from the table of the "third meal." Elissa called these presentations in good humor: the "*nareshkeit*" (worthless/silly, in Yiddish). Gedaliah described the Chabad students as sheep who eat whatever is given to them. But no one openly expressed a critical view. On the contrary, the young men were welcomed and congratulated for their contribution. Moreover, men and women appreciated their effort to walk the long way from Brooklyn and their commitment to Hassidic traditions.

Peretz responded to my obvious displeasure as we attended one of these simplistic homilies: "We are accepting." That attitude I believe was representative of the tolerance typical of the Stanton crowd. After all, it dawned on me, Jonathan's reading from a book in Yiddish and recounting honorable sages' stories, also was not fully comprehended by all present.

Sometime later, Peretz told me that about twenty five Chabad students who had arrived at Stanton on the evening service of *Simcaht Torah*. Their appearance made the service a convivial event, since they all enthusiastically danced with the Torah Scrolls. Peretz was grateful for the experience and personally made a long-distance phone call to the parents of one of the leading Chabad team at the *Simchat Torah* service, thanking them for their dedicated son.

CONFRONTING SOCIAL AND OTHER IMPEDIMENTS

A. Stubborn Congregants

For a while, the synagogue was in turmoil caused by a middle aged couple, the woman in particular, who accused the leadership of misusing the synagogue's funds. Moreover, the woman advertised her accusations by putting up fliers around the neighborhood and even beyond (at lower Manhattan's bus stops, etc.,) that claimed there was "corruption" at the Stanton Street Synagogue. The major allegation concerned the plan of repairing the leaking roof. The board decided to work with the State's agency (and its authorized contractors) that would have also assisted with funding the project and possibly might help to expand the renovation. The resentful couple contested this arrangement, demanding that the work be started immediately with the limited funds available. Was she "mad" as suggested by many in the congregation? or were they "professional trouble makers" as suggested by others? Actually they were longtime members who had taken an active part in the legal fight to save the synagogue. When I spoke to her husband, before the eruption of scandal, he seemed quite amicable and told me they had moved to the neighborhood about twelve years earlier and had decided to maintain a "Jewish home." They felt it was easy to join the Stanton synagogue crowd and its style of religiosity.

What made them fight now against the people who were investing so much effort to rebuild their synagogue? Was this a story from Jewish history, when people assumed they knew better than all others how to lead the community's affairs? In any case, when all requests and efforts to appease them failed, their membership was revoked and the board had to call on the police to keep them out of the synagogue. Jeff stood in front of the battle, which allowed Benny to keep away from the unpleasant affair. Abie also felt pain as he told me about the disturbances that had erupted when the woman entered the synagogue's space during service or later at the *kiddush*. Gedaliah just raised his voice in disdain: "we *daven* (pray) here!" Even Baruch, always convivial and forgiving, was upset and refused to officiate in his role as master of ceremony in the *kiddush* that followed one of these embarrassing affairs.

I was told that Baruch encouraged an older congregant to reveal his great voice and lead during the *kiddush* the Israeli national anthem "Hatikva" and then continue with "God Bless America." Baruch's playful experiment became a sort of secular ritual during the Sabbath *kiddush* from then on. The aging singer, who seemed at that stage of life and health little skilled in the Hebrew liturgy and poetical texts, took on the role most seriously. However, he usually distorted the rhymes to the extent that, in the beginning, made me uncomfortable when expected to rise in honor of the Israeli anthem. I gradually developed the tolerance other congregants showed toward him. They also usually tolerated his other habit of starting to sing beforetime, with his loud operatic voice, another popular prayer and song—Adon Olam—which ends the Sabbath morning service. During a large fund raising celebration, however, when visitors from other congregations and local dignitaries were also present, the same old singer was on the program with his role of launching the national anthems of Israel and the United States. As Elissa pointed out to me, the presence of the older congregants (regardless of their health and other capabilities) supported the notion of continuity, which the Stanton *shul* is all about.

B. Money for the Synagogue

The Stanton congregants had not been supported by a national organization or a private benefactor (such as a wealthy loyal congregant) to provide for the upkeep of the aging building or for running its regular activities. The annual dues remained for many years as low as $18. But also the modest raise accomplished by the new leadership ($100 for individual membership, $200 for family membership) was also insufficient to cope with the needs to renovate the site, improve its maintenance, and possibly appoint a rabbi to serve in a part-time position. The leadership planned and executed a long list of fund raising events that were also intended to attract visitors not affiliated with Stanton (dinners, lectures, musical performances, an auction, etc.,).

On a Sabbath preceding a celebratory dinner scheduled for September 11, Jeff, speaking from the *bimah*, encouraged all to come and invite other guests to join them. He ended his speech with an evocative conclusion: "On these days of great national disasters (referring to September 11, the war in Iraq, the Tzunami in Asia, the Katrina destruction of New Orleans, the disengagement from Gaza and the suicide bombers in Israel), we have only our *kehillah*, and we must help it survive." Jeff told me he found himself in the embarrassing position of a *shnorer* (Yiddish for a beggar). The active members had often contributed more than the others. It was frequently suggested to the membership that they honor fellow congregants and contribute to the synagogue on their personal and family happy or sad events (such as on birthdays, *shiva'* mourning events, etc.). There were a few occasions of greater generosity, such as when Peretz's parents made a substantial contribution on his birthday and on other events, large enough to undertake some serious work of renovation of the lower level hall.

During the major holidays, Benny and Baruch were conducting "the sale of honors." Benny's patriarchal dignity, and Baruch's straight-forward and humorous salesmanship, kept the audience jovial but under obligation to "buy" the honors as generously as they could afford. A great surprise awaited the couple on the *bimah* conducting the sale when an unknown older woman, a visitor from Texas, promised $1000 for an *aliya* honoring her son. The son, in his late thirties, was a newcomer to the neighborhood who had invited his visiting mother to attend prayers on Yom Kippur at Stanton. Benny, in good humor, though with a clear message, told a story of a man who made a generous pledge to his synagogue, but after the holiday when expected to materialize his promise, he excused himself claiming that he was drunk at the moment he made the pledge! The Texas guest, however, soon sent in the promised check. I spoke to her son who told me he had no religious inclinations but wished to express respect for his late father and widowed mother. I never saw him again.

c. Service Leaders and Cantors

For nearly two years, Akiva, Baruch's brother took on the role of rabbinic intern. Baruch also contributed a modest allowance to compensate Akiva for his dedicated work. Akiva, who was still in rabbinical school, gave the congregation a notion of religious leadership. His young age was no handicap for his acceptance under the legitimacy of Benny and other leading congregants. It was a problem to reckon with when he got married and left for another remote New York neighborhood. Although there were not sufficient funds anytime soon to support a full-time rabbi, it remained a desire nourished by many congregants, who considered the recruitment of an ordained rabbi as a symbol of community maturity. Jeff claimed that, with a rabbi, they would be respected among the Jewish constituency and would attract new congregants in the neighborhood.

The services were run by volunteers like Jeff, Jonathan, David, and other skilled congregants, including a congregant who was getting a rabbinical degree at a leading seminary. He did not plan to go into a rabbinical career, however. He was a certified accountant, which he believed would remain his major occupation. As he told me, he had no wish to engage in congregational politics—something an ordinary rabbi could never escape. Another more unusual character was Ira, a frequent visitor of Chassidic background, who often joined the congregation and took a leading position as cantor and service leader. In his ultra-Orthodox garb, all in black with a *shtreimel* (a flat fur hat as customary among Chassidic men), he cut a strange figure in the company of mostly mainstream American Jews at Stanton. I was surprised to see him there and for a while was uncomfortable with his style, which seemed to me too traditional, high-toned, and weepy. He also sometimes gave a *devar Torah* that reminded me of Chabad ideology. For example, he argued at one of his homilies that Abraham was chosen by God not because of his exceptional wisdom, but because every Jew is a chosen person. But, I gradually came to see the goodwill, not only naivety, on his part. I assume he had his own reasons to depart occasionally from his home synagogue. Did he contemplate becoming a religious leader at Stanton? He was only one among a number of occasional visitors who seemed somewhat odd, but all were welcome, honored during the service, and encouraged to come back.

D. The Minyan—"to be or not to be?"

Jonathan, one among the many congregants I observed, was at the same time himself an accomplished anthropologist. He welcomed my presence in his synagogue community and even encouraged me to conduct an ordinary ethnographic research. Jonathan wrote about the structure and the meaning of the *minyan* (relating specifically to the morning *shacharit* service) as he experienced it himself at Stanton (Boyarin 1996: 63-86). He posed the question: Is the *minyan* a quintessential Jewish form of a community? My interest was not as focused. I never participated at the morning *minyan* and I was not probing into the theological and sociological meaning of that institution in Judaism. I treated the *minyan* as a "social fact" to reckon with among the issues that the leadership had to cope with in order to perform all services successfully.

A major continuous thorny issue was the question at all services: "Have we a *minyan*?" (i.e., in order to start a fully-fledged public service with the required minimum of ten adult men). I was pleased to discover that at times I arrived to be counted as the tenth man for the *minyan*. For the *shacharit* services, however, Benny used to offer a lift to four or five other older men who would not have walked otherwise to the synagogue at that early morning hour. Only Abie preferred to walk, for health reasons, but also because he was uncomfortable with Benny's driving. A few younger men, like Jeff and Moishe, came regularly, and others, like Neal and Baruch attended a few mornings only. They came often because they felt obligated to Benny in particular. Even Moishe told me he would have preferred to stay in bed another hour, but he felt too guilty not to come on time. I was embarrassed to disappoint him, when Benny asked me to attend *shacharit* on a *Yortzeit* (a memorial day) for a close relative, and excused myself because of my remote residence.

The attainment of a complete *minyan* was often delayed on Friday evenings and sometimes was not complete even after a long hour of waiting. A few strategies were employed on these occasions. The simple one was to go out and recruit an extra one or two men from a synagogue around the corner (these might also volunteer to join the service even if they had already finished prayers at their own synagogue). Another way was to recruit accidental by-passers who seemed to be Jewish (in one case when two strangers volunteered to join a *minyan*, I discovered that one was not Jewish). A safer strategy was to call on sympathetic Israeli restaurant owners. Another less orthodox method employed on rare occasions, was to open the doors of the Holy Ark and let the Torah Scrolls stand for the missing tenth man. If the *minyan* remained deficient beyond an easy solution, the few attendees might walk to join another congregation (often also waiting to fill up a *minyan*). Otherwise, they would give up the expectation for a mandatory public service and end up praying as individuals. Jonathan described the various methods, the recruiting from or joining other congregations in particular, as "the Lower East Side synagogue economy" (Boyarin 1996: 70).

CHAPTER ELEVEN

On the Sabbath morning, there was always a *minyan* assembled sometime before or around 10 a.m., but rarely by the official time, at 9:30 a.m. The crowd of men might eventually include about twenty old and young attendants, some of whom arrived between the earlier *shacharit* and the later *musaf* services. At the afternoon and evening Sabbath services (*mincha* and *ma'ariv*), the *minyan* had often resembled the Friday evening service. However, these closing services of the Sabbath also benefited regularly (except for days of rough weather) from the late arrival of two young Chabad men who made their way from Brooklyn.

The Holiday services were usually well attended, but a surprise awaited me and others when the synagogue was packed with men and women on the Ninth day of the month of Av in the Jewish calendar, the memorial day of the destruction of the Temple in Jerusalem in 70 C.E. On that day, a few older men, who were absent from most other evening services, showed up. Baruch and Dov both reacted in a sarcastic tone to that massive attendance: "Jews love mourning." The *mechitza* was set aside, and an unusual blend of men and women seated randomly followed the public reading of *Eicha*, the Book of Lamentations.

However, the most sensitive issue concerned the smooth running of the morning daily services. Both Benny's fatherly pleading tone (which made one feel guilty for neglecting his request) and Jeff, in a more assertive tone, called on the congregants to make an effort and attend at least one *shacharit* service during the week. "The morning *minyan* is the soul of the synagogue," Jeff claimed one Sabbath in his appeal before the start of the *musaf* closing section. I asked him later why he considered the morning weekly service as the synagogue's soul. "In the *Shachrit* we *daven* (pray). The Sabbath service is social, which is good, but...". Jeff left the sentence unfinished.

Thus, Jeff revealed his deep commitment to the mandatory daily ritual "free" of the extra social and more celebratory style of the Sabbath services. In his view, those who regularly attended the *Shachrit* service, putting on the *tefillin* and making an effort to get to the synagogue in order to pray in a *minyan* before starting their day of work and other mundane tasks, displayed a deeper commitment to the endurance of Jewish culture.

Only a minority of the Stanton male congregants were able or willing to commit themselves regularly to that part of their synagogue life. Nevertheless, in the eyes of Benny and Jeff, the *Shacharit* service remained a must, the *raison d'être*, for the legitimacy of the synagogue's existence. It had to continue as sort of an eternal lamp lighting the path in a dark corridor, and to be known as such by the rest of the congregation. Neal told me he often had a bad conscience knowing that he might be the tenth missing man at the *shachrit* service. It happened on that same Friday morning, when no other man came after his arrival.

Already in November of 2005, Jeff had told me he was worried in case that anything should happen to Benny in his task of the morning driver bringing along a few older congregants: "The morning service will crash." Benny's car- load of men provided a reliable core for that service. Jeff's bad dream was materialized only a few weeks later when Benny lost consciousness during the Sabbath service. It happened as he was standing on the *bimah*, as he had done for so many years during the reading from the Torah. Luckily, he was saved from additional injury as he was supported by the rim of the *bimah* and the man who stood next to him. Although he soon regained his composure, he was taken to the closest emergency room and was hospitalized for nearly two weeks for a heart failure.

Only a few weeks earlier the synagogue celebrated, at the same happy party, Abie's at 94th birthday and Peretz's 40th. Elissa had opened the event with the story of baby Abie in his East European shtetel that was amusingly nicknamed "Duck Chatchkess." Benny had presided at the long *Kiddush* table in the basement hall (the *Beit Midrash*) packed with congregants and many guests. He told the crowd that, soon after he had managed to halt the sale of the synagogue, he received a phone call from one of Rabbi Singer's family who told him angrily: "We'll see if you'll manage to stay open one year." With great satisfaction, Benny had ended: "And now we are here!" He thanked Jeff and Elissa, in particular, for their dedication to the synagogue.

After Benny's collapse, Jeff assumed that, without Benny and his passengers, the next Sunday morning *minyan* was doomed, and he told Abie not to come. But Abie, responded immediately that he would be there as usual. I heard Jeff uttering, apparently to himself: "if Abie comes I must come."

The same evening, Jeff forwarded an urgent e-mail message asking the congregants to make an effort and come for the morning service. For the first time since the foundation of the synagogue in 1913, the chain of the *shachrit* services was in danger of being cut off. Jeff's plea was not only for himself, but, he considered that long honored tradition was important, in particular, for Abie and a few other older congregants. It was an essential part of their daily life program. If the synagogue was to operate only on the Sabbath, it did not justify the battle at court and the efforts made to keep the Stanton site alive as a fully-fledged Jewish institution.

A few days later Jeff forwarded a letter that was sent to him by a female congregant, but with the request to circulate it among the membership. I quote only a few lines from that evocative document:

> This is a desperate plea to ask people to come to the daily minyan. You may be wondering why this is so important to me since I can't be part of the minyan…we are like a family…I feel a commitment to the members of the shul…Especially now that he [Benny] is sick, to let the shul fall apart will be dishonoring who he is. We owe it to him to keep the shul going…Once a shul's daily minyan ceases to continue, many people stop coming to the Shabat minyan too… This is why I am begging people to attend the daily minyan…If people make a commitment to attend, I will make a commitment to supply cake and muffins several times a week for the morning minyan…
>
> *(Sharon Lebewohl, December 9, 2005)*

Sharon's letter attests to the position and feelings of women at Stanton as already stated above: "there are many ways for women to engage in an Orthodox synagogue." Elissa, Harriet, Anie, Sharon—the writer of the letter, and other women who were active in the synagogue did not seem deprived or abused by their peripheral role in ritual. Men go to *daven* as much as women breast feed the babies. It is all a collaborative family and communal project.

No doubt, the attainment of a *minyan* was not a problem that was specifically acute only at Stanton—it was the case for other synagogues in the Lower East Side as well as in other places. A few months later, I met a physician in Vancouver who, after joining a synagogue as tribute to his father who had passed away, felt obligated to also attend the morning services after the end of the period of mourning. He could not let them down knowing that he might be the tenth man missing in the *minyan* group. He concluded, however, that coming along had also a social benefit and this gave him a sense of supporting a cultural tradition.

I assume that the Stanton services will continue to be regularly conducted in spite of all difficulties. The older members might gradually drop out as much as the younger couples who have already moved to other localities (like Erik's family), but new synagogue seekers might move into the neighborhood or change synagogue loyalties. Actually, as I was writing these lines I got an e-mail from Jeff informing the congregation about the time table of the next Sabbath services, but also mentioning that Abie had had a nasty fall on his way to the synagogue for the early morning service and had been hospitalized. I felt as if a sacred totem pole had been stolen from an old temple or... a museum. I called up Elissa, who told me she visited Abie and had found him to be as alert and sharp as ever before. I got also a personal letter from Jeff telling me that the old pillars are falling down. Benny needed another operation, Gedaliah suffered from pains in his knees that often kept him at home, and Abie's daughter was planning to take him to stay with her in Brooklyn (which as he put it, "would be another fall for Abie").

However, a few months after I assumed I had completed my story of Stanton, on my return to New York in July 2006, I discovered that Jeff had departed with no explanation to other congregants. It was shortly after he saw his cherished goal realized—the appointment of a part-time rabbi. I met with him and discovered that he was tired of the continuing efforts to commit congregants to attend services regularly and on time. He was also disappointed with the demeanor of a few congregants who, he felt, were not engaged seriously enough in the routine of ritual activities and prayers: "They want to feel Jewish, but without the cost of persistence and work. It has become a men's club." In sum, he felt his efforts were not rewarded in religious terms fitting his expectation for a truly Jewish site of prayer. His friends among the congregants were hurt by his sudden withdrawal, particularly at the time when they were expecting the arrival of the rabbi (who was scheduled to start his mission in August 2006). I was told that Jeff revealed a controlling personality, unable to accommodate with other people's opinions, habits and life situations. Jonny, who felt betrayed by Jeff's departure, but an optimist as usual, looked around as we waited on a Sabbath morning at the beginning of the service, and commented: "You see, life goes on [also without Jeff]. Benny, Abie and Gedaliah were present. They looked somewhat older, but still alert and ready to continue with their life-long obligation at Stanton.

A week later Abie passed away. His funeral became a last celebration to commemorate his devotion to the Stanton synagogue. It was no less a display of the synagogue as a vital institution in the Lower East Side. Except for the first speaker, the grandson who spoke about Abie the affectionate grandfather, all other speakers, Benny, Jonny and Jeff, told the crowded funeral hall about Abie's dedication and hard work at the synagogue. Young and old, men and women, were in tears when the stories were told about the man of little physical stature but of great love for all people and for his religion, in particular. The funeral service became also an inaugural ceremony for the newly appointed rabbi at Stanton, who officiated for the first time in a public service.

PAST AND PRESENT IN THE LIFE OF A COMMUNITY

I did not present the Stanton Street Synagogue as a story about an Israeli who discovered his lost roots. I do not feel stripped of the authentic Jewish culture or indifferent to my ancestors' heritage. My Israeli education, in spite of the experience in a religious elementary school, had left me secular. But, my early religious schooling served me well, since it enabled me to integrate into the dynamics of synagogue life. Compared with Cowan (1982), who felt compelled to retrieve and reclaim his personal identity in Jewish history, I have had a clear notion of my place in the Jewish saga. Zionism had assigned my generation of *sabras* with a special role—that of the new Jews who master their destiny in an independent nation state. David's father's complaint about young Israelis, who have been removed from Judaism, had revealed that irony. The first generation of Zionist immigrants to Palestine and their *sabra* children recreated an Israeli culture in clear opposition to the East European Jewish heritage nourished at Stanton. Nevertheless, I was fascinated with the commitment displayed, by the younger people in particular, to revive the Stanton Synagogue. They seemed not much different from me in the background of close history, their professional careers, and world view. It was an "accident" that took their parents or grandparents to New York while, about the same time, my ancestors landed in Jaffa. It could have happened the other way around.

No doubt, thousands of Jews have converted during the generations and more have left the folds of practicing Jews of all shades. But many others, the Stanton crowd included, had, in Gedaliah's terms, displayed their "stiff necks," or had the Jewish virus "ingrained in their psyche." Recent studies have already indicated the religious resurgence and the rise of Orthodoxy among American Jews (e.g. Waxman 1983, Heilman and Cohen 1989, Don-Yehiya 2005). However, with not much probing, one could suggest that the Stanton congregants are not basically different from many millions of Americans—Christians, Jews, and members of other denominations—who congregate in small groups (e.g. Wuthnow 1994, Shokeid 2001). Religious organizations are still probably the most successful agencies for initiating support groups and responding to the quest for community, these days as in the past.

The proliferation of voluntary associations in American society, first identified by Tocqueville in the 1830s, has not lost its potency. The Stanton synagogue association seems also an expression of that American tradition of civic society. As already suggested by researchers, when people claim community membership they are simultaneously expressing their personal and social identities. True, concern about the decline of community in America over the last quarter-century was raised recently by Putnam (1995) in particular.

One expects an anthropologist to identify the shared personal characteristics that explain particular group participation and other specific common behaviors. My fieldwork at Stanton was of a shorter duration than my previous ethnographic projects. I do not refute the possibility that a more rigorous research might have identified some more definite social or psychological characteristics shared by the "Stantonites." But even had I been engaged with the Stanton congregation for a longer period, I believe that I would have confronted a few major problems. Are there really easily identifiable elements that might explain who the "joiners" are, and what separates them from the many thousands of Jews—married, single, men, women, heterosexuals, and homosexuals—in all parts of the city, who do not join a synagogue in any of the various Jewish movements? Similar queries have been raised also in other ethnographic studies of synagogue life (e.g. Heilman 1973, Prell 1989, Shokeid 1995)

What seems extraordinary in our case has been the great variety in the personal backgrounds and life styles of the younger congregants at Stanton. A few had a good Jewish education and were brought up in practicing families, like Baruch, David, Moishe, and Peretz. A few became Orthodox by their own choice, like Jeff, Erik, Jonathan, and Jonny. Others had a more standard American Jewish experience that could not foster their commitment to an Orthodox synagogue, like Neal, and Dov. But the practice of Orthodoxy by not a few among the participants had actually displayed a life-style and a level of ritual observance that might not have been easily condoned in other synagogues. That freedom, however, was usually tolerated by the more strictly observant at Stanton. "We are accepting" (Peretz), "No one tells you how to dress" (Neal), "No one comments about others' behavior" (Jeff), "I feel I am in wonder-land" (Moishe)—these are a few of the expressions of that social ambience in the synagogue.

In casual conversations, one is often told that people join synagogues because they are concerned about the cultural identity of their children (as stated by Neal). But a few among the more active members at Stanton were single or had no children, like Jeff, Peretz, David, and Moishe. However, they all came from a comfortable family background, were engaged in satisfying professional and economic positions, were mostly in a stable emotional state of mind, and had close relatives and friends beyond the borders of the Lower East Side. In sum, they seemed, to the accidental observer, as remarkably ordinary – just "normal."

Expressed in different terms, they all confessed a commitment to continue or even actively revive a cultural heritage. It was the respect and sentiment to honor those many generations of Jews, their ancestors, who had so adamantly and lovingly kept the *mitzvoth*, such as the taboos of *kashrut*, and the performance of the rituals of the services. Although most of the congregants were not directly related to the founders—those who had come from the shtetel of Brezezan—nevertheless, they felt it was the place of their own ancestors. Dov presented that position eloquently when he claimed that his association with the synagogue affirmed his identity in time and space. Elissa told me that she could not separate her identity from the Lower East Side, and from the Stanton Synagogue more specifically.

In sociological terms, it seems most appropriate to define the Stanton congregation "a community of memory".[2] The "Stantonites," maintained a rich web of memories rather than the usual application of the term to a specific source of a group's memory. The Jewish text of memories included naturally its religion, the painful history of the nation—most visibly illuminated with the tragedy of the Holocaust, life in the pre-Holocaust East European *shtetel*, the immigration to America, and settlement in the Lower East Side.

---

2   For example, Hawlbachs 1992, Myerhoff 1978, Rosaldo 1980, Bellah et.al. 1985, Boyarin 1991, Herzfeld 1991, Tonkin 1992, Zerubavel 1996, Climo and Gattell 2002, Shokeid 2007

CHAPTER ELEVEN

It was the old age of the site, the simple furniture, the cracks in the walls—all that seemed so shabby about the synagogue that gave it the aura of authenticity. The group had living representatives for the more recent dramatic experiences in that collective memory. The presence of the older congregants born in Eastern Europe, Benny and Abie in particular, made that connection to a past heritage and to the chain of generations more apparent. Having been born in Eastern Europe situated the older members as genuine agents of this connection.

For most groups defined as communities of memory, their members look to the past as a strategy for grappling with the present and preparing for the future. The past, reminiscent nostalgically and often glorified, endows the present with meaning and justifies daily routine activities. So too for the people in our account: preserving the heritage embodied in the Stanton synagogue engaged them in diligent work and investments for the sake of "our *kehillah*." The synagogue, as a site and as a social group, has become an extension of the territory of home as well as an expansion of the network of one's family and close friends. This work of imagination and true devotion endowed the "small shull" with a "big place" in Jonny's heart.

That record of the dynamics at Stanton, however, is not unrelated to the observer's own feelings. My attraction to the Stanton congregation communal project entailed also a fascination with what many Israelis miss in spite of the myth and practice of the Israeli "togetherness." Israelis often feel a sort of camaraderie at meeting their compatriots. They nurture many shared experiences—the army service, the wars, the suicide bombers, etc.—and in general, they have been nurtured in a small intimate society. They look for the company of their compatriots when they are among strangers. That has been observed, for example, in the "tribal" behavior of young adult Israeli backpackers, when they take their popular long journeys, after completing the mandatory army service, to the Far East or South America (e.g., Noy and Cohen 2005). That sharing, however, is not demanding in terms of building more stable associations and institutions. But, at home, Israelis have the State and other public agencies that take care of their national memories and provide the organizations and services that are frequently provided in the United States by voluntary associations. Israelis differ greatly from their American brethren in their lack of the motivation and skills for building and joining voluntary-communal societies and institutions. The hallmark of Israeli pre-State pioneer communalism, the kibbutz, has been lost long ago.

I observed that inability in my study of Israeli immigrants in New York. As described above in Chapter 8, they maintained informal networks of friends, but, unlike other groups of recent immigrants to New York, the growing Israeli constituency has not established its own communal organizations. They have also not joined the local Jewish institutions. In my own experience as an Israeli citizen, I can attest that Israelis love their close friends, but are not enthusiastic about joining and regularly contributing to the life of voluntary associations. In sum, I enjoyed the experience at Stanton of being so warmly adopted into a society of (Jewish) strangers. They made me feel as if I had been reunited with a group of lost relatives and with the history I share with them.

Jonathan, a congregant at Stanton and an anthropologist, had wrestled with contemporary proponents of the theory of community concerning the dilemma of the morning *minyan*, which I would summarize as: "is it, or is it not, a community?" Jonathan ended his story of a struggling *minyan* at the same Stanton place with "…we might dare call [the minyan] …Shhh!… community" (Boyarin 1996:86).[3] I reported above on that synagogue's life twelve-fourteen years later, in the "totality" of its *minyan* services and other social activities. I feel I do not need to wrestle any more with the sociological discourse about the feasibility of fitting the term "community" to my observations. Why not take seriously the "natives" when they talk about "our *Kehilla*" or "our community"? I believe, that Emil Durkheim, the great Jewish sociologist (and descendant of a distinguished rabbinical family) who taught us the basic elements of social organization, had he come for a visit to Stanton, would have confirmed the Stantonites' claim.

---

3 One could also refer to another ethnographic study of a *minyan* in New York City, in the South Bronx (Kugelmass 1986)) and ask: "is it a community of mourners" (saying *kaddish* for each other)?

PART FOUR.
GAY JEWS

CHAPTER 12.
THE TALMUD CIRCLE: IDENTITIES IN CONFLICT

*Like the last column of some ruined temple,
he remained standing mute and solitary in the middle
of the otherwise deserted room.*

Herman Melville, Bartleby

If a gay synagogue seems a paradox to the traditionalist, a gay Talmud class (*shiur*) can appear completely surreal. I remember the bewildered reaction of my colleague and Orthodox friend Shlomo Deshen who joined me for a lecture at the Congregation Beth Simchat Torah (CBST). He noticed a group of somber-looking men seated around a large table at the center of the community hall. When I told him they were studying the Talmud, he didn't believe me. "They can't be using a real Talmud text!", he exclaimed. "Go and see for yourself", I answered. "But how do they resolve the theological problem? How can people who consider themselves orthodox be gay at the same time?" This dilemma, introduced by a casual visitor, sets out the major issues of this chapter: Why do people whose behavior is considered abhorrent in the words of the Torah and the eyes of traditional Jews, enthusiastically endorse the text that is considered among the highest symbols of Jewish religious engagements and participate in a style typical of traditional orthodox synagogues.[1] And why are they tolerated by their fellow "sinners", who openly challenge the upholders of their shared stigma?

---

1   See, for example, Heilman, 1983.

The Talmud class I observed as part of my ethnographic study of spiritual and social life at CBST (Chapters 13, 14, 16),[2] was started in 1975 and consisted of a core of ten men in their late thirties to early fifties, most of whom had attended for many years. There were other men—and a few women—who were related to the group through their loyalty to and affection for its leader, Aaron. They rarely attended weekly classes but often participated in holiday parties. Both core and peripheral members were mostly professionals (computer programmers, educators, lawyers, etc.), with a few engaged in business. In contrast, to the majority of CBST members, the behavior and attire of the group resembled more traditional elements in Jewish society. Several wore black suits and hats, tzitzit[3] and yarmulkes. And they eschewed the hugging and kissing typical of CBST.

I was told that there had been a woman in the class, for nearly a year, who had learned Talmud from her father. A few other women joined briefly but, lacking her exposure, dropped out. Younger women who in recent years have gained a better Talmud education did not seem attracted to this traditional group of middle-aged males. I managed to keep up with the class, though with some difficulty, because of my elementary religious school training and knowledge of Hebrew.

The sexual orientation of the participants was not inquired into. During my time with the class an Orthodox man joined the group and was assumed to be gay. Later it was learned that he was not, but simply felt more comfortable there than in the mainstream Orthodox society, from which he was alienated. He untimely dropped out, for unrelated reasons, but remained on friendly terms with the members.

The class followed an unvarying routine: it met every Tuesday evening at 7:30 and ended at 9:30 after a short break for Ma'ariv prayers. The first ten or fifteen minutes were usually devoted to "schmoozing" about work, relatives, the health status of friends with AIDS, and political developments, particularly in the Middle East. With most of the members assembled, the class resumed the reading and discussion of the Talmud. In March 1989, for

---

2 See Shokeid 1995: 2003, for a comprehensive presentation of the ethnography of CBST.
3 Tzizit (Hebrew) are ritually tied fringes worn by observant Jewish males on four-cornered garments.

instance, several meetings were devoted to the issues of tithing (*ma'asrot*); a series in June 1990 probed the practice of shofar blowing; September 1990 was taken up with a discussion of whether an egg laid on the Sabbath could be consumed on the next day if it were a holiday.

These esoteric legal issues of ritual and practice were meticulously pored over until all the participants felt satisfied with the interpretation reached. The reading of the text was shared by most of the class including one Gentile who had learned Hebrew under the guidance of a knowledgeable member. Most also did homework to familiarize themselves with the text. The analysis often prompted far-reaching discussions related both to biblical and modern times. Aaron comparing tithing to income tax and inferred that not all Israelites were scrupulous in the observance of *ma'asrot*. Why else would Boaz's permitting Naomi and Ruth to glean be seen as an act of generosity to kin, when the law conferred this as a right? Another suggested that religious conflicts between the Pharisee and Sadducee sects might be comparable to the assault of the Reform and Conservative movements on the hegemony of one *halakhic* interpretation. A week later, still focusing on *ma'asrot*, an animated discussion of the Messiah ensued. Would the Jews rebuild the Temple and resume all rituals including animal sacrifice?

Linguistic queries often set off lively discussions. Edward, with his Ph.D., in classics, was particularly instrumental in revealing the philological and phonetic sources of the Hebrew and Aramaic Talmud. Wasn't the Hebrew term *yovel* (a cycle of fifty years) associated with the Latin *jubilee*? What was the source of the Hebrew term for rice *orez*? Edward assumed a Greek origin. After the Talmud class conversation continued as the members walked together to the subway or apartments in the neighborhood.

A different atmosphere dominated the Talmud class holiday parties, which were celebrated in the homes of the inner and outer circle. The Purim party of 1989 was given by a member who rarely attended regular meetings. His elegant East Side apartment offered a sharp contrast to the barren community room, notable for its lack of intimacy. Aaron brought a cassette of Hasidic songs to guide a sing-along. Its highlight was a Yiddish melody with the stanza "The rabbi commanded that one must be *freilach* [gay] every day until the last white day [the day one is buried in white shrouds]". The association of the rabbi's command for happiness with the term for *homosexual* caused much delight.

Joseph suggested that a man who is gay every day keeps the angel of death away. Someone invented another line adding to the amusement: "A gay every day keeps the doctor away". In the spirit of Purim Aaron offered an interpretation for the popular belief that King Akhashverosh invited Queen Vashti to attend a party dressed only in her crown. Apparently the king and his guests were completely drunk when someone in the crowd claimed the king was homosexual. He immediately challenged his accuser: "I'll call for Queen Vashti and you'll see for yourself if I am homosexual!" Such direct and humorous references to the sexual orientation of the participants were very rare in other meetings of the Talmud circle.

More typically, the following Passover the group was seated around a large table in Aaron's modest Upper West Side apartment for the final holiday meal. The participants were called on to discover new theological ideas in the Hagaddah text. It was nearly dusk when Aaron expressed his deep feeling for this holiday of freedom and the rebirth of nature. He pointed to the trees outside with their new-green leaves, a beautiful color unique to spring. Now, nearly dark, the Sabbath clock switched on the lights. All were intensely looking at Aaron as if by some magic he could prolong the last day of the holiday. The spell was only broken as Aaron bid the group join him for evening prayers at the nearby Spanish and Portuguese Synagogue. Gay identity had hardly been referred to in this celebration, which had lasted many hours.

The core of the Talmud class consisted of men who had been exposed in their youth to some form of Jewish life. Most had been raised in families affiliated with the Conservative movement, but others had come from orthodox and even ultra-orthodox backgrounds. A few had attended yeshiva. But at a later stage they had all abandoned Jewish life, unable to accommodate their sexual identity to Jewish dogma on homosexuality. Joining CBST was the first step they had taken toward reconciling their gay and Jewish identities.

Though differing in specifics, Ralph exemplified this pattern of Jewish departure and return. Described by Aaron as a "sixties leftist", Ralph told me that his return to New York from California was much influenced by his discovery of the Talmud class. He first heard about it from another member who was visiting San Francisco. Ralph thought how wonderful it must be to experience something more authentically Jewish. He was tired of the atmosphere in California and wished to return to something older and more stable. Ralph believed that Jewish identity could offer much more than gay identity: "What is gay identity—gay bars, Bette Davis movies, and a few other things of that sort?" When he came to New York, he immediately joined the Talmud class, which was his first introduction to that scholastic tradition. By the time I met him he attended services at CBST only occasionally, regretting that the synagogue wasn't more traditional and therefore, in his words, "more authentic". This differed from his initial assessment upon arrival in New York in 1983: "I was surprised that unlike the San Francisco gay *shul*, which was Reform or 'creative' in style, CBST was traditional, with lots of singing and a surprisingly large weekly turnout.[4]

In spite of Ralph's commitment to the Talmud class, he did not excel. He usually looked tired and had to make an effort to concentrate. He admitted he sometimes had second thoughts about his participation, but he did not give it up. Ralph's attraction to Talmud learning, despite his difficulties with the Gemara text, was eloquently expressed in the following: "It's like listening in on a long-distance telephone line to hundreds of Jewish conversations over the centuries. You feel as though you are suddenly connected to an uninterrupted Jewish channel of debate and discourse that goes back to Mount Sinai".

Ralph's disaffection with the CBST service—despite his commitment to the Talmud class—reflected the history and evolution of these two respective bodies and the individual who at one time united them. When Aaron began the Talmud class the synagogue itself was only two years old

---

4   The earlier interview with Ralph ('Ramifications' in the original text from 1983) appeared in a symposium on Judaism and homosexuality. See Rabinowitz, 1983.

THE TALMUD CIRCLE: IDENTITIES IN CONFLICT

and Aaron was its spiritual leader. Reminiscing about that time, Aaron told me he wanted to develop a community of people who would share major Jewish values. It was part of his perception of Judaism as a religion and a way of life that had to be practiced in community. He did not wish to see a synagogue that was essentially a cruising place where people showed up until they found a partner and disappeared.

This vision attracted a number of adherents who, along with Aaron, followed a path of increasing traditionalism. As expressed by one of his disciples: "Aaron hoped to develop full Jewish life. He wanted a place where gay Jews would feel comfortable at fulfilling Jewish life. He was ready to compromise for an interim period—he considered *yerida* for the sake of *aliyah* [a kabbalistic phrase meaning going down for the sake of going up]." But this traditionalism, as already described in an earlier chapter, was ultimately out of step with a congregation growing in number and diversity. As a result, Aaron left the congregation which took its own direction, but remained with the Talmud class on the periphery of CBST.

Since then, Aaron discovered he could fulfill his spiritual needs within the social context he had escaped many years before. He joined an orthodox *shul* in Manhattan. "It is my community; I pray with them; we talk and gossip together. True, I am somewhat peculiar because I am not married, but I don't advertise my sexual identity". Aaron went on to assert that most congregants in regular synagogues also have their own peculiarities: "It is foolish to assume that so-called orthodox are 100 percent Orthodox!"

This nonconfrontational strategy was also employed by a few others among the Talmud circle who joined Orthodox synagogues in Manhattan and Brooklyn. They claimed that the situation for gays had improved immensely in recent years. Nachman, a strictly observant *ba'al tshuvah* (one who turns from secular life to Orthodox Judaism), argued that as long as gays don't make a fuss, they can enjoy a tolerant atmosphere in many synagogues. Ten years ago gays were ostracized, and therefore CBST was very important. But now, he went on, "there are many CBST graduates in other synagogues".

Although Aaron described the Orthodox synagogue he adopted when he left CBST ten years earlier as "my community", he did not give up his deep involvement with the Talmud class. "It is a primary group", Aaron explained, defining the Talmud circle in sociological terms, "but this activity also carries some *kedushah* [holiness]". He went on to say that the members were close friends, often speaking to one another. He knew how important the meetings were to its members, for whom this was a very meaningful community. "When men are young the search for sex is their major goal; but when they reach the age of forty that drive declines, and then they discover loneliness". Aaron further observed that homosexuals don't constitute a community any more than the people on my block do". As Edward, another class member observed: "Someone who has never studied Gemara can't really understand the bond that is created among those who study together". Thus, in their religious life Aaron and the rest of the Talmud class belonged, in fact, to two, if not three, communities: the Talmud circle, and their primary synagogue—CBST for a minority, an Orthodox *shul* for the majority. But even among the latter a few remained associated with CBST through occasional attendance at religious and social events.

Tuesday evening was often a time for many busy activities at CBST. While the Talmud class met at the center of the community hall, other meetings might take place in the sanctuary, the library, the office, or in another part of the community hall. On June 26, 1990, for example, the Talmud circle prepared for the *siyum* celebration marking the completion of a volume of the Gemara. The big table was covered with a lavender tablecloth (a delicate reminder of gay identity) and loaded with a variety of salamis, salads, drinks, etc. In the sanctuary the trustees met for an executive board meeting. In the library the former presidents and a few other influential members were planning the inauguration ceremony of the Holocaust Torah scroll. At a later hour a few participants at the library meeting joined the celebrants at the Talmud table and were invited to partake of the food. Once the group was short two men for a minyan for the Ma'ariv service. Aaron went to the office and brought along the synagogue's secretary and another active member. On another Tuesday evening a large crowd attended a film in the sanctuary and a noisy meeting of the High Holiday Committee went on in the library. Morris, one of the committee's members, who years ago could not accommodate Aaron's growing orthodoxy, spent some time before the Talmud participants showed up chatting with Aaron about mutual friends and family affairs. Once the class began there were no further interruptions. The class carried on its business as usual, in spite of the noise of arguments heard from the library and the constant movement of people coming and going to the film, the rest rooms and the kitchen adjacent to the Talmud "corner".

After one Friday service I unexpectedly met an Orthodox Talmud class regular. He humorously derided the service and added that to his astonishment an earlier Gay Pride Week service he attended had introduced a Christian melody [in a bid for universality] and deleted the Amidah.[5] This skepticism about the quality of Jewishness at CBST formed one side of a smoked glass through which each group reflexively viewed the other. An incident on a busy Tuesday evening offered an observation from the other side: Leon, a past president, leaving a board meeting to make a phone call, paused on his way to the office when he heard voices coming from the library, through which he had to pass. Suspecting the Talmud class in an unaccustomed location, he asked in a timid, yet sarcastic voice—to the amusement of the other trustees—"Are the *Jews* there?"

The ambivalence, if not resentment, toward the Talmud class membership was not uncommon among the congregation. Simon, who still fondly remembered the first years with Aaron, nevertheless believed that he and his group were too ethnocentric: "They believe the Jews are better than anyone else…. They are too traditional; too confined to the words of the text". Simon was puzzled by the Talmud circle's growing Orthodoxy, a tendency no less evident among those with Gentile lovers. He saw Aaron's departure from CBST as proof of his failure to convert the congregation to his style of increasing Orthodoxy. He didn't see it as a conflict between

---

5   The *Amidah* is the core and main element of each of the prescribed daily services. The *Amidah* must be recited standing silently and no interruptions of any kind are permitted.

leading members but as an ideological and social split that left Aaron in the minority. Another former admirer of Aaron summed him up in a metaphor of Jewish New York geography: "Aaron first left Brooklyn for Manhattan, but then he made it all the way back to Brooklyn, though he stayed on in Manhattan!" A recent congregant commented, "I don't understand Aaron and his group who endorse Orthodoxy which denies gays and holds them in contempt".

But on another occasion Simon expressed his astonishment with Aaron's decision to carry on the Talmud class at CBST. He assumed that Aaron could hold meetings at his apartment and avoid the trouble of travel with no loss of attendants. Simon concluded: "This is Aaron's statement that he is still part of the synagogue". And when preparations were being made for CBST's eighteenth anniversary celebration, it was Simon who suggested that Aaron be invited to lead the commemorative Friday night service (an unusual gesture considering their latent competition, for when Aaron gave up his position at CBST Simon was among the first to take over his spiritual leadership). On the same note of reconciliation, a member of the education committee suggested that Aaron be invited to deliver a series of lectures on Judaism on a level equal to that of his Talmud class. The surprised committee agreed but had difficulty finding an intermediary to make the offer. Finally, I, a quasi outsider, was enlisted for this mission.

If these attempts were sometimes awkward, three members of the Talmud class regularly crossed the bridge over the schismatic divide. Despite decreased participation of the Talmud circle in CBST services, Edward and Dov were still regularly attending and, often, giving sermons. Nathan was a frequent visitor and occasionally acted as service leader. These three were the most active "go-between" members and were respected at CBST where they had close friends. They regularly brought back information to the circle about developments in the synagogue. During the Rosh Hashanah party, for example, Dov described the "super-feminist" service he had unhappily attended, which led to a discussion of the plan to appoint a professional rabbi at CBST, a position the leader of that service might fill. This radical proposal, announced by the synagogue's board several months before, was no less hotly debated by the circle than by CBST itself. Though they had grown apart, Talmud class and synagogue were not indifferent from one another. Despite its apparent alienation, as expressed by both sides, the Talmud class was still woven into the fabric of CBST.

THE TALMUD CLASS AS A SOCIAL TEXT

On reading Heilman's (1983) description of Talmud classes he observed in Orthodox and Modern Orthodox synagogues in Israel and the United States, I was struck by how closely the gay Talmud class I observed conformed to the general phenomenon of Talmud study (*lernen*) in traditional Judaism. It conformed in the structure of the social relationships, the content of the activity and its impact in terms of "cultural performance".[6] Aaron is not unique in his position as an admired teacher and moral guide. In all Talmud circles Heilman observed, the rabbi was a central figure, at once warm and authoritative. The notion of fellowship among the *learners*, their deep attachment and commitment to one another, was another shared characteristic. Applying an idea Clifford Geertz developed elsewhere,[7] Heilman interpreted the Talmud circle activity in the following—a description equally valid for the CBST group:

> Attending a *shiur* in the intimate atmosphere of the study circle may be understood as "a kind of sentimental education", during which what one "learns is what his culture's ethos and his private sensibility look like when spelled out externally in a collective text"(61).

---

6   See elaboration of 'cultural performance' in Chapter 9.
7   See Geertz, 1973.

Or,

> Both the process and product of such lernen provide "the structure of meaning through which men give shape to their experiences"..... The result of all this may be not so much a scholarly education as a sentimental one, an infusion of cultural ethos and worldview. In the cultural performance of lernen, men... express and act out Jewish beliefs and ideas... while exploring the contemporary in light of the tradition. (109)

If not for its location in a gay synagogue, the uninitiated might not be aware of the unconventional identities of the members of the Talmud circle at CBST. The visitor might notice that during class the learners wandered into subjects unrelated to the text, a process that enabled all to take part and made the Talmud study more relevant to contemporary life. But the difference between the CBST and other Talmud groups was more evident when the group met together outside the context of lernen. For other groups these social occasions were often dictated externally by events such as birth or death and involved family members not otherwise engaged with the group's activities. In contrast, the CBST circle's seasonal parties were opportunities for forceful expression of the members' unique identity and existential circumstance. The additional participants involved were not outsiders but a wider constituency supporting the core from which these activities grew.

Heilman was inclined to see Talmud *shiur* interaction in terms of Victor Turner's "social drama".[8] In the CBST circle I found less social drama during the analysis of the Gemara. The close relationships between the participants going back to their own past at CBST and the intimate knowledge they shared about members, old and new, muted any competition between actors as well as confrontations at difficult textual points. The bonds engaging the circle carried an emotional and moral commitment far stronger than that described by Heilman. The social drama I witnessed played to a wider audience and followed a different script.

---

8   See Turner, 1957, 1974.

The dramatic tension of the Talmud class was in its challenge to several worlds. As actors, the members forced their presence and particular configuration of religious and sexual identity on both their Orthodox and gay Jewish audiences. They were active in Orthodox synagogues but at the same time preserved their stronghold at CBST. True, they kept their sexual orientation secret in their newly adopted "Brooklyns", but it was a secret known to many non-gay fellow congregants. They were not revealed, nor were they denied the right to full participation in ritual and communal affairs. This unwritten compact was based on their acceptance of the basic tenets and ideals of traditional Judaism, including those most relevant to their existential situation.

Aaron told me he never gave up the hope of raising children. He had a dream of one day finding a woman who would cherish his promise of an affectionate relationship and devoted parenthood, but without sexual passion in their marital life. Aaron and his lover agreed that neither would stand in the other's way if this opportunity arose. I assume Aaron knew it was an impractical idea, even though he could relate a few instances where it had occurred, one involving a former member of the Talmud circle. Aaron admitted he was conservative in his view of Jewish life, and assumed that the continuity of Judaism required that of its people. He regarded his hope of fathering children - a belief that might materialize - as he did his strong conviction of the coming of the Messiah.

Aaron's vision was not shared by most of the other Talmud class members, who wished to adhere to Orthodox Jewish life without conforming to its norms of sexuality and reproduction. That approach was clearly expressed by Nahman: "Yes, there are problems, but a life of Torah and *mitzvos* is worth maintaining, even if one is negligent in one area of observance. Aren't there countless fine people in all committed Jewish circles who neglect one major mitzvah or another?" In another conversation Nahman differentiated between desire and action: "*Taieva* [lust] is not an *aveira* [sin]", only acting on it is. This distinction may be drawn from traditional assumptions that distinguish between transgressions forced on the individual by drives beyond his control and those deliberately undertaken with a free will. Rather than a clear-cut distinction between observance and sin, Nahman suggested an incremental scale in the failure to observe the halakhic prohibition against homosexuality. Though he himself did not long for offspring, Nahman, no less than Aaron accepted the normative expectations of a full Jewish life. Both endorsed the historical power of religious law, Halakhah, to preserve the Jewish people and culture precisely because it did not submit to frequent changes.

This doctrinal position was contested by several others in the Talmud circle, including Ralph and Dov. Ralph argued, "I refuse to believe that my loving a man is sinful. I think that the Halakhah is wrong in this area. Unfortunately, Halakhah changes very slowly". But only the strictly observant Gary refused to accommodate on any terms. He demanded that his Modern Orthodox congregation accept him as an openly gay Orthodox man. His claim was denied, and he was not supported in it by his gay friends in the same synagogue. But, at the same time, the straight congregants, who must have suspected the bonds between Gary and other unannounced gays, have not denied the others the honors and privileges of congregational life that Gary lost because of his conspicuous behavior.

The majority of CBST members did not differentiate between the delicate shades that colored the Talmud circle's theological position. Their synagogue was a haven (a "safe space") where they could express their Judaism as determined by gay Jews. The concealment of sexual identity in the house of prayer, where one comes for comfort, assurance and spiritual fulfillment, was considered a complete surrender to oppression. In this context the continuing presence of the Talmud members in the middle of CBST appeared like a scene from the theater of the absurd. "The Jews", as Leon derisively nicknamed them, appeared as "Orthodox impersonators" - gay men masquerading in the role of their major adversaries in Jewish society. Were they giving in to Orthodoxy? Or co-opting it, forcing it into the society and house of sinners?

Esther Newton (1972), who observed female impersonators, analyzed their impact on gay audiences and emphasized the duality they represent. They are evaluated positively "to the extent that they have perfected a sub-cultural skill and to the extent that gay people are willing to oppose the heterosexual culture directly. On the other hand, they are despised because they symbolize and embody the stigma" (104). Above all, the drag queen expresses the incongruity that is basic to the homosexual experience. The Talmud class was not performing in a rehearsed gay play but nevertheless contained elements of Esther Newton's portrayal. In the context of CBST this company of men seriously engaged in Talmud study, many in Orthodox garb, presented a social incongruity. But as skilled students of the Talmud they were also an implicit challenge to the tradition and institutions of Orthodox Judaism, which explicitly deny gays the status of moral personae. The return to Talmud study, which represents the highest intellectual achievement and purest scholastic occupation in Orthodox Jewish society, was a triumph gained after many years. From the vantage of the general CBST membership, however - much as they might applaud the Talmud circle's skill - the scene that it presented was taken from the most oppressive element of Jewish society. And as such it was a reminder of the stigma imposed by its people and theology. These mixed feelings of fascination and resentment, anger and affection that were often manifested by CBST observers poignantly communicated the duality embodied by the Talmud class.

My sociological imagination leads me to interpret the intricate relationships I observed at CBST's "Tuesday Play" in a Geertzian tradition - that of the images and cultural strategies employed to symbolize and give meaning to the individual's existential position and social identity. Resented or beloved by their spectators, Aaron and his circle embodied Orthodox authenticity at CBST. How else are we to understand the invitation to lead the commemorative service or to deliver a lecture series on Judaism? No doubt, nostalgia for the synagogue's early days played a role here. But if the Talmud shiur was a permanent reminder of CBST's institutional past, it was no less a reflection of the spiritual and social alternatives available to all Jews, gay included. For both audiences the Tuesday Talmud activity made possible a regular observation of their gradual development since their first reconciliation with, and open expression of, their yearning for Jewish life. That juxtaposition, irrespective of the growing difference and self-assertion on both sides, has offered a continuing link with the historicity of Jewish culture and Jewish identity on the part of CBST's congregants. And on the part of the Talmud class, their use of the premises of the expanding and prosperous gay synagogue has offered the vicarious experience of observing the unrestricted display and expression of homosexual identity in a Jewish milieu. Here they could witness the harvest of Jewish gay liberation, which they abandoned in their search for Jewish authenticity.

CHAPTER 13.
"THE WOMEN ARE COMING":
THE TRANSFORMATION OF GENDER RELATIONSHIPS IN A GAY SYNAGOGUE

Scholars who have explored the relationship between religion and the social order suggest that the invocation of the transcendence offers a key part of the process of legitimating gender hierarchy. The subordination of women in ritual activities and their denial of access to positions of religious leadership had been a powerful tool in most world religions in supporting the patriarchal order and the exclusion of women from the public forum. The religious sphere has thus constituted a major field for male domination, and a strategy to deprive women of public authority.[1] This issue has been succinctly addressed by Sered, who studied women's religions: "feminist anthropology has treated religion as the ideological foundation of and justification for patriarchy; through religious doctrine and ritual, women and men are persuaded of the rightness of male dominance"(1994:4). The gradual process of women's empowerment in mainstream religions and their entrance into roles of authority has engaged researchers in various denominations. For example, Lehman (1985;1993) who studied the position of female ministers in the United Presbyterian Church US, found that a minority of resentful male congregants could handicap the recruitment of female ministers. A supportive majority of church members might hesitate to nominate women to leading roles because they assumed that women would disrupt the harmony and cooperation in the congregation.

---

1 See, for example, Ortner 1974; Wallace 1997; Scott 1988; Jones 1993; Sered 1994,1998; Franzmann 2000.

CHAPTER THIRTEEN

For many generations, the synagogue was a male space in Jewish society. Following the code of *halakha*[2] that maintains men's superior status in religious affairs, women were relegated to secluded galleries and were not expected to take part in most ritual activities. The integration of women as equal partners in religious life has been an issue that, for many decades, engaged the more liberal Jewish denominations. Women's position in the Reform and the Conservative movements has undoubtedly changed dramatically compared with the status they still maintain in synagogues associated with the different shades of the Orthodox movement.[3] Even more radical have been from start the changes in the status of female participants in the Reconstructionist movement and the *havurah* congregations, the most radical genre of Jewish religious life.

The Reform movement synagogues had been the first to accommodate with a more egalitarian pattern of women's participation. These changes included the adoption of mixed seating early in the second half of the 19th century, and at later stages, the inclusion of women in the *minyan* quorum,[4] the development of bat-mitzvah ceremonies, allowing women to lead prayers and take part in handling the Torah, to be called up for *aliyot*,[5] and, in 1972, the ordination of the first female rabbi.[6] This process of female participation was considerably slower in the Conservative movement synagogues. However, even in those Jewish communal organizations where women did come to attain positions of leadership, their

---

2   Halakha - The entire body of Jewish law.
3   The orthodox position was clearly expressed by Rabbi Nisson Wolpin, editor of the *Jewish Observer*: *...abandonment of exclusivity of roles for men and women is not at all a liberation, as touted. It is the forcing of people into roles for which they are not suited, really limiting their opportunities for fulfillment* (1974: 15).
    There must be feminine answers [my emphasis--M.S.] *to Jewish women's continuing search for enrichment and fulfillment* (1974: 18).
4   Minyan - A minimum of 10 Jewish males required to be present to conduct a communal religious service.
5   Aliyot - The act of proceeding to the reading table (on the *bimah*) to bless on the reading of a portion from the Torah.
6   See, e.g. Lerner 1977; Pratt 1980; Wertheimer 1987; Fishman 1993.

path was sometimes painful. Their employment opportunities have been limited and they have had to confront a far more judgmental audience.[7]

My work at Congregation Beth Simchat Torah (CBST), the synagogue for gays and lesbians in New York, offered a most revealing case about the various themes relevant to gender equality in synagogue life. One might assume that gay men who had given up the most elementary responsibilities and privileges of their patriarchal position as household leaders and in the roles of husbands and fathers, would also ungrudgingly relinquish the privileges of males in religious life. One can wonder, therefore, to what extent a synagogue that caters to people who proclaim their same-sex orientation, reflects, or, alternatively, diverges from, the major patterns of gender-hierarchy relationships in mainstream synagogues?

As observed and documented in this paper, the entrance of women into the major arena of ritual and organizational life was not a simple matter, even at CBST. The congregants' sexual orientation--their "deviance" in terms of *halakhah* norms (which condemn homosexuality) and the shared experience of their rejection by mainstream Jewish congregations, did not immediately erase the vestiges of patriarchal religious traditions at CBST. Nor did these factors easily mitigate the resentments and competition that separate men and women in the various domains of synagogue life. I concentrate with the arena of public life, and, in particular, men's reactions to the emergence of "women's power," as represented in the growth of women's membership and their occupation of key positions of leadership and prestige.

The purpose of this chapter to identify the social dynamics that empowered the lesbian congregants to claim for an equal share with the men in ritual activities and in organizational decision making. I will explore

---

7   Fishman (1993:218) described the position of Jewish women in leading roles:
    Many women who have succeeded in acquiring positions of leadership in Jewish communal life have found that their competence and/or their executive methods are frequently challenged. Both female rabbis and female federation executives have found that their fiduciary skills, especially, are the subject of skepticism from male congregants or colleagues
    .

the circumstances that invested female candidates with leadership roles, and with authority, in both spiritual and institutional domains. Though not written from a feminist perspective, I believe my presentation contributes to the issues that have engaged the ongoing discourse about the dominant code of masculinity and women's struggle for legitimate authority in the public forum.

CBST REVISITED

I completed my CBST ethnography (Shokeid 1995) with the event that seemed among the most dramatic since the synagogue's foundation twenty years earlier--the inauguration, in September 1992, of Sharon Kleinbaum, its first pulpit rabbi. On my return to New York in 1995, when the book had already been published, I found the synagogue had gone through immense changes. I did not repeat the method of intensive observations I employed during my earlier association with CBST, and visited the synagogue only sporadically during 1995 and in later years. Nevertheless, I presume that I have sufficient data to allow me to describe some of the changes that have effected organizational life and relationships in the synagogue in recent years.

Since the inauguration ceremony of Rabbi Kleinbaum, the synagogue has gained much media attention. An eloquent public figure, skilled in promoting various issues related to the position of gay people in general, and in the Jewish communal arena in particular, the rabbi raised much enthusiasm. She also revealed a very captivating and persuasive personality. The number of female congregants expanded dramatically[8] and the rabbi became a subject of adulation by many women in particular. However, many men were also among her admirers.

It was not only the synagogue's demography that changed significantly since Rabbi Kleinbaum's inauguration. During the rabbi's first

---

8   By the end of the 1990s, the number of female congregants almost equaled that of the male constituency.

term in office, the board of trustees elected a woman as chair. Sheila,[9] strong willed, efficient and no less cunning than some previous powerful male leaders, became a close partner to the rabbi's agenda of congregational development. The only previous female President was actually a temporary episode, a compromise nominee during a conflict between two leading men and she survived in office for one year only during the early 1980s.[10] But in Sheila's case, she defeated the man who was considered her equal.

Soon after my arrival in New York, I met with my close friend Jeffery who told me he was no longer paying his annual fees to CBST. The people he wished to meet were not there any more, many had died (of AIDS), and he was not comfortable with the "political correctness" of the rabbi who was preaching: "have a family" (meaning, go through a commitment ceremony with your partner and raise or adopt children). He quoted a couple of close friends who had also moved away, who were close to Martin (the chair who orchestrated the search of Rabbi Kleinbaum and who had passed away one week before the inauguration ceremony), and who had told them before he died: "the women are coming!" Jeffery himself was not sure whether Martin meant to point out a fact, or if he was issuing a kind of warning. In any case, whatever Martin had actually said and meant on his deathbed, Jeffery used this prophecy in order to convey his feelings about the changes that took place since he and I had last met at CBST. No doubt, as I discovered on my first visit to a Friday service which coincided with CBST's 22nd anniversary, the crowd was composed of more women then ever before. The choir and its musical female director, who also played the piano, added an artistic element I had never experienced before at CBST's services. The rabbi, in the role of service leader, was welcoming the big crowd that showed up. At that service I met my old friend Ron who soon introduced me to a young man who had recently gone through a

---

9   Except for Rabbi Kleinbaum, I changed all names of male and female participants.
10 See Shokeid 1995:182.

commitment ceremony with his partner of nine years. Ron commented that the rabbi was influential in that direction. However, another veteran male congregant who overheard our conversation described the new trend as "an epidemic".

During the next months I attended services, board meetings and other events that became a stage for some major discourses and conflicts that evolved as consequence of the transformations the synagogue went through since the installment of Rabbi Kleinbaum. I attended a Sunday congregational brunch that was scheduled to allow the members to meet with the rabbi and board of trustees in order to discuss their expectations for the future. The board of trustees had also changed much since my last stay. With the new by-laws adopted sometime earlier, instead of the body of ten trustees that carried most public functions and headed most committees, it now included 9 men and 9 women, and was supposed to be composed of 24 members within a few years. The gender parity on the board was also a remarkable change compared with the poor representation of women during my earlier stay (when one, two or three women at most were on its ranks).

About fifty men and women showed up at this brunch and expressed their visions for the synagogue. The audience included many veteran members, but more were new faces, and mostly women. Many among the participants wished to see CBST in its own building with sufficient space to accommodate its growing membership and offer various activities for an heterogeneous constituency. Those who voiced that opinion seemed to perceive CBST in its present premises as somewhat invisible and outdated. A few veteran active members reacted indignantly. They considered that approach degrading and dismissive of the synagogue's history. Ron voiced more emphatically his feeling that the synagogue was already too big and was going to lose its special attraction with further plans of growth and gentrification. The rabbi concluded the discussion as she related to Ron's complaint; do they want to limit the synagogue's membership to those who are already there, or do they wish to see it preparing to welcome those many gays and lesbians who are "out there"?

"THE WOMEN ARE COMING"

A few weeks later I attended a major public event, the annual elections to replace and add new board members. That coincided with the announcement of the rabbi's new five year contract, the result of the negotiations that Sheila (the chair) had carried out with the rabbi and had already confirmed with her colleagues on the board. It was a contentious issue since a group of men and a few women, mostly from among the veteran membership, considered the package (to start with $103.000 a year and reach $129.000 on the fifth year) as too expensive and a burden on the synagogue's funds. A larger crowd than usual on these occasions showed up. Naomi and her partner told me that they changed their plans in order to attend that event. They heard that "Norman and his guys" were planning to contest the contract since they opposed both the rabbi and Sheila. Norman was a former chair who considered himself custodian of the synagogue founders' legacy. He hoped to retrieve the style of a lay-led congregation. Some of Norman's followers, Naomi explained, were practically unemployed or earned modestly, and therefore complained: "why should the rabbi get a lot of money?"

A few days later, as I was on my way out from a Broadway show, I met an older male couple who commented angrily about the exorbitant package the board bestowed upon the rabbi, "The American President gets $200.000, but the rabbi gets already $100.000!" They seemed also angry that the women so massively supported the rabbi, and told me they might resign from the synagogue.

THE "SEX SCANDAL"

The opposition that was simmering for some time against Sheila, the chair, because of her supposedly authoritative style of management that culminated with the controversial contract, reached a new zenith when a rumor spread about an extra marital affair that Sheila was having with another female congregant. To the delight of Sheila's opponents, it proved a more complicated entanglement than first rumored, and three couples were embroiled. Although all individuals concerned continued to participate in regular activities and no scandal exploded in public, juicy gossip circulated among both men and women. Norman saw the clumsy affair as almost a sign from heaven, and believed the time was ripe to unseat Sheila and avert the track of changes she was leading. His accusations against her regime and personal characteristics were now buttressed by his appeal to the breach of public morals inappropriate for a synagogue leader.

Norman was not alone to criticize Sheila for the turmoil she caused and the people she hurt. Even women among Sheila's supporters were offended by the salacious story that seemed to prove that women, despite stereotypes to the contrary, were not free of sexual misconduct. For many years and particularly with the devastation of AIDS, gay men were carrying the blame and stigma of promiscuity, something that seemed remote from the habits of lesbians. In a tone mixing astonishment and amusement, using Hebrew as form of disguise and familiarity, Jean asked me loudly: "*shama'ata al haskandal?*" Have you heard about the scandal? Sheila was present not too far away from our spot at the entrance to the synagogue.

Norman called upon a meeting at his apartment in order to negotiate Sheila's impeachment. He invited board members, men and women, those he believed were opposing Sheila's term or were offended by her recent misconduct. But to his disappointment he discovered there were not enough votes for a step to unseat Sheila. A few of the supposedly most conservative board members revealed a strong stand against public interference in private affairs. Even Carol, who was among the severest critics of expenditures, did not join forces with Norman's group. The same went for Ron, who was usually in the minority on the board and was not among Sheila's fans. They refused to adopt the role of moral prosecutors. The rabbi kept a distance from the embarrassing commotion, well aware of the different views and sensitivities of the parties involved and the rest of the congregation. I would have not related this affair, had it not been so poignantly expressive both of the more visible divisions and rivalries as well as the more latent opposing perspectives in the synagogue. I perceive the event and its repercussions as part of a "social drama," in the terms suggested by Turner (1996 [1957]).[11] It not only mirrored conflicts in the congregation, but it also served as a catalyst for an evolution that will be discussed below.

Sheila's adversaries also assumed it was her idea to change the by-laws that expanded the board of trustees. Critics of that change complained that the new system deprived the minority of any impact in decisions and policy making. They believed that Sheila hoped to get a better hold of the synagogue affairs through the new executive committee of close associates. In fact, it was mostly Leon who had initiated the change of by-laws as part of his usual concern with organizational development. But Leon was also influenced in that direction by the rabbi who had her own perception about stages of synagogue growth. They both believed the synagogue needed a larger board that would better represent a congregation that expanded so much since the original by-laws were first introduced. No doubt, Sheila was a willing partner to that move.

Sheila proved herself an effective and independent leader, the first woman to exhibit that extent of personal authority. Moreover, she had not reached that position supported only by the new wave of "lesbian power". Sheila consistently enjoyed the backing of a few leading men, Morris and Leon in particular. For many years Morris was the most influential congregant at CBST who served twice as chair, and was a leading figure in New York's gay community, while Leon, also a past chair, was an astute politician respected for his organizational skills and vast experience. Contrary to Norman and his friends, Morris and Leon believed there was not at this time a male candidate ready to take the role of chair. Too many of the generation of men that might have successfully competed for the job

---

11   Victor Turner divided the social process which constitutes the social drama into four major phases: (1) Breach of regular norm-governed social relations between persons or groups. (2) Mounting crisis with tendencies to extend and expose dominant cleavages within the relevant social group. (3) Redressive mechanisms, informal or formal, brought into operation by leading members. (4) Re-inegration of the disturbed social group, or recognition of an irreparable breach between the contesting parties (1996: 91-94).

were dead. On the other hand, a generation of women who had not an opportunity in earlier years was available and ready to take charge.

Morris and Leon did not abandon Sheila at this difficult time. They could also rely on the support of other influential men who would not join Norman's agenda and would tolerate though not condone Sheila's misdemeanor. Thus, in spite of the blemish she suffered as consequence of her unbecoming conduct, Sheila survived in office until the end of her term. Sheila represented the deep change in the position of women at CBST. Acting together in harmony with the rabbi, supported by some of the most astute male politicians and benefactors, she exhibited a transformation in public life that would have seemed a fantasy only a few years earlier. She seemed to have gained the type of personal and institutional authority hitherto denied from female congregants.

It is my premise that the "sex scandal" initiated a discourse that engaged both men and women in a subject that was rarely shared before. The men seemed pleased to have discovered that lesbians are sometimes no less involved than men in "sleazy" affairs. Moreover, they claimed that gay men couples had never separated with so much fanfare as happened with the couples involved in the "sex scandal." The women, however, noted that gay men carried on extramarital affairs either in agreement with their spouses or else they cheated on them without being revealed, protected by the far wider opportunities for sexual escapades in various specialized institutions and in public places. At the height of the Sheila affair, Norman argued disdainfully: "The men also fuck around, but not with their friends' boyfriends!" Carol, however, contended that gay men could more easily separate between the private and public domains, something that demonstrated again the differentiation of power between men and women. The lesbians were socializing in close networks that also often were the core groups of lesbian and gay organizations. That intensive socializing sometimes threatened the stability of couples. However, the scandal was contained, much due to the comportment of Sheila and her partner, who kept in complete silence the way they handled the crisis until they finally separated (they also demonstrated a civil demeanor months later when Sheila appeared in public with her new mate).

RECONCILING WITH CHANGE

In spite of Sheila's efforts to avoid further resentments, it was difficult to avoid contentious issues. For example, at one board meeting, Annette, a distinguished veteran congregant, informed her colleagues that the search committee she headed had interviewed the candidates for intern assistant rabbis and found two outstanding women candidates. Unfortunately, she explained, there were no male candidates. Sheila expressed hesitation about the prospect of these appointments and the subject was delayed for discussion at a later date. But at the next board meeting, Annette announced her committee's decision to hire these two excellent candidates. Quite agitated, Ron complained they had already three women and not one man in religious leadership positions. He continued: "You know I love our women, but I and many others are uncomfortable. Together with the toll of AIDS, we feel we are being wiped out." He went on to complain also about the change of the synagogue's name in official correspondence to "The Lesbian and Gay Synagogue". It was first "The Gay Synagogue," then it was "The Gay and Lesbian Synagogue", so, Ron exclaimed, "who takes these decisions?" Though less provocative in their reaction, in the eyes of not a few men, the leadership of women, installed in the positions of rabbi, chair, intern rabbis, and musical director, was representing the loss of a space that used to be their own creation and made for gay men. For these men, it was an invasion of guests who took over their home.

Nearly a year later Norman believed he could at last win back his losses, get elected to the board and lead the synagogue again "on the right track". As he told me at that time, he had enough votes to secure his election as well as supportive colleagues on the board that would nominate him as their chair. He promised friends and foes he had no plans to unseat the rabbi or the musical director. True, he thought the rabbi had surpassed the borders of her role within and outside the congregation. "She is not a pulpit rabbi"[12] he told me. But, he argued, he mostly wished to get people to work again and avoid extravagant expenditures. Despite his assurances, many congregants and in particular the women, believed Norman was planning a coup that would eradicate the major changes at CBST. Even Leon was worried, thinking that Norman as chair would create an atmosphere "uncomfortable" for the rabbi.

The elections proved Norman's worst experience in years. In a congregational meeting, as part of the election tradition, he also presented his agenda. He was "baited," I was later told by a man who attended that meeting, and he revealed his ill feelings against the apparent "feminist take over of the synagogue." "He made it clear he hated women!" Norman was booed unceremoniously by the large audience that showed up in fear of his planned coup. Soon afterwards Rebecca was elected to chair the board of trustees.

The expansion of the lesbian constituency and the increase of commitment ceremonies also meant that adoptions and birth of children became a new feature in CBST's public life. There were a few couples who had children prior to the rabbi's arrival. However, these were isolated cases that carried little impact in synagogue life. In recent years, though, twenty young children were considered as related to the synagogue. Even the rabbi was a parent to her partner's children, whom she brought along on special events. The synagogue's program included special activities for children and their parents.

I observed men reacting differently to that new phenomenon. Simon, my close friend and veteran active member, was very pleased with this change. He told me he considered the presence of children an important development of "normalization" in their life. Reproduction is the first *mitzvah* commended in the Torah, unfortunately denied from gay people. The arrival of children, he argued, brings them closer to mainstream synagogues. But at the same service when six children were continuously roaming around,

---

12 Pulpit rabbi – A rabbi who concentrates with the tasks of teaching and preaching sermons.

another veteran male congregant told me he felt the loss of a "safe space," he missed the atmosphere of an "all adult" synagogue. He was unhappy that CBST was moving closer to a mainstream synagogue. During Kol Nidre, the most evocative Yom Kippur prayer, Sheila walked around trying to pacify her crying baby. Nobody publicly commented about the disturbance, but Gershon, who often told me the lack of children was among the most painful losses of gay life, was obviously annoyed by the noise children caused during the Kol Nidre service. In a depressed mood he indicated that commotion as one of the things that have transformed CBST.

Gershon, had many reasons for his gloomy disposition. He felt he was part of a lost generation. Firstly, because many among his friends have died of AIDS. Secondly, because he was aging, and at 50 he felt the younger generation of men, and the women congregants in particular, did not share his memories. They also believed they knew everything better than the older men. Gershon thought the men were more sensitive to the feelings of women when the latter were in the minority, compared with the women's lack of understanding of men's sensitivities. For example, as service leaders, men were careful to call on women to read part of prayers. But the female service leaders, he often observed, called only their lesbian friends to come up to the *bimah*. Gershon felt he could not approach the rabbi with his personal "tzores"(afflictions), she is too busy. Even Larry, always amicable in his approach, claimed that the rabbi was too political, busy and remote, she is not "Sharon," she is "the rabbi." "We don't need a star," he told me, "but a spiritual leader."

No doubt, the congregation was far too big (about 800 dues paying members) and heterogeneous in the religious background and personal needs of its membership, men and women. It was impossible to satisfy all levels of Jewish experience and spiritual expectations among people who included some men in particular who had a wider knowledge in Judaism, and other congregants, including more women, who had only a limited exposure to Jewish religious education and rituals. Also women were sometimes disappointed, as Jane, for example, who admired the rabbi at start, but then thought she had not sufficiently integrated a feminist approach to her teachings and prayers. For example, the rabbi maintained as major text for Friday services prayer book, the Siddur, that was compiled by a three men committee in 1981. Another woman complained about the atmosphere of theatrical show that detracted from her cravings for spirituality, as happened, for example, on Yom Kippur when the rabbi tested the microphone system in a humorous style that was meant to entertain the congregation.

A few veterans among my close acquaintances left the synagogue because they resented the new mood at CBST. Zeev, former member of the religious committee, and Henry, former trustee and liaison to the Religious Committee, both had left for B'nai Jeshurun (an uptown famous Conservative congregation). The services at the uptown synagogue has become, in recent years, a major attraction among younger Jews. In addition, B'nai Jeshurun supported a gay social circle and advertised its activities in its synagogue's bulletin. Zeev, who joined B'nai Jeshurun, could not cope with the combination of women's growing dominance supported by the circle of men he was not part of. He could neither wholeheartedly join forces with Norman, whom he considered an old fashioned traditionalist. And frustrated, he told me the women would soon double their numbers at CBST, implying a cancerous bubbling of cells. But he could not also reconcile with a complete withdrawal from CBST. In the meantime, he maintained close ties with old friends and was a regular participant at the more intimate Sabbath morning services that have not changed much. These monthly services were still mostly attended by the old crowd, and the women who joined accommodated with its more traditional style. Here Zeev felt at home and a base to maintain his affiliation with CBST.

The rabbi was naturally aware of the attraction and the competition introduced by the gay-friendly atmosphere at B'nai Jeshurun. The services at that congregation were very impressive. The musical skills of its leaders made each visit an exceptionally uplifting experience with no comparison to other synagogues. Although Rabbi Kleinbaum claimed it was a good development that gays and lesbians could look for alternatives, nevertheless, her efforts to improve the quality of services at CBST showed her concern about the style of a lay-led congregation adopted at CBST. The appointment of a musical director was indeed one of the rabbi's more cherished innovations. At the same time, however, innovations in services and a somewhat stricter control over the competence of cantors and service leaders resulted in the resentment of the "traditionalists" who lamented the loss of the spirit of a lay-led congregation. For some members, it was probably easier to accommodate to a new congregation than tolerate change at their own synagogue. Thus, Henry, who opposed innovations at CBST, joined B'nai Jeshurun and did not show up again at CBST, even though he had been among its most dedicated members during my earlier stay in New York.

Another new development, implemented in 1996, was the change of the dues system. Instead of the $200 annual fees paid by all, it was decided to adopt a sliding scale structure based on income (starting with $275 for those who earn up to $20.000, $350 for the $20.001-$35.000 earning category, etc.). Those who opposed the present regime, symbolized by the rabbi and her supporters, considered the change another step that eradicated CBST's tradition of equality and open doors. Norman now claimed the rabbi preferred a small congregation of wealthy members. As proof, he indicated the growing respectability, elegance and more expensive entrance fees for the annual celebrations and the following sumptuous dinners. The board also decided to advertise the names of donors and the amounts of their contributions to the synagogue, instead of the old tradition of confidentiality that preserved equality in the congregation. Even supporters of the board like Carol (herself a trustee) were worried by the implications of heavier fees. But Leon had no doubt the synagogue must change the dues system and improve its financial structure similar to the norm in mainstream synagogues. Other gay synagogues, he emphasized, had fees that have often been more substantial compared with CBST. A modestly salaried female congregant told me the problem was not with those who could not afford the increase, but with those who could afford to pay more. She believed the dedicated members of modest incomes would make an effort to pay the basic fee, but that the wealthier would need to be encouraged to make a greater contribution.

CHAPTER THIRTEEN

Without doubt, the new system meant a major change: from an almost negligible contribution for fully employed professional men and women, to an admission of one's financial situation and payment of a share of income in a style similar to mainstream synagogues. It was a gamble taken by the leadership headed by women, but supported by the remaining active male congregants among the founding generation of CBST, Morris, Harvey and Leon in particular. Harvey was among the most generous members. It was his contribution that financed much of the intern rabbis and the musical director expenses. Also most other men of that generation remained loyal under the new regime.

I was standing in a crowded spot at Washington Square watching the Gay Pride Parade as it got close to Greenwich Village. I was happily greeted by the older couple whom I met at the theater a few months earlier, and who told me then they would leave the synagogue. Now they asked me, obviously proud, if I attended last Friday Pride service. A huge crowd attended the service, it was reminiscent of a Rosh Hashanah full house service. They had not left the congregation, even though the number of women was already probably equal to the men, and in spite of their conviction the congregation needed a social worker rather than a rabbi (to deal with the AIDS victims). It reminded me of Leon's assertion that Norman and his friends would not desert CBST: "Where else would they go to, this is their place!"

Norman himself, whom I met after his humiliating experience on the previous annual elections, told me he was attending services "out of spite," no one would drive him out of his synagogue! He told me about the nadir of his fall from grace as part of a concerted effort to drive him out of power. His close friend David, a generous donor to the synagogue funds, but who was among the most consistent opponents against extra expenses, never forgave the new leadership for his loss of influence in running the synagogue. On his death-bed, David made his friends promise him not to let the rabbi officiate at his funeral. Norman was using an opportunity to express his grievances during the Yom Kippur *drashah* (sermon) that he was still entitled to present as ex-chair. It was a personal privilege the High

Holiday committee did not deprive him of, in spite of his tarnished status. He was careful not to mention specific synagogue affairs until the last sentence of his address when he asked his audience to check out with their own conscience whether they did not owe an apology to anybody they might have offended during the passing year. As he told me, six people (the rabbi included) called him up a few days later and apologized for not interfering or considering his pain when he was booed at the election meeting.

The rabbi was supported by a circle of women. These were close friends of Rebecca, the chair, and whom she could call on at any time. They were younger women who joined in recent years and were mostly professionals in positions equal to the leading men, though no one among them had the financial resources at the disposal of Morris or Harvey for example. But these men, and others, dismissed the complaints about the women's take over of the synagogue. They claimed that the women were hard workers and were ready to do any job while men were looking for special tasks. Was it a unique commitment and affection to a charismatic lesbian rabbi that made women take over Norman's legacy of volunteer dedicated work?

When Rebecca finished her Presidential fund-raising address on Yom Kippur, Gershon was deeply touched. He forgot his frustrations and he hugged her with great affection. Although Rebecca was no less dedicated and forceful than Sheila, her predecessor in the office of chair, she was softer in her appearance and projected a more relaxed and warm demeanor. Her speech touched upon sensitive nerves shared by gay men and lesbians. She told about the painful experience of the rejection by her parents who did not speak to her for three years, the reconciliation and recent return to her hometown. She was particularly moving describing her visit to the cemetery where close to the tomb stones of her grandparents she discovered the new grave of a schoolmate who had died of AIDS. Rebecca, no less than Sheila, maintained a style of authority that did not show a weakness often ascribed to women, yet she managed to project an aura of "compassionate authority"(Jones 1993).

Jean, who represented the "feminists" in Norman's eyes, was indeed close to the rabbi and Rebecca. Her own view about the situation at CBST was more complicated. I told her I was writing about the changes in recent years and asked her to inform me about the ratio of actual membership of men and women. In her e-mail reply of September 1998, Jean told me "it is about 60% men to 40% women." However, she also quoted Rebecca that said it might be approaching 55%: 45%. But Jean added her own perceptive commentary about my project:

> What I must tell you is that I don't think having a woman rabbi is that much of an influence on the increase in women's membership. It may or may not help and some of the old-timer women still don't think we need a rabbi at all…even though those attitudes have changed for the most part. I think it's all about women's increased expressions for a spiritual community. This is seen in all branches of Judaism, lesbianism may have little or nothing to do with it.

Sometime earlier, however, Jean told me there were many women who fell in love with the rabbi.

Although more women than men seemed to admire the rabbi and express affection toward her, there were also men who were no less "under her spell." They enjoyed the rabbi's multifold services, and particularly the special events during the holidays, as she always succeeded in combining Torah study with play and raise an emotional excitement through group discussion. I have already mentioned Morris and Leon, but also Harvey, Simon and other men I knew before she came, thought Rabbi Kleinbaum did "a marvelous job." As the huge crowd was ready to leave the Javetz Convention Center[13] at the end of the Yom Kippur Ne'ilah service, Harvey with tears in his eyes asked me: "Isn't that a miracle?" He repeated the same question a year later on Simchat Torah[14] as the crowd led by the rabbi

---

13 In recent years CBST rented for the Yom Kippur service a large space at the Javetz Convention Center in order to accommodate a crowd of 3000 people, as part of its "open door" policy.

14 Simchat Torah—A festival that marks the completion of the annual cycle of the reading of the Torah in the synagogue.

continued the *haqafot*, parading with the Torah Scrolls late into the night, very joyful and exhilarated.

DISCUSSION

For over a century, the issue of gender equality in Jewish ritual and Jewish communal life has been tackled by the more liberal denominations in America. However, the evidence from mainstream synagogues and national Jewish organizations has often reported that the integration of women in leading positions has been slow even in the more liberal denominations. These accounts describe the resentful reactions of male congregants toward Jewish feminists, and recite claims that the presence of feminists will cause many men to leave the fold.[15]

In contrast, and in spite of the complaints by men reported above, the growth of the female constituency at CBST was almost immediately reflected by the entrance of women into all fields of public participation and their partaking in leading positions. Women were equally represented on the expanded board of trustees and two lesbian presidents had held office consecutively. The authority they gained was not ephemeral nor of a lesser weight compared with that hitherto exercized by male congregants. Moreover, they displayed an energy to initiate and support new projects and policies that were transforming the synagogue's organization, its decorum and style of ritual.

My observations reveal that the reaction of men toward the growing presence and roles of women was not unanimous. A minority was adamantly resentful and militant to the extent of trying to unseat the lesbian leadership and drive out the "feminists". Another, less identified group of men who were also uncomfortable, but not ready to join the militants. They either left for alternative synagogues (B'nai Jeshurun in particular), or remained discontented, feeling deprived of a "safe space," nevertheless, unable to give up what they considered their lawful inheritance and "home." But the majority of men, including the remaining members of their former

---

15   See, e.g. Cohen 1980; Wertheimer 1987; Horowitz et al. 1998.

cohort of leaders, were satisfied with the new energy stimulated by the female rabbi, the female officers and the dedicated lesbian crowd.

A most pertinent case to compare with CBST is offered by Prell (1989) in her study of a *havurah* congregation.[16] The *havurah* had probably attained the most egalitarian structure in Jewish congregations. As Prell discusses:

> Contrary to traditional law, women were given all the same ritual rights and obligations as men…The *havurah*, in essence, produced a generic Jew, male or female, whose religious participation no longer depended on gender (1987:173)

However, when Prell observed the *havurah* membership during the festival of Simchat Torah, she discovered the issue of gender was not neutralized: "Their explicit commitment to gender equality was nevertheless countered systematically…men not only dominated formal roles, but engaged publicly in humor that by any account was sexist"(174). Prell concluded that the eradication of gender was possible only as long as the participants maintained carefully assigned roles, "when the *havurah* scenario and the traditional Jewish scenario are carefully meshed"(187). Otherwise, the perceived traditional scenario, controlled by particular men, dominates in fact. Prell considered the field of Torah text humor a dangerous terrain that revived old prejudices and cleavages between the sexes in a heterosexual congregation. Her analysis left little doubt about the precarious gender balance apparently achieved at the *havurah* services: "every time gender relations are reintroduced in the *havurah*, when the generic is partitioned into male and female, hierarchy and exclusion result" (188). But, as observed at CBST, the field of humor seemed far less threatening as an agent for gender animosity in the company of gays and lesbians among whom sexual inversion, drag and other presentations of camp are important cultural features. The field of Torah humor lost here its discriminating relevance and not only

---

16 *Havurah* congregation – A movement of small, informal, prayer groups, first founded in Boston in 1968. I am not using the specific name Prell gave to the congregation she observed.

because of the culture of camp. The rabbi, a woman and a lesbian, proved her superior knowledge and sagacity, in presence of the synagogue's most learned attendants. She was also very skilled in the use of humor in and out the context of ritual.

My description of the relationship between men and women at CBST was not engaged with issues of ritual. The arena under observation for this presentation was mostly that of synagogue organization and leadership. I related to issues of ritual in my earlier work, for example, the elimination of *dukhanin* (1995:109-110). That important ritual, the blessing of the Cohanim (the clan of temple male priests),[17] was discarded completely already in the late 1980s, because the women considered it a male chauvinist tradition. During my visit at the 1997 Day of Atonement, all congregants, regardless of sex and association with the Cohanim clan, were invited by Simon to partake in the *dukhanin* ritual. It was thus completely stripped of its traditional elements, and was tolerated as a bad joke by some male traditionalists. Simon, who was often engaged in ritual innovations considered himself a feminist. None of the humor described by Prell that recalled a gender partition of the "generic Jew" was employed on that occasion. Though not intentionally, the *dukhanin* I observed on Yom Kippur turned a most sacred ritual into a campy performance. In conclusion, when CBST's congregants were called upon to choose between "having a gender or being Jewish in the way they believe is appropriate," as formulated by Prell (188), they seem to have chosen a different path from that displayed in the *havurah*. The field of ritual was far less contentious at CBST. The men were accommodating with changes in ritual and texts that were deemed necessary from the position of gender equality.

The choice of a female rabbi reveals a paradox in gender relationships at CBST. The attitude demonstrated by the majority of gay men did not reflect, in any way, the bitter observation that concluded Lacks' overview of the position of American Jewish women (1980: 196):

---

17   The Cohanim come up to the *bimah* and bless the congregation through a prescribed sacred ritual.

And even today, many are reluctant to accord the woman rabbi the kind of recognition she has earned. More and more congregations accept the idea of woman as rabbi intellectually, but have not yet fully endorsed that acceptance emotionally.

The respect accorded to Rabbi Kleinbaum signified the recognition of a woman's skills in the hitherto Jewish male scholastic domain and thus "degenderized" Jewish traditional scholarship. But the perception by men of the emerging lesbian *communitas* as consequence of her appointment seemed to contradict their egalitarian sensibility.

The apparently accommodating attitude of gay men toward the religious demands of the lesbian constituency seems natural for a society of homosexuals. After all, gay men share with lesbians a stigmatized identity and a hostile social environment. But while the majority of gay men seemed at ease with gender equality in the spiritual and ritual domain of synagogue life, nevertheless, many seemed less accommodating with the organizational and social implications of the expansion of the female population and their growing share in leadership positions. However, that reaction is not a unique phenomenon. Also Lehman (1985), in his study of the United Presbyterian Church, reported that male congregants resented women's performance in leading roles mostly because of organizational concerns.

For that ostensible incongruity at CBST, I suggest two major constraints that conditioned the response of gay men when confronted with the lesbians' claim for gender equality in their synagogue. Firstly, many gay men experienced synagogue life as children and adults in mainstream synagogues—not a few in Ultra Orthodox or Modern Orthodox congregations. Thus, they have been exposed to traditions that nurtured men to take a leading part in synagogue activities (Alpert 1997:68). Secondly, the founders of CBST were mostly men. For many years it was mainly a gay men's space.

Gays and lesbians working together in organizations and leading concerted political action in the public arena is relatively a recent phenomenon.[18] Even today the majority of gay men and lesbians in New York main-

---

18   See, for example, Sedgwick 1990: 255; M.Stein 1994: 87; A.Stein and Plummer 1996: 137.

tain and patronize separate bars and other same sex associations. From the point of view of many CBST congregants, their synagogue was for many years just one more place in the plethora of gay men's exclusive spaces in Greenwich Village. They could ignore the presence of a minority of lesbians who were usually self segregated in a few front rows and who usually left early during the social hour after prayers (Alpert 1997:68). Although gay men had sometimes developed close relationships with particular lesbian congregants, that did not detract from the perception of CBST as mostly a male territory. If we combine the effect of an early Jewish religious upbringing, with the later experience of male *communitas* nurtured in the exclusive gay men's associations and territories for social and sexual activities, we could expect even a stronger opposition against the growing presence and influence of women at CBST.

Anthropologists have identified the field of conflict as a major arena for their understanding of the dynamics of change in small tribal societies.[19] But this mode of interpretation, that often deducted macro-societal transformations from the micro/local reality, lost its attraction as it became associated with the genre of crude functionalism and positivism. Incidentally, rethinking the *havurah* phenomenon, Prell was attracted to the ethnographic work on gender relationships in African cultures, and ended her discussion (190) comparing the rites of women's role inversion and reversal in Zulu society (Gluckman 1965: 253-58) with the tradeoff of the innovations in ritual for the *havurah* women in America. I was also tempted to employ the conflict resolution mode of interpretation initiated in the studies of small-scale societies, as I tried to comprehend the relatively smooth, though not harmonious, process of gender accommodation that I had witnessed at CBST. For this line of interpretation, I return to the major events that colored the period of my observations in 1995. Norman, his friends and others, including some women, assumed that Sheila's sexual misconduct legitimized a drive for her impeachment. Her male foes also considered the case an opportunity for the return to a past when men

---

19 See, e.g. Middleton 1960; Gluckman 1963; Turner 1996/1957.

monopolized major activities and policies at their synagogue. But instead, I posit that the scandal—an event that I framed in Turner's terms of a social drama—helped to construct a new *modus vivendi* between the genders.

The lesbian congregants had often looked down on gay men for their alleged promiscuity and interest in "sleazy" sex. Gay men for their part, had also ambivalently perceived the far less provocative presentation of sexuality among their lesbian co-religionists. It was therefore startling, for both men and women, when a resourceful female President of a booming congregation was caught in an embarrassing extra-marital affair. Sheila seemed to display a mode of behavior that has been more often associated with gay men. Her defiant stand contested internalized beliefs about the norms dividing between masculinity and femininity.

It is my premise that the public turmoil, the moral debate, the containment of enmities, and the final reconciliation, helped to connect the separate worlds of sensuality and sociability as well as the shared obstacles and social pressures experienced by both genders in a same-sex oriented society. After all, it was the same problematic existential position concerning sexuality that made them build a joint community. At last, the "feminists" revealed their "true inner self," as lesbians, flesh and blood and …sexual.

The history of CBST tells us an interesting lesson. The gender equality gained there during the late 1990s was not the product of a more or less aggressive strategy aimed at political correctness. It was rather the culmination of some conditions and events that facilitated that process. I mention firstly the consequences of AIDS that diminished a cohort of male candidates for leadership, and opened the door for a generation of skilled women ready to claim for these positions. Secondly, the appointment of Rabbi Kleinbaum installed a female leader endowed with personal and scholastic attributes that could only be compared with the characteristics of Aaron, the first unofficial charismatic rabbi who led the congregation in the early 1970s (Chapter 12).[20] Indeed, Rabbi Kleinbaum contributed immensely to the self assertion of the lesbian audience as potentially equal to the male

---

20   For more details about Aaron, see, Shokeid 1995: 34-44.

crowd, also in the major field of their monopoly, that of Jewish learning. But, I emphasize no less the acceptance of women as equal sexual personae, and that on the basis of their comparable worlds of erotic life, independent of the male/female heterosexual syndrome and its hierarchies.

However, I presume the lesbian congregants maintained another advantage, as consequence of the more radical erosion in that religious context of the ideological premise that supports male authority in heterosexual society. As argued by feminists (e.g. Jones 1993:239), women have been denied of roles associated with masculinity as a result of the ideology of family and kinship that habituated us to identify paternal roles with authoritative roles. That ideology though eroded also in mainstream society, is evidently far weaker in a gay-lesbian social environment.

The testimony of gender equity in a gay/lesbian synagogue leads us back to Prell's notion of discontent about the precarious gender balance maintained at the *havurah* services. This contradiction raises a major dilemma: Since innovation in world religions must exist within a traditional ritual and textual structure, are Jewish women in mainstream communities inevitably contained by an explicitly male religious framework? Therefore, are heterosexual congregations inherently unable to erase the built in hierarchical gender partitions that characterize traditional religions? However, Scott's study (1988: 178-198) of the position of professional women historians, members of the American Historical Association, presents an interesting comparative case. The report from that society of distinguished academics recalls the structure of gender stratification observed in conservative religious organizations. Confronted with a male establishment, women historians employed strategies aimed to gain their own space of authority, for example, promoting the history of women. While there is an almost automatic assumption that religious institutions are resistant to gender equality, there is, it would seem, an equally quick presumption that secular institutions are able to eradicate inequality and become patriarchy free.

CHAPTER 14.
WHEN THE CURTAIN FALLS ON A FIELDWORK PROJECT: THE LAST CHAPTER OF A GAY SYNAGOGUE STUDY

In a recent article, Ruth Behar (2003:20) suggested that a notion of loss is the classical *raison d'être* ("the trope") of ethnographic practice. The mission of the ethnographic project is to save from extinction the books, culture, and social repertoire of the studied society. No doubt most ethnographic reports are chronicles of a time past and its lost realities.[1] In the epilogue to a new edition of my Gay Synagogue ethnography (Shokeid 2003:244-251) reporting on changes that took place during nearly ten years since I completed the observations for the 1995 edition, I suggested that we perceive our ethnographic texts as "layered ethnographies," a metaphor borrowed from archaeology. The synagogue society of the late 1990s was very different from that which I observed in the late 1980s and early 1990s. It is my contention, however, that anthropologists save also their own losses, as they record their memories and impressions of the worlds they observe and emulate during fieldwork. They do that already in the ethnographic texts that they publish on their return home; but more rarely, and evidently consciously, they express their manifold losses as they continue to study and revisit the sites and the people they introduced in their earlier ethnographies.

I intend now to narrate what I believe will be the final story to come from a research project in which I have been engaged for about 15 years. My association with Congregation Beth Simchat Torah (CBST) in New York has been an important component of my professional and emotional

---

1 Barbara Myerhoff introduced an exemplary case in her seminal ethnography (1978) of the life and memories of elderly Jews in Los Angeles.

life. During my last observations in the spring of 2004, however, I realized it was time to bid farewell to the institution that has been so dramatically transformed since I first passed through the doors of its sanctuary. It dawned on me that my ethnographic mission had been accomplished: I have exhausted my professional interest in that particular field. At the same time it seemed that I could not contribute any more to the people who now maintain the social and cultural scene of "my" fieldwork site.

When I first appeared in 1989 on the scene of CBST, at the Wesbeth complex in Greenwich Village (between Bethune and Bank streets), the congregants soon discovered they needed me in order to tell their story and enhance their claim of legitimacy in both the mainstream Jewish and gay worlds. On my part, I was excited by their determination, the audacity they demonstrated—the guts to challenge the institutional framework of the Jewish American establishment.[2] I admired their spirit of voluntarism. They seemed no less exotic and heroic than a "classical" fieldwork site in New Guinea. Fifteen years later, however, the premises of our mutual attraction were radically changed.

Before the era of reflexivity, ethnographic texts usually expressed the emotional notion of "from now to eternity"—the ethnographer remains permanently nostalgic and pained by the separation from his field. That separation was usually perceived as forced by the circumstances of geographic distance, research budget limitations, and other occupational constraints. Only a few famous "accidents" of strained relationships between the ethnographer and his/her subjects punctured that idyllic picture. Among these I recall the case of bad matching and mutual antipathy between Turnbull and his African hosts in a disintegrating Ik community (1972). Even more candid was Scheper-Hughes (2000) in her report of the aggressive reaction of her hosts in an Irish village who were offended by her published ethnography. The taken-for-granted conception of eternal

---

2   Until the late 1980s, except for the Reconstructionist movement, all other Jewish denominations had not openly acknowledged gay congregants in their synagogues. Since the 1990s, however, the Reform and the Conservative movements have made considerable efforts to welcome gay people to their congregations. But gay men and women remain ostracized by the Orthodox movement.

sentimental relationships between the ethnographer and "his/her people" became a sort of "must" in the records and ethos of anthropology. But that is now part of a disappearing professional reality of a one-time stretch of fieldwork stay in a remote and difficult to get to Third World location.

We usually feel obligated to present the stories of our "arrival" and "integration" into the field. It is generally assumed that this somewhat "traumatic" process deserves public knowledge because it might reflect on the quality of the data we have collected and presented in the final ethnographic report. Geertz's opening story ("The Raid"), in his Balinese Cockfight paradigmatic essay, is probably the most famous (1973: 412-417). Anthropologists, however, have far less frequently described their departure from the field. Turner's (1960) narration of his last meeting with his close African informant, Muchona, remains a landmark in the history of ethnographic writing. Read (1965) lamented his parting from New Guinea and particularly the separation from his informant and intimate friend Makis (his return visits to the site after an absence of nearly thirty years represent a different field of experience and personal circumstances).[3] So also does Abu-Lughod's (1990) description of the departure from a return visit to her hosts in Egypt and Wulff's (2000) last day of fieldwork at the Stockholm Ballet company. Most studies, however, end abruptly with the exit of the ethnographers, when the time and the budget allotted for their specific venture are spent. It is a job done, to be continued only if professional interest and circumstances encourage further research.

But that reality of work and feelings is much different for anthropologists who continue to visit and study the same community (often located in a closer territory). They experience more profoundly the dynamics and ever-changing circumstances of their research.[4] Not only the sites and patterns of life, but also the mutual relationships the ethnographer established with his or her subjects during fieldwork, change over time. That applies also to the varied and changing responses over time of our subjects, as well

---

3   See Read 1986.
4   See Kenna (1992), who returned to study a Greek island. Both the local economy and society, as well as her own personal status, changed over time.

as of those who have joined them at a later stage, to the ethnographic texts that introduced them to the world. The ethnographic text based on the observer's field notes, assumed to be accurate and disinterested, may not coincide with the participants' memories of the same event filtered through later developments and changing relationships among the participants.

I believe that we are equally obligated to our hosts, our readers, and ourselves to relate and analyze the experiences in the field and the continuing relationships with the people we study at later phases of our research and during the post-first-fieldwork journey. In sum, the stories of departure (in "love or conflict") and the "later-life" dynamics of fieldwork journeys are as important as the opening narratives in the saga of ethnographic writings. I proceed now to narrate the last scene of my observations and relationships, which I consider the end of the story, before the curtain falls on my role as ethnographer in my CBST project.

CBST REVISITED

After the publication of the 1995 ethnography, when Sharon Kleinbaum was first appointed as the first ordained rabbi at CBST, I wrote two more articles. A paper in *Current Anthropology* (Chapter 16) that displayed the process of writing the text of *A Gay Synagogue in New York* attracted the attention of *Lingua Franca* (Nussbaum 1998). To the extent that this discourse reached readers from CBST, I assume they appreciated its contribution to the reputation of their project.[5] Another article, published in *Ethnos* (Chapter 13), described the extensive changes that took place after the appointment of Rabbi Kleinbaum. The paper emphasized in particular the expansion of the lesbian constituency, the remarkable development of the formal organization, and the entrance of women to major roles of leadership. I described the bitter opposition of some of the veteran male congregants to the change of the gender bal-

---

5   See a supportive response ("A New York Observer") to my work at CBST by Regina Linder, an active member of CBST, in *Lingua Franca*, April 1998, p. 9.

ance of power led, in particular, by past-President Norman. My narrative displayed the abysmal defeat of Norman, who was isolated and ridiculed when other influential men from among the veteran core of the male leadership did not join his attack on the new leadership.

In the same article I summarized my observations of a somewhat embarrassing romantic complication among the lesbian constituency that involved a leading female congregant. Except for the unavoidable indication of the major character, I made no personal references to other women implicated in the story and gave no clues about the nature of the entanglement.[6] Employing Victor Turner's ideas of a social drama and the resolution of conflict, I related the event to a reconciliation process between the men and the women in the synagogue society. I posited that the incident presented men and women as sharing a similar plethora of intimate relationships and sensuality, instead of their stereotypical positioning as acutely contrasting in the domain of love and sex.

Although I assumed at the time that no one in the synagogue would ever come across this article published in a specialized European journal, nevertheless, I felt that my continuing relationships with the congregants obligated me to inform the leadership about my writings. I sent copies to Rabbi Kleinbaum, the current President—Rebecca, to Leon, a former President and a close informant, and last, to Jean, a close friend and a colleague (engaged in cultural studies) who was also active among the lesbian membership. I decided not to send a copy to Norman, who had shared with me his resentment and plans. I thought he might be offended by my report of his failure, and I wished to spare him further aggravation.

To my surprise, I discovered a year later that somebody had taken the initiative to anonymously circulate copies of my article among a wide membership of CBST, the women in particular. The rabbi and other participants suspected it was Norman's doing. According to that interpretation, Norman maintained the article proved that women were sexually

---

6 All names mentioned in my writings are pseudonyms, with the exception of Rabbi Kleinbaum and other two congregants who insisted on keeping their real names.

audacious and irresponsible. I was perplexed by that suggestion as I believed that my report was far less complementary to Norman. I did not meet Norman again and could not verify his role in trumpeting my article. His CBST membership was revoked some time later. In any case, the story of my *Ethnos* paper seemed to carry no repercussion on my relationships with the leadership during the occasions of my frequent sporadic visits to New York and to the synagogue in the early 2000s.

When I returned to New York for a two months stay in summer 2003, CBST had already relocated its Friday services to the larger and more attractive space at the Church of the Holy Apostles on 9th Avenue and 28th Street.[7] On my visit that summer to a Friday evening service, the first after a long absence, I was warmly approached by Ruth, the newly elected President. Ruth had not been a CBST member during the days of my fieldwork and was not mentioned in my earlier writings. The warm reception continued some time later when the rabbi, at the beginning of her sermon, told the audience that there were present a few guests, and she mentioned me as the author who "wrote about us," adding that a new edition of my book had come out just recently.

My experiences during the service made me aware of new tunes adopted for prayers and the introduction of trained cantors. During my "old days" at CBST, I was sometimes uncomfortable with the poor musical talent of amateur cantors. But, in spite of the professional performance of the two male cantors who officiated that evening, the unfamiliar tunes left me somewhat discontented. As I soon figured out, the new melodies were part of the rabbi's policy to improve musical standards at CBST, now led by a skilled musical director with a trained choir.

During the *kiddush,* the "social" hour after service, I met some of my old acquaintances, among whom were a couple of men in their late 50s who had joined the synagogue in the early 1990s. They were both successful professionals, and one of them, Abe, served on the synagogue executive board. Responding to my query about organization news, they

---

7   For more details about the change of location, see Shokeid 2003: 245-246.

commented, in a neutral tone, that leadership is mostly in the hands of women these days; however, Abe, the board member, continued that more women of better qualifications applied for the synagogue jobs. For example, heterosexual men would not apply for a rabbinical position in a gay synagogue, and that women were not worried that it might effect their future chances for a position in a mainstream synagogue. Moreover, he continued, women were ready to invest more time and work than men, for which he could attest by his own reluctance to take on the role of President. Abe confessed that he lacked the drive for that dedication.

I spoke to Ted, a respected veteran member, and a prominent professional in his field. I asked for his opinion about the changes he observed at CBST during the last few years. He told me, in a low tone meant to keep our conversation undetected by others standing nearby: "I am uncomfortable there are only a few men on the *bimah* [pulpit]." He mentioned the appointment of a female assistant rabbi. Ted agreed she was a good candidate, however, he believed that Rabbi Kleinbaum had a major role in her selection.

Ted looked around quickly screening the crowd of men and women and commented nostalgically about the late male Presidents I knew well, Martin and Morris, who he indicated could stand firm and fight for their positions on various issues. Unfortunately, he continued, Norman (among the few surviving former male Presidents) failed completely on the synagogue stage. He believed he could have his way at CBST, unchallenged by dissenting opinions. Martin and Morris he assumed would have had the stamina and sensitivity to stand up to the rabbi's preferences and check her power to mobilize the board to fully condone her wishes and plans for the synagogue.

Nathan, a veteran congregant and a friend who, during my fieldwork, had been editor of the synagogue newsletter, told me he continued to attend services although the inclusion of piano music disturbed his love of tradition. He also accommodated himself to other changes even though they had reduced much of the congregants' active participation in the services. On the subject of the men's loss of influence, Nathan humorously commented: "The men come and leave after they check out all those they could take to bed." By implication the lesbians were more seriously concerned with the synagogue than the men.

Daniel, who had often served as cantor during my 1990s fieldwork, remarked on the changes in the synagogue and the immense transformation with nine salaried employees (two rabbis, an executive director, office manager, music director, two part-time cantors, a social-worker and office staff). Nevertheless, he seemed content with the synagogue moving toward the structure of a mainstream synagogue. He was aware, however, that the changes at CBST possibly displayed a more general trend in the American gay movement by taking it closer to mainstream society.

As I looked around, listened, and reflected about the service, I asked myself: What has all that to do with the site, crowd, style of prayer, and leadership I was familiar with and wrote about? Moreover, I wondered; had I come today for the first time, how would I have reacted? Would I still have considered the place attractive for a fieldwork project? I tried to comprehend the sources of my disenchantment. Was it the loss of familiarity with the location (now at the Church of the Holy Apostles), the loss of my friends, or had I adopted the male perspective of the dispossession of their space? Alternatively, was the synagogue not exotic enough in its more elegant church premises, its professional style of leadership and more refined religious activities?

I decided to attend services at CBST's former site in the Wesbeth building complex, where those who refused to join services at the Church of the Holy Apostles (the Chelsea service) continued to pray in the old sanctuary that had been left intact (now called the Bethune Minyan). The membership at this service maintained the tradition of a lay-led congregation. They joined the main Chelsea crowd mostly on the major holidays in the Jewish calendar. For some time that congregation seemed to present a challenge to the synagogue's leadership. A few veteran men and women, with Norman at the helm, formed a visible constant protest against the desertion of CBST's "tradition" of a lay-led intimate congregation. But the growing attraction of the Chelsea service and Norman's failure in the contests for leadership brought about a serious decline of this congregation.

On my visit to the Bethune Minyan service the attendance was very small, numbering about fifteen men and women. Norman, whose membership had been revoked, had lost his last hold on the organization. Two veteran active members who continued to lead the service expressed their difficulties with the task of recruiting service leaders, cantors and *drashah* speakers. If the Chelsea service left me somewhat alienated because it was so radically transformed and lacked the cozy atmosphere of the early 1990s, the present Bethune event was indeed a depressing experience for me. The physical environment remained intact, but altogether the small group, the poor cantorial performance, and the joyless spirit displayed a shabby replica of the past crowded and lively, though sometimes hectic, services that had taken place at the same location. In conclusion, CBST of my ethnography could not be retrieved at the Chelsea church's gentrified site nor at Wesbeth (Bethune)—the "birthplace" and cradle of CBST. In any case, I soon went back to Tel Aviv[8] and left the issue dormant until my return a few months later for a six-month sabbatical.

FALLING APART

I was back for a Friday evening service late in February 2004. Ruth, the President, agreed to host me at the next Board meeting in March. I wished to attend a meeting of the board in order to compare notes with my observations years ago. I assumed it must have become a different institution with twenty-four members instead of the committee of ten trustees.

A few weeks later, relying on the President's friendly invitation to attend a Board meeting, I called on the synagogue office to verify the date and place. I arrived on time and was led by the office director to the meeting

---

8   I conducted my research during a 1989 visiting appointment at NYU, and during subsequent sabbatical leaves from Tel Aviv University.

room, which was already packed with more than twenty board members. As I took a side seat, I could identify only two or three faces. I remarked jokingly that I hoped I was not intruding. But in response, I was requested to leave for a minute and allow the members to discuss my presence. I left immediately accompanied by the executive director who informed me about the unexpected absence of the rabbi (whose sister was hospitalized) and the president (who had been hurt in a skiing accident).

I was taken aback when the executive director then returned to me, apologizing for the decision taken by the board not to let me observe the meeting. I departed in a civil manner, although offended and angry. I was vexed at how they could keep me out of their business meeting when I was the same person who wrote their history and was privy to many intimate stories relating to rank and file in the synagogue? What an irony. Only the other day I was requested to address the students of the Introduction to Anthropology class at NYU, who has been assigned to read my ethnography as a required text in the syllabus for the course. After all, I was invited by the President to attend the meeting. She was not there; nevertheless, I assumed, they must have known about me (although many of them joined the synagogue in recent years and had never met me before). I felt I could not attend again a CBST service knowing I would be met or seen by the people who had witnessed my disgrace.

A few days later I sent a letter addressed to the Board. I explained the unfortunate circumstances of my visit to the Board meeting and mentioned my previous work at CBST, the publication of the ethnography and its contribution to gay studies as well as to the reputation of the synagogue. I indicated my affection for the congregation and the feeling of public humiliation which my exclusion from the meeting had caused.

In the meantime I found on my answering machine a message from the President who apologized for the inconvenience I experienced in her absence. I called her back, but soon discovered that she had preferred not to let my letter reach the rest of the board members. With no further explanation, that was another aggravating revelation. Now, I forwarded the letter to Abe, my acquaintance on the Board. I got a long e-mail response. He indicated his personal indignation at the decision to prevent my attendance as consequence of the vote that was taken after I left the room. I learned that the board was informed I was not a member (I had not paid the annual fees since my departure in the early 1990s) and therefore I had no right to attend board meetings uninvited. But probably more detrimental to me, Abe explained, was the claim made by Rachel, an older board member, that my work offended the lesbian constituency. I could comprehend, though not sympathize, with the formal argument under the circumstances of the absentee President who had invited me. But the second accusation left me dumbstruck.

I called on Simon, my close friend who had opened the gate to my work at CBST. Simon, who played a major role in the spiritual development of the synagogue and was close to most members of the founding generation, considered my ethnography a most valuable achievement for CBST. At an early stage of my association with the synagogue he had hoped that I would write the story he wished he could write himself. At that time Simon was afraid his generation would all disappear under the havoc of AIDS and I was the witness left to tell the world about their project. He introduced me to the company of the synagogue's "*machers*" ("operators" in Yiddish) and convinced them to invite me to various business meetings and private social events. For a while he was my Doc, the remarkable assistant in Whyte's seminal *Street Corner Society* (1955).

When I saw Simon last, he was a loyal supporter and admirer of Rabbi Kleinbaum. He always considered himself a feminist and was pleased to observe the growth of the lesbians' involvement with the synagogue's affairs. Simon thought I should call on the rabbi and meet with her in order to clarify her position about the Board's vote against my presence, and possibly understand also the President's treatment of my letter to the Board. Accepting his advice, I called the synagogue office and made an appointment with Rabbi Kleinbaum.

By the time we met it was nearly three months after the annoying incident. I had cooled off, though I still harbored some resentment. The rabbi received me warmly and showed the office employees the two editions of my book. We had coffee at a nearby cafe and in a relaxed atmosphere discussed my story and other issues related to the synagogue and to Israel. The rabbi apologized for the circumstances that had kept her away from the Board meeting that had refused my attendance. It was negligence on the part of Ruth (the President), who did not inform the board about my visit. She also indicated the possible role of my *Ethnos* article and its account of romantic complications among a few female members in the CBST leadership.

As mentioned above, except for the major actor who could not be disguised and who shortly afterwards left the synagogue, none of the women implicated in the affair were identified in any way. Regardless of who had circulated the article, it was seen as evidence by some women that I had sullied the reputation of lesbians at CBST.

Before we parted the rabbi told me she would suggest to Ruth to invite me to present a lecture on my work and allow a discussion about my research methods and other issues. No doubt, Rabbi Kleinbaum made me feel far better about the consequences of the unfortunate Board meeting, but when I left New York in mid-August, about two months later, I had still not heard again from the President. I came to believe that Ruth preferred to avoid direct communication and its potential for further embarrassment. I kept my decision to stay away from public events at CBST. I attended only two services taking a back seat and left soon after prayers.

SHARING THE GRIEF

During the months that followed my failed visit to the board meeting I had some short communications with congregants on various occasions, but I also met with some close friends and informants who shared with me their feelings about their present association with CBST. The following sketches of a few of these encounters suggest a range of personal and institutional experiences that have affected my veteran "informants" since the days of my initial fieldwork at CBST and its impact on their view of the synagogue society. To some extent one can observe a convergence of life histories of the ethnographer and his interlocuters. Above all, it indicates their shared memories and shared sense of loss of a place, its people and a past social ambience that remain preserved in the ethnographic text.

Jeffrey, who was among the younger congregants when I first met him, was now in his mid 40s. Our relationship had become more intimate in recent years and I always called him on my visits. He introduced me to his new venues of social life and the ever-changing entertainment sites in the gay world. Jeffrey was never an active congregant at CBST in terms of taking a role on a committee or in other public activity; but he was quite popular in his somewhat all gay American boy macho appearance and friendly demeanor. He stopped attending services soon after the appointment of Rabbi Kleinbaum. He missed his old friends at the synagogue, the victims of AIDS, or those who had left for other places. He attended services only on the occasion of his mother's *yortzait* (annual date of death), the High Holiday services, and when he joined me occasionally on my visits. Whenever he mentioned the synagogue, he claimed the atmosphere at the place had turned "cold," or, he said: "It had become a Protestant Church."

Leon was among the most active congregants, having served twice as President and maintaining the position of senior statesman. He took part in all major decisions during the first decades of CBST's operation, and was instrumental in suggesting and operating the organizational changes such as the expansion of the board of trustees, the hiring of professional staff, etc. Leon was open with me about his expectations and plans for further changes in the synagogue organization. At a nearby Village restaurant, he surprised me as he told me he had moved away from the center of activities and now took on a marginal role. The appointment of the executive director in 2001 had taken over the work he used to do as volunteer.

Leon was not disturbed by the occupancy of most leading positions by women. He considered it a circumstantial development because women were the superior candidates available at that particular moment. But he felt he was not excited anymore about the place that used to be the center of his life (his own statement). During those days, he related, they used to fight about the positions of leadership. Today, in contrast, they had to look around and persuade men to be nominated for elections to the Board.

Leon knew about my exclusion from the Board meeting. He was not surprised the new generation at CBST were unaware of my contribution (alluding to a metaphor of "the new Pharaohs who knew not Joseph"). He believed, however, that the more consequential part in the event at the board meeting was played by Rachel, who had suggested that my article was hurtful to women. Although she had not been present during the period I was engaged with the synagogue—"before the era of feminism" as Leon referred to the days prior to the recruitment of Rabbi Kleinbaum, Rachel had appointed herself representative of the legacy of women at CBST. Listening to Leon, I thought, was not Rachel associating me with the privileged male majority of that era?

I met with Jack and Ron, a couple who have been together for nearly twenty years. They had met at the synagogue and were always active in religious and educational activities. For many years Jack served as chair of the religious committee. Jack was obviously the most knowledgeable congregant in Jewish liturgy and rituals. He was responsible for the allocation of all tasks during services throughout the year: that of service leaders, cantors, and *drashah* (sermon) speakers. He was also responsible for preparing the needed prayer books for all services. He taught classes of Torah-reading cantillation. Although Jack headed a committee of six to nine members, he did most of the work himself. I believe he was the most valuable unpaid officer at CBST. Jack carried that laborious operation in a modest manner. He accommodated with the changing regimes at CBST and came to terms with most innovations. He had a good working relationship with the rabbi, though the range and impact of his role had gradually diminished after her appointment.

Sometime before we met, Jack suggested to the rabbi to disband the religious committee altogether. As he concluded, many of the issues dealt with by the religious committee had gradually been taken over by the professional and administrative staff. In particular, Jack's major role of allocating the tasks of service leaders, cantors, and *drashah* speakers among lay-congregants was now mostly redundant. For example, the rabbi and the assistant rabbi were committed to present three sermons each month, while the two intern rabbis were scheduled to present two sermons each during their annual appointment. Thus, only seven slots remained available for lay *drasha* speakers to be allocated during the Friday services.

A similar situation emerged with the recruitment of two part-time salaried cantors. There was no longer much need for the non-professional cantorial volunteers. It remained Jack's job to deal delicately with the former volunteers who had lost their regular slots as active participants in the annual cycle of services. Among them were a few popular and respected congregants who had to share the limited openings left for the non-professionals.

Ron, was less accommodating than Jack, his partner. Although he was not among Norman's supporters, nevertheless, he preferred to stay on with the small crowd of congregants left at Wesbeth (the Bethune service). With the final departure of Norman he became more active in running that service; but he sometimes joined Jack at the Chelsea church. They used to come to the city on Friday evenings together, separate for the service and meet for a late dinner together with a few friends from the two services. Ron felt alienated by what he considered the extravagant style at the Chelsea service. He thought there was not really a need for the congregation to move out of Wesbeth. The move was justified because of the grant that enabled the synagogue to start an educational program, and the Wesbeth space was now used for the synagogue's administration and for classes. The old sanctuary, however, had been maintained intact, and Ron concluded it could still host the regular services. No doubt, Ron preferred a more intimate congregation, run less expensively and with a greater participation of lay congregants in religious tasks.

I have already mentioned Simon, my close friend among the veteran leadership. He had had a major role in compiling the prayer books still in use. He had made translations from Hebrew texts to English and had made many changes in liturgy in order to accommodate the special needs and taste of the gays and lesbians at CBST. As we were discussing my disturbing experience, however, Simon revealed that his relationships with the rabbi had their ups and downs. Simon felt the rabbi did not respond to the suggestions he had made during the last few years about changes in rituals and prayers. Actually, Simon was worried that he lacked the confidence to confront the rabbi and convince her about his innovative ideas for the synagogue. He felt somehow disempowered in the company of the rabbi. My first mentor and among the last survivors of the founding generation seemed to have lost his certitude in his home territory. But, he was more comfortable negotiating with the assistant rabbi. They shared the interest and task of degenderizing the prayer books.

At the same time, however, Simon accepted Ron's invitation to help the Bethune Street Minyan. The old place needed his skills as service leader, cantor, and *drashah* speaker. His presence could help revive the dwindling Bethune Minyan services. Simon could engage himself with that project, not having been associated with Norman's legacy and plans to unseat the lesbian leadership. He commented ironically that at the main congregation he was not considered suitable anymore to perform in major services, since "I am an amateur." Instead, he was going back to the sanctuary he had first entered to occupy again the role he had taken on nearly three decades earlier. The duality of working with the assistant rabbi on the prayer texts for the use of the wider CBST community of men and women, while at the same time helping out the Bethune smaller congregation, offered Simon a solution to accommodate a difficult situation. He need not withdraw from the institution that was so much part of his personal history and core identity as a Jewish gay man.

My old acquaintance Zeev suggested a more complex interpretation for the synagogue's style of the day and for his own mood of discontent. Going back to the days he had joined CBST and the years of his active participation (he served for many years on the religious committee), he described it as the era of radical youth who got their education in the 1950s. They were Leftists who resented bourgeois society and its institutions, synagogues included. He had joined CBST in terms of a lay-led congregation, a *chavurah* – a band of friends. Zeev believed that the guys who hired the rabbi assumed the power would remain with the President and all decisions would be approved by the Board. The role they designed for their rabbi was mostly pastoral work to help the victims of AIDS. They wished to leave the jobs of service leaders and other tasks at ritual to be performed mostly by volunteers

However, Zeev concluded, that did not happen for various reasons. First of all, the board of directors got "bigger" [in number] but with "smaller" people. In contrast, Rabbi Kleinbaum became a charismatic figure with increased power and authority. The organization expanded and needed more money for its operation. They had to improve the performance at services and beautify the synagogue's decor in order to attract more members, heterosexuals included. And this was how things had come along: the change of space, the hiring of a music director and cantors, the expansion of the rabbinical staff, etc. But finally, Zeev returned to his main argument, that all this could happen because the generation of men and women who inherited his cohort were raised under more comfortable circumstances. For them, bourgeois society was not marked anymore by stigma; on the contrary, it represented a challenge to join and emulate. "They" want to be accepted into mainstream society and this is why they wished to gentrify the synagogue, and appoint rabbis and other functionaries. In sum, Zeev concluded, they want "confirmation."

Debbie had been one of the most active women during my early days at CBST. She was convivial, assertive, and maintained close friendly relationships with the core of the male leadership. Debbie had often served on the Board and had been visible in the public forum; however, she had disappeared from the weekly services during my later visits to the synagogue. I met her on my last unplanned attendance at the celebratory CBST annual concert (Shabat Shira) held in February 2005. She greeted me during the intermission, and seemed to be relieved at the opportunity to express her disappointment with the present regime. I was surprised by her bitter tone as she described the removal of volunteers from most roles and public visibility at CBST. As a lesbian close to the former male leadership, Debbie expressed her dismay at the "complete" takeover of all positions and spheres of authority by women. She told me she attended services only very rarely. Had she been a man, Debbie added, she would have stopped coming altogether.

Obviously, Debbie did not represent the wider constituency of lesbians who had joined the synagogue at a later stage and who felt at home because it was not dominated by a male leadership. The following opinions of Jean are more representative of the viewpoint of women who experienced enhanced empowerment after the decline of men's authority in the synagogue organization.

Jean remained a close friend from the day she discovered my presence at a High Holidays service when I was called to the *bimah* to read the blessing for the State of Israel. It was her first visit to CBST and she knew my name as author of research on Moroccan Jews. We had also met in later years during her visits to Israel. More than anyone else at the synagogue, Jean was aware of my interests and the precepts of my work. She appreciated the contribution of my writings, for CBST in particular. Jean was close to Rabbi Kleinbaum, whom she admired, and she could call upon and meet her with no delays.

Jean was among the first readers of my *Ethnos* article. Actually, she was also quoted in my description of the event that annoyed Rachel. Jean's support was my proof that I had not "erred" in terms of ethnographic ethics. It was also a personal consolation that I was not considered a misogynist by a woman I respected and liked, a proud lesbian, a feminist, and an active CBST member. Jean assumed that Rachel and also Ruth could not appreciate the professional rules of ethnographic report and the analytical strategies of my work. She believed there was no need to be a member of the congregation (or of any other organization) in order to conduct research.

CONFRONTING THE ETHNOGRAPHER'S DISPUTANT

Immediately after the embarrassing affair at the Board meeting I felt I could not call on Rachel and directly explore her viewpoint. I was angry at what I considered an insult. Nevertheless, I could not erase a nagging thought that I must speak to her. It seemed to me a professional and a personal failure to rely only on rumors about her claims during the meeting. I discussed the matter with Simon in particular. He volunteered to join me at a meeting with Rachel and serve as go-between in order to maintain a cordial atmosphere. I declined Simon's kind suggestion, and finally, in mid-July, I called the synagogue and left a message asking Rachel to return my call.

Rachel called me back one morning a few days later. I told her I wished to understand her complaint about my work. Rachel responded sharply that she joined the discussion about my presence when somebody else inquired about the right of a non-member to attend a board meeting. She voted against my attendance and explained her position to the board members based on her reading of my *Ethnos* article (which she had found in her mail box sometime earlier). In sum, she liked my thesis about the gender conflict over the allocation of authority and power in the synagogue organization, but my description and interpretation of the romantic scandal she considered "voyeuristic" and "unprofessional." There was, however, no time to continue a conversation as she was on her way to a medical appointment. Before ending that tense conversation, I asked Rachel if she saw my letter to the board or the epilogue to the new edition of my ethnography. She now requested that I send her these items "as a matter of courtesy."

A few days later Rachel called back. Again in a brief exchange, she thanked me for the effort and acknowledged that the epilogue was far better than the article (it did not include my comment on the romantic complication). I thanked her for the cordial response. And that was our last communication.

When I came to write this paper, I found in my files an article Rachel had published a few years earlier in *Outward*, a newsletter of the Lesbian and Gay Aging Network. Here she told about her late coming out and joining CBST at the age of 60 (in 1993). Throughout the article Rachel expressed a strong plea for empowering aged lesbians to become vital members of Jewish communities. She called on "old lesbians" to be assertive, even if this might raise the stereotype of "loud-mouthed Jewish women."

FAREWELL TO CBST

In spite of the discomfort I must have caused for both of us, I was glad I had gotten in touch with Rachel. It helped me comprehend the personal and professional encounter I had experienced as perceived by "the native" who had initiated much of my embarrassment. I could now better comprehend that "an honest" report from the "ethnographer's point of view" is not necessarily the historicity of the life experiences and the social circumstances as apprehended by the subjects of his research,[9] or by those who joined their community at a later stage. The reality of events as recorded by the observer is not always the narrative unanimously expected by the membership of the group observed. Rachel (and probably other women who saw my article) was offended by the exposure in print of a type of behavior she considered private, although it engaged active members on the synagogue's stage and was a matter of public debate.

That incident reflected, *inter alia*, great changes in the composition of congregants and gender relationships at CBST. Inevitably, these transformations also affected my own position reminiscent of Callaway's query (1992: 30):

> What are the implications of the anthropologist as a gendered knower? Of field research as a process of personal interaction and flawed understandings, involving what may be vastly different—and not always easily recognised—patterns of gender relations between that of the anthropologist and the society being studied? In what ways does rational inquiry have gendered dimensions?

Moreover, the public revelation of my allegedly ethnographic misdemeanor, the debate at the Board, and its consequences, exemplify Dumont's (1978: 12) and Hastrup's (1992: 117) claims that the ethnographer in the field is the locus of a drama that is the source of his/her anthropological

---

9   See also Scheper-Hughes, 2000.

reflection. The feelings of injury on my part have also sharpened my awareness and sensitivity about the feelings of loss as experienced by the veteran congregants presented in this paper.

In retrospect, I now realize that I might have overreacted. After all, I was unknown to the majority of the board members (who had joined CBST in recent years), and I was not a fee-paying member. Unfortunate coincidences kept both the President and the Rabbi away from the meeting. Their absence left me out in the cold waiting for the vote. Without the presence of these two leading women, Rachel was, by default, installed in the position of an authoritative female voice. Nevertheless, I can now also better apprehend her complaint. I emulate a novel insight to the situation from Hastrup's (1992: 122) proposition that the drama of fieldwork implies a degree of "violence" on the ethnographer's part:

> Because any scientific discourse must take claims to speak over and above the acts observed or heard, there is an inherent hierarchy in the relationship between the interlocutors. To deny this is also to remain insensitive to the violence inherent in fieldwork.

As much as it is difficult for me to sympathize with Rachel's position, I tell myself that it deserves a measure of empathy on my part. I am reminded of Wolf's assertion (1992:13):

> No matter how careful, I fear all of us who do research must be prepared to be the resented Other to the "objects" of our study.

It took me a few months to reach that moment of wisdom and reconciliation. Nevertheless, some irreversible damage was done to what I naively considered a state of unconditional love. The poignant experience, probably misconceived or exaggerated, became a trigger for my realization that the place and the society I had come to study in 1989 had changed almost beyond recognition. One can claim, metaphorically, that "I signed a contract for research" with another business partner. As it turned out, I came to rely on the vestiges of the memories of my participation preserved only by a minority of participants, and on the assumed reputation of my book that many may not have read. In the words of Leon, I was surrounded by a generation of men and women, "the Pharaohs," who had not known Joseph.

With the loss of the warm familiarity if not of the sense of privileged relationships, it was time to ask myself: Am I still interested in the present working style of the organization, in the type of spirituality and sociability at CBST? Moreover, I felt that my excitement would not have been revived even if the board and the President had publicly expressed regret for my embarrassment. In sum, it was time to move on. As I once told Simon, my failed visit to the board meeting liberated me from an obsession that had lost its target. In the final analysis, Rachel's complaint helped to facilitate my exit from the field.[10] Naturally, it was soothing to discover that my disenchantment was shared with several individuals among the "natives" who, to some extent, had represented the society I had observed during the initial period of my fieldwork.

I decided to write this report on the process of my departure, and the assumed end of my CBST research, not to 'get back' at anyone in the community. On the contrary, I take my final title from a celebrated Chinese film that I have watched more than once, "Farewell To My Concubine," an evocative presentation of a love story expired under the tragic circumstances of traumatic cultural and social changes.[11] Anthropologists often fall in love with the communities they study.[12] Often the separation dictated by the inevitable constraints of distance as well as time and budget apportionments, keep their love stories intact, saved for posterity from the ravages of the circumstances of daily life.

---

10 I occasionally attended services during subsequent visits to New York, but no longer with the intention of doing research.
11 *Farewell To My Concubine*, a film released in 1993, directed by Chan Kaige, based on a novel by Lilian Lee.
12 See Dominguez 2000.

I started this paper with Behar's suggestion of loss as a basic notion in the work of ethnographers who salvage the stories of the people they study. However, I am not writing a requiem to CBST in a manner reminiscent of Read's (1986) description of two brief summer trips he made to his New Guinea site after an absence of nearly thirty years. Read portrayed a vanished world, as if he had returned to visit a tomb commemorating a place, its people, and a way of life. In Geertz's ironic expression, Read's *Return to the High Valley* is "cast in something of a where-are-the-warriors-of-yesterday idiom" (Geertz 1988: 99). In real life, people, places, fieldwork sites, ethnographers, and their informants change, and in that inevitable process, they all lose their innocence.

Reporting the full cycle of an ethnographic project, from start to close—a "holistic representation" in a new sense of the term—could enrich our work. I advocate an enterprise that includes more rigorously the later phases of communication with one's subjects of research. Such a presentation would introduce the anthropologist's perspective on the transformations that have taken place in the field, as well as in the patterns of mutuality—rapport, affection, commitment, etc.—between the observer and the observed. As much as we record the life history of the people we study, these ethnographic records also constitute a major part of our own life history. They contribute immensely to our professional careers, to our personal identity, to our pride, our failures, and our inevitable losses.

I feel I can best conclude this exiting paper by repeating the last lines in the text of my ethnography (Shokeid 1995/2003: 243), a quote from an evocative 1990 Day of Atonement sermon given by Gilbert, a founder member of the congregation. The name of the particular service is *Ne'ilat She'arim*—the closing of the gates—associated with the symbolic closing of the heavenly gates at the end of the period of God's yearly judgment:

> Ne'ilah not only signals the end of our role in the spiritual drama of the Days of Awe, it likewise signals the beginning of a new role for us in living the drama of our everyday lives. Ne'ilah is one last

act after which the curtain does not fall; it goes up! — to which one hardly knows whether to say "Amen" or "Break a leg!"

Gilbert moved to Florida some time before my arrival in 1989. But, he continued to attend High Holiday services at CBST and we met at these annual occasions. He regularly served also as cantor at a major Day of Atonement service. Then he stopped coming a few years ago. He felt the place had changed too much and he was not needed anymore to perform as cantor or deliver sermons. Always an optimist, joking and smiling, I consider the final words in his *Ne'ilah* sermon appropriate for the story and the message of my essay.

CHAPTER 15.
CLOSETED COSMOPOLITANS: ISRAELI GAYS BETWEEN CENTER AND PERIPHERY

The chapter presents observations of gay life conducted in Tel Aviv in 1993 and again, a few years later, in 1998 when the scene of gay life in Tel Aviv seemed much different. The introduction of two stages of observation displays also the dynamic nature of social phenomena that ethnographers might often confront in their present-day research projects.

More than most other spheres of social behavior, gay life, seems to epitomize the "Global Ecumene" (Hannerz 1989, Featherstone 1990), that new order with its continuous flow of shared values, goods and experiences. A sexual expression which for centuries has been suppressed in Western cultures, within a short period since World War II, has become a clear mark of modern urban cosmopolitan life (e.g. Weeks 1991:108; Plummer 1992:17). The emergence of highly visible gay institutions and enclaves in most major metropolitan cities in Western countries should be of interest to those studying the processes of the global dissemination of new technologies, cultural genres, behavioral modes and life styles.

The gay traveler finds a familiar landscape of gay life soon on his arrival in a new metropolitan city in America or Europe. He often carries a guide-book with him informing him of the exact location of the places to visit: bars, restaurants, baths, film theaters, book stores, parks, beaches and other available sites, facilities and gay organizations. The decor and decorum in these places may differ, but that only adds to the visitor's enjoyment. He has no difficulty adjusting to the role of client or participant in these new locales around the Western globe.

The locus of Center versus Periphery in this gay map is somewhat vague. Amsterdam, for example, earned the reputation as a haven for homosexuals before San Francisco became the new Mecca. However, New York, London, Paris, Copenhagen, Brussels and many other cities almost simultaneously developed a similar repertoire of attractions and commodities for both the citizen and the visitor. But regardless of the hierarchy of the cities on the gay map, this chain of dominant urban metropolis has become the "Center" for the periphery at home and abroad.

The major metropolitan centers have continuously drawn immigrants and visitors from the more peripheral areas in the Western and non-Western world. Wulff (1993), for example, described the young, and mostly straight, Swedes attracted to Manhattan. But for homosexuals, in particular, the visits to these sites embody some clear elements of a pilgrimage, though secular, to the temples of gay life. The gay traveler has a clear conception of the places to visit and his participation for a while, diminishes temporarily his identity as stranger in this new environment. The regular tourist, unless on an extended visit, remains mostly an alien voyeur. But the gay traveler, as soon as he enters any of the gay establishments on his journey, proceeds into a liminal type of existence comparable to pilgrims on a religious voyage (e.g. Turner 1973, Myerhoff 1974). Back home, he looks forward to the opportunity to return and relive the sensation so basic to his inner being.

Hannerz's paper for the ICAES conference (1993)[1] started with the story of "Baby U.K." the comic-tragic heroine of a Nigerian novel who was willing to pay any price in order to get to England, the land of her dreams where most of her friends have already migrated. The story of "Baby U.K." well serves the theory of globalization.[2] The better educated or better informed individuals in the periphery yearn to get to the world's major stages.

---

1   It was Ulf Hannerz's invitation to participate in the session "The Center in the Periphery" which he convened for the International Congress of the Anthropological and Ethnological Sciences (ICAES) 1993 meeting in Mexico City, that tempted me to conduct the observations for this paper. However, since I prepared the first version for the presentation in 1993, some important changes have occurred in the public life of gay people in Israel.
2   See, for example, Hannerz 1989; Featherstone 1990.

When I began my research among gays in Israel, I assumed that most gays would be looking for any opportunity to move to a metropolitan center free from the constraints on gay life in Israeli society. My paper is mainly engaged with an examination of that "centricity orientation" supposition, namely, the yearning of people from peripheral regions, and particularly those apparently in disadvantaged circumstances, to move out and get closer to the Center.

GAY RIGHTS IN ISRAEL

The status of homosexuals in Israel is somewhat ambiguous. Judaism has traditionally condemned homosexual practices as explicitly stated in Leviticus, 20:13: "Two men who have sexual intercourse with each other have committed an abomination: they shall be put to death..." Only in 1988 did the Israeli Knesset repeal the British Mandate's rule making homosexuality a criminal offense. The new liberal legislation had little practical effect, however, since the old discriminatory rule was never enforced. Homosexuals were not persecuted for their private acts, and men and women served in the military as long as their conduct was kept secret (Gal 1994; Kaplan 1999).

Although Israel has been developing under the impact of Western influence, that has not been reflected in the sphere of family life. The family still maintains important traditional characteristics in Israeli society. Historical, cultural, ideological, social, political, geographical and many other factors typical of a small society have preserved family values to an extent unknown in most Western societies.[3] In particular, marriage and birth rates are relatively high. The permanent state of conflict with the Arab world and the pivotal position of the army have contributed to the strength of the family and to what is often referred to as a "Macho" ethos (e.g. Kaplan 1999). A survey of homophobic attitudes, comparing Israeli and American students

---

3   See, for example, Peres and Katz 1981.

(Lieblich and Friedman 1985), revealed Israelis to be more conservative in sex-role identification and more homophobic than Americans.[4]

Public attitudes have usually discounted the likelihood of a substantial homosexual minority among Israelis. While single women are tolerated somewhat for their unmarried status because it is still considered the men who can make the choice, men have little excuse for not getting married. The least a single gay man can do, is not advertise his unorthodox sexual preference for his own gender. Marcia Freedman, an American immigrant who became a leading feminist and Knesset member, discovered she was painfully isolated after she revealed her lesbian orientation. "...All but a handful are carefully closeted...Israel is a hostile and barren climate for dykes" she wrote on her return to the United States (Freedman 1982:214, 221).

In Tel Aviv, where the pace of life and the variety of entertainment compare favorably with major metropolitan centers, until recently gay life has been almost invisible. The only national gay organization until 1999 carried the unobtrusive name of: The Society for the Protection of Personal Rights—SPPR. For many years its leaders were careful to avoid public attention which might prompt official action (Luzato 1984). Its membership has remained limited, 376 men and women were on its list for January 1993, of whom 30% maintained the status of unidentified supporters under the category of "friends". In a study on same sex couples, the author (Mizrachi 1990) claimed that most of the people she studied were reluctant to expose themselves in political activity and have expressed resentment toward SPPR. That reaction was seen as stemming from the stigma Israeli gays and lesbians have internalized.

The major step taken by gays and lesbians in Israel to make a claim for their identity and civil rights took place only in February 1993. As a few active members of SPPR argued, that would not even have happened had their cause not been taken up by the outspoken Labor member of

---

[4] A tentative explanation for Israeli homophobic attitudes (also suggested by Robert Paine) might be the deeply implanted pioneering ethos; one's first commitment to the needs of the community and the priority of collective goals over individual desires.

the Knesset Yael Dayan, who invited a group of homosexuals to appear at a Knesset forum to address the committee she chaired on women issues. The major spokesman was Uzi Even, a professor of chemistry at Tel Aviv University, a man in his early fifties. His impressive appearance, which was also shown on public television, left a strong impact on many people who for the first time watched a gay man announce his sexual preference. Uzi Even told the story of his dismissal from his scientific army assignment which he had successfully fulfilled for many years, once his homosexuality was revealed. While it took a group of angry drag queens in a New York bar (the Stonewall, June 27, 1969), to ignite the movement for gay rights in America, a serious, masculine looking professor seems to have been the more appropriate hero for an Israeli Stonewall.[5]

OBSERVATIONS IN TEL AVIV

My report introduces an exploratory study I carried out during several months in 1993. I observed the activities of a network of religious gay men (HOD)[6] with the core of fifteen members and interviewed another ten men, mostly members of SPPR.[7] Those interviewed were mainly professionals and artists. The membership of HOD was more varied in its socio-economic composition and included a group of American immigrants. The majority of those interviewed and observed were economically comfortable and often traveled to America

---

5   The impact of Uzi Even's performance was later eloquently described by his partner who also specializes in communication studies, as follows:
    To sum up, the 1993 Knesset convention was a historical event which triggered constructional changes in the geography of the Israeli public sphere. A new map has been laid out. One that demarcates a distinct gay territory which, until the mid-1980s, was *terra incognita* (Kama 2000: 156).

6   An acronym for Religious Homosexuals that carries also the meaning of "splendor."

7   I am grateful to Amit Kama who facilitated my interviews with members of the national gay organization—SPPR.

or Europe. The men I observed and interviewed were mostly in their mid 20s up to early 40s.

Israelis are frequent travelers, a phenomenon customarily attributed to their life in a small country under siege. They are observed in many highlights of modern tourism in proportion far beyond the size of that nation. A popular topic of conversation among Israelis is their experiences as tourists in other countries. Israeli youth have developed their own style of travel, journeying for many months to the Far East, South America and the United States soon after completing their army service (e.g. Jacobson 1987; Noy and Cohen 2005). There is little doubt that many, if not a majority of gays in Israel have had some experience visiting the centers of gay life in Europe and America.

Over the years, one or two gay bars usually operated in Tel Aviv, but as told to me by everyone I spoke to, these never became permanent locations for a gay clientele. Without a stable crowd to keep them going, the bars had frequently opened and closed down. These places attracted a large turnout only on the one day weekend in Israel. The crowd seemed to include "the same faces," since too many were reluctant to show up in a public gay space, and the business was also slow because Israelis are not accustomed to consuming alcoholic drinks. They usually end up an evening in a bar with one bottle of beer or a soft drink.

So, if the bars have been for many years the major pre-Stonewall institution in gay Western society (Murray 1984:34), that has certainly not been the case in Israel. I was often told by the people I interviewed that Israeli gays prefer to entertain at home in the company of their friends. It seems gays have adopted the major form of socializing in mainstream Israeli society which entails meeting a close networks of friends at home particularly during the weekend.

The baths, another major gay institution were almost absent in Israel. The only gay sauna open in Tel Aviv during my 1993 survey, operated in what was a small apartment and its clientele was often described to me derogatorily as: "mostly the old and ugly, and some youngsters attracted to the old."⁸ A public bath in Jerusalem which also attracted gays, was closed down under the pressure of the many Orthodox residents in the neighborhood. As explained to me by my acquaintances, gay saunas can not draw a large clientele in locations where customers might meet people they know. The closely-knit Israeli society eliminates the impersonal atmosphere expected in most sites for anonymous sex:

> A gay bath needs an anonymous crowd. Here you walk naked, this is the very top of the meat market and it might embarrass you to show up in the nude in front of a friend...you might be uncomfortable in his company even if not naked, because of the sexual tension of the place.⁹

The man who made that statement, an artist in his early thirties had frequently traveled abroad where he always enjoyed to search the attractions of gay life. He had patronized the baths in other countries, but refrained from visiting the one in Tel Aviv close to his neighborhood.

There are no gay bookstores or gay cinemas in Tel Aviv, though a few erotic film theaters also attract some gay people. But the major places where gays can meet, and which are also listed in the one Israeli gay magazine (*Maga'im*) in the early 1990s,¹⁰ are a few parks in Tel Aviv and other larger cities. Independence Park, along the coast in Tel Aviv, has become probably the largest of its kind in the Western Hemisphere, a relatively safe cruising site. With Israel's mild weather, except for a short winter, that scenic site close to Tel Aviv's major shopping center, hotels and restaurants, continued to offer ample opportunities for anonymous sex and the hope of meeting with candidates for a more lasting relationship. The park is easy to reach and the safety it normally offers even late at night

---

8   During the late 1990s, however, that sauna moved out to a new larger facility. Also another sauna opened at that time in down-town Tel Aviv. But both establishments are small in size compared with those in Europe and the US (e.g. Tattelman 1999).

9   See Bolton's (1995) description of his happy experiences in a gay sauna in Brussels.

10 Not untypical, *Maga'im* ("Contacts"), did not survive for long, and in 1995 a new publication appeared in the market, titled *Tat Tarbut* ("Sub Culture") to be replaced a year later by *Hazman Havarod* ("Pink Time").

stands in striking contrast to the fear and danger which have left most parks deserted in other Western metropolitan cities.

The popularity of Independence Park versus the poor registration with the one gay association was explained to me by an active SPPR member in the following words:

> This is a symptom of internalized homophobia; When you open the door of the association's quarters you admit to yourself that you are gay. But you can go to the park, get fucked, and go back home pretending that nothing had really happened.

My research during the early 1980s among Israelis in New York (Chapters 8, 9) had shown that in spite of a strong national ethos and the stigma of becoming "Yordim" ("those who go down"—the disparaging nickname for those who have left Israel), nevertheless, many young and older Israelis have emigrated, in particular, since 1967. But among that group, I met no gay "Yordim". Most of the Israeli emigrants I met have left because of instrumental reasons. Only a few were motivated to leave because of political pressures or ideological convictions. Also, during my late 1980s study in New York's gay and lesbian synagogue, only a few Israeli gays and lesbians showed up occasionally. The initiative to start an Israeli group at the Gay and Lesbian Community Center in Greenwich Village attracted a small number of men and women. But some among the Israelis I met at the synagogue and the Village Center told me they have been in contact with other Israelis at informal gatherings of close networks of friends in the style of entertainment similar to their practice in Israel.

Considering the suppressed identity of homosexuals in Israeli public life and its poor state compared to gay life in Western metropolitan cities, I assumed my interviews in Tel Aviv would reveal a resentful attitude toward the local gay scene and express emphatic hopes to join friends and acquaintances who had already left for the "Center." Along with "Baby U.K." from Nigeria, I expected to find "Baby-Gay N.Y." desperate to leave the Promised Land for the Land of Promise.

CHAPTER FIFTEEN

Luckily, from the anthropologist's point of view, human life is more complex than an academic's rational predictions prompted in part by social scientists' fascination with the "Center." I do not claim to present a sample of Israeli gay men, but the majority of the men I observed and interviewed did not express a wish to pack up and move out to the Western havens of gay life.

I met with Uzi Even, the chemistry professor who had "come out" publicly and asked him hadn't he been tempted to leave Israel after his humiliating discharge from his army position. I assumed it would have been relatively easy for a scientist with his credentials to find a suitable job elsewhere. His response reiterated by other gays I met, was:

> I am here, firstly, because I am an Israeli. Secondly, it is not that difficult to be gay in Israel, it is probably easier! Why do the Jews organize in New York? why did they establish their own clubs? because they were discriminated against. This is also the reason the gays are so actively organized in America. There is gay bashing in New York, but there is no gay bashing in Tel Aviv!

As proof of the actual tolerance in daily life, he mentioned that since making his public appearance, he and his partner have not confronted open bigotry. There were no threatening phone calls, no angry letters, no attempts to disturb them in their apartment.

During the same conversation, Amit Kama, Uzi's companion mentioned that when they had spent a Sabbatical in an American city of the size of Tel Aviv, they counted fifteen gay institutions. That phenomenon, so different from the Israeli experience, had not deterred them from returning to Israel where they entertain mainly at home in the company of close friends. They both argued that although going out to restaurants and pubs had been increasing in recent years among straight Israelis (as indicated in a national survey of leisure activities), the gay population had mainly preserved its habits. They mentioned the absence of gay book stores in Tel Aviv, but added that many gays bring home books and magazines they purchased abroad (though they are sometimes worried the publications might be confiscated by the custom officers). It was also suggested that gays travel more often abroad where they find whatever they miss in Israeli gay life.

Another artist I interviewed, who lived in Paris for nearly two years, argued as he evaluated gay life in Israel:

> Homosexuality is not only fucking. True, for the sake of fucking it is much easier to go abroad, you can find it there for twenty four hours without a break.

He himself refrained from visiting Tel Aviv's few bars, the sauna and Independence Park. He considered it humiliating to look for sexual satisfaction and the illusion of lasting friendship in those few places of anonymous sex. He met his gay friends in the company of heterosexuals or homosexuals without the compulsion to search for them in notoriously gay sites. Many years ago he had considered the possibility of immigration, but gave up the idea although he might have gained materially. He thought he would always be handicapped in a new land without his mother tongue. He knew only one gay man who had left in recent years for Amsterdam "because he wanted to be free". He did not complain of harassment of gays, but blamed gays themselves for having internalized the old Eastern European attitudes, "Jewish-Polish" values and fears (relating to roots in Eastern Europe) which keep them so closeted. They do not dare disappoint their parents and are worried about what their neighbors might think of them. This is the reason he thought Israeli homosexuals do not join the one active gay organization and prefer to remain invisible.

The claim of public tolerance in Israel, earlier expressed by Uzi Even, was repeated in most interviews by both younger and older respondents. The following is representative:

> In the United States there is much hatred toward gays, therefore they need organizations. They need to demonstrate and march in provocative parades. We don't need parades, we have no gay bashing.

The young man, in his late twenties, who made this statement travels frequently, and mentioned his visits to Amsterdam in particular, where one can spend the day between various gay establishments and where sex is continuously available: "But after a few days you've had your fill."

Another professional, in his early thirties who could easily "pass" in an English or French speaking society, explained the pros and cons of gay life in Israel by relating his own experiences. He remained "closeted" to his family, at work and in his army unit. He found it difficult to form a relationship with another man because gay male couples who live together are easily identified. "If the world today is a village, Israel is one co-op apartment building," was the metaphor he used to describe the social constraints on gays in Israel who can not freely display their true identity. (He was careful to maintain his anonymity meeting me in a public place.) Nevertheless, he did not contemplate the idea of immigrating. "A man is the product of the landscape of his native country," he quoted a well known Israeli poet.[11] He loved the landscape, the people and particularly his friends in Tel Aviv. Nowhere else could one find the kind of friendship one could find among Israelis, interpolating an American term he declared: "There are no 'buddies' like Israeli 'buddies.'" He also told me about an Israeli friend who had recently returned after living for three years in San Francisco. Although good looking and successful at work, he was disappointed by what seemed to him the emotional distance between people in the United States. His friend missed the closeness and comradeship of Israeli life. He went on to explain the tolerance of Israelis toward gays:

> The Americans are terrible people; There is no gay bashing here, people have too many problems to bother about – the Arabs, the politics, the economy, etc. – they don't bother about the gays.

Although he assumed the closetness of Israeli gays negatively effected the prevalence of gay couples and increased the frequency of cruising, he considered it easy to find sexual mates and form friendships anywhere.

---

11   Saul Tchernichowsky.

And in any case, Independence Park was always available for the desperate gay loner. He concluded that for many gays, their homosexual identity and needs are only part of a wider set of identities and expectations. He socialized with heterosexual as often as with gay networks of friends and had no difficulty accommodating these apparently incongruous worlds.

I met with the American partner of one of the Israelis quoted above. An artist, in his mid twenties, he had arrived in Israel a few years earlier from Rochester. He compared the gay scene in Tel Aviv with that in Rochester and revealed many paradoxes: While he considered Rochester far less cosmopolitan than Tel Aviv, it maintained a far more active gay life. Tel Aviv is still bustling at 2 A.M. while Rochester is already asleep, but the gay establishments there are operating till morning. Israeli society is tolerant, but Israeli families are reluctant to accept gay or lesbian children.[12] In contrast, in the United States, the family is far more understanding, but society at large is homophobic. In Rochester he was always careful when he left a gay bar, but in Israel there is no gay bashing and he feels safe. Gay life in Israel is invisible, but a lot is going on under the surface and people can find company. Not many Israelis go to gay bars, because that would represent an acknowledgment of their gay identity both to themselves and others. But many choose to go to Independence Park from which they can return home, leaving the unresolved problem of sexual identity behind. Israelis seriously lag behind gays in America who have long ago come out of the closet and claimed their rights. But happy at work, content with his partner, enjoying the safety and the cultural life in Tel Aviv, he had no plans to go back to America.

DISCUSSION

I must confess I was taken by surprise at concluding my interviews in Tel Aviv. For more than a year I carried out observations at New York's gay and lesbian synagogue (Congregation Beth Simchat Torah)

---

12 A recent study demonstrates the painful process of Israeli parents' accommodation with their children's homosexuality (Mizrachi 2002).

and was impressed with the continuing struggle of homosexuals to claim their personal and communal rights. I never considered Israeli society, by and large, tolerant and liberal in sexual matters. Starting a family, having children and grandchildren are among the major societal expectations. No doubt, there have always been well known individuals, particularly in the arts, whose marital or sexual life style did not conform to mainstream morality. But these I believed were the exception, tolerated under the special category of "bohemians". I assume that the overall invisibility of Israeli gays and lesbians in terms of a well defined community and political force, corresponding to the realities of the Euro-American Center, had influenced my own perception of the lives of Israeli homosexuals as dominated by stigma and deprivation.

The gay scene in Mexico as described, for example, by Taylor (1985) reveals a few similar characteristics. Although Mexican society is incomparable to Israel in its sheer size and its closeness to a world Center, nevertheless, gay life is closeted, invisible and mainly acted out in public places not specifically defined as gay. Moreover, Taylor reports that for more than a hundred years homosexuality in Mexico has been considered a private matter with no legal prohibitions. But Mexican homosexuals consider their closeted life style superior to gay life in the United States. They claim that gay behavior in America separates homosexuals from their families and confines them to a ghetto society. In contrast, they feel they are part of mainstream Mexican society and consider it easy to step in temporarily and move out of "Ambient" – gay environment and code of behavior. That pattern differs greatly from Humphreys' (1970) description of married homosexuals in America who frequent public restrooms, but who otherwise are dissociated from gay life. I assume that institutionalized Mexican pattern of a dual life style of sexuality and demeanor (which does not also correspond to the common perception of bisexuality) may also be the case in other "Peripheral" societies, in South America in particular (e.g. Lancaster 1988; Murray 1992).

As I have already suggested, gay populations in certain peripheral societies can be compared to the pilgrims who went off to visit sacred monuments or the tombs of saints which introduced them to the Center of their spiritual life and often the political center of the world of their day (Turner 1973, Turner and Turner 1978). The anthropological literature on tourism had been engaged for some time in a debate about the similarities and differences between tourists and pilgrims (e.g. Smith 1992, Eade 1992, Cohen 1992). The gay traveler, however, represents a type of "tourist-pilgrim" absent from that discourse and its tourists versus pilgrims paradigm, which relates primarily to secular tourists in traditional sacred pilgrimage sites. Aware of the incongruities of that analogy, nevertheless, I posit that the secular gays consummate their visit to gay attractions in a fashion which could be compared with the catharsis experienced by the pilgrims to sacred sites in various parts of the globe.

Locked in time and space during their ecstatic visits, the gay tourist-pilgrims accept their remoteness from the Center with equanimity, and content to return to their home society without revolutionize or publicly deviating from its norms. We could probably borrow Turner's (1973:204) perception of pilgrimage as "symbolic antistructure".

Paraphrasing Hannerz's description (1990) of the "cosmopolitan" who plays a prominent role in the new world ecumene, I am tempted to define the gays I met in Israel in 1993 as "closeted cosmopolitans." They shared a "subculture," holding to two codes, one they experienced on their travels to the Center and one they displayed at home. As for their Israeli environment, as perceived and experienced by the gay men we observed, our findings revealed an unexpected paradox: public tolerance and civility which conflicted with both the societal familial-communal ethos, and the pressures endured in the more intimate circles, close family and work in particular. This pattern of asymmetry between the intimate and the public arenas seemed to contradict the experience of gays in America in particular. That divergence suggests an insight into some essential differences in moral and social codes of these respective societies. However, it needs further examination before we can expand on the source and meanings of these societal incongruities.

But the map of gay attractions and pilgrimages does not exclude the periphery. The visitors from the Center whose search for adventure, archaeology, religion and other attractions (such as a trip to Israel for American Jews) leads them to sites in the Periphery, are also well informed about the gay scene in these places. A visit to Independence Park in Tel Aviv is an exciting experience for men who have mostly abandoned that type of cruising in their own cities. The safety of cruising in public places in Israel, Mexico, Thailand and other countries in the Periphery which also assures anonymity to the outsider, retrieves a lost paradise for guests from the Center. The majority of gays who visit Israel, Jews in particular, combine a journey to the land of their ethno-cultural roots and its sacred monuments with a taste of gay life in Tel Aviv's famous park as much as they do on trips to other countries in the Periphery. Most of my acquaintances in New York's gay synagogue who have visited Israel have also journeyed to the gay sites in the Promised Land. Thus the Center and the Periphery in the map of gay tourists-pilgrims carry on a continuing exchange of visitors, images, world views and ideas. My observations suggest that one aspect, at least, in the new world ecumene is not fully constructed by the inequality usually associated with the "Center-Periphery" paradigm. A thorough examination might reveal other spheres of exchange that sustain that global division and communion.

POSTSCRIPT

Since I first concluded my 1993 observations, the gay scene in Israel has changed dramatically. I present now a few observations from May 1998 that highlight these developments.

On May 5, 1998, Dana International, a transgendered person,[13] won the Eurovision song contest for Israel. The good news was spontaneously celebrated that night by a crowd of several hundred young gays and lesbians, as well as others who joined the impromptu happening in Tel Aviv's main public space – Rabin Square. The international gay rainbow flags

---

13 Formerly a man named Yaron Cohen.

were happily raised on the poles usually used for the national and city flags. Male couples kissed in front of the television cameras to be screened in days later on the newscasts. Dana International, a provocative and outspoken person, visited the Knesset and was received by the Minister of Tourism who served also as Deputy Prime Minister. Dana announced her commitment and devotion to the Israeli gay community.

Two weeks later, the Wigstock happening, a fund raising event to support the battle against AIDS attracted a big crowd (estimated by participants as of 3,000-4,000 people, mostly young gays and lesbians), that took over part of Independence Park. The event started on Friday (May 22) at 2 p.m. and was scheduled to end early in the evening. I was attending in the company of Uzi Even and his partner. They were aware of the change that had taken place since Uzi had first publicly announced his homosexuality. The late 1990s witnessed also the emergence of a few more stable gay venues in Tel Aviv. In particular, four or five bars for gays and lesbians managed to operate more regularly than ever before. Uzi and Amit were impressed by the size of the crowd that greatly surpassed all past public events. The name of Dana International was mentioned by the participants who approached Uzi, and some claimed that "we are witnessing historical days." They implied that the impact of Dana's achievement on the changing status of homosexuals in Israel was significant. Dana's winning song, Diva, was often performed during that afternoon on a stage built for the occasion.

I could not avoid comparing the two heroes of gay public life in Israel who emerged within the gap of five years, from the solid professor of chemistry standing next to me to the provocative transsexual singer. That transition seemed also to epitomize the bravado of the crowd of young gays and lesbians who came out into the open. As Uzi Even also noticed, gays of older generations kept away from this conspicuous display of homosexual identity.

As I left for home late in the afternoon, I did not suspect that the event, which had seemed peaceful and jolly, would end up in violence. But, as it turned out, the police insisted on closing the celebration "on time" at

7 p.m., before the official start of the Sabbath. The organizers, however, assumed they had been given permission to close at 8 p.m. Although the organizers agreed to cut off the loudspeakers, a popular protest erupted spontaneously. Several hundred participants poured down the street in front of Independence Park and blocked the traffic at a nearby major junction. In the ensuing conflict with police officers who handled the crowd with plastic gloves (thus symbolizing both prejudice and ignorance), four men were detained for a few hours.

A few days later I met on campus with two male students who participated in the demonstration and one of whom was detained. They admitted it was the expression of suppressed anger of a discriminated group, rather than provocation by the police, that caused the violent reaction. It was a feeling of empowerment encouraged by Dana's triumph, they thought, that evoked the rank and file to take action. But, I assume, that impromptu revolt was stimulated also by a chain of recent events in the Israeli public arena linked to the growing estrangement between the secular and orthodox constituencies. (The conflict got to a boiling point when a leading dance company, canceled its performance at a major Independence Day celebration because the dancers were pressed to change their stage dress in order to accommodate the modesty code of orthodox politicians). The violent demonstration of gays and lesbians on the Sabbath evening, seemed to combine the old grievances of a stigmatized minority with prevalent public anger at the growing power of the religious parties in the government coalition and the notion of abuse of the secular citizenry often associated in the national folklore with a Tel Aviv milieu. That convergence of social resentments probably endowed the gay demonstration with some wider legitimacy and intensified the feeling of witnessing "historical days".[14] In 1999, the SPPR was renamed as The Agudah—Israel Gay, Lesbian, Bisexual and Transgender Association.

We cannot consider the case of the gay minority in isolation from other major societal developments, as well as from the political, cultural

---

14 One year later Tel Aviv hosted the first Gay Pride Parade.

and ideological discourses that dominate the public arena. It has become a standard reaction by observers to comment about the loss of ideological and cultural consensus in contemporary Israeli society. In particular, the growing division in daily life between seculars and orthodox, and no less, the bitter conflict between Right and Left in national politics. These cleavages are sometime described in the Israeli intellectual discourse as representing the consequences or marks of "post-Zionism" (e.g., Taub 1997). Rather than relating the growth of gay empowerment solely to the idea of globalization, the theme of my treatise, or to the popular supposition about the impact of "postmodernism," we ought first to consider the social context within which these worldwide influences take place. Israel has become the stage of contested ideologies since the mid-1990s; major political and social myths have continually been deconstructed and reconstructed. I like in particular the term *prima,* "tear up", suggested to me as related to the decline, or the break up, of the Israeli mainstream ethos. The tear up of a dominant cultural hegemony opens up the public arena and allows hitherto marginal groups to claim the space and articulation they have long been denied.

The Israeli case offers us an opportunity to sensitize our assumptions about the agents and means of globalization. Thus, for example, the geographical closeness or remoteness from the Center is not imperative in order to explain changes in the Periphery. Equally, the exposure to the international media, or the extent of travel from the Periphery to the Center are only secondary variables in a chain of changes that are no less, or even more, influenced by the evolution of the local social context and its cultural representations.

PART FIVE.
ON METHODOLOGY

CHAPTER 16.
NEGOTIATING MULTIPLE VIEWPOINTS THE COOK, THE NATIVE, THE PUBLISHER AND THE ETHNOGRAPHIC TEXT

In recent years, anthropology has become a battered profession, and many of its practitioners have enthusiastically joined in the ritual of devouring their own enterprise. First, and not without some patricidal and matricidal satisfaction, the works of the ancestors were discarded. Soon thereafter, anthropologists lost faith in their core belief about the reliability, the morality and the usefulness of their own efforts. Nevertheless, by and large, we still maintain that anthropology must survive. Deep down we still believe its major role in revealing the human condition in locales both near and far cannot be abandoned because of methodological shortcomings, postmodernist epistemological doubts, or changing circumstances in the traditional fieldwork sites. Some have also come to realize that although anthropologists continue to talk mostly to their own folk, there are new audiences interested in their endeavor that they cannot afford to ignore. Not the least of these is the audience embodying the "object of study" itself.

Its emergence is one more indication that the old relationship between ethnographers, their "informants", and other groups sharing their agenda has significantly changed. I believe it deserves to be further restructured—not just to facilitate the researchers' personal situations during and after fieldwork, to bolster their ethical position, or to ameliorate the stigma and guilt of colonialism but because the painfully gained "truth" of the ethnographic text can no longer be judged exclusively by the verdict of our colleagues or even of sages from other critical disciplines. To the extent that the anthropologist's labor carries authority in representing another reality, it must also stand the test of its subjects. Can they identify themselves in the ethnographic hall of mirrors, as distorted as that image might be in their own eyes? This is probably a far more crucial test of the reliability, morality and usefulness of our work. The full acknowledgement of what has been only an idea simmering among anthropologists in recent years may offer a more constructive revolution in our practice than the fashionable debunking of the ethnographic project.

In keeping with the current spirit of soul-searching, anthropologists have often described the difficulties they experienced with their ethnographic projects. Most of their revelations have focused on their fieldwork. Crapanzano (1977), Rabinow (1977) and Dumont (1978), among the first of many in this genre, pointed out the elements of personal confrontation involved in that undertaking. These chiefly centered on issues related to the ethnographer's identity and relationship with major informants in the field. In my recent study of Congregation Beth Simchat Torah [CBST]—*A Gay Synagogue in New York*—I explored my own experience during fieldwork. In its introductory chapter I discussed the dilemmas and difficulties of integrating into an alien field—of self-presentation and acceptance by the subjects of the study—and the significant role played by key informants.[1]

In the context of this chapter, however, it is not the challenges I faced in doing this fieldwork that I would like to address. Rather, it is those I encountered during the nearly two years it took to transform fieldnotes into a published volume—the "ethnographic text", in current parlance. This was a period of considerable tension and discourse—and a type of confrontation—unlike any I had experienced before. It seemed to bear out Kennedy's (1995: 31) suggestion that this is "a time of problematizing the concept of the isolated individual .... of seeing research itself as a process of inter-connection between the researcher and 'object of study'". I describe my experience in the belief that it raises issues that will be increasingly relevant to the construction of contemporary ethnographies.

---

1   I had also discussed these issues in two earlier ethnographies (Shokeid 1971, 1989).

Some of these problems were succinctly addressed in Brettel's recent volume (1993). Most contributors, however, related to the reactions of the researched to the published ethnographies. Nevertheless, we can learn from their reports and conclusions on the complex relationships ethnographers and the "ethnographed" maintain beyond the formal perception of their respective roles and the delimited period of fieldwork. Illuminating, for example, is Jaffe's assertion: "The experience of writing about people who read what we write and then talk and write back to us undermines our ability to construct an unproblematic Other, and hence, an unproblematic self" (1993: 52). A few participants in Brettel's volume provided some evidence to illustrate their exchange with informants whom they engaged with their texts. (Horwitz, for example, signed his major informants on release forms). However, I intend to introduce an ethnographic approach to represent the discourse between the partners in the ethnographic project that is comparable with other presentations by anthropologists "from the field".

Instrumental in this confrontation between researcher and "object of study" were two individuals who entered the project at the manuscript stage. Each evolved a role as reader and commentator, and each significantly shaped the final work. Though neither was a true "native" of the field, both were insiders in ways I was not, and this conferred authority on their views on content that their roles might not have otherwise. One, "Mark", was informally the first-draft editor of my manuscript, the other, "Jane", my editor at Columbia University Press. Together they achieved a position unique in my ethnographic experience—one predicted, however, by critical anthropologists.[2]

"NATIVE" CHALLENGES AUTHOR'S PREMISES

I met Mark through mutual Israeli friends—a straight couple—toward the end of my stay in New York observing CBST, the gay and lesbian synagogue in the West Village. He, I soon learned, was both gay and

---

2   For example, Marcus and Cushman, 1982, Rosaldo 1989, Sanjek 1993.

a nominal member of CBST, though completely absent from its scene. Early in our friendship I asked him to look over a journal article I was about to submit. He did, and gingerly took correction fluid to a couple of typos. When later I wrote up my first observations of CBST in the form of a paper on the Talmud class, I asked Mark to read it as well, and he did. He was now involved with that ethnographic project and subsequently read the manuscript chapters as they were written.

If Mark's first effort had been confined to a light brush stroke, his work on the CBST ethnography was undertaken with a heavier hand and resulted in extensive changes to the wording and structure of major parts of the manuscript. Initially deferential, Mark ultimately became an alter ego, questioning some of the study's major observations on gay life as well as the theoretical position that framed its approach. A milepost in that journey was a note that he stuck on the wall above the computer during one of our early sessions together. "This is Moshe Shokeid's book". It was both a reminder to himself and a notice to me that he was aware he should not overstep the bounds of his role, but toward the end of the project I felt that as author I was gradually losing my authority. In a number of instances Mark challenged what he saw as my acceptance of the majority—heterosexual—culture's frame of reference. But one of the most fundamental and persistent points of contention between us was one that he felt reflected a different bias: an Israeli conception of Judaism. Its note was struck as early as the opening paragraph of the Talmud-class paper (chapter 12) with which we began our collaboration. The paragraph began:

> If a gay synagogue seems a paradox difficult to comprehend, a Talmud shiur [class] in the real sense of the term seems completely surrealistic for an outsider. I remember the bewildering reaction of my colleague and Orthodox friend Shlomo Deshen ... "How can people who consider themselves Orthodox be gay at the same time?"... This dilemma, introduced by a casual visitor, sets out the major issues of our discussion: Firstly, why do people whose behavior is considered abhorrent in the words of the Torah and in the eyes of Orthodox Jews voluntarily endorse,

CHAPTER SIXTEEN

and how do they accommodate, the text, the norms and the style of life which squarely advertise their stigma? Secondly, why are they tolerated by their fellow "sinners" who openly challenge the upholders of their shared stigma?

Mark immediately objected to the statement that "a gay synagogue seems a paradox difficult to comprehend" and I accepted the qualification "a paradox to the traditionalist".

Some weeks later, back in Israel, I received a letter from him returning to that paragraph:

> Something still bothers me… I'm sure it's the assumption that Judaism and homosexuality are antithetical, and the more one is of the former the less one can be of the latter…. Shlomo Deshen's …. Sounds like a theological question, but its answer probably has more to do with the nature or religion in America as non-canonical and self-defined. How can Catholics consider themselves devout and practice birth control? Easily…. You are introducing an investigation of a culture from a pretty strongly biased vantage… When the overflow CBST crowd convenes at the Javits Center for Yom Kippur, I dare say they are not asking for atonement for their homosexuality …. And if it isn't an issue to the subjects of the study, should it be a framing question for the observer? Does this say more about him than them?

Mark went on to explain that in his experience (in a Conservative suburban temple), Judaism had not been an agent in the transmission of the deep societal antipathy to homosexuality, whose existence he did not question. In this he distinguished his experience from that of the Talmud class members, who frequently reported having felt alienated from Judaism on discovering their homosexuality.

In our ongoing debate over this issue, Mark argued that I brought an unacknowledged bias to my observations, one having nothing to do with sexual orientation: it was the Israeli view of Judaism, which, even among those who identify themselves as secular, accepts the Orthodox interpretation of Judaism as the true faith. No doubt this was the case, but it was also true of many of the earliest and most active members of CBST, who were my informants. In fact, Mark's experience ran counter to that of many CBST members, whose experience could be summed up by Naomi's comment: "I had minimized my connection with Judaism shortly after coming out; the term 'lesbian Jew' felt like an oxymoron".

For Mark, a gay synagogue was no more paradoxical than a synagogue parking lot filled with cars, whose drivers had, in a traditional interpretation, violated the sabbath's rest. For me, the Levitical prohibition against homosexuality was an underlying tension, a motive force, which had propelled CBST's founding and was at the core of its being. It was also a reason often given for having joined the congregation. As an anthropologist and ethnographer, this paradox was what drew me to it.

If I could not embrace Mark's view, I could not dismiss it entirely either, and it made its effect felt in a number of ways in the manuscript. Most directly, I cited Mark's experience as one exception to the frequenct pattern of Jewish alienation and return and quoted him extensively in a footnote. Included was his comment that "believing Jews to be 'essentially liberal and tolerant', he was 'amazed and mortified'… when he read …. Of the Conservative movement's vote against ordaining gay and lesbian rabbis…. Mark heatedly declared: 'They are cheapening my religion—making it the moral equivalent of Cracker Barrel'.[3] I also tacitly acquiesced when in reshuffling the chapter entitled "Why Join a Gay Synagogue?" its original introductory paragraph was lost: "A gay synagogue suggests a direct confrontation not only with Jewish theology, but no less, with major Jewish perceptions of social life. It is not mainly the notion of 'sin' which separates gay and lesbian Jews from the Jewish moral community, but they seem to challenge the Jewish normative order by their betrayal of the ideal of family life". In this instance—though not always—I accepted Mark's

---

3   This is a reference, as Mark explains it, to "a restaurant chain at one of whose Georgia locations gay and lesbian employees were fired as inimical to the 'family' character of the establishment, an action they were legally able to take but which prompted a series of protests".

adamant view that in portraying antipathy between homosexuality and Judaism the voice could be that of God or individual CBST congregants but should not be the author's. As Mark explained in retrospect, the vehemence with which he objected to the portrayal of Jewish homophobia reflected his personal experience as well as a defensive desire to think well of his "people", Jews. During one of our arguments at the time he complained, "You are alienating me from my religion"!

Another chapter opening, which I could not change, contained a somewhat similar dichotomy and remained a contentious issue between us:

> The mere title of "a Gay Synagogue" seems to raise an immediate contradiction of which the most direct designation might be: spiritually and cruising? Can one add it to the list of other gay institutions which almost automatically offer an opportunity for blatant or more latent cruising such as the gay bar and restaurant, the gay sauna and beaches as much as many other gay circles whose titles are less conspicuously sexual?

This opened a chapter originally entitled: "Cruising, Bonding and Talking Sex". Mark was so unhappy with its exclusive focus on male sexuality that he deferred editing its copy until it was too late. On his recommendation, however, I did broaden the scope of the chapter to an exploration of the social component of CBST generally and included material on couples and commitment ceremonies that originally formed a separate chapter.

In another area, Mark attempted to shape the manuscript by giving added visibility to women. This was an attempt to redress the manuscript's tilt toward males, who were then present in greater numbers than females in the synagogue and much more so in leadership roles. Toward this end, he organized a brunch in his apartment in January 1993 to coincide with a visit I was making to New York. His neighbors Naomi and Susan, who were very much involved in CBST, were asked to invite a cross section of women members. The eight who attended were among the most active at CBST. Mark did not intervene in the discussion, and after a few leading questions I took a passive role. The women themselves then engaged in an intense conversation about their experiences in the synagogue and their memories of it. (One younger participant decided, as a result of the meeting, to take a more active role in CBST and ran successfully for a seat on the board of trustees). Mark made a tape recording of the meeting—there was no objection—but was later embarrassed to discover that, in his words, "clanging dishes, overlapping conversation, and ultimately a tired battery diminished its utility somewhat"—words that I included verbatim in the text.

EDITOR CHALLENGES AUTHOR'S GENDER-SENSITIVITY

The question of the visibility of women in the manuscript formed the major issue in the discourse with the other significant partner in the production of the final work, my manuscript editor. The first indication that this might be so came in the form of a warning I received in September 1993, some time after I had signed a contract with Columbia University Press and nearly a year before I had completed the manuscript. In it, the executive editor commented on what she described as an excellent recently published study on gay men in corporate America: "The author explains at the start of the book why he felt it practical to focus only on men. Nevertheless, reviewers are taking him severely to task for slighting women ... I'd hate to have the same thing happen to your book".

In June 1994, after submitting the completed manuscript, I received a warm letter from the executive editor praising the work for its professional contribution and evocative personal voice. After reporting that the manuscript had been favorably reviewed for both form and content, she nevertheless expressed her concern about it: "As it currently stands, the book is vulnerable to the charge of too often rendering the lesbians of CBST invisible". She concluded that the press wished to go ahead and release the manuscript for editing but with the understanding that my editor would not only copy-edit it but also continue to raise questions and make suggestions that addressed the sensitivities of the lesbian congregants.

My editor would also review the use of terminology that might be considered offensive from a feminist or lesbian viewpoint. The manuscript editor whom she recommended was "someone eminently qualified to do this with sensitivity and care. Jane is acquainted with CBST; she identifies herself as bisexual, she has spent time in Israel, she knows and respects your work, and she has been interested in this project from the time we reviewed the prospectus".

I wrote back with some ambivalence (June 20, 1994):

> I am glad you have Jane who is enthusiastic about the topic and appreciative of my work. But wouldn't she carry the issue of male/female "equal representation" and the exactness of terminology too rigorously? I went through many heated arguments with "Mark" who read through most chapters and tried to root out my Israeli and other biases. As much as I was grateful for his contribution I sometimes felt the text lost my personal voice. I dread another experience of the sort.
>
> I have no doubt my work might have been a different product had the synagogue been observed and the manuscript written by a woman, an American man, a Gentile or by any other master identity. After all we can only project a perspective knowledge.
>
> I agree I should be more careful at designating my references to "gay men", "lesbians" and "homosexuals". But would not a thorough regimentation of terms, which sometimes seems to me a matter of "political correctness", spoil the "humanity" of the style and detract from the impact of the ethnography?
>
> I hope that Jane would consider my intimate feelings toward the text, which is for me a double creation—the construction of a social reality, and its communication in a specific personal voice.

In response to the issues raised by the press, I submitted additional text for the chapter on methodology. This effort was acknowledged by the executive editor (August 8, 1994): "Your new paragraphs on your presentation of the women of the congregation are a step in the right direction".

In the ensuing six months, as the press prepared the manuscript for publication, letters were exchanged between the manuscript editor and myself consisting of her comments on the text and my response. This dialogue of collaboration gives evidence of a deep engagement in a joint venture but also—still largely concerned with the issue of gender balance—of a confrontation of conflicting positions and, at times, mutual irritation. Excerpts from this correspondence follow:

> Manuscript editor. Commenting on the urging of a leading informant, Simon, that I record CBST's story ("As he told me later, he was scared that AIDS would wipe out his generation and he wanted the story of the synagogue to survive. He came to believe I could be relied on to be their witness"): *Of course this is representing a generation and a congregation as being made up of only its male members. This seems tacitly insensitive, particularly in the phrase "he wanted the story of the synagogue to survive", to the female members of the congregation who have now changed its character entirely.*

> Author: I disagree, I report ... the authentic feelings of a member of the founding generation that ... was mostly composed of men... I think you observed the congregation in 1994 and assume it looked similar during 1989—1991. I was amazed on my visit to CBST last February to note that the number of women had increased enormously.

> Manuscript editor, on the author's questioning Simon about the poetic loss of naming seven matriarchs and patriarchs, each preceded by "God of", a practice which led another congregant to close his prayer book and continue in silence: *It would seem from your remark to Simon you are virtually egging on the male congregants to express retrograde patterns—is this male bonding?*

CHAPTER SIXTEEN

... You could balance an account such as this with the impact the issues might have on some of the women congregants. You seem to prefer to review the reactions of a rather old-fashioned clique.

Author: I wished to understand the perceptions of congregants who were active and influential in the field... One can claim I got a wrong selection of people. However, I could not be everywhere in the synagogue or produce my research through a "representative sample".

Manuscript editor, on Aaron's claim that for the sake of gender equality the last paragraph in the Purim megillah (Book of Esther), as read at CBST, had lost its humor and fun: *For women, watching Vashti die and Esther manipulate men through dangerous special pleading, it is not a "lighthearted culmination"... you let this guy who isn't really representative of the congregation anymore ... an exotic of halakhic Jew and homosexual, get in the last word.*

Author: I also thought the megillah a bizarre and unethical text when I read it again many years ago. But I am not in the position to include or reject it from Jewish liturgy ... Aaron, that "exotic..." made CBST a haven for many people. Quoting him does not mean I accept his ideas.

Manuscript editor, on the question Mark had objected to earlier framing the chapter on the Talmud class ("Why do people whose behavior is considered abhorrent in the word of the Torah and the eyes of Orthodox Jews...?"): *I would say your attitude is very Israeli, ... rather condescending to the spectrum of attitudes towards acts of homosexuality within, if you like, "Orthodoxy".* [Where Mark had objected to what he believed was my failure to recognize other attitudes besides Orthodox, Jane faulted what she viewed as my omission of them within the Orthodox].

Author: You may not like those men ... but I did not create them through my wild Israeli imagination. The audiences in those

[Orthodox] synagogues are not as "thoughtful" as you suggest and even the gay participants were aware of that.

Manuscript editor, on a question I posed at the brunch—Why were women still reluctant to run for office even though CBST has changed to their advantage—and my interpretation of their response, which was that women did not consider this an important outlet for self-expression and creativity: *The framing of this question comes across as condescending and so does your analysis of the answer: after all, 1, the "natives" were talking to a man, 2, this is a small sampling of women at the synagogue—and old-timers at that ... This is a way of saying that men made women's lives miserable within organizational politics at the synagogue.*

Author: Your reaction comes across as condescending toward that group of women... I am amused by my being portrayed as representative of the oppressive part of humanity... Why not conclude that women are smarter than men and save their time for some more gratifying goals? Don't you thus also accept men's list of priorities?

Manuscript editor, responding to Mark's characterization of the brunch recording—quoted above—which had been inserted in the text: *You ought to delete the remark entirely or revise it carefully. I fear an analogy can be made between that tired battery... and your general awareness of these women while writing our book—not to mention the possible stereotype to be drawn from "clanging dishes, overlapping conversations"...* [Following Jane's advice, I deleted the comment entirely].

Manuscript editor, on the title and content of the "Cruising...." section: *The word cruising has no cachet in the women's community... you have not treated women and men equally in this chapter; you have relied on men's eyes and men's histories, even as you have employed women's eyes and women's histories to buttress your discussion, you have counted on the men for much, much more.*

Author: This is true of course, but a book is not a complete shopping mall .... if the word "cruising" has no cachet in the women's community, does that justify its omission? [Some time later I took some comfort for my inhibited relationships with the lesbian congregants and the limited exposure of female sexuality in my ethnography by citing (p. 245) Gregor's (1985) admission of his deficiency as a male researcher in reporting on women's sexuality, despite the villagers' candor about sexual conduct. Most of the material on that topic, he revealed, was elicited by his wife!].

Manuscript editor, responding to a male congregant's complaint about the synagogue's AIDS programs, now that both its rabbi and its board chair are women: *The women in many of these men's eyes—eyes you use to see CBST—cannot win, they can only lose.* [Accepting Jane's criticism, I deleted from the body of the text the entire section on the impact of AIDS on the position of women in the synagogue—an update on the book's observation period. My suggestion that the demise of leading male congregants opened the way for women to attain leadership positions was transferred to a footnote].

As much as Jane managed to improve the ethnography's balance between men and women, that objective could be only partially achieved. As I pointed out in the book, my data were far more concentrated on the male population, and it was too late to return to the field and expand my work on the women.

At about this time, I composed a letter I intended to send to the executive editor detailing my give-and-take with her manuscript editor. After acknowledging Jane's diligent work and the improvements she made to the manuscript, I commented: "You might appreciate the difficult task we shared. I hope you did not expect me to adopt a feminist viewpoint. I do not consider my role as judge of the behavior I observed, nor do I pretend to introduce all voices." That same day, I received a fax from Jane reacting to some of my responses to her earlier comments: "As I'm sure you are aware.... I am performing a job here, though I enjoy merging some of my personal identity into the process. I'm not as radical as you might think: I happen to be a feminist who is very interested in Halakhah. I believe you succeeded beautifully in what you intended to do ... I appreciate the story you have told profoundly and respect its players".

About a month later, Jane and I met for the first time in New York. I think we were both surprised to discover we liked each other, and we immediately developed a personal rapport. (After the book was published, Jane met Simon, whose observations as reported in my ethnography she had often resented, and they developed a warm relationship. As a result of her work on the book, Jane became active at CBST, where she now teaches a course on women and Judaism).

REHASHING A DEBATE

While in New York, I gave Mark a copy of the corrected galleys I had approved in my meetings with Jane and the executive editor. After returning to Israel in December, relieved that the book was complete, I received a lengthy fax from him. It began:

> I spent a good deal of last weekend reading through your work with mixed emotions. A lot of it flows well and is quite readable. Other of it, to my eyes, needs to be polished and more structured. Some few parts I find wrong-headed and offensive. All in all it represents an immense effort and because it does, it bothers me that it isn't as good as it could be... It frustrates me that you studied gemology, bought the equipment, made the trip halfway around the world, spent years digging in the mine, finally brought out the diamond rock, and then didn't have the

> energy to give it a few taps with the hammer. ... why don't you come to New York in February and spend the first month working on the book? Let its publication be delayed?

In his fax, Mark—who had hoped and expected that the Columbia editor would champion his causes — continued to raise questions we had wrestled with during the previous months. These, I thought, had been sorted out already, or at least I assumed that we had reached a compromise, in style and terms, to satisfy both Mark's feelings and my own professional convictions. Returning to the Talmud-class chapter, he quoted a sentence — "Above all, the drag queen expresses the incongruity that is basic to homosexual experience" — expressing an idea I had borrowed from Esther Newton's Mother Camp (1972). "I do not know what that is", Mark wrote, and went on: "Having a same-sex attraction in a culture where opposite-sex attraction is the norm? That is the only 'incongruity', if that is the right word, I can identify with". He then criticized a passage in the text — "As such it [the Talmud class] was a reminder of the stigma imposed by its people and theology" — as follows:

> It doesn't remind me of the stigma, it reminds me of the prejudice, the stigmatization. [stigma: (a) a mark burned into the skin of a criminal or slave; brand (b) a mark or token of infamy, disgrace or reproach]. To me homophobic Jews have stigmatized themselves by their prejudice and narrow-minded outlook. Their bigotry is their stigma. They are not a reminder of my "shame" as, it seems to me, you suggest.

Mark's complaint revived a long-standing discourse — apparently still unresolved. I am unable now to pinpoint the revisions I had already made to various parts of the manuscript in order to accommodate Mark's discomfort with my use of Goffman's (1963) exposition of "stigma" and its implications. Had I fully accepted his position, that term would have disappeared completely, but I was convinced that this would have robbed the chapter of much of its impact and its special role in the ethnography. I also took heart from the knowledge that, despite his complaints,

Mark found my description of the Talmud class evocative. A number of its members, including its leader, had—except for this class—left CBST for more Orthodox synagogues. And my portrayal of the group as a persistent, anomalous, and not entirely welcome presence in the center of CBST's community hall prompted Mark to suggest a quotation from Herman Melville's Bartleby the Scrivener as an epigraph—the only one in the book: "Like the last column of some ruined temple, he remained standing mute and solitary in the middle of the otherwise deserted room".

In any case, delaying publication for the sake of further deliberations and changes was impractical, as Mark himself soon realized when he had his first contact with the press, delivering some CBST photographs in my absence. He wrote: "My train was derailed this afternoon when I asked the editors to what extent the present stage permits revision. They were not encouraging (to say the least)". As for myself, I had neither the intention nor the stamina to rewrite parts of the manuscript again. About a week later I faxed Mark from Tel Aviv (January 17, 1995): "I am able at last to express my feelings about your amazing ability to digest again my description of CBST .... You remind me of a man who suggests that a pregnant woman delay giving birth for a day or two in order to improve the IQ of her baby". In reply, Mark, with his formidable sense of humor, suggested that I keep his additional improvements for a later date: "When you're Israel's 'Anthropology Laureate' and the gilt-edged reissue of your complete works is being planned, we'll be ready with the revised, re-arranged and improved version". This was our last exchange until we saw the book in print.

Looking back on it then, I was surprised that Mark and I had managed to maintain our friendship intact. Indeed, some time earlier Mark had told me that he wanted to be removed from the acknowledgements. My first thought was that he didn't want his name revealed, didn't want to be "outed", but he immediately explained that he felt he couldn't be identified with a book with which he was not in full agreement. (I learned only much later that it was the introduction to the "Cruising" chapter, quoted above, that was the camel's back-breaking straw). As much as I wished to acknowledge Mark's generous contribution to my life and labor in New

York, I decided not to press the issue. I was relieved, however, a day later when he changed his mind and requested only that I alter the wording of the original acknowledgement. I accepted his amendation (shown in italics), and it became: "Edward Pass – Mark, in my text – was more than my first-draft editor: this would have been another book without his efforts (*and if up to him, yet another*)". It was now made clear that the "wrongheaded" stuff was not his responsibility. This remained the status quo between us, and despite his reservations he later endorsed the book and purchased a number of copies to give to close friends. I cannot report on how Mark felt about our collaboration, but for myself it was, as I wrote in the introductory chapter (p. 14), "a process of pleasure and agony combined. He proved a severe critic with no tolerance for anthropological jargon ... he often suspected me of expressing mainstream ideology and stereotypes, a theme that resulted in hectic arguments and textual alterations ... Mark's involvement gave me the assurance that I was listening to a voice from the field in a way I had never done before".

CONCLUSION

The experience I have described raises a number of issues relevant to the construction of contemporary ethnographies. Some of them were touched on recently by W.F. Whyte, author of the most celebrated urban ethnography, first published in 1943: "Whose voice does the researcher use when reporting results that were collaboratively generated? Can the researcher ever represent anyone but himself/herself?" (Whyte: 1995: 298). Whyte's second question, in particular, does not sound new to an audience of anthropologists beset by doubts about the credibility of "I-witness" ethnography (see Geertz 1988: 79), but from the vantage of over a half-century in the discipline this pioneer ethnographer is confident enough of his methodology to confront the current malaise. Yes, he answers, the researcher can represent others: by actively engaging representatives from the field in the research process.[4]

---

4   A research strategy that Whyte terms "participatory action research".

While my own recent study of CBST did not involve partners from the field in the actual production of the ethnographer's observations, its textual construction drew on the viewpoints of many from the field. Two of those have been highlighted above, but they were not alone. My confrontation with contending viewpoints had, in fact, begun earlier, during fieldwork.

Before presenting my paper on the Talmud class (Chapter 12)—at a meeting of the American Jewish Studies Association—I asked Aaron, the group's leader and a key informant, to read it and give me his comments. He was pleased with my description of the group's activities, the bonds formed between its members, and the atmosphere of the meetings but was surprised, if not disturbed, by the resentment of his group on the part of other congregants that I portrayed. He was also unhappy with my metaphorical comparison of the Talmud disciples to drag queens in their impact on the larger CBST community. Nevertheless, in somewhat Talmudic fashion, he seemed to reason that the benefits of my presentation outweighed its liabilities.

Another early experience with contending viewpoints was prompted by a sermon reprinted in the synagogue's newsletter which, to me, seemed to make a clear—and profane—sexual allusion (see Shokeid 1995: 11-12). I was puzzled. Had the speaker consciously intended this? Or had I imposed this interpretation on his text? I approached a few congregants, including the author of the sermon, to find out how they perceived the piece. They expressed various views, ranging from a complete dismissal of any sexual innuendo to an outright conviction of its presence. What I had believed was an interpretation representing "the natives' point of view" did not necessarily correspond to their own understanding—however attractive it may have been to the anthropologist's mind. Moreover, the natives—contrary to their portrayer—had no single point of view but, rather, multiple viewpoints. I was left with a nagging dilemma: What is to be done when the natives' version is less evocatively revealing about their worldview than that suggested by the observer? How many insights acquired by anthropologists would have been lost had they communicated their findings to their subjects and accepted the natives' verdict on them? This question carries Clifford's argument (1983: 132) about the banishment from the final representative text of discursive situations and of individual interlocutors into far deeper layers of the ethnographic encounter.

Seen more broadly, this experience—like those described earlier—gives rise to the dilemma of multiple viewpoints, a dilemma expressed succinctly in Whyte's first question: "Whose voice does the researcher use?" Mark, Jane, key informants like Simon and Aaron and other congregants made an effort to bring their own worlds—gay, lesbian, feminist, liberal and traditional Jewish—into my story. Faced with their multiple viewpoints—their sometimes competing voices—as well as those of my own gender, sexual orientation, nationality, religious experience and profession, through which theirs were inevitably filtered and reshaped, how successful a course did I thread? Was I too receptive to their efforts or not receptive enough? Did I succumb too easily to the pressures exerted upon me? Or did I prove too stubborn or prejudiced to accept the advice and observations offered by authentic voices from the field?

In the case of the classic ethnographies, only rarely have the "objects of study" reacted to the works that encompassed their lives; this was beyond their reach. And in the many decades since the establishment of modern anthropology, most of its practitioners have looked mainly to their colleagues as potential readers. Only a few have aimed at a broader audience of educated readers as well and then almost always excluded their subjects of research. Even when Crapanzano claimed that the writer of an ethnography addressed two audiences—the audience of other professionals, "his own people", and the silent audience, "those illiterate others on his fieldwork"—from which he affirmed his identity as an ethnographer and obtained his sense of self (1977:72), the balance between the two audiences still obviously privileged the audience of other professionals.

This is not ancient history. Lederman's account (1990:89) of the experience of the anthropologist returning home from a distant field (often geographically but moreover representing an alien culture) reveals the traditional constraints that still dominate our tools and our perspective in the construction of the ethnographic text:

> Once we are home… the scales tilt overwhelmingly in one direction. The commitments we have made to people in our field community are subjected to intense if contradictory competition with commitment to our professional community, which for most of us exerts a more persistent influence. Our conversations, formal and informal—in seminars, conferences and hallways, and indirectly on the pages of journals and books—are constrained by common anthropological idioms.

At the same time, however, anthropologists of the "exotic, puzzling and distant" do now confront a growing awareness in their subjects of the political dimension of their ethnographies (Myers 1986: 152). And the balance has been dramatically changing since anthropologists started to look for fields closer to home. Thus, Ginsburg, who studied the pro-life/pro-choice women activists in a small American town, expressed her experience as follows: "I had to consider a complex readership which included other anthropologists and feminist scholars, as well as my informants and other activists on both sides of the abortion debate" (1993: 174-75). In recent years anthropologists have increasingly been engaging in research relevant to contemporary issues and of interest to new audiences, including the subjects of their fieldwork.[5] And as the fields of "other illiterates" gradually diminish, anthropologists will increasingly encounter their subjects as both enthusiastic readers and competent reviewers. It seemed somewhat remote when Clifford suggested that "it is intrinsic to the breakup of monological authority that ethnographies no longer address a single general type of reader" (1983:141). This was certainly the case with my recent project.

Never before had an ethnography I had written received such a warm reception from the people studied. The book was immediately discovered by CBST members and avidly purchased. Congregants told me how they took copies from remote sections of bookstores and placed them up front. It was their story, and they felt that it deserved greater visibility in their

---

5   See, for example, Ginsburg 1989, Kennedy and Davis 1993, Newton 1993.

city. I lost my position of obscurity in the synagogue. I was asked to speak on the book after a Friday night service and more than one congregant told me, "You are now a celebrity".

The emergence of such new readers, including those from the "colonized object of study", may also effect change within the publishing world. Traditionally, publishers of ethnographic monographs—academic presses, in particular—have been principally concerned with professional peer review. However, as a new audience of readers develops, publishers will increasingly take their new customers' special sensitivities into account. As they do, anthropologists and their publishers may find themselves more and more involved in a web of contentions and dilemmas of the sort I have reported. This will inevitably affect the ethnographic project.

A few years before my current ethnography on CBST, when I was studying Israeli immigrants, I already felt the inescapable changes in the circumstances of our work. I wrote then (1988: 45), "Anthropologists and their informants are inextricably bound together in producing an ethnographic text that integrates the impact of their unique personalities, their social incongruities and dreams". The experience I have reported on here suggests this even more strongly.

CHAPTER 17.
WHAT IS THERE TO A NAME?
THE ETHNOGRAPHER AND HIS
MOROCCAN SUBJECTS IN SHOKEIDA

Over the last two decades we have witnessed the continuing attraction of anthropologists to an analytical perspective and a literary style known as the genre of reflexivity.[1] As reported in a few previous chapters (10, 14, 16) I contributed my own share to that growing shelf of books and articles. I discussed my difficulties and position during fieldwork, my concerns about my ethnographic presentations, and finally, my relationships, and sometimes conflicts, with informants, editors and friends. This time, however, I would like to share some of the feelings and the personal consequences that I am conscious about as related to my long-term ethnographic research in one community of immigrants from the Atlas Mountains who arrived in Israel in 1956 and settled in a Negev village (presented in chapters 2-6).

I feel no urge to transform the ethnographic experiences presented in this closing note into a prototype for a professional career, for identity construction or for any other cultural process that deserves a name.[2] I see myself as narrator of a "true story" deeply interwoven with the historical

---

1   Actually, we are familiar with a "pre-reflexivity" tradition among anthropologists who chronicled seductive stories about their own or about other ethnographers' works and lives. They have usually tried to retrieve an instructive lesson for their academic audience (e.g., Levi-Strauss 1973 [1953]; Powdermaker 1966; Geertz 1988).

2   I could, probably, frame my presentation in terms of the anthropology of experience, and delve into the world of meanings explored by anthropologists, philosophers and historians, in the ongoing discourse about the position and the construction of experience (e.g., Dilthey 1976 [1914], Dewey 1934, Abrahams 1986, Turner 1986, Scott 1991, Shokeid 1992).

events initiated by the emergence of modern Zionism. A lifelong eventuality, that brought together an anthropologist, born in Israel into a family that came from Eastern Europe, with a community of Jewish immigrants from a Moslem country. However, it is also the story of my cohort of Israeli anthropologists who, during the 1960s and 1970s, were mostly engaged in the study of the mass immigration of Jews from the Middle East and North Africa. Among them, for example, Goldberg (1972) who, simultaneously with my own fieldwork assignment, conducted a similar ethnographic project in a farming community of Jewish immigrants from Libya.

I first encountered "my" community in 1961; as a sociologist working for the Jewish Agency Land Settlement Department, I had been assigned to study the villagers' economic situation. I was absolutely fascinated by those people who, to me, represented the "quintessential Jewish *other*." Four years later, now a Ph.D. candidate in anthropology, with a research grant sponsored by the late Max Gluckman of Manchester, I decided to return to that Negev village for 18 months of fieldwork (October 1965-April 1967). It became a lasting professional relationship and remained a critical turning point in my outlook and perception of my subsequent life experiences. It was not the only field I studied throughout my professional career. I had a few other demanding fieldwork engagements: among Israeli Arabs in Jaffa,[3] among Israeli "Yordim" in New York and, more recently, in the gay synagogue also in New York. However, I never completely departed from the Negev village that I dubbed Romema. I returned twice for a few months of fieldwork in each of the summers of 1976 and 1988. I have revisited particular families again and again, and have also continued to publish on various issues of Romema's public life.

But more important, it became part of my personal identity since the day I adopted my family name "Shokeid". About the time I was preparing for the publication of my first ethnography, based on my Ph.D. dissertation, I decided to drop my surname, Minkovitz, which located my family's roots in a Lithuanian landscape, in favor of a Hebrew name. Many Israelis

---

[3] Not reported in this volume. See Shokeid and Deshen, 1982.

in this period were similarly changing their Diaspora names for Hebrew names. Typically, their new names were derived from their old ones by a process of shortening, translation, or linguistic manipulations. Atypically, the name I chose had no connection to my old name, bearing no resemblance to it in form, sound, or meaning. In addition, it was somewhat eccentric in its linguistic construction. It was not a noun or adjective, as was the norm, for example, Mandelbaum became "Shaked" (almond), Stein became "Even" or "Avni" (stone), Weisbrod became "Lahmi" (my bread), etc. Instead, Shokeid, is the present tense of the verb "being diligent." This bit of invention has come at a price: to my annoyance, it is sufficiently unusual to be continually misread and mispronounced as Shaked, Shokad, or Shukad. It requires my frequent correction.

As inventive as it was, my new name did not emerge from whole cloth. And here I will let you in on a private matter which, in the old anthropological tradition, I have never publicly revealed before. The Moroccan immigrant village I had dubbed "Romema," was in fact called "Shokeida."[4] Actually, I was extremely embarrassed (and sometimes offended) when somebody mentioned it, insinuating the origin of my name.

In an article that seems to have preceded the era of reflexivity, I presented a somewhat vague statement: "My decision to adopt a new Hebrew surname, associated with Romema's original name, proved and expressed, at least as regards my feelings at that time, the deep sympathy and respect I felt for the Romemites" (1971:118). I assume that it was no less an act of personal self assertion, a strategy to claim for my self-made positioning against a cultural, socio-ethnic and family background. That act seemed somewhat bizarre when, later in my career, I became similarly engaged with other people's lives. In particular, my most recent work in the gay synagogue was equally rewarding. Nevertheless, the change of name I had made at an early stage of my professional life became a stamp of identity

---

4   For many years I assumed the name Shokeida was adopted from a biblical source related to the term "shokeid." But only recently, as I wished to mention here the accurate source I discovered it was not the case. The various geographical guides indicate: "It is a symbolic name" (e.g., Reuveni 1999:911).

I could never change nor become indifferent to. It made my occupation and a particular project a permanent part of my identity.

What is there to a name? I assume that most people take theirs for granted. I do not know how women who adopt their husband's name feel about it. I do not consider the choice of a name an ontology,[5] but, for the last 35 years I have constantly been aware of my name in a similar way to that which I feel about some other characteristics of my appearance and behavior that must affect my daily life and communication with family, friends and strangers. Whatever this may mean in psychological or literary terms, I can claim, in the strict sense of the term, that "I made my name" with my first fieldwork experience.

My interest in the lives of the Romemites never faded, even as my personal status and life experiences changed very radically since I first came there for fieldwork as an aspiring novice, in what is often considered the major *rite de passage* for anthropologists. Though only sporadically, I continued to observe their personal and communal destinies that have been greatly transformed since my fieldwork in the 1960s.

Actually, before I completed writing up my first research there, I had planned to return to the village and work on a second ethnography. I already had a title: "A Portrait of a Traditional Man." It was to focus on the life and beliefs of one informant and close friend, the late Haviv Dehan.[6] Haviv and his wife, who often invited me for meals, were childless, and we frequently traveled together to various doctors and healers, looking for a remedy or miracle that would beget them an offspring.[7] Haviv was my teacher in the various cultural and religious spheres of Moroccan Jewish life. We developed a close relationship based on mutual affection, and I believed that he would happily cooperate on my next project. On hindsight, it seems I envisioned an ethnography somewhat like Crapanzano's

---

5   See Walzer's comment (1989:117) on George Orwell's choice of his name.
6   The names of the people I mention in the text are not identical with those ascribed to them in earlier publications.
7   See Shokeid 1974a.

Tuami (1980).⁸ But to my great regret and personal loss, shortly before my return to Israel from England, Haviv was killed in a road accident. I assume he would have interpreted that fatal, freak collision between two bicycles on the night before the Day of Atonement as a message directed from the world above or from the world of spirits below. However, it was a clear message for me. I will never write the book I hoped might introduce a novel approach to the presentation of Moroccan Jewish culture.⁹

On my visits in recent years, I have been disappointed with how stagnant, economically and socially, the village has become, compared to the incredible growth I witnessed during the 1960s and 1970s. Already by the late 1970s, I could identify the process of decline and to an extent predict the consequences. In 1976 I spent the summer in Shokeida and witnessed the farmers' adamant refusal to allocate farms to six young native sons who wished to settle in their village. The farmers claimed that they had to reserve the farms for later allocation to the younger children still at home. At that time, I heard the few more perceptive farmers who warned their neighbors and relatives that by opposing the absorption of the six candidates the village would end up as an old-aged home. By the late 1980s, I could see this coming true: no sons (daughters were never candidates for farms) wished to settle there, and also those few young farmers who settled during the early 1970s, had since moved away, looking for places promising a more attractive social environment (Shokeid, 1990).

I visited Shokeida a few times in recent years (2000-2008). I enjoyed a warm and jolly reception from my old friends who had aged as I had. But, in spite of the happy reunion, I could not avoid a feeling of sadness. I did not want to contemplate the prospects for a place where the majority of its residents consisted of aging farmers who have already reduced their activity, widows, and only a very few younger settlers, whom their

---

8 Tuami introduced Crapanzano to the world of Moroccan mystical beliefs.
9 On the publication of a revised edition of *The Generation of Transition* (1999), co-authored with Shlomo Deshen, I was able to offer a late token of gratitude and affection to a friend and a cultural role model I still miss on my visits to Shokeida. I dedicated to Haviv my part in the book.

CHAPTER SEVENTEEN

neighbors described as "failures" who could not successfully adjust anywhere else.

It was particularly prognostic to see a few of the most active farmers during the 1960s and 1970s, who had become full or part-time vendors, as well as owners of shops, in Beersheba and other close or remote markets. They trade mostly in fresh vegetables and fruit which they grow on their farms or purchase regularly from other farmers in Shokeida and nearby villages. I had an opportunity to watch one of the grocers at work when I visited Beersheba and went to see my friend Nathan at his shop in the local market. The shop, however, turned out to be a fruit stand in a cramped line of market stalls. One would imagine a similar scene of vendors, shoppers, voices and smells in other Middle Eastern and third world markets. It suddenly struck me: have "my people" returned to their traditional trades in the Atlas Mountains? Though now they travel by Peugeot or Subaru vans instead of the donkeys that carried their merchandise across the hilly trails to the villages of their Berber clients and down the mountains to Demnate, the major town closest to their home village. Reckless Israeli drivers, rather than belligerent Berber tribesmen, are the dangerous foes they might confront on their daily journeys loaded with tomatoes or cucumbers.

That thought had crossed my mind as I remembered the story from the Atlas Mountains recorded by Geertz (1973: 15) in his exploration of the terms of our constructions about the lives, and the interpretations through which other people formulate their experiences. The *dramatis personae* in that case engaged a Jewish trader, a Berber sheikh, robbers from a neighboring tribe who had attacked the trader and his guests, and a French colonial officer. I must confess that I was somewhat disillusioned as I listened to the former Atlas Mountains native Jews who explained that their present market activity was indispensable to supplement their income, since "you can't survive these days from farming!" I pondered on why the most active farmers have adopted that economic view. At the same time, however, I questioned my own skeptic reaction: have I also been brainwashed by Zionist ideology that denigrated the role and image of shopkeepers as reminders of the "classical Diaspora Jew?"

The transformation of Jews, from peddlers, traders and craftsmen into farmers, has been among the major goals of modern Zionism.[10] Jews in the Atlas Mountains were not allowed to own land and only very rarely were directly engaged in agricultural tasks. The settlers of Shokeida, who became successful farmers and plowed the wilderness of the Negev, seem now to have lost their enthusiasm for that Zionist passion. But also the country they had come to, its leadership, the economy, the conditions of agriculture and major national goals, have changed dramatically since the early days of my fieldwork.

However, regardless of the present decline in farming, no doubt, "my village" proved to be a success story in its ability to provide the founding generation with a good living, and their children (in families that mostly had no less than five sons and daughters) with the education and skills to adjust comfortably in other locales. The older immigrants and their children have done far better than many of their compatriots who settled in the "development towns" of the mid-1950s. Most of these towns have remained underdeveloped and turned into enclaves of poverty. Nevertheless, Shokeida, the once prosperous village, now looked, to me, somewhat shabby and neglected. When my wife and I visited the home of one of my closest friends, a man of my own generation, his wife, Sara, who was among the best educated women of her cohort, told us she missed the noise and activity of the earlier days: "You hardly see people walking around now." All her grown children had left the village. Only the youngest daughter, who was still in the army, and a teenaged son remained--but for how long? Their home was immaculate and looked affluent, with its modern equipment and furniture. But when a widowed relative came by for a late afternoon chat, reminiscing about the old days, it suddenly struck me that I might eventually be named after a vanished world!...

I went to see my close friend Aaron. He now needed a walking stick for support, but still seemed as agile as usual and happy to see me. He apologized for his limp, mentioning that now he was 85. I had never

---

10   See Weingrod's (1966) portrayal of the immigration of Moroccan Jews.

thought about him as an old man. And, true to my image of him, he told me that just last year he had gone back to Morocco for the first time. For one day, he and another Shokeida settler had rented a Land-Rover and drove to their old village in the Atlas Mountains. When they reached the place, they found that it looked exactly as they had left it nearly half a century earlier. Still no electricity and no running water. They met only one man of their generation there, apparently having outlived the others, who remembered that there had been Jews in the community. Proud of the life they had made in Israel, Aaron told the government officer who approached them for documents, that the farm of the least successful settler in Shokeida looked more prosperous than the whole village they had come to visit.

I was happy for Aaron, my reliable informant and friend. He had proved again his ability and courage. Despite his age, he was the first to initiate that trip back to Morocco. Long ago he suggested that one day we might go together to visit their former home in Morocco. Sara and her husband followed his lead, but the younger people had no urge to see the land their parents had come from. (I had made the trip with the first groups of Israeli tourists allowed to enter Morocco, but unfortunately, I had no one to lead me to the village the people I describe had come from).

Life and habits have changed in Shokeida over the years. Sara pointed out that now one can see cars coming and going on the Sabbath. Ironically, she reminded us that when I stayed with them, I did not dare move my car on that day. Shrewd but generous, Sara had known all along that it was not Orthodox observance that had motivated me. But the Moroccans I knew were never religiously fanatic.[11] I met them long before the growing influence of the SHAS party among North African Jews.[12]

---

11 See chapter 7 for my exploration of the religiosity of North African Jews that seems to have been more tolerant and accommodating in daily life compared with Ashkenazi Orthodoxy.

12 SHAS--a successful party that has emerged since the late 1980s. Appealing mostly to voters of Middle Eastern and North African extraction, the party leadership has presented its goals and identity in religious terms.

When I stopped to visit David, the most influential and uncompromising member of the Biton kin group, we were joined by his unmarried son, a modern-looking man in his mid-20s. He did not hesitate to mention, in his father's presence, that he watched videos on the Day of Atonement, and he proclaimed his resentment of Bibi Netanyahu, the ousted prime minister who enjoyed the support of SHAS and other religious parties. David reacted humorously to his son's conspicuous secularism, adding that he himself did not believe in the holy men leading SHAS. But David emphasized that he still goes on pilgrimage to Meron (the burial site of Rabbi Shimeon Bar Yohai)[13] three times a year, and recalled the trip to Meron we took together many years ago (we went there in 1966, in the company of his mother and younger brother).[14]

Nearly forty years ago we had traveled to Meron. One, an aspiring Ph.D. student of anthropology, the other, a strong-minded immigrant from the Atlas Mountains, never-in-doubt farmer, father and believer. Now, at the age of 70, David could congratulate himself on his achievements in farming and raising a family of twelve children, though these educated children would no longer tolerate his strict patriarchal authority. As for the enthusiastic ethnographer, I could say that I had accomplished a satisfactory academic career. But I could not claim that anthropology had made a serious impact in Israeli cultural life.

Israeli anthropology, except for the few early pioneers (Weingrod, Willner, and Rosenfeld, in particular),[15] came late to the universities and despite professional achievements and international recognition, has remained somewhat marginal in Israeli social sciences.[16] Its focus on ethnic cultures ran contrary to the agenda of the "melting pot" ideology of

---

13 Meron--a village in the Galilee, the burial site of Rabbi Shimeon Bar Yohai, the most important post-biblical figure in Jewish folk tradition. Famous as a scholar and patriot, tradition also ascribes to him the writing of the *Zohar* (The major work of Jewish gnosticism).

14 See Shokeid, 1974b.

15 See, for example, Weingrod 1966, Willner 1969, Rosenfeld 1968.

16 See Shokeid 2004.

the first decades. But also the later growing awareness of the persistence of deep socio-economic gaps between Sephardim and Ashkenazim, did not raise much interest in the subjects introduced in the corpus of ethnographic work. Rarely were anthropologists called upon to engage in public discourse. These days, however, when ethnicity and religiosity have dramatically emerged as powerful forces in Israeli public life, one can look back comfortably and acknowledge the contribution made by most Israeli anthropologists who worked among North Africa and other Middle Eastern communities of immigrants (Faige 1998).

I sometimes think that rather than anthropology, had I and my colleagues concentrated our efforts instead on studying the life of Israel's leading politicians, the history and strategy of its major political parties, or the voting habits of its people, we would have garnered a far wider audience. For more than anything else, Israel is a country obsessed with politics. But then, I cannot imagine having chosen LIKUD, MAPAI or SHAS for my family name, or to have fallen in love even with MERETZ![17]

In truth, I have never regretted the choice of my first field and the adoption of its name. An American friend who saw an earlier draft of this story, commented humorously: "Like an intoxicated sailor who on leave has himself tattooed with the name of his first love, you bear the name of your first professional love – or at least, long-term relationship." As much as I sometimes doubt the work, both past and present, done in the name of anthropology, I still would have chosen anthropology as my vocation. Shokeida and Shokeid are a reminder of what I cherish in the craft of ethnographic fieldwork. And besides, there are even a few innocent, young souls who assume their parents' village is named after me!

Naturally, compared with my other ethnographic missions, I never felt that the time was ripe to relinquish my close association with, and interest in the people, as well as with the progress or decline of Shokeida. I am convinced that I will not write a farewell chapter to inform about the end of my professional engagement on this site. Only recently I pub-

---

17 MERETZ--a political party that appeals mostly to educated, secular, Left-wing Israelis.

lished a paper relating the story of my exit as a researcher from the gay synagogue in New York (Chapter 14). Whenever invited, I will return to attend weddings and speak at memorial services set up by the relatives of my deceased old friends of Shokeida, or on the occasion of public events such as the celebration scheduled for August 2007 to commemorate the 50th anniversary of the founding of the village (in 1957).

I assume that a notion of deep obligation and an interminable emotional affinity engulf many anthropologists, everywhere in academia, whose first fieldwork venture became the hallmark of their professional career and a major component of their personal identity. Those feelings, however, seem more potent for Israeli anthropologists whose first fieldwork venture took place during the "era of creation" (1950s-1970s), when the process of nation-building was greatly affected by the mass exodus of Jews from remote diaspora lands. I mention, for example, Bilu, Deshen, and Goldberg, who continued to study the people they encountered many years earlier and never lost interest in their destinies. They have traced the social and cultural transformations of their subjects of research since they arrived in the country and became residents of villages and towns, mostly in the periphery of Israeli social geography.[18] In sum, ethnographic work, in the real sense of the term, often entails a life-long commitment on the part of its practitioners.

---

18   Bilu continuously studied the cult of saints among Moroccan Jews (e.g. Bilu 1987, 2003), Deshen continued to inquire into the culture of Tunisian Jews (e.g. Deshen 1974, 1997), and Goldberg never parted from his work with Libyan Jews (e.g. Goldberg 1972, 1994).

BIBLIOGRAPHY

Abrahams, Roger D. (1986). "Ordinary and Extraordinary Experiences," in V.W. Turner and E.M. Bruner (eds.) *The Anthropology of Experience*. Urbana: University of Illinois Press, pp. 45-72.

Abu-Lughod, Lila (1990). "Shifting Politics in Bedouin Love Poetry," in C.A. Lutz and L. Abu-Lughod (eds.), *Language and the Politics of Emotion*. Cambridge: Cambridge University Press, pp. 24-45.

Alpert, Rebecca (1997). *Like Bread on the Seder Plate: Jewish Lesbians and the Transformation of Tradition*. New York: Columbia University Press.

Amir, M., and S. Shihor (1975). "Ethnicity and Juvenile Delinquency in Israel," *Crime and Social Deviance* 3: 1-15 (Hebrew).

Arian, A. (1981). "Elections 1981: Competitiveness and Polarization" *Jerusalem Quarterly* 21; 16-20.

Bakan, D. (1971). *Slaughter of the Innocents*. San Francisco.

Bar-Asher, S. (1981). "The Jews in North Africa and Egypt," in S. Ettinger (ed.) *History of the Jews in the Islamic Countries*. Jerusalem: Zalman Shazar Center, pp. 172-3 (Hebrew).

Bar-Yosef, R. (1959). "The Moroccans: The Background of a Problem." *Molad* 17: 247-51 (Hebrew). Revised English version 1970, in S.N. Eisenstadt et al. (eds.), *Integration and Development in Israel*. Jerusalem: Israel Universities Press, pp. 419-28.

Bar-Joseph, R. (1968). "Desocialization and Resocialization: The Adjustment Process of Immigrants," *International Migration Review* 2: 27-45.

Bar-Yosef, Y. (1976). "Actual and Potential *Yordim*," *Moznaim* 42: 83-86. (Hebrew).

Barth, F. (1969). *Ethnic Groups and Boundaries*. Boston, MA: Little Brown and Company.

Behar, Ruth (2003). "Ethnography and the Book that was Lost," *Ethnography* 4(1): 15-39.

Bellah, Robert N., Richard Masden, William Sullivan, Ann Swidler, and Stephen Lipton (1985). *Habits of the Heart: Individualism and Commitment in American Life*. Berkeley, CA: University of California Press.

Ben-Ami, Issachar (1977). "The Folklore of War: The Motif of Saints," in, S. Verssess et al. (eds.) *Dov Sadan*. Tel Aviv: Hakibbutz Hameuhad, pp. 87-104 (Hebrew).

Ben-Ami, Ilan (1992). "Shleppers and Car Washers: Young Israelis in the New York Labor Market," *Migration World*. 20: 18-20.

Ben-David, Joseph (ed.) (1964). *Agricultural Planning and Village Planning in Israel*, Paris: UNESCO

Benedict, Burton (1957). "Factionalism in Mauritian Villages," *British Journal of Sociology* 8: 328-42.

Ben-Tolila, Y. (1983). *The Sociophonology of Hebrew as Spoken in a Rural Settlement of Moroccan Jews in the Negev*. Ph.D. thesis. The Hebrew University (Hebrew).

Berler, A. (1970). *New Towns in Israel.* Jerusalem: Israel Universities Press (Hebrew).

Bernstein, D. (1978). "A Critical Review of a Dominant School in Israeli Sociology." *Mahbarot le'Mehkhar ule-Vikoret* 1: 5-19 (Hebrew).

Bilu, Yoram (1979). "Demonic Explanations of Disease among Moroccan Jews in Israel," *Culture, Medicine and Psychiatry* 3: 363-380.

Bilu, Yoram (1987). "Dreams and Wishes of the Saint," in H. Goldberg (ed.) *Judaism Viewed From Within and From Without: Anthropological Exploration in the Comparative Study of Jewish Culture.* New York: State University of New York Press, 285-314.

Bilu, Yoram (2003). *The Saints' Impresarios: Dreamers, Healers and Holy Men in Israel's Urban Periphery.* Haifa: Haifa University Press (Hebrew).

Bohannan, P. (1960). *African Homicide and Suicide.* Princeton.

Boissevain, Jeremy (1964). "Factions, Parties and Politics in a Maltese Village," *American Anthropologist* 66: 1275-87.

Bolton, R. (1995). "Tricks, Friends, and Lovers: Erotic Encounters in the Field," in *Taboo: Sex, Identity, and Erotic Subjectivity in Anthropological Fieldwork*, D. Kulick and M. Willson (eds.). London: Routledge, pp. 140-167.

Boyarin, Jonathan (1992). *Storm from Paradise: The Politics of Jewish Memory.* Minneapolis, MN: University of Minnesota Press.

Boyarin, Jonathan (1996). *Thinking in Jewish.* Chicago, IL: The University of Chicago Press.

Brettel, Caroline B. (ed.) (1993). *When They Read What We Write: The Politics of Ethnography.* Westport, Conn.: Bergin and Garvey.

Bryce-Laporte, R.S. (ed.) (1980). *Sourcebook on the New Immigration.* New Brunswick, NJ: Transaction Books.

Burawoy, M. et al. (1991). *Ethnography Unbound: Power and Resistance in the Modern Metropolis.* Berkeley: University of California Press.

Burke, E. (1976). *Prelude to Protectorate in Morocco.* Chicago: University of Chicago Press.

Buyra, Janet M. (1973). "The Dynamics of Political Action: A New Look at Factionalism," *American Anthropologist* 75: 132-52.

Callaway, Helen (1992). "Ethnography and Experience: Gender Implications in Fieldwork and Texts," in J. Okely and H. Callaway (eds.), *Anthropology and Autobiography.* London: Routledge, pp. 29-49.

Caroli, B. Boyd (1982). "Recent Immigration to the United States," *Trends in History* 2: 49-69.

Chouraqui, A.C. (1968). *Between East and West.* Philadelphia: Jewish Publication Society.

Clifford, James (1983). "On Ethnographic Authority," *Representations* 1: 118-46.

Climo, Jacob J. and Maria G. Cattel (Eds.) (2002). *Social Memory and History: Anthropological Perspectives.* Walnut Creek, CA: Alta Mira Press.

Cohen, Albert (1955). *Delinquent Boys: The Culture of the Gang.* Glencoe.

Cohen, Abner (1965). *Arab Border-Villages in Israel.* Manchester: Manchester University Press.

Cohen, Abner (1969). *Customs and Politics in Urban Africa.* London: Routledge & Kegan Paul.

Cohen, Abner (ed.) (1974). *Urban Ethnicity,* A.S.A. Monograph 12. London: Tavistock.

Cohen, Abner (1980). "Drama and Politics in the Development of a London Carnival," *Man,* 15: 65-87.

Cohen, Erik (1972). "The Black Panthers and Israeli Society," *Jewish Journal of Sociology* 14: 93-109.

Cohen, Erik (1992). "Pilgrimage Centers: Concentric and Eccentric," *Annals of Tourism Research* 19:33-50.

Cohen, M. Steven (1980). "American Jewish Feminism: A study in Conflicts and Compromises," *American Behavioral Scientist* 23: 519-558.

Cooper, S. (1978). *Newgate: An Old-New Town in the Negev.* Ph.D. Dissertation, The Catholic University of America.

Cowan, Paul (1986). *Orphan in History.* New York, NY: Bantam Books.

Crapanzano, V. (1977). "On the Writing of Ethnography," *Dialectical Anthropology* 2: 69-73.

Crapanzano, Vincent (1980). *Tuhami: Portrait of a Moroccan*. Chicago: University of Chicago Press.

Davis, Fred (1979). *Yearning for Yesterday: A Sociology of Nostalgia*. New York: Free Press.

Deshen, Shlomo (1969). "The Ethnic Synagogue: Patterns of Religious Change in Israel," in S.N. Eisenstadt and A. Zloczower (eds.) *The Integration of Immigrants from Different Countries of Origin in Israel*. Jerusalem: Magnes Press, pp. 66-73 (Hebrew).

Deshen, Shlomo (1970). *Immigrant Voters in Israel: Parties and Congregations in a Local Election Campaign*. Manchester: Manchester University Press.

Deshen, Shlomo (1974). "The Memorial Celebrations of Tunisian Immigrants,." in S. Deshen and M. Shokeid (eds.) *The Predicament of Homecoming: Cultural and Social Life of North African Immigrants in Israel*. Ithaca: Cornell University Press, pp. 95-121.

Deshen, Shlomo (1974). "Political Ethnicity and Cultural Ethnicity in Israel during the 1960s", in A. Cohen (ed.) *Urban Ethnicity*. London: Tavistock, pp. 281-309.

Deshen, Shlomo (1978). "Israeli Judaism: Introduction to the Major Patterns", *International Journal of Middle East Studies* 9: 141-169.

Deshen, Shlomo (1980). "Religion among Middle Eastern Immigrants in Israel", in A. Arian (ed.) *Israel A Developing Society*. Assen: Van Gorcum, pp. 235-246.

Deshen, S. (1983). *Individuals and the Community: Social Life in 18th-19th Century Moroccan Jewry*. Defense Ministry, 1983.

Deshen, Shlomo (1997). "Near the Jerba Beach: Tunisian Jews, An Anthropologist, and Other Visitors," *Jewish Social Studies* 3: 90-118.

Deshen, Shlomo and M. Shokeid (1974). *The Predicament of Homecoming: Cultural and Social Life among North African Immigrants in Israel.* Ithaca, N.Y.: Cornell University Press.

Deshen, Shlomo and M. Shokeid (1984). *Jews of the Middle East.* Tel Aviv: Shocken Publishing House (Hebrew).

Dewey, John (1934). *Art as Experience.* New York: Minton, Balch and Co.

Dilthey, W. (1976)[1914]. *Selected Writings.* H.P. Rickman (ed. and trans.). Cambridge: Cambridge University Press.

Diner, Hasia R. (2000). *Lower East Side Memories: A Jewish Place in America.* Princeton, NJ: Princeton University Press.

Diner, Hasia R., Jeffrey Shandler, and Beth S. Wenger. (Eds.) (2000). *Remembering the Lower East Side: American Jewish Reflections.* Bloomington, IN: Indiana University Press.

Diskin, A. (1982). "The 1981 Elections: Public Opinion Polls," *Jerusalem Quarterly* 22: 99-104.

Dominguez, Virginia (2000). "For a Politics of Love and Rescue," *Cultural Anthropology* 15(3): 361-393.

Don-Yehiya, Eliezer (2005). "Orthodox Jewry in Israel and in North America," *Israel Studies* 10(1): 157-187.

Douglas, M. (1966). *Purity and Danger.* London: Routledge & Kegan Paul.

Dumont, Jean-Paul (1978). *The Headman and I: Ambiguity and Ambivalence in the Fieldworking Experience.* Austin: University of Texas Press.

Durkheim, Emile (1964). *The Division of Labor in Society.* New York: The Free Press.

Eade, J. (1992). "Pilgrimage and Tourism at Lourdes, France." *Annals of Tourism Research* 19:18-32.

Eickelman, Dale F. (1976). *Moroccan Islam.* Austin: University of Texas Press.

Eickelman, Dale F. (1981). *The Middle East: An Anthropological Approach.* Englewood Cliffs: Prentice Hall.

Eidelheim, H. (1969)."When Ethnic Identity is a Social Stigma". in F. Barth (ed). *Ethnic Groups and Boundaries.* Boston, MA: Little Brown and Company, pp. 39-57.

Eisendstadt, S.N. (1954). *The Absorption of Immigrants.* London: Routledge & Kegan Paul.

Eisendstadt, S.N. (1968). *Max Weber on Charisma and Institution Building.* Chicago and London: The University of Chicago Press.

Elam, Y. (1973). *The Sexual Roles of Hima Women.* Manchester: Manchester University Press.

Elam, Y. (1978). "Use of Force among Moroccan and Georgian Immigrants," *Megamot* 24: 169-185 (Hebrew).

Elizur, D. (1980). "Israelis in the United States: Motives, Attitudes and Intentions". in M. Himmelfarb and D. Singer (eds), *American Jewish Yearbook.* New York: The American Jewish Committee, pp. 53-67.

Epstein, Arnold L. (1961). "The Network and Urban Social Organization," *Rhodes-Livingston Journal* 29: 29-62.

Epstein, Arnold L. (1981). *Urbanization and Kinship*, London and New York: Academic Press.

Featherstone, M. (1990). "Global Culture: An Introduction," *Theory, Culture & Society* 7:1-14.

Feige, Michael (1998). "Archaeology, Anthropology and Development Towns: The Construction of Place in Israel," *Zion* 63: 441-459 (in Hebrew).

Fein, A. (1978). *The Process of Migration: Israeli Emigration to the United States.* Ph.D. Thesis. Cleveland, OH: Case Western Reserve University.

Feld, Steven (1982). *Sound and Sentiment: Birds, Weeping, Poetics and Song in Kaluli Expression.* Philadelphia: University of Pennsylvania Press.

Feshbach, S. (1964). "The Function of Aggression and the Regulation of Aggressive Drive," *Psychological Review* 71: 257-272.

Firth, Raymond (1957). "Factions in Indian and Overseas Indian Societies," *British Journal of Sociology* 8: 291-95.

Firth, Raymond (1961). "Suicide and Risk-Taking in Tikopia Society," *Psychiatry* 24:1-17.

Fisher, M.P. (1980). "Indian Ethnic Identity: The Role of Associations in the New York Indian Population," in P.Saran and E. Eames (eds), *The New Ethnics: Asian Indians in the United States.* New York: Praeger, pp. 179-192.

Fishman Barack, Sylvia (1993). *A Breath of Life: Feminism in the American Jewish Community.* New York: The Free Press.

Flamand, P. (1959). *Diaspora en Terre d'Islam: Les Communautés Israelites du Sud Marocain.* Casablanca: Presses des Imprimeries Reunies.

Foner, N. (ed.) (1987). *New Immigrants in New York.* New York: Columbia University Press.

Franzmann, Majella (2000). *Women and Religion.* New York and Oxford: Oxford University Press.

Freedman, M. (1982). "A Lesbian in the Promised Land," in E. Torton Beck (ed.), *Nice Jewish Girl.* Watertown, Mass., Persephone Press.

Freud, Sigmund (1975) (first published 1930). *Civilization and its Discontents.* London.

Friedlander, D. and C. Goldscheider (1978). "Immigration, Social Change and Cohort Fertility in Israel," *Population Studies* 31: 299-317.

Gal, R. (1994). "Gays in the Military: Policy and Practice in the Israeli Defence Forces" in W.J. Scott and S.C. Stanley (eds.) *Gays and Lesbians in the Military:Issues, Concerns, and Contrasts.* Hawthorne, NY: Aldine de Gruyter, pp. 181-189.

Gans, H.J. (1979). "Symbolic Ethnicity: The Future of Ethnic Groups and Cultures in America," *Ethnic and Racial Studies* 2: 1-20.

Geertz, Clifford (1968). *Islam Observed: Religious Development in Morocco and Indonesia.* New Haven and London: Yale University Press.

Geertz, Clifford (1973). *The Interpretation of Culture*. New York: Basic Books.

Geertz, Clifford (1980). *Works and Lives: The Anthropologist as Author*. Stanford CA: Stanford University Press.

Geertz, H. (1979). "The Meaning of Family Ties," in C. Geertz, H. Geertz, and L. Rosen (eds.) *Meaning and Order in Moroccan Society*. New York: Cambridge University Press, pp. 315-91.

Gellner, E. (1969). *Saints of the Atlas,* London: Weidenfeld and Nicolson.

Gellner, E. (1972). "Political and Religious Organization of the Berbers of the Central High Atlas," in E. Gellner and C. Micaud (eds.), *Arabs and Berbers*. Lexington: Heath, pp. 59-66.

Ginsburg, Faye (1989). *Contested Lives: The Abortion Debate in an American Community*. Berkeley: University of California Press.

Glazer, N., and D.P. Moynihan (1970). *Beyond the Melting Pot: The Negroes, Puerto Ricans, Jews, Italians and Irish of New York City*. Cambridge, MA: The M.I.T. Press (first published 1963).

Glazer, N., and D.P. Moynihan (eds.) (1975) *Ethnicity: Theory and Experience*. Cambridge MA: Harvard University Press.

Gluckman Max (1963). *Custom and Conflict in Africa*. Oxford: Basil Blackwell.

Gluckman Max (1965). *Politics, Law and Ritual in Tribal Society*. Chicago: Aldine.

Goffman, Erving (1961). *Encounters*. New York: Bobbs-Merrill.

Goffman, Erving (1968). *Stigma: Notes on the Management of Spoiled Identity.* Harmondsworth, Middlesex (UK): Penguin Books Ltd., (first published 1963).

Goitein, S.D. (1967). *A Mediterranean Society,* 4 vols. Berkeley: University of California Press.

Goitein, S.D. (1974). *Jews and Arabs: Their Contacts Through the Ages.* (first published 1955) reprinted, New York: Schocken.

Gold, S.J. (1997). "Transnationalism and Vocabularies of Motives in International Migration: The Case of Israelis in the United States," *Social Perspectives* 40(3): 409-27.

Goldberg, Harvey (1972). *Cave Dwellers and Citrus Growers: A Jewish Community in Libya and Israel.* Cambridge: Cambridge University Press.

Goldberg, Harvey (1977). "Introduction: Culture and Ethnicity in the Study of Israeli Society", *Ethnic Groups* 1: 163-186.

Goldberg, Harvey (1978). "The Memuna and Minority Status of Moroccan Jews", *Ethnology* 17: 75-87.

Goldberg, Harvey (1994). "Jerba and Tripoli: A Comparative Analysis of Two Jewish Communities in the Maghreb," *Journal of Mediterranean Studies* 4: 278-299.

Goldscheider, C. (1986). "Family Change and Variation Among Israeli Ethnic Groups," in S.M. Cohen and P.E. Hyman (eds.) *The Jewish Family: Myth and Reality.* New York: Holms and Meier, pp. 131-147.

Gothalf, Y. (1976). "The *Yordim* who Torment Nation and Land," *Davar*, 16 January, pp. 11, 19 (Hebrew).

Gregor, Thomas (1985) *Anxious Pleasures: The Sexual Lives of an Amazonian People*. Chicago: University of Chicago Press.

Gross, Daniel R. (1973). "Factionalism and Local Level Politics in Rural Brazil," *Journal of Anthropological Research* 29: 123-44.

Halper, J. and H. Abramovitch (1984). "The Saharanei Celebration in Kurdistan and Israel," in S. Deshen and M. Shokeid (eds.) *Jews of the Middle East: Anthropological Perspectives on Past and Present*. Tel Aviv: Shocken, pp. 260-270.

Hannerz, Ulf (1989). "Notes on the Global Ecumene." *Public Culture* 1:66-75.

Hannerz, Ulf (1990). "Cosmopolitan and Locals in World Culture." *Theory, Culture and Society* 7:237-251.

Hannerz, Ulf (1993) (n.d.). *Introduction: Varieties of Centers and Peripheries in the Global Ecumene*. Session on "The Center in the Periphery" 13th International Congress of the Anthropological and Ethnological Sciences, Mexico City, August 1993.

Hansen, M.L.(1938). *The Problems of the Third Generation Immigrant*. Rock Island: Augustana Historical Society.

Hansen, M.L. (1952). "The Third Generation in America," *Commentary* 14: 492-500.

Har-Even, Y. (1989). *Emigration as a Social Problem: Emigration from Israel as Reflected in "Letter to the Editor" of Ha'aretz, 1949-1987*.

Unpublished M.A. Thesis. Tel Aviv: Tel Aviv University, Department of Sociology and Anthropology. (Hebrew).

Hart, D.M. (1972). "The Tribe in Modern Morocco," in E. Gellner and C. Micaude (eds.), *Arabs and Berbers*. Lexington: Heath, pp. 25-58.

Hart, D.M. (1976). *The Aith Waryushun of the Moroccan Rif: An Ethnography and Histoy.* Texas: University of Arizona Press.

Hartman, N. and H. Ayalon (1975). "Ethnicity and Stratification in Israel," *Megamot*: 124-129 (Hebrew).

Hawlbachs, M. (1992). *On Collective Memory*. Chicago, IL: The University of Chicago Press.

Heilman, Samuel C. (1973). *Synagogue Life: A Study in Symbolic Interaction*. Chicago, IL: The University of Chicago Press.

Heilman, Samuel. C. (1983). *The People of the Book*. Chicago: University of Chicago Press.

Heilman, Samuel C. and Steven M. Cohen (1989). *Cosmopolitans and Parochials: Modern Orthodox Jews in America*. Chicago: The University of Chicago Press.

Herman S.N. (1970). *Israelis and Jews: The Continuity of an Identity*. New York: Random House.

Herzfeld, Michael (1991). *A Place in History: Social and Monument Time in a Creatan Town*. Princeton, NJ: Princeton University Press.

Herzog, H. 1984. *Political Ethnicity: Image versus Reality*. Tel Aviv (Hebrew).

Horowitz, Bethamie, Beck Pearl and Charles Kadushin (1998). *Power and Parity: Women on the Boards of Major American Jewish Organizations.* Ma'yan: The Jewish Women's Project and The Center for Jewish Studies at the Graduate School and University Center, CUNY.

Humphreys, L. (1970). *Tearoom Trade: Impersonal Sex in Public Places.* Chicago: Aldine Publishing Company.

Hustrup, Kirsten (1992). "Writing Ethnography: State of the Art," in J. Okley and H. Callaway (eds.), *Anthropology and Autobiography.* London: Routledge, pp. 116-133.

Inbar, M., and C. Adler (1977). *Ethnic Integration in Israel.* New Brunswick, NJ: Transaction Books.

Isaacs H.R. (1975). "Basic Group Identity: The Idols of the Tribe," in N. Glazer and D.P. Moynihan (eds.) *Ethnicity: Theory and Experience.* Cambridge, MA: Harvard University Press, pp. 29-52.

Jacobson, Y. (1987). *Secular Pilgrimages in the Israeli Context: The Journey of Young Israelis to Distant Countries.* M.A. Thesis, Tel Aviv University, Department of Sociology and Anthropology (in Hebrew).

Jones, B. Kathleen (1993). *Compassionate Authority: Democracy and the Representation of Women.* New York/London:Routledge.

Kama, A. (2000). "From *Terra Incognita* to *Terra Firma*: The Logbook of the Voyage of Gay Men's Community into the Israeli Public Sphere," *Journal of Homosexuality* 38: 133-162.

Kaplan, D. (1999). *David, Jonathan and Other Soldiers: Identity, Masculinity and Sexuality in Combat Units in the Israeli Army.* Tel Aviv: Hakibbutz Hameuchad (in Hebrew).

Kass, D. and S.M. Lipset (1982). "Jewish Immigration to the United States from 1967 to the Present: Israelis and Others," in M. Sklare (ed.), *Understanding American Jewry*. New Brunswick, NJ: Transaction Books, pp. 272-294.

Katz, J. (1961) *Tradition and Crisis: Jewish Society at the end of the Middle Ages*. New York: The Free Press of Glencoe.

Katz, J., and Z. Zloczower (1958). "Ethnic Continuity in the Second Generation: A Report on Yemenites and Ashkenazim in a Small Israeli Town," *Megamot* 9: 187-200 (Hebrew).

Kaufman, David (2000). "Constructions of Memory: The Synagogues of the Lower East Side," in Dinner, Hasia R, et al. (eds.), *Remembering the Lower East Side: American Jewish Reflections*. Bloomington, IN: Indiana University Press, pp. 113-136.

Keinan, A. (1976). "A Letter to a *Yored*". *Yedioth Ahronoth*, 4 April, Passover Issue Supplement, p. 5 (Hebrew).

Kenna, Margaret E. (1992). "Changing Places and Altered Perspectives," in J. Okley and H. Callaway (eds.), *Anthropology and Autobiography*. London: Routledge, pp. 147-162.

Kennedy Lapovski, Elizabeth (1995) "In Pursuit of Connection: Reflections on Collaborative Work," *American Anthropologist* 97: 26-33.

Kennedy Lapovski, Elizabeth, and Madeline D. Davis (1993). *Boots of Leather, Slippers of Gold: The History of a Lesbian Community*. New York: Routledge.

Kessner, T. and B. Boyd Caroli (1981). *Today's Immigrants, Their Stories: A New Look at the Newest Americans*. New York and Oxford: Oxford University Press.

Korazim, J. (1983). *Israeli Families in New York City: Utilization of Social Services, Unmet Needs and Policy Implications*. Ph.D. Thesis. New York: Columbia University, School of Social Work.

Kugelmass, Jack (1986). *The Miracle of Intervale Avenue*. New York, NY: Schocken.

Lacks, Roslyn (1980). *Women and Judaism: Myth, History and Struggle*. New York: Doubleday Company, Inc.

Lancaster, R.N. (1988). "Subject Honor and Object Shame: The Construction of Male Homosexuality and Stigma in Nicaragua," *Ethnology* 27: 111-126.

Langer, Susanne K. (1953). *Feeling and Form*. New York: Scribner's.

Lederman, Rena (1990). "Pretexts for Ethnography: On Reading Fieldnotes," in R. Sanjek (ed.) *Fieldnotes: The Makings of Anthropology*. Ithaca: Cornell University Press, pp. 71-91.

Lehman, C. Edward (1985). *Women Clergy: Breaking Through Gender Barriers*. New Brunswick: Transaction Books.

Leon, Nisim (2008). "Ethnic Synagogues of Mizrahi Jews in Israel: Ethnicity, Orthodoxy, and Nationalism," *Sociological Papers*. Bar Ilan University, 30: 6-23.

Lerner Lapidus. Ann (1973). "'Who Has Not Made Me a Man': The Movement for Equal Rights for Women in American Jewry," in

M. Fine and M. Himmelfarb (eds.) *American Jewish Yearbook 77*. New York and Philadelphia: American Jewish Committee and Jewish Publications Society of America, pp.3-38.

Lev Ari, L. (2008). *The American Dream for Men Only?: Gender, Immigration and the Assimilation of Israelis in the United States*, L.F.B. Scholarly Publishing.

Levi-Strauss, Claude (1974) [1955] *Tristes Tropiques*. New York: Atheneum.

Levy, R.I. (1973). *Tahitians: Mind and Experience in the Islands*. Chicago: University of Chicago Press.

Liberson, S. and M.C. Waters (1988). *From Many Strands: Ethnic and Racial Groups in Contemporary America*. New York: Russel Sage Foundation.

Lieblich, A and G. Friedman (1985). "Attitudes Toward Male and Female Homosexuality and Sex-Role Stereotypes among Israeli and American Students," *Sex Roles* 12:561-570.

Liebow, E. (1968). *Tally's Corner*. Boston: Little Brown.

Light, I. (1985). "Immigrant Entrepreneurs in America," in N.Glazer (ed.) *Clamor at the Gates: The New American Immigration*. San Francisco, CA: Institute for Contemporary Studies, pp. 161-180.

Loeb, L.D. (1976). "Dhimmi Status and Jewish Roles in Iranian Society," *Ethnic Groups* 1: 89-105.

Luzato, D. (1984). *Features of a Voluntary Organization: Homosexuals in Israel.* M.A. Thesis, Tel Aviv University, Department of Sociology and Anthropology (in Hebrew).

Malinowski, B. (1967). *A Diary in the Strict Term.* New York: Harcourt, Brace and World.

Marcus, G.E. (1982). "Rhetoric and the Ethnographic Genre in Anthropological Research," in J. Ruby (ed.), *A Crack in the Mirror.* Philadelphia: University of Pennsylvania Press, pp. 163-171.

Marcus, G.E., and P. Cushman (1982). "Ethnographies as Texts," *Annual Review of Anthropology* 11: 25-69.

Marx, E. (1976). *The Social Context of Violent Behavior: A Social Anthropological Study in an Israeli Immigrant Town.* London: Routledge & Kegan Paul.

Matras, J. (1965). *Social Change in Israel.* Chicago: Aldine.

Matras, J. (1973). "On Changing Matchmaking, Marriage, and Fertility in Israel: Some Findings, Problems, and Hypotheses," *American Journal of Sociology* 79: 364-88.

Mayer, Adrian C. (1957). "Factions in Fiji Indian Rural Settlements," *British Journal of Sociology* 8: 317-28.

Mayer, Adrian C. (1961). *Peasants in the Pacific.* London: Routledge and Kegan Paul.

McNamara, T.F. (1987). "Language and Social Identity: Some Australian Studies," *Australian Review of Applied Linguistics*, 10(2).

Mead, M. (1935). *Sex and Temperament in Three Primitive Societies.* New York.

Meyer, Leonard B. (1956). *Emotion and Meaning in Music.* Chicago: University of Chicago Press.

Meyers, A.R. (1966) [1977]. "Patronage and Protection: The Status of Jews in Precolonial Morocco," in S. Deshen and W.P. Zenner (eds.) *Jews Among Muslims: Communities in the Precolonial Middle East.* Macmillan Press, pp. 83-97.

Middleton, John (1960). *Lugbara Religion: Ritual and Authority among an East African People.* London: Oxford University Press.

Mittelberg, D. and M.C. Waters (1992). "The Process of Ethnogenesis among Haitians and Israeli Immigrants in the United States," *Ethnic and Racial Studies* 15: 412-435.

Mizrachi, S. (1990). *Same-Sex Couples Coping with Stigma.* M.A. Thesis, Tel Aviv University, School of Social Work (in Hebrew).

Mizrachi, S. (2002). *The Gay's Sad Family: The Construction of Reality in a Family with a Gay Offspring.* Ph.D. Thesis, Tel Aviv University (in Hebrew).

Montagne, R. (1930). *Les Berberes et le makhzen dans le sud du Maroc: Essai sur la transformation politique des Berberes sedentaires.* Paris: Felix Alcan.

Montagu, A. (1976). *The Nature of Human Aggression.* New York: Oxford University Press.

Morris, H.S. (1957). "Communal Rivalry among Indians in Uganda," *British Journal of Sociology* 8: 306-17.

Murray, O.S. (1984). *Social Theory: Homosexual Realities.* New York: Gai Saben Monographs No.3.

Murray, O.S. (1992). "The 'Underdevelopment' of Modern Gay Homosexuality in Mesoa America" in K. Plummer (ed.) *Modern Homosexualities.* London: Routledge, pp. 29-38.

Myerhoff, Barbara (1974). *Peyote Hunt: The Sacred Journey of the Huichol Indians.* Ithaca: Cornell University Press.

Myerhoff, Barbara (1978). *Number Our Days.* New York: Simon and Schuster.

Myerhoff, Barbara and J. Ruby (1982). "Introduction," in J. Ruby (ed.), *A Crack in the Mirror.* Philadelphia: University of Pennsylvania Press, pp. 1-35.

Myers, Fred (1986). "The Politics of Representation: Anthropological Discourse and Australian Aborigines," *American Ethnologist* 13: 138-53.

Nettleship, M.A., R.D. Givens, and A. Nettleship (eds.) (1975). *War, Its Causes and Correlates.* The Hague and Paris: Mouton Publishers.

Newton, Esther (1972). *Mother Camp: Female Impersonators in America,* Chicago: University of Chicago Press.

Nicholas, Ralph W. (1965). "Factions: A Comparative Analysis," in Banton, Michael (ed.), *Political Systems and the Distribution of Power.* ASA Monograph 2, London: Tavistock, pp. 21-61.

Noy, C. and E. Cohen (eds.) (2005). *Israeli Backpackers and their Society: A View from Afar.* New York, NY: SUNY Press.

Noy, D. (1964). *Jewish Folktales from Morocco.* Jerusalem:Bitfuzot Hagolah.

Nusbaum, Emily (1998). "Return of the Natives: What Happens When an Anthropologist's Manuscript is Edited by his Subjects?" *Lingua Franca* 8(1), February: 53-56.

O'Nell, C.W. (1979). "Nonviolence and Personality Dispositions Among the Zapotec: Paradox and Enigma," *The Journal of Psychological Anthropology* 2: 301-322.

Ortner, Sherry B. (1974). "Is Female to Male as Nature is to Culture?" in M.Z. Rosaldo and L. Lamphere (eds.), *Woman, Culture, and Society.* Stanford: Stanford University Press, pp. 67-88.

Ovadia D. (1975). *The Community of Sefrou.* Jerusalem: Center of Moroccan Studies (Hebrew).

Palgi, P. (1966). "Cultural Components of Immigrants' Adjustment," in H.P. David (ed.), *Migration, Mental Health and Community Services.* Washington, pp. 71-82.

Park, R.E. and H.A. Miller (1925). *Old World Traits Transplanted.* Chicago: Society for Social Research, University of Chicago.

Paz, Octavio (1981). *The Labyrinth of Solitude.* New York: Grove Press.

Peres, Y. and R. Katz (1981). "Stability and Centrality: The Nuclear Family in Modern Israel," *Social Forces* 59: 687-704.

Peters, E.L. (1967). "Some Structural Aspects of the Feud among the Camel-Herding Bedouin of Cyrenaica," *Africa*, 37: 261-282.

Plummer. K. (ed.) (1992). *Modern Homosexualities*. London: Routledge.

Powdermaker, Hortense (1966). *Stranger and Friend: The Way of an Anthropologist*. New York: W.W. Norton & Co.

Pratt, Norma Fain (1980). "Transitions in Judaism: The Jewish American Women through the 1930s," in J. Wilson James (ed.), *Women in American Religion*. University of Pennsylvania Press, pp. 207-228.

Prell, Riv-Ellen (1989). "Sacred Categories and Social Relations: The Visibility and Invisibility of Gender in an American Jewish Community," in H. Goldberg (ed.) *Judaism Viewed from Within and from Without*. Albany: State University of New York, pp.171-194.

Prell, Riv-Ellen (1989). *Prayer and Community: The Havurah in American Judaism*. Detroit: Wayne State University Press.

Putnam, Robert D. (1995). "Bowling Alone: American Declining Social Capital." *Journal of Democracy*: 65-78.

Quanty, M.B. (1976). "Aggression Catharsis: Experimental Investigations and Implications," in R.G. Green and E.C. O'Neal (eds.), *Perspectives on Aggression*. New York, pp. 99-132.

Rabinow, Paul (1977). *Reflections on Fieldwork in Morocco*. Berkeley: University of California Press.

Rabinowitz, Henry (1983). "Talmud Class in a Gay Synagogue," *Judaism* 32: 437-39.

Radcliffe-Brown, A.R. (1952). *Structure and Function in Primitive Society.* London.

Ram, Uri (ed.) (1993). *Israeli Society: Critical Perspectives.* Tel Aviv (Hebrew).

Read, Kenneth E. (1965). *The High Valley.* New York: Columbia University Press.

Read, Kenneth E. (1986). *Return to the High Valley: Coming Full Circle.* Berkeley, CA: University of California Press.

Reuveni, Immanuel (1999). *Eretz-Israel Lexicon.* Tel Aviv: Miskal-Yediot Ahronot Books (Hebrew).

Ritterband, P. (1969). "The Determinants of Motives of Israeli Students Studying in the United States," *Sociology of Education* 42: 330-349.

Ritterband, P. (1986). "Israelis in New York," *Contemporary Jewry* 7: 113-126.

Roche, J.P. (1984). "Social Factors Affecting Cultural, National and Religious Ethnicity: A Study of Suburban Italian-Americans," *Ethnic Groups* 6: 27-45.

Romanucci-Ross, L. (1973). *Conflict, Violence and Morality in a Mexican Village.* Palo Alto.

Rosaldo, Renato (1980). *Ilongot Headhunting 1883- 1974: A Study in Society and History.* Stanford, CA: Stanford University Press.

Rosaldo, Renato (1989). *Culture and Truth: The Remaking of Social Analysis.* Boston: Beacon Press.

Rosen, Lawrence (1972). "Muslim-Jewish Relations in a Moroccan City," *International Journal of Middle Eastern Studies* 3: 435-449.

Rosen, Lawrence (1979). "Social Identity and Points of Attachment," in C. Geertz, H. Geertz and L. Rosen (eds.) *Meaning and Order in Moroccan Society.* Cambridge: Cambridge University Press, pp. 19-111.

Rosenfeld, Henry (1968). "Changes, Barriers to Change, and Contradictions in the Arab Village Family," *American Anthropologist* 70: 732-752.

Rumbaut, R.G. and A. Portes. (1990). *Immigrant America.* Berkeley and Los Angeles, CA: University of California Press.

Sanjek, Roger (1978). "A Network Method and Its Uses in Urban Anthropology," *Urban Anthropology* 37: 257-268.

Sanjek, Roger (1988). The People of Queens from Now to Then. New York: *Asian/American Working Papers,* Queens College, CUNY.

Sanjek, Roger (1993). "Anthropology's Hidden Colonialism: Assistants and their Ethnographers," *Anthropology Today* 9: 13-18.

Saran and J. Leonhard-Spark (1980). "Attitudinal and Behavioral Profile," in P. Saran and E. Eames (eds.), *The New Ethnics: Asian Indians in the United States.* New York: Praeger, pp. 163-176.

Saran, P. and E. Eames (eds.) (1980). *The New Ethnics: Asian Indians in the United States.* New York: Praeger.

Scheper-Hughes, Nancy (2000). "Ire in Ireland," *Ethnography* 1: 117-140.

Schneider, Jane (1971). "Of Vigilance and Virgins: Honor, Shame, and Access to Resources in Mediterranean Societies," *Ethnology* 10: 1-24.

Schryer, Frans J. (1975). "Village Factionalism and Class Conflict in Peasant Communities," *Canadian Review of Sociology and Anthropology* 12: 290-302.

Scott, J.P. (1958). *Aggression*. Chicago:The University of Chicago Press.

Scott, Joan Wallach (1988). *Gender and the Politics of History*. New York: Columbia University Press.

Scott, Joan Wallach (1991). "The Evidence of Experience," *Critical Inquiry* 17: 773-797.

Sedgwick, Eve (1990). *Epistemology of the Closet*. Berkeley: University of California Press.

Sered, S. Susan (1994). *Priestess, Mother, Sacred Sister*. New York/Oxford: Oxford University Press.

Sered, S. Susan (2001). "Religiosity Doing Gender: The Good Woman and the Bad Woman in Israeli Ritual Discourse," *Method and Theory in the Study of Religion* 13: 153-176.

Sharot, S. (1976). *Judaism: A Sociology*. London: David and Charles.

Shenhar, A. (1972). *Family Confrontation and Conflict in Jewish Folktales*. Ph.D. Thesis, The Hebrew University.

Shils, Edward A. (1958). "The Concentration and Dispersion of Charisma: Their Bearings on Economic Policy in Underdeveloped Countries," *World Politics* 11: 1-19.

Shoham, S. and G. Rahav (1967). "Social Stigma and Prostitution," *Annales Internationales de Criminologie* 6: 479-513.

Shokeid, Moshe (1968). "Immigration and Factionalism: An Analysis of Factions in Rural Israeli Communities of Immigrants," *The British Journal of Sociology*, xix: 385-406.

Shokeid, Moshe (1971). *The Dual Heritage: Immigrants from the Atlas Mountains in an Israeli Village*, Manchester: Manchester University Press (augmented edition, 1985. New Brunswick, N.J: Transaction Books).

Shokeid, Moshe (1971a). "Fieldwork as Predicament Rather Than Spectacle," *Archives Européennes de Sociologie*, XII: 111-122.

Shokeid, Moshe (1971b). "Social Networks and Innovation in the Division of Labour Between Men and Women in the Family and in the Community: A Study of Moroccan Immigrants in Israel," *Canadian Review of Sociology and Anthropology* 8: 1-17.

Shokeid, Moshe (1974a). "The Emergence of Supernatural Explanations for Male Barrenness among Moroccan Immigrants," in S. Deshen and M. Shokeid, *The Predicament of Homecoming*. Ithaca: Cornell University Press, pp. 122-150.

Shokeid, Moshe (1974b). "An Anthropological Perspective on Ascetic Behavior and Religious Change: Cultural and Social Life of North African Immigrants in Israel," in Deshen, S. and M. Shokeid, *The Predicament of Homecoming*. Ithaca, N.Y.: Cornell University Press, pp. 64-94.

Shokeid, Moshe (1976). "Conviviality Versus Strife: Peacemaking at Parties Among Atlas Mountain Immigrants in Israel," *Political Anthropology* 1: 101-21.

Shokeid, Moshe (1980a). "Reconciling with Bureaucracy: Middle Eastern Immigrants' Moshav in Transition," *Economic Development and Cultural Change* 29: 187-205.

Shokeid, Moshe (1980b). "Ethnic Identity and the Position of Women Among Arabs in an Israeli Town," *Ethnic and Racial Studies* 3: 188-206.

Shokeid, Moshe (1988a). *Children of Circumstances: Israeli Emigrants in New York*. Ithaca, N.Y.: Cornell University Press.

Shokeid, Moshe (1988b). "Anthropologists and Their Informants: Marginality Reconsidered," *Archives Européennes de Sociologie*, XXIX: 31-47.

Shokeid, Moshe (1988-89). "The Manchester School in Africa and Israel Revisited: Reflections on the Sources and Method of an Anthropological Discourse," *Israel Social Science Research*, 6:9-23.

Shokeid, Moshe (1990). "Generations Divorced: The Mutation of Familism among Atlas Mountains Immigrants in Israel," *Anthropological Quarterly* 63: 76-89.

Shokeid, Moshe (1992a). "Commitment and Contextual Study in Anthropology," *Cultural Anthropology*, 7: 464-477.

Shokeid, Moshe (1992b). Exceptional Experiences in Everyday Life," *Cultural Anthropology*, 7: 232-243.

Shokeid, Moshe (1995). *A Gay Synagogue in New York*. New York: Columbia University Press.

Shokeid, Moshe (1997). "Negotiating Multiple Viewpoints: The Cook, the Native, the Editor, and the Ethnographic Text," *Current Anthropology* 38(4): 631-645.

Shokeid, Moshe (2001). "'Our Group Has a Life of its Own': An Affective Fellowship of Older Gay Men," *City & Society* XIII (1): 5-30.

Shokeid, Moshe (2004). "Max Gluckman and the Making of Israeli Anthropology," *Ethnos* 69: 387-410.

Shokeid, Moshe (2007). "Anthropological Texts: Mirrored Memories of Researcher and Subjects," in D. Mendels (ed.) *On Memory: An Interdisciplinary Approach*. Oxford: Peter Lang Publishers, pp. 275-298.

Shokeid, Moshe and Shlomo Deshen (1982). *Distant Relations: Ethnicity and Politics among Arabs and North African Jews in Israel*. New York: Praeger and Bergin.

Shokeid, Moshe and Shlomo Deshen (1977, expanded edition 1999). *The Generation of Transition: Continuity and Change Among North African Immigrants in Israel*. Jerusalem: Yad Izhak Ben-Zvi (in Hebrew).

Shtal, A. (1975). "The Order of Seating in the Synagogue as Reflection of the Type of Service," in Y. Ilan et al. (eds.) *Mikdash Me'at*. Jerusalem: Ministry of Education, pp. 46-56 (Hebrew).

Shtal, A. (1978). "Prostitution among Jews as a Symptom of Cultural Transition," *Megamot* 24: 202-25 (Hebrew).

Siegel, Bernard J. and Alan Beals (1960a). "Pervasive Factionalism," *American Anthropologist* 62: 395-417.

Siegel, Bernard J. and Alan Beals (1960b). "Conflict and Factional Dispute," *Journal of the Royal Anthropological Institute* 90: 107-17.

Silverman, Marilyn and R.F. Salisbury (eds.) (1977). *A House Divided: Anthropological Studies of Factionalism*. St. Johns: Institute of Social and Economic Research, Memorial University of Newfoundland.

Singer, Milton (1955). "The Cultural Patterns of Indian Civilization," *Far Eastern Quarterly,* 15: 23-36.

Siu, P.C.P. (1952). "The Sojourner," *American Journal of Sociology*, LVIII: 34-44.

Slouschz, N. (1927). *Travels in North Africa.* Philadelphia: Jewish Publication Society.

Smith, E.M. (1978). "The Case of the Disappearing Ethnics," in E.L. Ross (ed.), *Interethnic Communication.* Athens, GA: The University of Georgia Press, pp. 63-77.

Smith, V.L. (1992). "Introduction: The Quest in Guest." *Annals of Tourism Research* 19:1-17.

Smooha, S. (1978). *Israel: Pluralism and Conflict.* Berkeley: University of California Press.

Sobel, Z.B. (1986). *Migrants from the Promised Land.* New Brunswick, NJ: Transaction Books.

Spilerman, S., and J. Habib (1976). "Development Towns in Israel: The Role of Community in Creating Ethnic Disparities in Labor Force Characteristics," *American Journal of Sociology* 81: 781-812.

Spooner, Brian (1965). "Kinship and Marriage in Eastern Persia," *Sociologus* 15: 22-31.

Statistical Abstract of Israel (1980). Jerusalem: Central Bureau of Statistics.

Stein, Arlene and Ken Plummer (1996). "'I Can't Even Think Straight': 'Queer' Theory and the Missing Sexual Revolution in Sociology," in S. Seidman (ed.) *Queer Theory/Sociology*. Cambridge and Oxford: Blackwell, pp.129-144.

Stein, Marc (1994). "Sex Politics in the City of Sisterly and Brotherhood Loves," *Radical History Review*. 59: 59-92.

Steinmetz, S.K. and M.A. Straus (eds.) (1974). *Violence in the Family*. New York: Harper & Row.

Stillman, N. (1977). "Muslims and Jews in Morocco," *Jerusalem Quarterly* 5: 74-83.

Stonner, D.M. (1976). "The Study of Aggression: Conclusions and Prospects for the Future," in R.G. Green and E.C. O'Neal (eds.) *Perspectives on Aggression*. New York, pp. 235-260.

Storr, A. (1968). *Human Aggression*. London: Allen Lane the Penguin Press.

Styles, J. (1979). "Outsider/Insider: Researching Gay Baths," *Urban Life* 8: 135-152.

Svirsky S. and D. Bernstein(1980). "Who Worked Where, for Whom and for What: Economic Developments in Israel and the Emergence of an Ethnic Division of Labor" *Mahbarot le'Mekhar ule-Vikoret*: 45-66 (Hebrew).

Swarts, Norman B. (1969). "Goal Attainment Through factionalism:A Guatemalan Case" *American Anthropologist* 71: 1088-1108.

Swedenburg, T. (1989). "Occupational Hazards: Palestine Ethnography," *Cultural Anthropology*, 4: 265-272.

Swedenburg, T. (1992). "Occupational Hazards Revisited: Reply to Moshe Shokeid," *Cultural Anthropology,* 7: 478-495.

Tattelman, I. (1999). "Speaking to the Gay Bathhouse: Communicating in Sexually Charged Spaces," in W.L. Leap (ed.) *Public Space/Gay Space.* New York: Columbia University Press, pp. 71-94.

Taub, G. (1997). *A Dispirited Rebellion: Essays on Contemporary Israeli Culture.* Tel Aviv: Hakibbutz Hameuchad (in Hebrew).

Taylor, L. C. (1985). "Mexican Male Homosexual Interaction in Public Contexts." *Journal of Homosexuality* 11:117-136.

Tessler, M.A. (1978) "The Identity of Religious Minorities in Non-Secular States: Jews in Tunisia and Morocco and Arabs in Israel", *Comparative Studies in Society and History* 20: 359-374.

Thernstrom, S. (ed.) (1980). *Harvard Encyclopedia of American Ethnic Groups.* Cambridge, MA: Harvard University Press.

Thomson, J. (1889). *Travels in the Atlas and Southern Morocco.* London: George Philip.

TIME (1985). "The Newest Americans," *Time,* 8 July.

Tocqueville, Alexis de (1956). *Democracy in America* (Richard D. Heffmen, ed.). New York: Mentor Books.

Tonkin, Elizabeth (1992). *Narrating Our Past: The Social Construction of Oral History.* Cambridge, UK: Cambridge University Press.

Turnbull, Colin (1972). *The Mountain People.* New York: Simon and Schuster.

Turner, Victor W. (1957). *Schism and Continuity in Ndembu Society*. Manchester: Manchester University Press.

Turner, Victor W. (1960). "Muchona the Hornet," in J. Casagrande (ed.), *In the Company of Man*. New York: Harper, pp. 334-355.

Turner, Victor W. (1973). "The Center Out There: Pilgrim's Goal." *History of Religions* 12:191-230.

Turner, Victor W. (1974). *Drama, Fields and Metaphors: Symbolic Action in Human Society*. Ithaca: Cornell University Press.

Turner, Victor W. (1986). "Dewey, Dilthey, and Drama: An Essay in the Anthropology of Experience," in V.W. Turner and E.M. Bruner (eds.) *The Anthropology of Experience*. Urbana: University of Illinois Press, pp. 33-44.

Turner, V. and E. Turner (1978). *Images and Pilgrimages in the Christian Culture*. New York: Columbia University Press.

Tzabar, N. (1996). "Kibbutz L.A." Tel Aviv: *Hakibutz Hameuchad* (Hebrew).

Ugalde, A., F.D. Bean and G. Cardenas (1979). "International Migration from the Dominican Republic: Findings from a National Survey," *International Migration Review* 13: 235-254.

Van den Berghe, P.L. (1981). *The Ethnic Phenomenon*. New York: Elsevier North Holland.

Van Teeffelen, T. (1978). "The Manchester School in Africa and Israel: A Critique," *Dialectical Anthropology*, 3: 67-83.

Varma, B.N. (1980). "Indians as New Ethnics: A Theoretical Note," in P. Saran and E. Eames (eds.) *The New Ethnics: Asian Indians in the United States*. New York: Praeger, pp. 29-41.

Wallace, A. Ruth (1997). "The Mosaic of Research on Religion: Where Are the Women?" *Journal for the Scientific Study of Religion*. 36:1-12.

Walters, M.C. (1990). *Ethnic Options: Choosing Identities in America*. Berkeley, CA: University of California Press.

Walzer, Michael (1989). *The Company of Critics*. London: Peter Halban.

Waxman, Chaim I. (1983). *American Jews in Transition*. Philadelphia: Temple University Press.

Weber, M. (1947). *The Theory of Social and Economic Organization*. New York: Oxford University Press.

Weeks, J. (1991). *Against Nature: Essays on History, Sexuality and Identity*. London: Rivers Oram Press.

Weingrod, Alex (1960). "Moroccan Jewry in Transition," *Megamot* 10: 193-208 (Hebrew).

Weingrod, Alex (1966). *Reluctant Pioneers: Village Development in Israel*. Ithaca: Cornell University Press.

Weingrod, Alex (1979). "Recent Trends in Israeli Ethnicity," *Ethnic and Racial Studies* 2: 55-65.

Weintraub, Dov and M. Lissak (1964). "Social Integration and Change" in J. Ben-David (ed.) *Agricultural Planning and Village Community in Israel*. Paris: UNESCO.

Weintraub, Dov, Lissak, M., and Atzmon, Y. (1969). *Moshava, Kibbutz and Moshav: Patterns of Jewish Rural Settlement and Development in Palestine.* Ithaca and London: Cornell University Press.

Weintraub, Dov et al. (1971). *Immigration and Social Change: Agricultural Settlements of New Immigrants in Israel.* Manchester: Manchester University Press.

Wertheimer, Jack (ed.) (1987). *The American Synagogue: A Sanctuary Transformed.* Cambridge: Cambridge University Press.

Whyte, William Foote (1943). *Street Corner Society.* Chicago: University of Chicago Press.

Whyte, William Foote (1995). "Encounters with Participatory Action Research." *Qualitative Sociology* 18: 289-300.

Willner, D. (1969). *Nation Building and Community in Israel.* Princeton: Princeton University Press.

Wirth, L. (1928). *The Ghetto.* Chicago: The University of Chicago Press.

Wolf, Margery (1992). *A Thrice Told Tale: Feminism, Postmodernism and Ethnographic Responsiblity .* Stanford: Stanford University Press.

Wolfgang, M.E., and F. Ferracuti (1967). *The Subculture of Violence: Towards an Integrated Theory in Criminology.* London.

Wolpin, Nisson (1974). "Jewish Women in a Torah Society: For Frustration? or Fulfillment?", *The Jewish Observer* X (Nos. 5-6): 12-18.

Wulff. Helena (1993) (n.d.). *Moratorium on Manhattan: Young Swedes and Globalization*. University of Stockholm, Department of Social Anthropology.

Wulff, Helena (2000). "Access to a Closed World: Methods for a Multilocale Study on Ballet as a Career," in V. Amit (ed.), *Constructing the Field: Ethnographic Fieldwork in the Contemporary World*. London: Routledge, pp. 147-161.

Wuthnow, Robert (1994). *Sharing the Journey: Support Groups and America's New Quest for Community*. New York, NY: The Free Press.

Yadava, J.S. (1968). "Factionalism in a Haryana Village," *American Anthropologist* 70: 898-910.

Yancey, W.L., E.P. Ericksen and R.N. Juliani (1976). "Emergent Ethnicity: A Review and Reformulation," *American Sociological Review* 41: 391-403.

Yancey, W.L., P. Ericksen and G.H. Leon (1985). "The Structure of Pluralism: 'We're all Italian Around Here, Aren't We, Mrs. O'Brian?'" *Ethnic and Racial Studies*. 8: 94-116.

Yehoshua, A.B. (1981). *Between Right and Right*. Garden City, NY: Doubleday & Company.

Youth Probation Service Annual Reports (1977, 1978). Jerusalem: Ministry of Labor and Welfare.

Zenner, W.P. (1965). "Saints and Piecemeal Supernaturalism among the Jerusalem Sephardim," *Anthropological Quarterly* 38: 201-217.

Zerubavel, Eviatar (1996). "Social Memories: Steps to a Sociology of the Past," *Qualitative Sociology* 19: 283-299.

INDEX OF NAMES

A

Abrahams, Roger	341
Abu Hatzeira, Aaron	128
Abu-Lughod, Lila	278
Adler, C.	86
Almagor, Dan	176
Alterman, Nathan	171-172
Amir, M.	81
Arian, A.	116
Ayalon, H.	115

B

Bakan, D.	64
Bar-Yosef, R.	62, 81, 150
Barth, F.	145, 189
Beals, Alan	44, 58-59
Behar, Ruth	276, 298
Bellah, Robert	231
Ben-Ami, Ilan	144
Ben-Ami, Issachar	130
Ben-David, Joseph	98
Ben-Tolila, J.	82
Benedict, Burton	58
Berler, A.	82
Bernstein, D.	115-116
Bilu, Yoram	74-75, 130, 351
Bohannan, P.	63, 75
Boissevain, Jeremy	44
Bolton, R.	306
Boyarin, Jonathan	201, 204, 208, 222-223, 231, 233
Brettel, Caroline	322
Bryce-Laporte, R.S.	146

Burawoy, M. 17
Burke, E. 40
Buyra, Janet 44

C

Callaway, Helen 295
Caroli, B. 143, 146, 153
Cattel, Marcia 231
Chazan, Robert 115
Chouraqui, A.C. 30
Climo, Jacob 231
Cohen, Abner 20, 44, 60, 116, 119, 145
Cohen, Erik 81, 232, 305, 313
Cohen, Steven 230, 269
Cohen, Percy 16
Cohen, Yinon 149
Cooper, S. 78, 82, 86
Cowan, Paul 204, 229
Crapanzano, Vincent 21, 191, 321, 338, 344-345
Cushman, P. 25, 322

D

Dana International 314-315
Dahl, Gudrun 14
Davis, Fred 185
Davis, Madeline 339
Dayan, Yael 304
Demnate 33-34, 36, 97, 346
Deshen, Shlomo 10, 16, 20-22, 33-34, 65, 82, 84, 88, 90, 96, 105, 111-112, 115, 117-122, 124, 130, 132, 134-136, 145, 147, 188-189, 200, 236, 323, 324, 342, 345, 351
Dewey, John 341
Dilthey, W. 341
Diner, Hasia 204
Diskin, A. 116
Dominguez, Virginia 297
Dor, Moshe 177
Douglas, M. 152

Dumont, Jean-Paul   191, 295, 321
Durkheim, Emil   233
Dushman, Yisrael   180

E

Eames, E.   144
Eickelman, Dale   21, 57, 61, 106
Eidheim, H.   145
Eisenstadt, S.N.   14, 18, 110, 116, 142
Eitan, Rachel   196, 198
Elam, Yitzhak   18, 63, 77
Elizur, D.   149
Ericksen, E.P.   116, 136, 139, 143, 145, 164-165
Even, Uzi   304, 308-309, 315

F

Featherstone, M.   300, 302
Fein, A.   149
Feld, Steven   185, 187
Ferracuti, F.   64, 75
Feshbach, S.   64
Firth, Raymond   18, 44, 58-59, 63
Flamand, P.   31, 35-36
Franzmann, Majella   251
Freedman, Marcia   303
Friedlander, D.   80, 85
Friedman, Menachem   115, 303

G

Gans, H.J.   116, 164
Geertz, Clifford   21, 23, 32, 63, 84, 106, 186-189, 191, 199, 245, 249, 278, 298, 336, 341, 346
Gellner, Ernest   24, 35, 40, 106
Gerholm, Tomas   14
Gila'd, Zerubavel   172
Ginsburg, Faye   339
Givens, R.D.   63
Glazer, N.   146, 165
Gluckman, Max   16-18, 20, 63, 76, 273, 342

Goffman, Erving	26, 161-162, 187, 334
Goitein, S.D.	133-134
Goldberg, Harvey	31, 111, 116-117, 131, 342, 351
Goldscheider, C.	80, 85
Gregor, Thomas	332
Gross, Daniel	58

H

Habib, J.	82, 115
Hannerz, Ulf	14, 300-302, 313
Hansen, M.L.	139, 164
Har-Even, Y.	150
Hart, D.M.	35, 40-41
Hartman, M.	115
Hastrup, Kirsten	295-296
Hawlbachs, M.	231
Hayerushalmi, Levy Itzhak	128
Hefer, Hayim	173
Heilman, Samuel	186, 189, 229-230, 236, 245-246
Herzfeld, Michael	231
Herzog, H.	138
Horowitz, Bethamie	269

I

Isaacs, H.R.	144

J

Jones, B.	251, 267, 275
Juliani, R.N.	116, 136, 139, 145

K

Kaige, Chan	297
Kama, Amit	304, 308
Kass, D.	149
Katz, Jacob	80, 105, 115, 118, 134, 302
Kenna, Margaret	278
Kennedy-Lapovski, Elizabeth	321, 339
Kessner, T.	143, 146, 153
Kipnis, Levin	170

Klatchkin, Refael	173
Kleinbaum, Sharon	254-256, 264, 268, 272, 274, 279-280, 282, 286-289, 292-293
Korazim, J.	147, 149
Kugelmass, Jack	233

L

Langer, Susanne	184
Lee, Lilian	297
Leon, G.H.	140, 143, 164-165
Leonhard-Spark, J.	144
Lieblich, A.	303
Liebow, E.	147
Light, I.	144
Lipset, S.M.	149
Lissak, M.	116
Loeb, L.D.	39-40

M

Malinowski, B.	19, 190
Manor, Ehud	177
Marcus, G.E.	25, 191, 322
Marx, E.	62-63, 69, 76-77, 82
Matras, J.	88, 122
Mayer, Adrien	44, 58
McNamara, T.F.	164
Mead, Margaret	63
Meyer, Leonard	185
Meyers, A.R.	31
Middleton, John	17, 273
Miller, H.A.	142
Mitchell, Clyde	17
Mizrachi, S.	303, 311
Mohar, Yechiel	174
Montagu, A.	63
Morris, H.S.	58
Moynihan, D.P.	146, 165
Myerhoff, Barbara	190, 231, 276, 301

N

Nettleship, M.A.	63
Netzer, Ephi	169
Newton, Esther	248-249, 334, 339
Nicholas, Ralph	44
Nini, Yehuda	127
Noy, C.	232, 305
Noy, D.	106

O

O'Nell, C.W.	63
Ortner, Sherry	251
Ovadia, D.	134

P

Paine, Robert	303
Palgi, P.	63, 81
Park, R.E.	142
Parsons, Talcot	14
Pass, Edward	336
Paz, Octavio	185
Peres, Y.	80, 302
Peters, Emrys	17, 19, 63
Plummer, K.	272, 300
Pniel, Noah	170
Portes, A.	146
Powdermaker, Hortense	341
Pratt, Norma	252
Prell, Riv-Ellen	230, 270-271, 273, 275
Putnam, Robert	230

Q

Quanty, M.B.	64

R

Rabbi Ovadia Jossef	140
Rabin, Yitzchak	150, 314
Rabinow, Paul	21, 191, 321
Rahav, G.	81

Ram, U.	116
Read, Kenneth	278, 298
Rebee Al'Aziz	107-108, 110-111
Reuveni, Immanuel	343
Ritterband, P.	147, 149
Roche, J.P.	164-165
Romanucci-Ross, L.	66
Rosaldo, Renato	231, 322
Rosen, Lawrence	21, 30-31, 40, 42, 61, 63, 132
Rosenfeld, Henry	349
Rotblit, Jacob	174
Rumbaut, R.G.	146

S

Salisbury, R.F.	44
Sampson, Elissa	201-202
Sanjek, R.	147, 322
Saran, P.	144
Scheper-Hughes, Nancy	277, 295
Schryer, Frans	44, 58
Scott, J.P.	64
Scott, J.W.	64, 251, 275, 341
Sedgwick, Eve	272
Sered, S.	251
Shalmoni, Hayim	177
Shandler, Jeffrey	204
Shapira, Rachel	175
Shemer, Naomi	159, 169, 178-179
Shenhar, A.	74
Shihor, S.	81
Shils, Edward	59
Shoham, S.	81
Shtal, A.	81, 94
Siegel, Bernard	44, 58-59
Silverman, Marilyn	44
Siu, P.C.P	142
Smith, E.M.	153
Smith, V.L.	313
Smooha, S.	115-116

Spilerman, S.	82, 115
Spooner, Brian	57
Stein, A.	272
Stein, M.	272
Steinmetz, S.K.	64
Stillman, N.	30-31, 42
Storr, A.	78
Straus, M.A.	64
Styles, J.	163
Svirski, S.	115
Swartz, Norman	58

T

Tattelman, I.	306
Tessler, M.A.	127
Tonkin, Elizabeth	231
Turnbull, Colin	79, 277
Turner, Victor	17, 20-21, 246, 259, 273-274, 278, 280, 301, 313, 341
Tzabar, N.	149

V

Van den Berghe, P.L.	143, 145, 161, 164-165
Van Velsen, Japp	17

W

Wallace, A.	251
Walzer, Michael	344
Waters, M.C.	146, 161
Weber, M.	106
Weeks, J.	300
Weingrod, Alex	45-46, 63, 65, 81-82, 98, 114, 117-118, 131, 347, 349
Weintraub, Dov	18, 46, 98, 116
Wenger, Beth	204
Wertheimer, Jack	252, 269
Whyte, W.F.	147, 286, 336, 338
Willner, D.	31, 46, 65, 82, 105, 107, 349
Wirth, L.	153

Wolfgang, M.E.	64, 75
Wolpin, Nisson	252
Wulff, Helena	278, 301

Y

Yadava, J.S.	58
Yancey, W.L.	116, 136, 139, 143, 145, 164-165

Z

Zenner, W.P.	114
Zimmels, H.J.	134

INDEX OF SUBJECTS

A
Asamer	33-37, 39, 42, 65, 67-68, 70, 73, 76, 97-99, 101, 105-114
Ashkenazi	80, 87, 95, 115, 198, 350
Orthodoxy	118-120, 122, 126, 129, 131, 133-134, 137, 139-140, 186, 348
Secularism	21, 91, 94, 120, 123, 129, 136, 138-139, 163, 166, 176

B
Baraka	21, 40, 106, 123

C
Chabad	217-218, 222, 224
Community of Memory	231
Congregation Beth Simchat Torah	8-9, 236-237, 239-250, 253-256, 259-260, 262-274, 276-277, 279-299, 321-333, 335, 337, 339-340
Cultural Performance	23, 184, 186-187, 245-246

D
Development Towns	15, 81-82, 84, 86, 138, 347
Dhimmi (Status of Jews)	30

E
Ethnic	
Associations	153
Organizations	143, 164
Parties	
See Shas, Tami	
Ethnicity	
Affective	23

Cultural	117
Emergent	116, 121, 139-140, 165
One-Night-Stand	23, 164-165
Submerged	144, 165
Ethnographic Text	24-25, 198, 276-277, 279, 288, 320-321, 338, 340
Extended Case Method	17, 19, 23

H

Hamula Groups (Kinship Groups)	9, 44-45, 53, 55-56, 59, 61
Havurah	252, 270-271, 273, 275, 291
Human Aggression	78
Physical	64, 66-67, 71, 75
Verbal	64, 66-67, 69-70, 75

I

Independence Park	306-307, 309, 311, 314-316
Informants	9, 14, 24-25, 38, 41, 148, 163, 190, 287, 298, 320-322, 325, 338-341

J

Jewish Agency Land Settlement Department
7, 15, 46, 48, 50, 77, 342

K

Kehillah	105, 217, 220, 232

L

Labor Party	116, 128-130, 138, 304
Likud	116, 129, 181, 350
Lower East Side	9, 149, 201, 203-204, 208-209, 212, 215, 223, 227-228, 231

M

Manchester School	16-17, 20, 25
Masoret Religiosity	128-129, 135, 137-140
Melting Pot	21, 46-47, 56, 94, 138, 176, 349
Modernization Theories	116, 143
Moshav Pattern	44-45, 65

N

Nostalgia	167, 185-187, 249

P

Pilgrimage	
Religious	113, 130, 137, 349
Secular	84, 301, 313-314
Reflexivity	24-25, 190, 200, 277, 341, 343
Religious Leadership	
Israel	108-109, 113, 117
Morocco	97, 104-106, 123, 134
United States	221, 251, 261

S

Sex, Impersonal	162-163
Shas	140, 348-350
Sociability, Impersonal	162-163, 165
Social Drama	246, 259, 274, 280
Stanton Street Synagogue	9, 201, 203-204, 218, 228
Synagogue Life	130-131, 134, 136, 225, 229-230, 253, 262, 272

T

Tami	115, 121, 129, 138-140

W

Women's Participation in Synagogue Life	87, 252-253, 259, 262-263, 267, 269-275, 279-280, 283, 286, 293

Y

Yerida	146, 150, 153, 166, 192-195, 241
Yordim	9, 146, 148-153, 155-156, 160-161, 164, 166-167, 183-184, 187, 192, 194-197, 199, 307, 342

Z

Zekhut Avot	21, 105-109, 123, 126

Breinigsville, PA USA
22 January 2010
231221BV00004B/6/P